The Future of Child-Friendly Justice and Children's Rights in Vietnam

Nguyen Binh An · Luong Van Tuan ·
Nguyen Thi Bich
Editors

The Future of Child-Friendly Justice and Children's Rights in Vietnam

Springer

Editors
Nguyen Binh An
University of Finance - Marketing
Ho Chi Minh City, Viet Nam

Luong Van Tuan
Judicial Academy
Ha Noi City, Viet Nam

Nguyen Thi Bich
Hochiminh City University of Law
Ho Chi Minh City, Viet Nam

ISBN 978-981-95-3520-0 ISBN 978-981-95-3521-7 (eBook)
https://doi.org/10.1007/978-981-95-3521-7

This Springer imprint is published by the registered company Springer Nature Singapore Pte Ltd.
The registered company address is: 152 Beach Road, #21-01/04 Gateway East, Singapore 189721, Singapore

Preamble

This volume, *The Future of Child-Friendly Justice and Children's Rights in Vietnam*, represents our scholarly effort to conduct an in-depth analysis and evaluation aimed at improving legal systems, policies, and practices for the better protection of children's rights and interests. By combining theoretical approaches, comparative international perspectives, and empirical research, we hope that the contributions in this volume will enhance understanding and promote innovative policy reforms in the field of child-friendly justice.

The first theme focuses on foundational concepts and approaches from a comparative international perspective. The chapters in this section not only analyze international standards and principles but also situate Vietnam's legislative reforms within the global context. This allows us to see more clearly the necessity of ensuring that domestic regulations are consistent with international commitments while remaining responsive to Vietnam's unique socio-cultural context.

The second theme addresses children's rights in the context of labor and business. The authors in this section examine necessary reforms to protect working children, strategies for eliminating child labor, and ways to integrate children's rights into corporate social responsibility. We pay particular attention to theoretical debates as well as in-depth analyses of specific sectors, including risks within global supply chains, thereby offering concrete reform suggestions.

The third theme delves into judicial and administrative processes. The chapters in this section assess child-friendly procedures in both administrative and criminal justice, the role of legal professionals in safeguarding minors' right to a fair trial, and the treatment of children as victims or witnesses. Through these discussions, we emphasize the importance of procedural safeguards to ensure that children's rights do not merely exist on paper but are effectively protected in practice.

The final theme examines emerging challenges. This section highlights children's rights in cyberspace, data protection issues in the context of artificial intelligence, the legal dimensions of international trade disputes involving products affecting children's rights, and the right to education for children from ethnic minority communities. These chapters demonstrate that child-friendly justice must continually adapt to new technological, economic, and social realities.

The completion of this volume has been made possible through the support and professionalism of Springer Nature, together with the editorial and production teams who have guided us throughout the publication process. We express our deepest gratitude to them.

We recognize that this volume is only a starting point in an ongoing academic and policy dialogue. We warmly welcome feedback, critiques, and suggestions from readers and colleagues, with the conviction that continuous exchange will contribute to the fuller and more effective development of child-friendly justice in Vietnam and worldwide.

Nguyen Binh An
Luong Van Tuan
Nguyen Thi Bich

Contents

Part I Theoretical and Comparative Foundations of Child-Friendly Justice

1 **Understanding Child-Friendly Justice: Concepts, Principles, and International Standards** 3
Nguyen Binh An

2 **Child-Friendly Justice in Civil Judgment Enforcement: Legislative Reform in Vietnam** 21
Hoang Thi Thanh Hoa

3 **The Future of Child-Friendly Justice on Property Rights of Minors in Vietnam's Civil Law** 35
Doan Thi Ngoc Hai and Luu Tran Phuong Thao

Part II Children's Rights in Vietnamese Law and Justice

4 **Labour Rights of Vietnamese Children: Legal Reforms for a Child-Friendly Justice Approach** 47
Nguyen Hien Phuong and Nguyen Minh Ha

5 **Eliminating Child Labour in Vietnam: Legal Framework and Policy Solutions** 63
Nguyen Binh An

6 **Children's Rights in the Business Field—Some Theoretical and Legal Issues in Vietnam** 79
Ha Thi Ut

7 **Advancing Child-Friendly CSR: Protecting Minor Workers Under Vietnam's Labor Law** 91
Nguyen Thi Bich

8 **Corporate Social Responsibility and the Protection of Children from Labor Exploitation in Vietnam's Textile Supply Chain** ... 109
Nguyen Binh An

Part III Child-Friendly Justice in Judicial and Administrative Processes

9 **Child-Friendly Administrative Justice for Children in Conflict with the Law in Vietnam** ... 131
Ha Thi Phuong Nguyen

10 **Lawyer Skills in Guaranteeing Fair Trial Rights for Juvenile Drug Offenders in Vietnam** ... 145
Luong Van Tuan and Nguyen The Vinh

11 **Child-Friendly Justice for Child Victims in First-Instance Criminal Proceedings in Vietnam** ... 161
Hieu Thi Ngoc Tran

12 **The Model of Child-Friendly Trial Under Vietnamese Criminal Procedure Law** ... 175
Pham Minh Trang

13 **Preventing Sexual Abuse of Children Under 16 Through Criminal Justice Mechanisms** ... 193
Thao Huyen DIEP

Part IV Emerging Challenges to Children's Rights in Vietnam

14 **Protecting Children's Privacy Rights in Cyberspace Under Vietnamese Law** ... 211
Dang Thi Hong Tuyen

15 **Protecting Children's Rights in International Trade Disputes: A Legal Perspective from Vietnam on Products Infringing Intellectual Property Rights** ... 227
Tran Minh Chien, Pham Hoang Phuc, and Huynh Thi Ngoc Diem

16 **Protecting Children's Data Privacy in the Age of AI: Legal Lessons from the U.S. And EU** ... 249
Le Ho Trung Hieu and Vu Thi Bich Hai

17 **The Right to Education for Ethnic Minority Children in Vietnam** ... 261
Nguyen Thi Thu Huong

18 **Business Cooperation Contracts and Education Rights of the Child in Vietnam** ... 277
Vu Thi Bich Hai and Le Ho Trung Hieu

Part I
Theoretical and Comparative Foundations of Child-Friendly Justice

Chapter 1
Understanding Child-Friendly Justice: Concepts, Principles, and International Standards

Nguyen Binh An

Abstract This chapter explores the theoretical and legal foundations of child-friendly justice as an emerging trend in global legal and judicial reform. Drawing on insights from human rights law, the sociology of law, and developmental psychology, it argues that child-friendly justice represents a shift away from traditional juvenile justice models toward frameworks that prioritize children's rights and meaningful participation. The discussion identifies five key principles that underpin this approach: the best interests of the child, the right to be heard, non-discrimination, humane and accessible justice, and procedures that reflect the child's age and development. These principles form the normative core of a child-sensitive legal system.

1.1 Introduction

The idea of child-friendly justice grew out of the United Nations Convention on the Rights of the Child (CRC) and has become a central theme in contemporary legal thinking about children. It goes beyond technical legal reform to reflect a deeper change in how legal systems view and treat children involved in proceedings. Importantly, child-friendly justice is not limited to juvenile criminal law. Its scope extends to civil and administrative procedures, including enforcement mechanisms, whenever children are affected. This chapter examines these dimensions and highlights how a child-focused perspective can improve both the fairness and effectiveness of legal processes. This constitutes a prevailing trend vigorously promoted in the recommendations of the United Nations, the Council of Europe, and numerous other international organizations, compelling member states to undertake a rigorous

Article history: Received 05 April 2025; Revised 10 July 2025; Accepted 05 August 2025.

N. B. An (✉)
Doctor of Laws, University of Finance - Marketing, Ho Chi Minh City, Viet Nam
e-mail: an.luatsu@gmail.com

N. Binh An et al. (eds.), *The Future of Child-Friendly Justice and Children's Rights in Vietnam*, https://doi.org/10.1007/978-981-95-3521-7_1

review and harmonization of their national legal systems in accordance with these internationalized principles.

However, a prerequisite for the effective application and domestication of these principles is a comprehensive understanding of the conceptual essence, foundational values, and core standards of child-friendly justice. Accordingly, this chapter will focus on elucidating three critical areas: (i) the theoretical underpinnings and conceptual evolution of child-friendly justice; (ii) the fundamental legal principles that form the bedrock of this judicial model; and (iii) the system of widely recognized international standards. This will serve as the crucial theoretical predicate for the subsequent chapters, which will analyze the Vietnamese legal system and propose orientations for its future development.

1.2 The Theoretical Foundations of Child Friendly Justice

1.2.1 The Concept, Characteristics, and Role of Child Friendly Justice

1.2.1.1 The Concept of Child Friendly Justice

The notion of "Child Friendly Justice" has been formulated and has evolved over the past three decades, emphasizing the imperative to construct a modern legal system oriented toward protecting the rights and welfare of children throughout all judicial processes.

At the international level, a significant starting point is the United Nations' Beijing Rules (1985), formally titled the Standard Minimum Rules for the Administration of Juvenile Justice. This instrument placed particular emphasis on the objective of securing the well being of juveniles, while concurrently encouraging states to avoid the detention of children unless absolutely necessary (United Nations General Assembly, 1985). Consequently, the deprivation of liberty is to be employed only as a measure of last resort and for the shortest possible duration (Kishita Gupta, 2021). Subsequently, although the CRC does not explicitly use the term "child friendly justice," the substantive content of this concept is clearly articulated through its key provisions. Accordingly, Article 3 sets forth the principle of the best interests of the child, Article 12 affirms the right to participation and expression of views, while Articles 37 and 40 underscore the critical aspects of juvenile justice (United Nations General Assembly, 1989). The United Nations, through Unicef Ecaro (2018), has stated that child-friendly justice refers to a judicial system designed to effectively respect and uphold the rights of children. This understanding highlights the need for procedures that are accessible, appropriate to the child's age, conducted without unnecessary delay, and responsive to the specific needs and rights of children. Such systems are expected to guarantee core rights, including the right to a fair trial, the right to be heard and to understand proceedings, respect for private and family life, and the protection of dignity and integrity. General Comment No. 24 of the Committee on the Rights of the Child (2019) further clarifies that child-friendly justice gives effect to the principles of the Convention on the Rights of the Child and related international standards by ensuring the full implementation of children's rights within judicial processes.

At the regional level, child-friendly justice has been interpreted and applied in different ways, shaped by the legal traditions, cultural norms, and institutional practices of each region.

The European region is regarded as a pioneer in the conceptualization and institutionalization of child friendly justice as a distinct and structured legal model. The Council of Europe (2010) perceives child friendly justice as a justice system that guarantees respect for and the effective implementation of all children's rights at the highest possible level, taking into account the principles listed below and with due regard to the child's level of maturity and understanding as well as the circumstances of the case.

In the Asian and African regions, despite the absence of a binding regional convention comparable to that in Europe, the concept of child friendly justice is progressively being given substance through policy discourses and guidance documents. Rather than advancing a technical legal definition, many documents in these regions articulate the concept as a guiding principle aimed at ensuring that children, as distinct legal subjects, can access justice in a manner that is equitable, humane, and suited to their developmental characteristics. For instance, the ASEAN Human Rights Declaration (2012) and the regional guidelines of the African Union both indirectly reflect the spirit of this concept by emphasizing the protection of children from violence, the elimination of cruel treatment, and the promotion of effective access to justice for children in vulnerable situations (Moïra Phuöng Van de Poël, 2024). Herein, child friendly justice is envisioned as a system capable of safeguarding the integrity and dignity of the child throughout the entire legal process, from investigation and adjudication to the enforcement of sentences, without losing sight of its educational and social reintegration functions.

Although the modes of expression may vary across regions, the commonality in these regional approaches is a paradigm shift from a purely punitive judicial model to one that is child centered. Child friendly justice, therefore, is not a matter of mere clemency but rather the recognition of a child's status as a rights holder, accompanied by a corresponding legal and institutional framework designed to ensure the substantive efficacy of those rights in all judicial contexts.

Building upon these established approaches, Goldson và Muncie (2012) discuss child friendly justice by citing official guidance from the Council of Europe. They describe it as an "integrated multidisciplinary approach to justice systems which places the best interests of the child at the centre, which respects the child's right to participate, and which prioritises restoration over punishment". Nevertheless, the authors also candidly highlight the divergence between the rhetoric of human rights and the actual circumstances that children confront.

Continuing this perspective, Ton Liefaard (2016) concurs with the concept of "child friendly justice" as advanced by the Council of Europe. He emphasizes that this concept originates from viewing children as subjects of rights within human rights law, representing a balance between the rights intended to protect children and their right to participate in all matters affecting them. This perspective, therefore, is directly linked to the legal status of children under international human rights law, acknowledging them as rights holders rather than merely as objects of care and protection.

Meanwhile, Ilona Kronberga (2017) analyzes the concept of "child friendly justice" within the practical context of law enforcement, connecting it to international law and European Union law. The author posits that every child possesses a fundamental right to live in a friendly legal environment, meaning an environment not negatively impacted by crime. Kronberga further contends that a child friendly justice system must extend beyond judicial authorities to encompass any institution or process with which a child may come into contact.

Aoife Daly (2024), however, extends the application of child friendly justice principles into the domain of climate crisis litigation involving children and young people. The author notes that "child friendly justice" is an emerging concept, developed by the Council of Europe to make justice systems more accessible and appropriate for children.

Synthesizing the academic viewpoints presented above, which, despite their different emphases and perspectives, converge on the core idea of a justice system centered on the rights and interests of the child. Aggregating these arguments, the concept of 'child friendly justice' can be identified as follows: "*Child friendly justice is a legal system designed and operated based on respect for the human rights and specific needs of children at all stages of the proceedings to ensure their effective access to justice, including the right to be informed, the right to representation, and the right to be heard in a meaningful way, thereby creating a legal environment that is safe, supportive, and conducive to their physical, psychological, and cognitive development*".

1.2.1.2 The Characteristics of Child Friendly Justice

From the explicit definition provided above, child friendly justice can be more concretely identified through the following distinctive characteristics:

Firstly, it is a system of justice that respects the rights and dignity of the child.

This characteristic underscores that all judicial processes and decisions must emanate from the recognition of children as subjects of fundamental human rights, while always ensuring their dignity is absolutely respected. Indeed, Article 40 of the United Nations Convention on the Rights of the Child (1989) stipulates that every child accused or convicted of infringing the penal law shall be treated in a manner which promotes their sense of dignity and worth. Therefore, a friendly justice system must prioritize the best interests of the child and avoid any action or procedure that could violate their dignity or inflict psychological harm. Children must be treated equitably, without discrimination, and their opinions and wishes must be heard during the proceedings (Dao & Dandurand, 2023). Concurrently, their legitimate interests and right to privacy must be protected to preserve their honor and dignity.

Secondly, child friendly justice constitutes an adaptive justice system responsive to the needs of children.

A crucial characteristic is the system's obligation to accommodate the distinct requirements of each child engaging with the judicial process. Accordingly, investigative, prosecutorial, and adjudicatory procedures must be adjusted to align with the psychological, physical, and situational specificities of children (Unicef Ecaro, 2018). For instance, prosecuting authorities may employ child friendly interrogation and statement taking methods, avoiding the induction of fear or undue pressure; similarly, juvenile court proceedings should be structured flexibly and intimately to foster a sense of security for the child, foregoing overly formal judicial attire that might induce anxiety, and permitting the accompaniment and support of psychological professionals or guardians throughout the proceedings (Liefaard, 2016). Furthermore, children in special circumstances (such as those with disabilities, from ethnic minority groups, or who have experienced trauma) necessitate the application of appropriate support and adaptive measures, ensuring that all children's needs are met equitably.

Thridly, it is an accessible justice system.

An "accessible" justice system reflects the characteristic of providing convenient and equitable access to justice for all children. Barriers related to language, cost, geographical distance, or administrative procedures must be minimized or eliminated to ensure that children and their families encounter no impediments when seeking legal protection (Liefaard, 2019). Consequently, information concerning rights and legal processes must be communicated in simple, comprehensible language for children; related forms and documents should be designed in a child friendly manner, appropriate for their cognitive developmental stage. Children possess the right to avail themselves of support services such as free legal aid or appointed counsel, guaranteeing that even children in challenging circumstances can utilize the justice system to protect their interests (Goldson & Muncie, 2012). Moreover, the establishment of specialized courts (e.g., family courts and juvenile courts) and dedicated adjudicatory procedures for children represents a significant measure to enhance accessibility, thereby helping children feel more secure and confident when participating in legal proceedings.

Fourthly, child friendly justice is an age appropriate justice system.

This characteristic is discernible when the child friendly justice system ensures that procedures and decisions are tailored proportionally to the age and maturity level of each child. Communication methods and explanatory content during legal proceedings are adjusted so that children of every age can comprehend their rights, obligations, and the unfolding of matters related to them (Council of Europe, 2010). For example, when explaining procedural steps or allegations to a child, officials should use everyday language, avoiding complex legal jargon; for younger children, visual aids or engaging tools can be employed to facilitate better understanding. This characteristic reflects the flexibility to accommodate children's "evolving capacities": older children may be afforded opportunities for deeper participation, and their opinions must be respected, whereas younger children require specific support to avoid disadvantage in legal proceedings (Hanson et al., 2025). Even the handling of juvenile misconduct must account for the age factor. Accordingly, the legal framework should stipulate lower levels of criminal responsibility or apply restorative and educational measures instead of severe punishment for juvenile offenders (Daly, 2024). This approach reflects the recognition that children's cognitive abilities and behavioral control differ by age, and the primary objective for juveniles is education and assistance in rectifying mistakes rather than punitive measures (United Nations General Assembly, 1985).

Fifthly, child friendly justice is a swift and careful justice system.

A distinct characteristic of child friendly justice, compared to conventional justice, is its timely and swifter resolution, primarily because prolonged proceedings can negatively impact a child's development and psychological well being (Unicef Ecaro, 2018). Therefore, cases involving children must be prioritized for early processing, avoiding all unnecessary delays, to mitigate anxiety and instability for the children. This characteristic embodies not only the protection of children's rights (for instance, children separated from their families have the right to early reunification, or child victims have the right to timely compensation), but also enhances the effectiveness of child education and rehabilitation processes (Kronberga, 2017). Concurrently with the demand for swiftness, legal proceedings must ensure requisite carefulness. All decisions concerning children must be thoroughly considered, based on comprehensive information and profound expert assessment, so that rapid resolution does not come at the expense of errors or infringement upon children's legitimate rights and interests (Committee on the Rights of the Child, 2019).

1.2.1.3 The Role of Child Friendly Justice

Based on the characteristics analyzed, it is evident that child friendly justice is not merely a legal system with specific attributes but also assumes a vital role in practical legal implementation and the comprehensive protection of children's rights, specifically:

Firstly, it ensures children's right to participation and to be heard.

Child friendly justice designs procedures to fully inform children of their rights, enabling them to genuinely voice their perspectives. The Council of Europe has steadfastly affirmed the child's right to participation as a cardinal principle, requiring children to be "informed of their rights, advised and heard" at every stage of proceedings (Council of Europe, 2010). Research demonstrates that child friendly justice not only enhances child protection but also renders children's participation more meaningful in adjudication processes.

Secondly, it creates a safe and supportive judicial environment.

Child friendly justice guarantees child friendly legal procedures, minimizing stress and psychological risks. Accordingly, the United Nations' Beijing Rules (1985) mandate that juvenile proceedings be conducted "in an atmosphere of understanding" to safeguard the child's best interests. Similarly, the Council of Europe (2017) recommends adopting a multidisciplinary approach to comprehensively assess a child's legal, psychological, social, emotional, physical, and cognitive status, thereby aligning legal processes with their developmental needs.

Thirdly, it ensures the right to information and legal representation.

Child friendly justice assists children in comprehending legal information and having representatives protect their interests. EU Directive 2016/800 (2016) stipulates children's right to attend and participate in hearings, receive timely information about their case, obtain legal representation and assistance, and mandates individual assessment for each child. These provisions aim to ensure children genuinely access justice in accordance with their capacities and specific needs.

Fourthly, it affirms children as subjects of human rights.

Child friendly justice embodies a human rights perspective, treating children as full subjects of rights. The CRC (1989) mandates that children must be afforded "the opportunity to be heard in any judicial and administrative proceedings affecting the child," asserting their right to express opinions in related decisions. Child friendly justice operationalizes this principle by placing the child's best interests and voice at the center of legal procedures and decisions.

1.2.2 The Genesis and Evolution of Child Friendly Justice Globally

1.2.2.1 Historical Ideologies and Institutions from the Twentieth Century to the Present

The historical development of child friendly justice is the culmination of a protracted transformational process in legal, political, and societal perceptions concerning the status of children within legal systems. Until the early twentieth century, children who infringed upon the law were treated similarly to adults, both in terms of adjudicatory procedures and applied sanctions. The traditional view that children were "incomplete adults" led criminal law to disregard the psychological, behavioral, and circumstantial differences of minors (Goldson, 2013).

The establishment of the first Juvenile Court in Chicago in 1899 marked a pivotal turning point in legal thought, stemming from the early twentieth century social reform movement in the United States (Fuller, 2015). This model inaugurated a novel concept: that children required a distinct approach to justice, one that was simultaneously protective and educational. Subsequently, nations began to establish institutions and judicial procedures specifically for minors, laying a robust foundation for the concept of child friendly justice (Smith, 2010).

However, it was not until the emergence of international instruments with legally binding force upon member states that the legal paradigm concerning children's rights truly became globalized. The Beijing Rules (1985) represented one of the initial endeavors to establish international standards for handling children who infringe upon the law. This instrument not only emphasized the child's right to fair and humane treatment but also established the principle of restorative approaches, maximizing the limitation of deprivation of liberty (Liefaard, 2016). Following this, the CRC (1989) erected the foundational pillar of human rights theory for children within legal systems. By recognizing children as "rights holders," the CRC fundamentally altered traditional legal logic. Provisions such as Article 3 concerning the best interests of the child, Article 12 concerning the right to be heard, and Article 40 concerning child friendly criminal justice established irreversible principles in international law. Many scholars, such as Kilkelly (2008b) contend that the CRC served as a "conceptual lever," transforming the perception of children from passive objects of protection to active rights bearing subjects in legal proceedings.

Regional and international initiatives vigorously propelled the development of child friendly justice. In 2010, the Council of Europe issued its Guidelines on Child Friendly Justice. This instrument underscored that the justice system must ensure children's access to justice without detriment, while designing procedures appropriate for their age and cognitive abilities (Council of Europe, 2010). This was the first document to present a comprehensive definition and a systematic framework of the characteristic principles of child friendly justice, notably highlighting five fundamental criteria: accessibility, age appropriateness, swiftness and carefulness, adaptability to children's needs, and respect for children's rights and dignity (Daly, 2024). Additionally, organizations like UNICEF play a crucial role in supporting and encouraging nations to implement child friendly justice systems through training programs and legal reforms. Kilkelly (2008a) emphasized that children's participation in legal processes is not merely a legal requirement but also a critical factor fostering their psychological and social development.

Evidently, the history of the formation and evolution of the philosophy of child friendly justice reflects a transformation in how society perceives children. From viewing children as passive objects requiring protection, modern legal systems increasingly recognize children as autonomous and participating rights holders. This transformation represents not only a legal advancement but also an ethical commitment to ensure that children are treated with respect and dignity in all facets of the justice system.

1.2.2.2 Stages of Development and Transformation from Juvenile Justice to Child Friendly Justice

The concept of child friendly justice did not emerge as an independent idea but rather as a result of the transformation from the juvenile justice model, which was once regarded as a progressive legal reform achievement (Muncie, 2007). This process can be divided into three primary stages, each marking significant accomplishments in protecting and promoting children's rights.

The First Stage (1950s–1980s): This period witnessed the strong institutionalization of juvenile justice, particularly in Western countries. Juvenile courts, child prosecutors, correctional facilities, and non criminal measures symbolized this model.

However, procedures often remained confidential and lacked transparency, with children having virtually no voice in the proceedings. Despite purporting to act "for the child's benefit," this model maintained a "top down protective" nature, failing to reflect the spirit of modern human rights (Goldson & Muncie, 2012).

The Second Stage (1989–2010): Following the adoption of the CRC, the understanding of children's legal status underwent a fundamental shift. The recognition of children as rights holders meant that reform demands extended beyond mere procedures or court models to encompass the entire justice system. This necessitated the comprehensive integration of children's rights into legal procedures, not only when children were offenders but also when they were victims, witnesses, or related parties in civil and administrative disputes (Smith, 2010).

The Third Stage (2010 to Present): Child friendly justice has distinctly materialized as a separate theoretical framework. The Council of Europe's Guidelines (2010), along with regional legal instruments such as EU Directive 2016/800 on the rights of children in criminal proceedings, expanded the concept from the criminal domain to other areas like civil and administrative proceedings, and even environmental dispute resolution (Daly, 2024). The appearance of this concept in judgments of the European Court of Human Rights and the Inter American Court of Human Rights demonstrates its emergence as a minimum standard in international legal practice (Mazzinghy, 2020). Many scholars are currently advocating for the "actualization of child friendly justice" through institutional reform, interdisciplinary professional training, and the application of child centric methodologies in substantive and procedural law. Liefaard (2016) posits that a genuine transformation from juvenile justice to child friendly justice requires a flexible legal structure, readily adaptable to children's diverse living circumstances and linked to national obligations to ensure the implementation of children's rights not only on paper but also in legal practice.

1.2.3 The Philosophical and Sociological Jurisprudence Underpinnings of Child Friendly Justice

The conceptualization of child friendly justice originates from a transformative shift in the perception of children's legal status within society generally and the justice system specifically. Its philosophical foundation centers on the recognition of children's rights as a universal value, transcending the perspective that views children as passive recipients of state or familial protection. Accordingly, children's rights are affirmed as an inseparable component of the international human rights system.

The CRC of 1989, ratified by 196 nations (United Nations Treaty Collection, 2025), has acknowledged children as autonomous rights bearing subjects, possessing the capacity to engage in legal actions commensurate with their level of maturity and cognitive ability. This recognition dismantles traditional paternalistic thinking, establishing the principle that "children are not the property of parents, nor are they the objects of charity, but are human beings with full rights" (Freeman, 1983).

Consequently, all policies, laws, and judicial procedures pertaining to children must be constructed on the premise of treating children as equal subjects of rights. This acknowledgment reflects a universal humanitarian spirit, whereby children's rights are protected on par with the general human rights of all citizens.

The principle of the best interests of the child serves as a foundational pillar within the entire conceptual framework of child friendly justice, reflecting a consistent, dialectical ideological current between existential protection and the actualization of developmental potential. The first dimension embodies the moral imperative of the legal system to protect children from all risks of physical, psychological, and dignitary harm throughout legal proceedings. Meanwhile, the second dimension requires that the rule of law provide conditions that support children's cognitive, emotional, and social development, whether they are involved in proceedings as accused persons or as litigants (Adami et al., 2023). This perspective reflects a significant shift in judicial thinking, moving away from approaches centered on sanction and punishment toward models that emphasize rehabilitation, education, and reintegration. Justice, in this sense, is no longer understood solely as a mechanism of coercion but as a normative space designed to foster the overall growth of minors and to help them build personal integrity and social competence (An, 2024).

In line with this understanding, the CRC and other international human rights instruments consistently underscore the goal of promoting children's full and balanced development. The CRC, in particular, guides states to create environments that enable children to develop materially, intellectually, emotionally, morally, and socially from an early age. Protecting and promoting the best interests and harmonious development of the child is therefore recognized as a central principle, requiring that all policies and decisions concerning children be assessed with their well-being as the primary consideration. This responsibility rests not only with families but also with the entire legal and social system, from prosecuting authorities to the community, because any decision can have long lasting effects on a child's life and development.

Concurrently, children's right to be heard and to participate is a core component of the CRC and international standards. Children are empowered to express their views on matters affecting them, and those views must be given due weight commensurate with their age and psychological development. Child friendly justice actualizes this right within the legal environment. Accordingly, prosecuting authorities must adjust their language, environment, and working methods to ensure children feel safe, respected, and able to participate actively. Ton Liefaard (2019) notes that the goal of child friendly justice is to make the justice system "more child rights centered, more child interest sensitive, and more responsive to child participation."

In other words, child friendly justice not only protects but also fosters children's agency within legal processes, transforming children from passive objects to capable subjects who can participate in and influence proceedings. From a sociological jurisprudence perspective, this is an embodiment of the law's shift towards inclusion and humanization. In modern society, which values the full development of individuals from childhood, the law cannot remain age-neutral but must reflect children's specific psychological and social needs. Empirical sociological research has shown how children's cognitive and emotional development differs significantly from that of adults, and how applying legal procedures designed for adults can perpetuate inequalities and limit children's access to justice. A child-friendly legal framework recognizes that law should not be seen as an inflexible set of rules but as a dynamic instrument designed to support children's development and well-being. Child-friendly justice, therefore, goes beyond procedural adjustments to reflect a broader commitment to integrating children's rights and needs into the core objectives of the legal system.

1.3 Fundamental Principles of Child Friendly Justice

1.3.1 The Principle of Ensuring the Best Interests of the Child

The best interests of the child is the cornerstone of any child-friendly justice system. This principle requires not only clear legal standards but also flexible and context-sensitive assessments in individual cases. Article 3 of the CRC obliges State Parties to ensure that all decisions concerning children prioritize their protection and development. Judges applying this principle must consider three key factors: (1) the child's own wishes, taking into account their age and maturity; (2) the risk of harm that the decision may cause; and (3) the potential for the child's rehabilitation and reintegration (Mahmoudi et al., 2015).

This principle marks an important shift in legal thinking, viewing children as active rights-holders rather than passive recipients of protection. It challenges the traditional assumption that children's interests align automatically with parental or state decisions and instead requires independent scrutiny of any intervention in children's lives (Alston, 1994). To properly assess the best interests of the child, courts are expected to rely on multidisciplinary evidence and to ensure that children are actively involved in the process. This calls for a justice system that is flexible, attentive to power dynamics between the state and families, and responsive to the individual circumstances of each child.

1.3.2 The Principle of Respect for the Right to Participate

Article 12 of the CRC sets out the right of children to participate in all proceedings that affect them, reflecting a shift from a purely protective approach to one based on empowerment. States are obliged to give children a meaningful opportunity to express their views and to consider those views in line with the child's age and maturity (Nylund, 2019). This principle emphasizes that children are not merely passive beneficiaries of adult decisions but active participants in shaping outcomes that affect their lives.

The right to participate is not simply an indicator of progress but a core component of a child-centered legal system. It recognizes that children have unique knowledge of their own needs and challenges the outdated notion of their limited capacity. The UN Committee on the Rights of the Child stresses that participation must be meaningful, going beyond symbolic gestures, and requires courts and authorities to adapt their procedures to each child's communication abilities and understanding (UN. Committee on the Rights of the Child, 2009).

Ultimately, this principle requires robust mechanisms to ensure that children can express their views freely and without undue influence. Genuine participation is essential not only for respecting children's rights but also for ensuring that the legal process is fair, legitimate, and effective. The active presence of children helps to correct unconscious biases in adult judgments and rebalance the often asymmetrical power relationship between the state and children (Alminde, 2024). Ultimately, respecting children's right to participate is a form of civic empowerment from an early age. This fosters the development of critical thinking, decision making abilities, and a sense of responsibility in children. This is not merely a manifestation of inclusivity in legal thought but also a step forward in humanizing the legal system, bringing the rule of law closer to the dynamic reality of human life. Children are no longer silenced but become active participants with a voice.

1.3.3 The Principle of Ensuring the Right to Protection and Non Discrimination

Within the framework of child friendly justice, the principle of ensuring the right to protection and non discrimination plays a central role. It forms the foundation for all legislative, executive, and judicial activities concerning children. This principle originates from the CRC, particularly the convergence of Article 2 (prohibition of discrimination), Article 19 (protection from violence), and Article 34 (protection from sexual exploitation). These provisions establish a three tiered obligation for the state: preventing risks through a comprehensive legal framework; intervening promptly when children's rights are threatened; and rehabilitating victims through specialized services (UN. Committee on the Rights of the Child, 2011).

Legally, this principle requires the justice system not only to establish regulations prohibiting discriminatory acts but also to actively design mechanisms for preventing, detecting, and redressing inequalities. Children in vulnerable circumstances, such as ethnic minority children, migrant children, children with disabilities, or children in alternative care systems, must have access to specific protective measures to ensure equitable and effective access to justice. This principle reflects the acknowledgment of diversity and heterogeneity in children's legal experiences. Designing an equitable justice system requires understanding that social factors such as poverty, gender discrimination, or cultural inequality can create significant barriers to children's exercise of their rights (Kronberga, 2017). Therefore, protecting children does not equate to applying a uniform standard but necessitates a flexible approach based on interdisciplinary analysis.

The principle of non discrimination is a prerequisite for the substantive realization of other children's rights. Without eliminating the factors that lead to inequality, all efforts to protect children's rights will remain merely formal. Thus, a truly child friendly justice system creates conditions for all children, regardless of their background, to have the opportunity for adequate and equal protection under the law.

1.3.4 The Principle of Friendly and Humane Access to Justice

Within the framework of child friendly justice, the principle of friendly and humane access to justice is not merely a procedural requirement but also an expression of respect for children's dignity and human rights throughout the entire judicial process. This principle demands that the justice system be designed and operated in a manner appropriate to children's age, developmental stage, and specific circumstances, to ensure that all children can access justice effectively, equitably, and without harm (Fernández-Molina et al., 2021).

Although the CRC does not directly refer to the right to access justice as an independent right, many provisions within the convention, particularly Articles 12, 37, and 40, have laid a solid foundation for ensuring this right. Specifically, Article 40(3) of the CRC requires state parties to develop special procedural safeguards "appropriate to the child's age and circumstances." Other international instruments such as the Beijing Rules (1985), the Havana Rules (1990), and the Council of Europe Guidelines on Child Friendly Justice (2010) have concretized the requirements for a child appropriate justice system. These instruments emphasize ensuring procedural rights, the right to be heard, and the right to be protected from all forms of cruel, inhuman, or degrading treatment.

Accordingly, the principle of friendly and humane access to justice encompasses four main obligations: first, ensuring prompt case resolution to minimize prolonged psychological harm, as concretized in the Beijing Rules (1985); second, designing a non threatening judicial environment by limiting contact with accused individuals, using age appropriate language, and arranging separate spaces (Council of Europe, 2010); third, providing multidisciplinary support including psychological services, interpretation, and specialized legal aid (United Nations General Assembly, 1989).

The UN Committee on the Rights of the Child, in its General Comment No. 24 (2019), explains that humanity in child justice requires a shift in mindset from punishment to rehabilitation. Judges must prioritize educational measures over detention, consistent with neuroscientific research on the incomplete brain development of adolescents.

1.3.5 The Principle of Age Appropriate and Individualized Adjudication

The principle of age appropriate and individualized adjudication focuses on tailoring and personalizing legal procedures based on a child's developmental characteristics, complementing the principles of humanity and nondiscrimination within child friendly justice. This principle stems from the pervasive requirement in the international human rights system to ensure that participation in the judicial process causes no harm and is commensurate with a child's cognitive, emotional, and social capacities (Alston, 1994).

This principle represents the scientific pillar of child friendly justice, demanding that all legal procedures be designed based on the physiological, psychological, and cognitive developmental attributes of each child. The CRC establishes a binding obligation for states to "promote the establishment of laws, procedures, authorities and institutions specifically applicable to children alleged as, accused of, or recognized as having infringed the penal law," emphasizing "age" and "developmental circumstances" as grounds for adjustment. The Beijing Rules (1985) concretize this obligation by requiring judges to consider a child's "level of maturity," "cognitive capacity," and "communication ability" when determining the form of legal proceedings.

General Comment No. 10 of the Committee on the Rights of the Child (2007) underscores that the justice system must establish age appropriate procedures, including: (i) legal terminology must be presented in a manner suitable for children to comprehend at each developmental stage; (ii) diverse consultation methods must be established, such as using pictures, diagrams, or visual aids for children under 10 years of age; and (iii) legal procedures must be differentiated by age, for example, children under 14 years may not be required to take an oath as they may not yet grasp the concept of legal responsibility (Committee on the Rights of the Child, 2019), (Council of Europe, 2010).

1.4 International Standards on Child Friendly Justice

1.4.1 The United Nations Convention on the Rights of the Child (CRC) and Related Resolutions

The Convention on the Rights of the Child (1989) plays a central role in constructing a child friendly justice system. Liefaard (2016) argues that the CRC imposes a legal obligation on State Parties to adapt their entire justice system to protect the dignity and fundamental rights of children, while simultaneously promoting restorative rather than punitive justice.

The evolution of child-friendly justice is deeply rooted in a progressive clarification and expansion of the CRC principles through a series of significant United

Nations resolutions. A key milestone in the development of child-friendly justice was the adoption of United Nations General Assembly Resolution 45/112 (1990), known as the United Nations Standard Minimum Rules for the Administration of Juvenile Justice (the Beijing Rules). This document set out essential standards for the treatment of children in conflict with the law, emphasizing alternatives to detention, promoting rehabilitative measures such as education and reintegration, and encouraging the establishment of specialized juvenile courts and procedures (Fuller, 2015).

Building on this, Resolution 45/113 (1990), the United Nations Guidelines for the Prevention of Juvenile Delinquency (the Riyadh Guidelines), shifted attention to prevention, highlighting the roles of families, schools, and communities in addressing the causes of juvenile delinquency. It underlined that child-friendly justice must include not only procedural safeguards but also preventive and supportive social measures (Dao & Dandurand, 2023).

The treatment of children deprived of liberty was addressed in Resolution 65/229 (2010), the United Nations Rules for the Protection of Juveniles Deprived of their Liberty (the Havana Rules), which made clear that detention should only be used as a last resort and for the shortest appropriate period (Adami et al., 2023).

To further strengthen these standards, Resolution 67/169 (2013) called on states to establish specialized institutions and ensure that personnel working with children in the justice system receive appropriate training. In response, several developed countries have created integrated centers offering coordinated legal, psychological, and educational services tailored to children involved in criminal, civil, and administrative proceedings (Kronberga, 2017).

The Committee on the Rights of the Child has also elaborated on these standards in its General Comments, particularly No. 12 (2009) and No. 24 (2019). General Comment No. 12 stressed that children must have meaningful opportunities to participate in legal proceedings and that this requires effective mechanisms to ensure their views are heard and taken seriously. General Comment No. 24 expanded on this by emphasizing the need to protect children from secondary victimization through measures such as single interviews, child-friendly interview rooms, and independent verification of age and identity beyond relying solely on documents.

1.4.2 Regional Legal Instruments

At the regional level, child-friendly justice has become an important part of efforts to shift justice systems away from punitive approaches and toward protection, support, and empowerment of children. Regional bodies such as the European Union (EU) and the Association of Southeast Asian Nations (ASEAN) have played a significant role in promoting these reforms. They have sought to ensure that children are treated as rights-holders whose voices and needs are actively recognized.

In Europe, EU Directive 2016/800 introduced minimum standards for safeguards for children who are suspects or accused in criminal proceedings. The directive requires member states to provide clear legal information, ensure access to legal counsel from the earliest stage, and adapt procedures to the child's age and maturity. Research by Liefaard (2016) documents how the directive has influenced reforms in national justice systems, including the creation of specialized juvenile courts with child-appropriate facilities and trained personnel. The Council of Europe's Guidelines on Child-Friendly Justice (2010) further advanced this approach by promoting measures that protect children's mental health and respect their dignity throughout legal processes (2008b).

In Southeast Asia, ASEAN has incorporated child-friendly standards into its regional human rights framework. The ASEAN Human Rights Declaration (2012) affirmed that human rights apply equally to children and other vulnerable groups and condemned the exploitation of children. The ASEAN Declaration on the Rights of Children in the Context of Migration further highlighted the need for child-sensitive procedures, including appropriate legal and psychological support for migrant children.

1.5 Conclusion

Child-friendly justice is not only a modern approach to justice but also a significant advancement in the understanding of human rights. By examining its key concepts, principles, and international standards, this chapter has outlined the theoretical foundation for integrating child-friendly practices into legal systems.

While international standards offer consistent benchmarks, their implementation must be adapted to each country's cultural, institutional, and social context. For Vietnam, developing a child-friendly justice system is an essential part of broader judicial reform and international integration efforts.

Successfully applying these principles in Vietnam will require systematic, multidisciplinary, and evidence-based approaches. These critical issues will be explored in greater depth in the following chapters of this book.

References

Adami, R., Kaldal, A., & Aspán, M. (Eds.). (2023). *The rights of the child: Legal*. Political and Ethical Challenges.

Alminde, S. (2024). Listening to children: A Childist analysis of children's participation in family law cases. *Social Sciences, 13*(3), 3. https://doi.org/10.3390/socsci13030133

Alston, P. (Ed.). (1994). *The best interests of the child: Reconciling culture and human rights*. Oxford University Press.

An, N. B. (2024). Empowering access: Legal assistance as a safeguard for the right to justice of persons with disabilities in Vietnam. In A. Nguyen Binh, N. H. Phuong, & L. V. Tuan (Eds.), *Sustainable legacies: A legal inquiry into PwDs' rights in Vietnam's development* (pp. 85–101). Springer Nature Singapore. https://doi.org/10.1007/978-981-97-9566-6_6

Committee on the Rights of the Child. (2019). *General comment No. 24 (2019) on children's rights in the child justice system*. OHCHR. https://www.ohchr.org/en/documents/general-comments-and-recommendations/general-comment-no-24-2019-childrens-rights-child
Council of Europe. (2010). *Guidelines of the Committee of Ministers of the Council of Europe on child friendly justice*. https://search.coe.int/cm#{%22CoEIdentifier%22:[%2209000016804b2cf3%22],%22sort%22:[%22CoEValidationDate%20Descending%22]}
Daly, A. (2024). Child and youth friendly justice for the climate crisis: Relying on the UN convention on the rights of the child. *The International Journal of Children's Rights, 32*(3), 632–661. https://doi.org/10.1163/15718182-32030002
Dao, L. T., & Dandurand, Y. (2023). Social, cultural and systemic barriers to child justice reform: Lessons from Vietnam. *Youth Justice, 23*(1), 29–48. https://doi.org/10.1177/14732254211036196
European Union Agency for Fundamental Rights. (2017). *Child-friendly justice :perspectives and experiences of children involved in judicial proceedings as victims, witnesses or parties in nine EU Member States: Annexes*. Publications Office. https://data.europa.eu/doi/10.2811/516162
European Union. (2016, May 11). *Directive—2016/800—EN-EUR-Lex*. https://eur-lex.europa.eu/eli/dir/2016/800/oj/eng
Fernández-Molina, E., Bermejo, M., & Baz, O. (2021). Observing juvenile courtrooms: Testing the implementation of guidelines on child-friendly justice in Spain. *Youth Justice, 21*(2), 192–209. https://doi.org/10.1177/1473225420918027
Freeman, M. D. A. (1983). *The rights and wrongs of children*. UNKNO.
Fuller, J. R. (2015). *Juvenile delinquency: Mainstream and crosscurrents*. Oxford University Press.
Goldson, B. (Ed.). (2013). *Dictionary of youth justice* (0th ed.). Willan. https://doi.org/10.4324/9781843925972
Goldson, B., & Muncie, J. (2012). Towards a global 'child friendly juvenile justice. *International Journal of Law, Crime and Justice, 40*(1), 47–64. https://doi.org/10.1016/j.ijlcj.2011.09.004
Hanson, K., Liefaard, T., Ruggiero, R., Patrizi, E., Klep, K., & Opoka, L. (2025). *International Children's Rights Instruments*. Brill|Nijhoff. doi:https://doi.org/10.1163/9789004681224.
Kilkelly, U. (2008a). Youth courts and children's rights: The Irish experience. *Youth Justice, 8*(1), 39–56. https://doi.org/10.1177/1473225407087041
Kilkelly, U. (2008b). Youth justice and children's rights: Measuring compliance with international standards. *Youth Justice, 8*(3), 187–192. https://doi.org/10.1177/1473225408096458
Kishita Gupta. (2021, August 16). *Implementation of the Beijing Rules, 1985 in the Juvenile Justice (Care and Protection) Act, 2015*. iPleaders. https://blog.ipleaders.in/implementation-beijing-rules-1985-juvenile-justice-care-protection-act-2015/
Kronberga, I. (2017). Life without crime as a fundamental right of the child: On the prevention of juvenile delinquency. *Juridica International, 25*, 74. https://doi.org/10.12697/JI.2017.25.08
Liefaard, T. (2016). Child-friendly justice: Protection and participation of children in the justice system. *Temple Law Review, 88*(4), 905–927.
Liefaard, T. (2019). Access to justice for children: Towards a specific research and implementation agenda. *The International Journal of Children's Rights, 27*(2), 195–227. https://doi.org/10.1163/15718182-02702002
Mahmoudi, S., Leviner, P., Kaldal, A., & Lainpelto, K. (Eds.). (2015). *Child-friendly Justice*. Brill. https://brill.com/edcollbook/title/31892
Mazzinghy, Á. (2020). Child-Friendly Justice Behind Bars: A Comparative Analysis of the Protection Mechanisms of the Rights of Arrested Children in the Practice of the Working Group on Arbitrary Detention and of the European and Inter-American Courts of Human Rights. *American University International Law Review, 35*(2). https://digitalcommons.wcl.american.edu/auilr/vol35/iss2/6
Moïra Phuöng Van de Poël. (2024). International Rules of Justice for Children. *Humanium*. https://www.humanium.org/en/international-rules-justice-children-2/
Muncie, J. (Ed.). (2007). *Criminal justice and crime control*. SAGE Publications Ltd..

Nylund, A. (2019). Children's right to participate in decision-making in Norway: Paternalism and autonomy. In T. Haugli, A. Nylund, R. Sigurdsen, & L. R. L. Bendiksen (Eds.), *Children's constitutional rights in the Nordic countries* (pp. 201–224). Brill| Nijhoff. https://doi.org/10.1163/9789004382817_012

Smith, R. (2010). Book Reviews: John Muncie, Youth & Crime (3rd Edition), SAGE, London, 2009, £22.99 Pb, ISBN 978—1—84787—432—0. *Youth Justice, 10*(3), 306–308. doi:https://doi.org/10.1177/14732254100100030703.

UN. Committee on the Rights of the Child (Ed.). (2009). *General comment no. 12 (2009), The right of the child to be heard*. UN. https://digitallibrary.un.org/record/671444

UN. Committee on the Rights of the Child (Ed.). (2011). *General comment no. 13 (2011), The right of the child to freedom from all forms of violence*. UN. https://digitallibrary.un.org/record/711722

UN. Committee on the Rights of the ChildGeneva (Ed.). (2007). *General comment no. 10 (2007), Children's rights in juvenile justice*. UN. https://digitallibrary.un.org/record/599395

UN. General Assembly (Ed.). (1990). *United Nations Rules for the Protection of Juveniles Deprived of Their Liberty: Resolution*. UN. https://digitallibrary.un.org/record/105555

Unicef Ecaro. (2018). *Guidelines On Child-Friendly Legal Aid*. Unicef. https://www.unicef.org/eca/media/5171/file

United Nations General Assembly. (1985). *United Nations Standard Minimum Rules for the Administration of Juvenile Justice (The Beijing Rules)*. OHCHR. https://www.ohchr.org/en/instruments-mechanisms/instruments/united-nations-standard-minimum-rules-administration-juvenile

United Nations General Assembly. (1989). *Convention on the Rights of the Child*. https://www.ohchr.org/en/instruments-mechanisms/instruments/convention-rights-child

United Nations Treaty Collection. (2025). *United Nations Treaty Collection*. https://treaties.un.org/

Chapter 2
Child-Friendly Justice in Civil Judgment Enforcement: Legislative Reform in Vietnam

Hoang Thi Thanh Hoa

Abstract In addition to the investigation, prosecution and adjudication stages, the stage of judgment enforcement plays a very important role in protecting the lawful rights and interests of minors. Within the scope of this article, the author focuses on analysing certain provisions of the law on civil judgment enforcement related to minors in Viet Nam, comparing them with the legal systems of some other countries, and from that proposing improvements to the law to better ensure the lawful rights and interests of minors in the process of organising civil judgment enforcement, contributing to the building of a child-friendly justice system in Viet Nam.

2.1 Introduction

Building a child-friendly justice system is an objective and essential requirement for every country, especially in the current context of integration and globalisation. Viet Nam was the first country in Asia and the second in the world to ratify the United Nations Convention on the Rights of the Child (UNCRC). It has also recognised many other international instruments on human rights in general and children's rights in particular, all of which recommend strengthening the development and improvement of laws on juvenile justice. Directive No. 28-CT/TW dated 25 December 2023 of the Politburo on "strengthening the care, education and protection of children to meet the requirements of developing a prosperous and happy country" has put forward the solution of "developing a child-friendly justice system and protecting children". Article 37 of the 2013 Constitution of the Socialist Republic of Viet Nam also affirms that "Children are protected, cared for and educated by the State, family and society; and have the right to participate in matters relating to children."

Article history: Received 23 April 2025; Revised 22 July 2025; Accepted 20 August 2025.

H. T. T. Hoa (✉)
Judicial Academy, Ha Noi City, Viet Nam

Vietnam National University, Hanoi – University of Law, Ha Noi City, Viet Nam

N. Binh An et al. (eds.), *The Future of Child-Friendly Justice and Children's Rights in Vietnam*, https://doi.org/10.1007/978-981-95-3521-7_2

Civil judgment enforcement is the stage where judgments and decisions are implemented in practice, directly affecting the rights and obligations of the parties involved, including minors. This is a group of subjects with special characteristics in terms of age and cognition, yet the current legal provisions on civil judgment enforcement in Viet Nam have not paid much attention to this group. In the context that Viet Nam is building a child-friendly justice system, improving the legal provisions on civil judgment enforcement related to minors is of great importance and necessity.

2.2 General Issues on Minors in Civil Judgment Enforcement

2.2.1 Concept and Characteristics of Minors

2.2.1.1 Concept of Minors

International law does not use the term "persons under 18 years old" but rather uses the terms "child" and "minor." International legal instruments relating to minors such as the United Nations Convention on the Rights of the Child adopted by the United Nations General Assembly on 20 November 1989; the United Nations Standard Minimum Rules for the Administration of Juvenile Justice (Beijing Rules) adopted on 29 November 1985; and the United Nations Guidelines for the Prevention of Juvenile Delinquency (Riyadh Guidelines) adopted on 14 December 1990, all refer to children and minors. Article 1 of the Convention on the Rights of the Child provides that "For the purposes of the present Convention, a child means every human being below the age of eighteen years unless under the law applicable to the child, majority is attained earlier." According to the international view, a child is a person under 18 years old, a juvenile is a person from 15 to under 18 years old, youth refers to persons from 15 to 24 years old, and young persons include children, juveniles and youth. To designate the subjects protected under the Convention, international legal documents do not use entirely uniform terminology. Alongside the term "child" used in the Convention and its three optional protocols, other terms include "juvenile," "adolescent," and "youth," which are widely used in various rules, guidelines and general comments. Despite such differences, these instruments share the common goal of protecting persons under 18 years old or those who have not yet reached adulthood. It can be seen that, in defining "child" or "minor," international law does not rely on psychological or physiological characteristics but directly or indirectly determines by age. Both terms generally set the limit at under 18 years old while allowing States to provide for a lower age depending on their socio-economic conditions, culture and traditions.

Vietnamese law currently uses several terms, including "child" (meaning a person under 16 years old under the 2016 Law on Children), "minor" (meaning a person under 18 years old under the 2015 Civil Code, also used in the 2015 Civil Procedure Code and the 2012 Law on Handling Administrative Violations as amended in

2020 – this term is also used in the name of the specialised court for persons under 18 years old, namely the Family and Juvenile Court). The Penal Code and the Criminal Procedure Code use the phrase "person under 18 years old." The Convention on the Rights of the Child and other international standards use the terms "child" and "minor" to refer to persons under 18 years old.

Thus, the terms "child" and "minor," though not completely identical, are generally used to refer to the same group of persons under 18 years old. In the context of Vietnamese law, the concepts of "child" and "minor" participating in legal proceedings are now considered equivalent, with the age threshold being under 18 years. This provision is consistent with international law on the judicial rights of children.

2.2.1.2 Characteristics of Minors

First, regarding psychological and physiological development: Research on age-related psychology and physiology shows that during the ages of 11, 12–17 and 18, particularly from 12 to 15, there are complex changes and developments. This results from new elements of maturity, bodily changes, self-awareness, relationships with adults and peers, learning activities, and social engagement, all of which influence cognition and behaviour. Rapid physical development can affect tendencies to commit violent acts as a way to show strength, which may lead to criminal offences such as intentional injury or resisting law enforcement officers.

Second, regarding emotions: Minors are easily influenced by life circumstances. In addition to family factors such as family disharmony, parental divorce, or lack of shelter, there are external influences such as peer pressure or exposure to negative issues in society or the media. Their emotions are often unstable, easily agitated, impulsive and subject to change – this is a basic age-related characteristic of minors.

Third, regarding cognition: Minors do not have fully developed cognitive abilities and often lack life experience. Their psychological and physiological states are unstable, and their understanding of social matters, particularly legal awareness, is still limited or even incorrect. Therefore, minors tend to be impulsive, competitive and reckless when influenced by external factors.

2.2.2 The Role and Legal Status of Minors in Civil Judgment Enforcement

In Viet Nam, the estimated number of minors involved in legal matters each year is approximately 84,000, including 13,000 who commit administrative or criminal violations, 2000 who are victims, and 69,000 involved in divorce cases. Civil judgment enforcement is the activity that ensures the full and timely implementation of legally effective civil judgments and decisions in accordance with the order and procedures prescribed by law. In this stage, depending on the specific case, a minor may participate in civil judgment enforcement legal relations in the capacity of the judgment creditor (an individual entitled to the rights and interests specified in the judgment or decision to be enforced), the judgment debtor (an individual obliged to perform duties specified in the judgment or decision to be enforced), or a person with related rights and obligations (an individual, agency, or organisation whose rights and obligations are directly related to the enforcement of the rights or obligations of the parties) (Clauses 2, 3, 4 of Article 3, the Law on Civil Judgment Enforcement). When participating in civil judgment enforcement legal relations, minors have rights and obligations prescribed by law such as the right to request enforcement, the right to be notified of enforcement, and the right to reach agreements on enforcement (Articles 7(a, b), Law on Civil Judgment Enforcement). A minor exercises these rights and performs these obligations through his or her guardian or legal representative.

2.3 The Current State of Vietnamese Law on Minors in Civil Judgment Enforcement in Comparison with the Legal Systems of Certain Other Countries

2.3.1 The Right of Minors to Request Judgment Enforcement

Viet Nam was the first country in Asia and the second in the world to ratify the United Nations Convention on the Rights of the Child. In doing so, Viet Nam committed to guaranteeing four fundamental groups of children's rights as provided in the Convention, namely the right to survival, the right to development, the right to protection, and the right to participation. The right to request judgment enforcement is also encompassed within the fundamental rights of citizens, as recognised in the Constitution of the Socialist Republic of Viet Nam, expressed as human rights and citizens' rights in the political, civil, economic, cultural, and social spheres, including the right to have lawful residence, the right to the inviolability of one's domicile, and the right to ownership of lawful property. These rights are recognised, respected, protected, and guaranteed by the State under the Constitution and the law (Article 14(1), the Constitution of the Socialist Republic of Viet Nam). According to Clause 3 of Article 8 of the 2015 Civil Code, judgments of the court or decisions of other competent authorities as provided by law constitute one of the bases for the establishment of civil rights. Therefore, to restore infringed civil rights, based on the court's decision, the judgment creditor and the judgment debtor have the right to request enforcement in order to protect their civil rights.

Pursuant to Article 31 of the Law on Civil Judgment Enforcement of 2008 as amended in 2014, 2018, and 2022 (hereinafter referred to as the Law on Civil Judgment Enforcement), a party may directly submit a written request, present an oral request, or send a written request by post, either personally or through an authorised representative. In cases where the party is a legal entity or a minor, or a person with limited legal capacity, the head of the civil judgment enforcement agency shall issue the enforcement decision at the request of the lawful representative of that party. Where the party is a person lacking legal capacity, or a minor who has no parents, whose parents are unknown, or whose parents have both lost or have limited legal capacity, have difficulties in cognition or behaviour control, have been restricted by the court in parental rights, or are unable to care for or educate the minor, the head of the civil judgment enforcement agency shall issue the enforcement decision at the request of the guardian. Under Article 44 of the 2015 Civil Code, guardianship is the arrangement in which an individual or legal entity provided for by law, appointed by the commune-level People's Committee, designated by the court, or determined under Clause 2 of Article 48 of the Civil Code, carries out the care and protection of the lawful rights and interests of a minor, a person lacking legal capacity, or a person with difficulties in cognition or behaviour control.

This provision is similar to that of certain other countries. Under the German Civil Code (Bürgerliches Gesetzbuch), a minor's civil capacity is limited. Specifically, persons under seven years old have no legal capacity and must act through their legal representative, while persons from seven to under eighteen years old may perform certain legal acts but require the consent of their guardian, usually their parents or other lawful representative. Clause 2 of Article 1596 of the German Civil Code on recognition and consent in cases of lack or limitation of business capacity provides that for a minor lacking legal capacity or under fourteen years old, only the legal representative may give consent or recognition. German law also accords considerable respect to the views of minors. Under Article 1746 of the German Civil Code, for a child without legal capacity or under fourteen years old, only the lawful representative may give consent. A child may give consent personally; however, such consent must be approved by the lawful representative. If the child is at least fourteen years old and not lacking legal capacity, the child may withdraw consent before the decision becomes binding on the family court. The withdrawal must be publicly notarised and does not require the legal representative's consent. If the guardian or custodian refuses consent or approval without justifiable reason, the family court may replace such refusal, without requiring a declaration from the parents.

Vietnamese law clearly provides the method by which a minor may exercise the right to request judgment enforcement (through the guardian). However, it does not yet impose specific obligations on the guardian regarding the exercise of this right, nor does it prescribe sanctions to be applied where the guardian fails to act or acts inadequately in exercising such right. Therefore, in order to best ensure the right of minors to request judgment enforcement, the law should provide additional provisions on the responsibilities of the guardian in this regard, as well as specific sanctions in cases where the guardian fails to exercise or inadequately exercises this right.

2.3.2 Minor as Judgment Debtor

Under Vietnamese criminal law, "A minor committing a crime is a person from full fourteen years of age to under eighteen years of age, possessing full criminal responsibility capacity, who commits socially dangerous acts as prescribed in the Penal Code, with fault, infringing upon social relations protected by criminal law, and must bear criminal responsibility for his or her acts". Article 12 of the 2015 Penal Code as amended in 2017 provides that the age of criminal responsibility in Viet Nam is from full fourteen years of age. Persons from full fourteen years to under sixteen years of age shall bear criminal responsibility only for very serious crimes or particularly serious crimes. This differentiation of criminal responsibility age corresponds to the general principle that at different ages, minors have different levels of perception.

The German Juvenile Courts Act (JGG) also provides that a juvenile is a person from fourteen to seventeen years of age, with criminal responsibility starting at the age of fourteen (Article 19 of the Penal Code–Article 40(III) of the United Nations Convention on the Rights of the Child), but with a mandatory individual assessment of maturity under criminal law (Article 3 JGG). For young adults from eighteen to twenty years of age, certain restrictions on penalties apply under the JGG depending on the circumstances of each case.

Point d of Clause 1 of Article 12 of the 2015 Civil Procedure Code provides that children are exempt from paying advances on court costs and court fees. The Law on the Protection, Care and Education of Minors states that "Children as defined in this Law are Vietnamese citizens under sixteen years of age." Accordingly, if the defendant is from full fourteen to under sixteen years of age and commits an offence, he or she shall be exempt from court fees (both criminal and civil) when tried. If the defendant is from full sixteen to under eighteen years of age and commits an offence, in criminal proceedings the defendant must bear criminal court fees and civil court fees in accordance with the 2015 Civil Procedure Code and Articles 23 and 26 of Resolution No. 326/2016/UBTVQH14 on collection rates, exemptions, reductions, collection, payment, management and use of court fees and charges.

In addition, minors must compensate for damage in accordance with Clause 2 of Article 586 of the 2015 Civil Code. Where a person under fifteen years of age causes damage and still has parents, the parents must compensate for the entire damage. If the parents' property is insufficient for compensation and the minor has his or her own property, that property shall be used to compensate for the shortfall. Where a person from full fifteen to under eighteen years of age causes damage, he or she must compensate with his or her own property. If there is insufficient property to compensate, the parents must compensate for the shortfall with their own property.

In principle, a minor as judgment debtor may bear obligations relating to property such as compensation for damage, court fees, fines and similar obligations. In practice, enforcement of such obligations encounters considerable difficulty because minors often do not have money or property for enforcement, while in many cases their lawful representatives (the parents) try to evade enforcement obligations. Therefore, the court may consider other types of penalties (apart from monetary penalties) which are more appropriate for minors and more feasible for enforcement.

In relation to determining alternative penalties, in the Netherlands when a minor commits an offence, alternative sanctions are considered and applied. These sanctions may replace not only imprisonment but also traditional penalties such as fines or suspended sentences. There are two types of alternative sanctions applied to minors: community service projects and training projects. These sanctions may be applied to all types of offences committed by minors and to any minor offender, regardless of whether it is a first offence or a repeat offence, and regardless of gender.

Regarding enforcement procedures, the current Law on Civil Judgment Enforcement applies a uniform order and procedure to all judgment debtors without distinguishing cases where the judgment debtor is a minor. The principles for applying security measures and coercive enforcement measures do not specifically address the protection of the lawful rights and interests of this group. In Germany, enforcement against minors is regulated in a very strict manner, with special protection for the rights and development of the child. Procedures must ensure that minors have legal protection and are not subject to coercive measures beyond what is necessary to protect their interests. This is also an experience that Viet Nam may refer to in formulating principles for applying coercive measures in judgment enforcement.

2.3.3 *Handover of Minor to Custodian*

The handover of a minor to the custodian under a judgment or decision is a specific type of enforcement case arising in matrimonial and family cases. In the context of an increasing trend of divorce cases, the number of enforcement cases involving the handover of minors to custodians is also rising. This is a particularly complex type of enforcement case because the subject of enforcement is not money or property but a human being. Coercive enforcement of handing over a minor to the custodian is usually sensitive, affecting the psychology and emotions of the judgment creditor, the judgment debtor and the minor. It may even face obstruction or resistance from many quarters such as family members, relatives and local public opinion, making implementation difficult.

2.3.3.1 Person Granted Direct Custody by the Court

Under the interpretation in Article 3 of the Law on Civil Judgment Enforcement, the judgment creditor is an individual, agency or organisation entitled to the rights and interests in the judgment or decision to be enforced. In judgments and decisions of the court resolving matters relating to child custody, it can be understood that the person with the right to directly raise the child is identified as the judgment creditor. Accordingly, in principle, they have the right to renounce or not accept their rights and interests. This interpretation may not be entirely appropriate when viewed in the relationship between parent and child. Under the provisions of the Law on Marriage and Family, the care, upbringing and education of a minor child or an adult child who has lost legal capacity or is incapable of working and has no property to support himself or herself (hereinafter referred to as the child) (Articles 70, 71, the Law on Marriage and Family) is both the right and the obligation of the parents. When the spouses divorce, the spouse granted custody not only holds a right but also bears a duty. In the relationship with the other spouse, the custodial parent is identified as the judgment creditor, but in the relationship with the child, this person is both the rights holder and the person with the obligation to care for, raise and educate the child.

Under point e of Clause 1 of Article 48 of the Law on Civil Judgment Enforcement, the head of the civil judgment enforcement agency shall decide to postpone enforcement where the person granted custody has been duly notified twice of the handover but fails to appear to receive the child. In such case, if the judgment debtor voluntarily hands over the child but the custodial parent does not come to receive him or her, the enforcement agency shall postpone enforcement. However, when enforcement is postponed, the person obliged to hand over the child continues to care for, raise and educate the child, whereas under the judgment or decision of the court this responsibility should have been transferred to the other person. In this case, the lawful rights and interests of the child and of the parent who is not granted custody will not be guaranteed. This situation raises several issues as follows:

First, should the person granted the right to directly raise the child, who has not yet received or refuses to receive custody without a justifiable reason, be subject to any sanction? The Law on Civil Judgment Enforcement and its guiding documents do not contain provisions on this matter. In the author's view, in this case the receipt of custody under the court's judgment or decision is both a right and an obligation. Therefore, the failure or refusal to receive custody constitutes a violation of the provisions of the Law on Marriage and Family, specifically a breach of the parental obligation to care for, raise and nurture the child. The law should provide sanctions for such cases to compel this person to fulfil the obligation to assume custody.

Second, does the person obliged to transfer custody have the right to initiate a lawsuit to request the court to protect his or her rights when performing the care and upbringing that should rightfully belong to the custodial parent? The care and upbringing of a child is both a right and an obligation of the parents. The obligation to raise the child is a joint obligation of the parents, and therefore the property obligations arising from transactions for the purpose of raising the child are considered joint obligations of the spouses. Under the provisions of civil law and the law on marriage and family, the spouses are jointly responsible for performing this obligation. Where one party has fully performed the obligation, he or she has the right to request the other party to fulfil his or her share of the joint obligation (Article 288, the Civil Code; Articles 27, 37, 69, 71, the Law on Marriage and Family). Accordingly, it is reasonable for the person obliged to transfer custody to request the custodial parent to reimburse part of the expenses for raising the child. In practice, there have been cases where the judgment debtor voluntarily performed his or her obligation, but the judgment creditor failed or refused to receive the rights and interests. In such circumstances, in the author's opinion, the person obliged to transfer custody has the right to initiate a lawsuit to request the court to protect his or her rights, to require the custodial parent to reimburse part of the expenses for raising the child where the obligation to hand over the child was voluntarily performed but the transfer could not be completed due to the fault of the custodial parent. This should also be considered a basis for requesting a change of custody in accordance with the provisions of the Law on Marriage and Family.

2.3.3.2 Coercive Enforcement of the Handover of a Minor to the Custodian under the Judgment or Decision

In France, in matters concerning visitation rights or custody, if one of the parents fails to comply with a court decision, the minor may request the intervention of the family court judge (Juge aux Affaires Familiales). The court may order enforcement, including measures such as fines or the handover of the child to the party entitled to custody, but must always adhere to the principle of protecting the healthy development of the child. The judge may adopt measures to ensure that the child's relationship with each parent is maintained continuously in practice. In particular, the judge may order that the parents' passports be annotated with a prohibition on removing the child from French territory without the consent of both parents. This prohibition is also entered in the prosecutor's list of persons sought (Article 373–2–1, the French Civil Code).

In Viet Nam, the coercive enforcement of handing over a minor to the custodian under a judgment or decision is provided in Article 120 of the Law on Civil Judgment Enforcement. Where the judgment debtor or the person keeping the minor refuses to hand the minor over to the custodian, the bailiff issues a decision to impose a monetary fine, setting a time limit of five working days from the date of the fine decision for the person to hand over the minor. Under Clause 3 of Article 64 and Clause 3 of Article 85 of Decree No. 82/2020/ND-CP, the act of "failing to perform an act required by the judgment or decision" is subject to a fine of between 3,000,000 and 5,000,000 VND. However, the maximum fine that a bailiff is authorised to impose is 500,000 VND. Therefore, the power to impose administrative sanctions for the act of failing to hand over the minor under a judgment or decision does not fall within the bailiff's authority but within the authority of the Director of the provincial Civil Judgment Enforcement Department. The bailiff must prepare a record of administrative violation and request the Director to issue an administrative sanction decision. In practice, this procedure consumes a considerable amount of time for the bailiff and the civil judgment enforcement agencies.

According to Clause 2 of Article 120 of the Law on Civil Judgment Enforcement, upon expiry of the time limit set in the administrative sanction decision (five working days) without compliance, the bailiff proceeds to coercive enforcement of the handover or requests the competent authority to initiate criminal proceedings for the offence of failing to comply with a judgment. Article 380 of the 2015 Penal

Code as amended in 2017 provides that a person who, having the ability to comply, fails to comply with a court judgment or decision that has taken legal effect, after having been subjected to coercive measures under the law or having been administratively sanctioned for this act, shall be liable to imprisonment from three months to two years. If the offence falls under certain circumstances, such as resisting the bailiff or the person performing official duties, the penalty is imprisonment from two to five years. The offender may also be subject to a fine. In practice, requesting the competent authority to initiate criminal proceedings for the offence of failing to comply with a judgment still faces many difficulties. The bailiff must carry out numerous procedures to prepare the request file, but the public security agency and the people's procuracy at the same level may not necessarily agree to process it. Although Article 169 of the Law on Civil Judgment Enforcement provides for the duties and powers of the Ministry of Public Security in civil judgment enforcement, it has not addressed coordination between the public security agency and the civil judgment enforcement agency in the investigation and prosecution of crimes arising in judgment enforcement activities.

2.3.4 Enforcement of Child Support Obligations for Minors

Child support is the obligation of a person to contribute money or other property to meet the essential needs of another person with whom he or she does not live but to whom he or she is related by marriage, blood or adoption, in cases where that person is a minor, an adult incapable of working and without property to support himself or herself, or a person in difficulty or destitution as provided by law (Clause 24 of Article 3, the Law on Marriage and Family).

Under Clause 1 of Article 30 of the Law on Civil Judgment Enforcement, the limitation period for requesting enforcement of a periodic child support obligation is calculated for each period (monthly) and each period has a limitation period of five years from the due date of the obligation. To protect the interests of the person entitled to support, Clause 2 of Article 2 of the Law on Civil Judgment Enforcement provides that judgments and decisions on child support are enforceable immediately even if they are subject to appeal or protest. Therefore, for judgments and decisions on child support, the civil judgment enforcement agency must accept requests for enforcement even when the court judgment or decision has not yet taken legal effect.

The current law has relatively clear and specific provisions on receiving requests for enforcement and issuing enforcement decisions for judgments and decisions on child support obligations. However, there is still a lack of provisions on monitoring the use of child support funds. Monitoring and ensuring that child support is used for the correct purposes, such as healthcare, tuition, and living expenses, is an important requirement to safeguard the lawful rights and interests of minors. This is a practical issue that requires further research and improvement.

Regarding criminal liability for persons with a child support obligation who fail to perform it, Article 152 of the 2015 Penal Code as amended in 2017 provides for the offence of refusing or evading the obligation of child support: "Any person who has the obligation to provide child support under the law and has the actual ability to do so but deliberately refuses or evades the obligation, causing serious consequences, or who has been administratively sanctioned for this act and repeats the violation, shall be subject to a warning, non-custodial reform of up to two years, or imprisonment from three months to two years." This provision has many similarities with Article 227–3 of the French Penal Code (Code Pénal) on the offence of failing to perform a child support obligation, under which any person who is obliged to provide support for his or her children or spouse but fails to do so despite having the ability shall be liable to imprisonment of up to two years and/or a fine of up to 15,000 euros.

2.4 Certain Recommendations for Improving the Law on Minors in Civil Judgment Enforcement in Viet Nam

First: Provide specific principles to protect minors in civil judgment enforcement.

The improvement of the Law on Civil Judgment Enforcement must ensure special principles to protect minors, such as: safeguarding the best interests of the minor; ensuring friendly enforcement procedures; equal treatment; the right to full and timely information; ensuring prompt and timely access by minors to their legal representatives and legal aid providers; minimising the application of security measures and coercive enforcement measures; improving enforcement procedures to reduce psychological impact on minors.

A minor is a person who has not fully developed physically, emotionally, and cognitively. This is a vulnerable group in society and thus requires special protection and care, particularly in enforcement activities. Accordingly, policies in the field of civil judgment enforcement concerning minors need to adopt a specialised approach that is appropriate to the child's age and level of awareness. It is necessary to establish a specific enforcement procedure for cases involving minors in order to minimise negative psychological effects on the child. When deciding on enforcement measures, psychological factors and the development of the minor must be considered, rather than focusing solely on legal factors and neglecting the child's mental state. The participation of psychologists and child protection specialists should be encouraged. In certain cases, such specialists may assist the enforcement agency in assessing the psychological impact on the minor and in proposing appropriate protective measures.

Second: Design enforcement procedures consistent with the needs of minors and the Juvenile Justice Law.

It is necessary to ensure that children's rights are protected throughout the enforcement process, including the right to access legal services, the right not to be subjected to cruel treatment, and the right to protection from abuse. The right of minors to participate and express their views must be guaranteed and respected. Although minors do not have full decision-making capacity in many legal matters, in certain cases their right to participate in civil judgment enforcement proceedings and to present their views is of great importance. Mechanisms should be established for minors to participate in decisions affecting their interests in ways appropriate to their age and cognitive ability. Clearer provisions should be made on the rights and obligations of minors, especially in enforcement cases concerning property, inheritance, and maintenance. The identification and protection of the lawful rights and interests of minors should be specified in detail, with clear guidance to avoid situations in which minors are disadvantaged or unprotected during enforcement.

Amendments and supplements to certain provisions on enforcement procedures involving minors should be made based on the approach of child-friendly justice. This is particularly relevant given that Viet Nam has enacted the Juvenile Justice Law (Article 36), which provides for diversion measures such as warnings, apologies to victims, compensation for damage, and community-based education at the commune, ward, or township level. The Law on Civil Judgment Enforcement should be further supplemented with provisions relating to these diversion measures in the future.

Mechanisms for monitoring and protecting the rights of minors in civil judgment enforcement should be strengthened. A special monitoring mechanism should be established for cases directly involving minors. In addition to the lawful representative of the minor in civil judgment enforcement proceedings, organisations for the protection of children's rights should also participate to ensure that the lawful rights and interests of minors are not infringed.

Third: Training and capacity building for authorised enforcement personnel in cases involving minors.

Enhancing the capacity of enforcement authorities is a crucial factor in ensuring humanity, fairness, and efficiency in the legal system. Training should focus on specific areas such as international principles and legal provisions relating to children, especially the United Nations Convention on the Rights of the Child and the rules on handling juvenile offenders; legal provisions concerning the enforcement of judgments involving minors, ensuring that enforcement measures respect the rights and development of minors; and understanding the psychology and development of minors so as to apply suitable methods and enforcement measures.

Furthermore, the handling of enforcement cases involving minors requires coordination among multiple entities such as courts, enforcement agencies, social organisations, child protection agencies, and families. Therefore, training in inter-agency coordination for cases involving minors is necessary, with emphasis on the responsibility of agencies, organisations, and individuals in enforcement activities relating to minors.

Fourth: Strengthen international cooperation and learn from international experience in enforcement involving minors.

Viet Nam can learn from and refer to international experiences to improve its domestic legal system, contributing to better protection of minors' rights in civil judgment enforcement. This includes compliance with international cooperation on principles and standards, with the United Nations Convention on the Rights of the Child serving as an important legal basis for States in protecting children's rights, particularly in enforcement proceedings. It is necessary to strengthen cooperation between countries in adhering to these principles, ensuring that enforcement measures involving minors conform to international standards.

Experience should be shared in applying the principles of the United Nations Standard Minimum Rules for the Administration of Juvenile Justice (Beijing Rules) and the Convention on the Rights of the Child to ensure that the legal system does not merely punish but also educates and reintegrates children into the community. Participation in international organisations such as the International Labour Organization (ILO), UNICEF, and other organisations specialising in the rights of children and youth should be promoted to exchange experience and learn effective models for enforcement involving minors. Enforcement measures must not infringe upon the lawful rights and interests of minors while promoting policies and laws to protect minors in enforcement cases. The application of international standards and coordination between judicial bodies, child protection agencies, social organisations, and communities should be promoted to address issues related to enforcement involving minors.

2.5 Conclusion

Improving the law on the protection of minors in civil judgment enforcement is an important and urgent task to ensure their rights and interests. Viet Nam needs to implement a set of coordinated solutions, particularly amendments and supplements to the current provisions of the Law on Civil Judgment Enforcement in a direction that is friendly to minors, thereby contributing to the comprehensive and effective protection of their rights and interests.

References

Bình, N. H. (2024, 6 10). *Major orientations in developing the Juvenile Justice Law in Viet Nam.* Tạp chí Cộng sản. https://www.tapchicongsan.org.vn/media-story/-/asset_publisher/V8hhp4dK31Gf/content/nhung-dinh-huong-lon-trong-xay-dung-luat-tu-phap-nguoi-chua-thanh-nien-o-viet-n-1

Bình, V. N. (1996). Juvenile justice and children's rights. In *Juvenile justice and childrens rights* (p. 13). National Politics Publishing House.

Châu, L. V. (2018, 08 28). *Handling cases where the judgment creditor fails or refuses to receive custody of the child under the court's judgment or decision.* https://tapchitoaan.vn/xu-ly-truong-hop-nguoi-duoc-thi-hanh-an-khong-hoac-chua-tiep-nhan-quyen-truc-tiep-nuoi-con-theo-ban-an-quyet-dinh-cua-toa-an?

Đức, L. B., & Hương, P. Q. (2022, 09 20). *Causes and conditions of juvenile crime and preventive solutions.* Retrieved from 12 29, 2024. https://danchuphapluat.vn/nguyen-nhan-dieu-kien-pham-toi-cua-nguoi-chua-thanh-nien-va-giai-phap-phong-ngua

Đức, N. M. (2014). Causes and conditions of minors committing criminal offences and preventive solutions. *Justice.*

Government. (2020). Report No. 217/BC-CP on the implementation of policies and laws on prevention and combat of child abuse. Báo cáo. Retrieved from 05 14, 2020. https://datafiles.chinhphu.vn/cpp/files/vbpq/2020/05/217.signed.pdf

Hải, Đ. T. (2019, 1 31). *The rights of minors committing crimes under international law and Vietnamese law*. Ministry of Justice Portal: https://moj.gov.vn/qt/tintuc/Pages/nghien-cuu-trao-doi.aspx?ItemID=2420

Hiếu, Q. N. (2018). *Enforcement of decisions on the application of provisional urgent measures*. In Master's thesis in law (p. 31). Ho Chi Minh City University of Law.

Hoa, H. T. (2017, 10 16). *Administrative sanctioning in civil judgment enforcement–Why is it ineffective?*. Retrieved from 12 29, 2024. http://baophapluat.vn/hoi-dap-phap-luat/xu-phat-vi-pham-hanh-chinh-trong-thi-hanh-an-dan-su-vi-sao-kem-hieu-qua-360854.html

Hoàng, C. V., & Hiếu, a. N. (2015, 9 28). Certain issues on child-friendly justice. http://hvta.toaan.gov.vn/portal/page/portal/hvta/27676686/27677461?p_page_id=27677461&pers_id=28346379&folder_id=&item_id=122284560&p_details=1

Hoàng, Đ. Q., & Hiền, N. T. (2024, 6 27). *The right to development of children in Viet Nam*. Retrieved from 12 28, 2024. https://www.xaydungdang.org.vn/nhan-quyen-va-cuoc-song/quyen-duoc-phat-trien-cua-tre-em-tai-viet-nam-21119

Ministry of Justice & Unicef. (2019). Research report on law relating to prevention, handling, rehabilitation and community reintegration of minors committing legal violations and the situation of minors committing legal violations in Viet Nam.

Ministry of Justice; Supreme People's Court; Supreme People's Procuracy. (2016, 8 1). Article 1. Joint Circular No. 11/2016/TTLT-BTP-TANDTC-VKSNDTC.

Ngân, K. (2017, 10 02). *Why is the divorce rate increasing?* Retrieved from 01 03, 2025. http://baovinhphuc.com.vn/xa-hoi/43199/vi-sao-tinh-trang-ly-hon-ngay-cang-gia-tang.html

NH Quang & Associates Law Office. (2024). In *Research on the formation and operation of the Family and Juvenile Court in Viet Nam within the framework of the programme* Enhancing the Rule of Law and Justice in Viet Nam (EU JULE) (p. 8). Lao Động.

Phong, V. (2023, 15 06). *Training workshop on handling cases involving minors*. https://tapchitoaan.vn/kinh-nghiem-quoc-te-trong-viec-giai-quyet-cac-vu-an-lien-quan-den-nguoi-chua-thanh-nien8761.html

Quốc hội nước Cộng hòa xã hội chủ nghĩa Việt Nam. (2013). Điều 37, Hiến pháp nước Cộng hòa xã hội chủ nghĩa Việt Nam.

Thanh, P. V., Hải, N. T., Công, L. M., Thức, N. M., & Công, N. T. (n. d). *Preventing minors from committing legal violations–current situation and solutions*. Ho Chi Minh City National University Publishing House.

Thông, T. Q., & Đức, H. M. (2017). *Juvenile criminal justice in Viet Nam today–certain theoretical and practical issues*. People's Public Security Publishing House.

Thủy, M. T. (2022). *Diversion measures for persons under 18 committing crimes under Vietnamese criminal law*. In Doctoral thesis in law, (p. 28). Ho Chi Minh City University of Law.

Tiến, B. Đ. (2018). *Implementation of law on coercive civil judgment enforcement in Viet Nam*. In Doctoral thesis in law (p. 31). Vietnam Academy of Social Sciences.

UNICEF. (2015). Training material on child justice for judges.

United Nations. (1989). The united nation convention on the rights of the child.

Chapter 3
The Future of Child-Friendly Justice on Property Rights of Minors in Vietnam's Civil Law

Doan Thi Ngoc Hai and Luu Tran Phuong Thao

Abstract Within the scope of this research, the authors focus on analyzing certain provisions of Vietnamese civil law regarding the property rights of minors, thereby proposing several recommendations to improve the provisions of civil law in order to better ensure the property rights of minors in civil life. This is to contribute towards building a child-friendly justice system for minors in Viet Nam in the coming period.

3.1 Introduction

Building a justice system that is friendly to minors is an objective and inevitable requirement, and is highly necessary for every nation and territory, especially in the context of deep international integration at present. Viet Nam is the first country in Asia and the second in the world to ratify the United Nations Convention on the Rights of the Child (UNCRC). It is also a country that has recognized many international instruments on human rights in general and children's rights in particular, all of which recommend promoting the construction and improvement of laws on juvenile justice. Directive No. 28-CT/TW dated 25 December 2023 of the Politburo on strengthening the work of care, education and protection of children to meet the requirements of developing a prosperous and happy country has set out the solution of "developing a child-friendly justice system and protecting children". Article 37 of the Constitution of the Socialist Republic of Viet Nam 2013 affirms: "Children shall be protected, cared for and educated by the State, family and society; and shall be allowed to participate in issues concerning children". It can be said that Viet Nam has carried out

Article history: Received 27 April 2025; Revised 09 July 2025; Accepted 23 August 2025

D. T. N. Hai (✉) · L. T. P. Thao
Vietnam Women's Academy, Ha Noi City, Viet Nam
e-mail: haidtn@hvpnvn.edu.vn

L. T. P. Thao
e-mail: Thaoltp@vwa.edu.vn

N. Binh An et al. (eds.), *The Future of Child-Friendly Justice and Children's Rights in Vietnam*, https://doi.org/10.1007/978-981-95-3521-7_3

many important reforms, most notably the effort to codify the legal system towards building a child-friendly justice system for minors.

The property rights of individuals in general, including minors, are one of the fundamental civil rights. Every individual has the right to own their property. However, for minors, Vietnamese civil law has not clearly and specifically provided for their property rights, although the Civil Code, 2015, the Law on Children, 2014, and the Law on Marriage and Family, 2014 have mentioned the property rights of minors. Therefore, in the context where Viet Nam is building a child-friendly justice system for minors, improving the provisions of the law on property in general, including those relating to minors, is both important and necessary.

3.2 General Overview of Property Rights in Civil Law

From the perspective of legal science, up to now there are still many different views in Viet Nam on property rights. According to Assoc. Prof. Dr. Nguyen Ngoc Dien, "property rights in the positive law of Viet Nam are understood as legal relations different from ownership relations, where on the basis of such other relations, an interest valued in money is formed and belongs to a subject of such relation" (Nguyen Ngoc Dien, 2005). Assoc. Prof. Dr. Phung Trung Tap believes that "property rights can be understood in a broad sense as a collection of rights and interests of the subject in controlling and managing property, including the owner and persons having other rights over the property" (Nguyen Van Cu & Tran Thi Hue, 2017). Author Nguyen Hoang Long, in an article published in the People's Court Journal, asserts that "property rights are a special type of intangible property". Thus, from a theoretical point of view, there remain many differing interpretations of property rights, so it is very necessary to provide an exact definition of property rights in the Civil Code. However, determining how to define it accurately and reasonably is not simple, and requires research and comparison with the laws of some countries and with the practice in Viet Nam.

According to the Textbook of Ho Chi Minh City University of Law, "property rights are a specific form of property, not existing in a tangible material form, and are a type of civil right with economic content, which can be valued in money, that the right holder may exercise themselves or request others to perform in order to satisfy the material or spiritual needs of the right holder". This definition summarizes the characteristics of property rights as a form of property, namely that they are civil rights of an intangible nature and can be valued in money. Thus, although not explicitly stated, when viewed in the aspect of rights, the definition of property rights only covers ownership rights (as a form of property) over intangible things, and does not include other rights and interests, meaning certain real rights are not regarded as property. The definition also indicates the way in which the right holder can act, either by themselves (right in rem) or by requesting another person to act (right in personam).

From the perspective of foreign law, property rights are a type of subjective right (Nguyen Ngoc Dien, 2005). The concept of property rights is constructed within the framework of the institution of subjective rights, which is considered the backbone of the private law systems in countries of the Romano-Germanic legal tradition. Subjective rights are understood as the restriction of others' freedom under the provisions of law, for the benefit of the subject in exercising the rights recognized in a certain field. For example, ownership of income-generating property is the owner's exclusive right to use the property, collect its fruits and dispose of it; everyone must respect that right, and any act of infringement may be subject to sanctions under the law.

Based on the criterion of whether the right can be valued in money, subjective rights are divided into two types: rights that cannot be valued in money, called personal rights, and rights that can be valued in money, called property rights. In principle, property rights can be transferred in civil transactions and therefore serve as security for obligations established by the right holder. In certain cases, there are rights that have property value but are attached to the person and therefore cannot be transferred or seized. A typical example is the right to claim maintenance.

What kind of property right is regarded as property? According to a definition of property in the Deluxe Black's Law Dictionary, "property is a term to describe everything that is the subject of ownership" (Bryan A. Garner, 1999). Under the current provisions of Viet Nam, ownership includes three basic powers of the subject: the right to possess, the right to use, and the right to dispose. Therefore, something that is the subject of ownership means that it can be possessed, used and disposed of by a certain subject. In many countries, ownership consists of the rights to use and dispose, while possession of property is regulated as a factual condition with respect to property. According to the theory of Harold Demsetz and actual practice, a property right may be exercised by many different subjects. Property rights can be exercised by various persons, and in specific cases "the exercise of such rights has no meaning and is not appropriate for the establishment of ownership" (SMH Law School Summaries I, Third Edition, SMH Inc, 1987). From this perspective, we can explain why rights such as mortgage, pledge, assignment, priority in payment, right of recourse, and other rights, while having economic value, may not be considered as property.

In addition, determining which rights are the subject of ownership depends on the legislative perspective of each country. For instance, under Vietnamese law, the right of usufruct is not regarded as the subject of ownership; it is a right established over another person's property, forming part of the owner's rights to the property, but not separated into an independent property with full ownership powers. The holder of the usufruct right is not recognized as having the right to sell, pledge or mortgage the property (Article 261 of the Civil Code, 2015), so the holder cannot exercise such powers (Article 160 of the Civil Code, 2015). However, under the law of the French Republic, the right of usufruct is also a right established over another's property, but French law affirms that the usufructuary may sell the usufruct right. This shows that the usufruct right itself is also the subject of ownership and is property. Similarly, under Vietnamese law, the land use right is property in the form of a property right, while in the law of many countries the land use right is a power within land ownership. The Civil Code of China considers that "A person who has a beneficial real right in accordance with the provisions of law is entitled to possess, use and derive benefits from immovable property or movable property owned by another person in accordance with the provisions of law" (Article 323 of the Civil Code of China, 2020).

3.3 Identifying Property Rights under the Perspective of Vietnamese Positive Law

Article 115 of the Civil Code, 2015 provides: "Property rights are rights that can be valued in money, including property rights over objects of intellectual property rights, land use rights and other property rights." From this provision, it can be seen that, according to the drafters of the Civil Code, 2015, property rights are now characterized only by one distinctive feature, namely "can be valued in money". That is, any right that brings economic value to a person will be considered a property right. They take the view that the nature of property rights should be regarded only in terms of their economic value (that is, their monetary valuation), while the matter of whether they can be transferred or cannot be transferred in civil transactions serves only to determine which property rights will be the object of civil transactions, and is not itself a characteristic of property rights. Article 115 of the Civil Code, 2015 also lists types of property rights including: rights over objects of intellectual property rights, land use rights, and other property rights. In the end, this provision is not a complete definition of property rights; rather, it lies somewhere between a definitional provision and a provision of enumeration.

In addition to Article 115, the Civil Code, 2015 also contains Article 450 referring to the purchase and sale of property rights, which provides that (i) the right to claim a debt is a type of property right, and (ii) "the time when ownership of a property right is transferred is the time when the purchaser receives documents concerning ownership of that property right or from the time of registration of the ownership transfer, if the law so provides". The term "documents concerning ownership" should be understood broadly, to include all papers and vouchers relating to the property right.

Clause 7 Article 6 of Circular No. 08/2018/TT-BTP dated 20 June 2018 of the Ministry of Justice guiding certain matters on registration and provision of information on security measures, contracts and exchange of information on registration of security measures at the Transaction and Property Registration Centers of the National Registration Agency for Secured Transactions under the Ministry of Justice provides that property rights under Article 115 of the Civil Code, except land use rights, include: (i) property rights arising from copyright, industrial property rights, rights to plant varieties; rights to claim debts; rights to exploit natural resources; rights to compensation for damage arising from contracts; (ii) property rights arising from contracts for the lease of shipbuilding; rights to compensation for damage arising from contracts for the sale of aircraft and ships; rights to benefit from insurance under insurance contracts relating to aircraft and ships; (iii) property rights such as rights to claim debts, rights to request payment, rights to compensation for damage, rights to benefit from insurance arising from contracts for the sale of housing, contracts for capital contribution for housing construction, contracts for investment cooperation or business cooperation in housing, contracts for lease or lease-purchase of housing (including social housing) between organizations and individuals or between organizations, individuals and real estate business enterprises in housing construction projects under the housing law; property rights such as rights to claim debts, rights to request payment, rights to compensation for damage, rights to benefit from insurance arising from contracts for sale, capital contribution, investment cooperation, business cooperation, lease or lease-purchase of construction works between organizations and individuals or between organizations, individuals and real estate business enterprises in construction projects under the law on real estate business; (iv) other property rights under the law. Thus, Circular No. 08/2018/TT-BTP does not recognize land use rights as a property right.

Alongside property rights, the Civil Code, 2015 also recognizes other rights over property, whereby "other rights over property are the rights of a subject to directly hold and control property belonging to the ownership of another subject. Other rights over property include: rights to adjacent immovable property, rights of usufruct, and rights of superficies" (Civil Code, 2015, Article 108). The sign for identifying other rights over property is the status of the subject directly holding, exploiting the utility, and enjoying the fruits and income from the property. If a person is not the owner of the property but has the right to hold, exploit the utility, and enjoy the fruits and income from property belonging to another's ownership, they are determined to be a holder of other rights over property.

Other rights over property is a new concept used to distinguish from the concept of ownership and the concept of property rights, and it encompasses rights to adjacent immovable property, rights of usufruct, and rights of superficies. There is a viewpoint that the concept of other rights over property is not a constituent part of the concept of property rights. To explain this view, some scholars point out that the approach to the concept of property in the Civil Code of Viet Nam is constructed in the direction that "property is the object of ownership", and ownership is defined by the Civil Code through listing the specific powers of the owner to be exercised over their property. Other rights over property, in some sense, are understood as a "sharing" of ownership, since the owner has transferred certain powers to the holder of other rights over the property. However, not in every case does the owner share their ownership; depending on the case, the owner may transfer to another person the right to possess, to exploit the utility, and to enjoy the fruits and income from the property.

Another viewpoint holds that other rights over property are in fact "limited real rights" (Ho Chi Minh City University of Law, 2019), a term used to distinguish from the concept of "real rights" which refers to ownership. In practice, there are cases where subjects do not have the capacity or do not have the need to directly exercise the powers of the owner to exploit and enjoy their property. Conversely, there are subjects who do not have property or wish to use, exploit and enjoy property belonging to another owner. Through specific transactions, the needs of these subjects meet. In other words, the owner allows a non-owner to use, exploit the functions and utility, and enjoy the benefits of their property. Although they also have powers over the property, the nature of these rights is that they are established on the basis of the owner's consent, so the scope of the rights of the holder of other rights over property is very limited. In this context, the term "limited real rights" is used to describe the powers of a non-owner over property belonging to another's ownership to satisfy their personal or consumption needs arising in civil transactions.

Therefore, in the narrow sense, the concept of other rights over property as understood under the Civil Code, 2015 refers to the specific powers and obligations arising for a non-owner when they hold and control property belonging to another's ownership. In short, the Civil Code, 2015 defines other rights over property as "the right of a subject to directly hold and control property belonging to the ownership of another subject" (Civil Code, 2015, Clause 1 Article 159).

3.4 The Current State of Vietnamese Civil Law on the Property Rights of Minors and Proposals for Legal Improvement

The Civil Code, 2015, the Law on Children, 2014, the Law on Marriage and Family, 2014, and a number of related legal instruments all recognize that minors have their own property and have ownership rights over their property. Article 75 of the Law on Marriage and Family, 2014 provides that minors have the right to own separate property. The separate property of a minor includes property inherited individually, property given individually, income from the labor of the minor, fruits and income arising from the minor's separate property, and other lawful income. Property formed from the separate property of a minor is also their separate property. In addition, Article 20 of the Law on Children 2016 also provides that children have the right to own, inherit, and exercise other rights with respect to property. Vietnamese positive law provides that the subject being a minor has ownership rights over their separate property, and civil transactions involving large property must be made through their legal representative. They also have the three basic powers of the owner over property, namely the right to possess, the right to use, and the right to dispose.

However, when approached from the perspective of the property rights of minors, there remain many matters that require clarification. Article 115 of the Civil Code, 2015 provides that "Property rights are rights that can be valued in money, including property rights over objects of intellectual property rights, land use rights, and other property rights." Although Article 115 of the Civil Code, 2015 determines that the above rights are "rights that can be valued in money", not every right that can be valued in money is regarded as an object of property. In other words, the law does not always establish the ownership right over such property rights for the subject, but rather treats them purely as real rights, as a component of ownership. Article 159 of the Civil Code, 2015 recognizes three types of real rights called "other rights over property" which are the rights of a subject established over property "belonging to the ownership of another subject", including rights of usufruct, rights of superficies, and rights to adjacent immovable property. These are rights separated from ownership to become independent rights. Notably, the rights of usufruct and superficies are rights that can be valued in money and can be easily transferred in civil circulation. According to Nguyen Ngoc Dien, "Separated from ownership to become an independent right, major real rights that are not ownership rights are temporary in nature: at some point these rights must disappear or return to ownership" (Nguyen Ngoc Dien, 2016). Article 115 of the Civil Code, 2015 provides a general regulation on property rights, within which the property rights of minors are included.

First, the property rights of minors over objects of intellectual property rights. Minors have intellectual property rights like any other subject, but the right to dispose of property rights related to such intellectual property objects may be restricted, especially in important transactions such as transfer, lease, or use for business purposes. Minors may be authors, owners of copyright, or owners of industrial property rights or plant variety rights. They have the right to enjoy the property rights arising from intellectual property rights, such as the right to receive royalties, remuneration, and the right to use and exploit works, inventions, and industrial designs. However, while minors have intellectual property rights, they may be restricted in disposing of property rights related to intellectual property objects. In practice, minors participate in labor relations at a very early age. Article 145 of the Labour Code 2019 provides that "A labor contract must be concluded in writing with a person under fifteen years old and their legal representative", which means that a person under fifteen years old already has the right to conclude a labor contract, to earn property to support themselves, and in some cases individuals in this age group are the main breadwinners of the family. However, the law restricts their rights when engaging in certain civil transactions with their own property.

For property rights that are the subject of intellectual property rights, including the rights of the holder of a protection title over inventions, utility solutions, industrial designs, trademarks, trade names, layout designs of semiconductor integrated circuits, and plant varieties; copyright over literary, artistic, and scientific works; rights of the copyright owner and the rights of related rights holders, when a minor is the owner of such rights and wishes to establish a transaction, the law requires that this be done through their legal representative. The Civil Code, 2015 and several other laws restrict the rights of minors over their property rights when establishing and performing civil transactions, including property rights in respect of intellectual property objects. Therefore, the law should be adjusted to ensure the property rights of this group of subjects.

Second, the property rights of minors with respect to land use rights. In Viet Nam at present, land is under the ownership of the entire people with the State acting as the representative owner, and the State uniformly manages the land. The State allocates land to individuals, legal entities, and other subjects for use in constructing houses and other structures for a certain period or for long-term use (residential land is land used on a long-term basis). Accordingly, the subject with land use rights is the owner of a type of right, namely the right to use land. This is a very distinctive feature of Viet Nam's land regime compared to other countries. For example, under Chinese civil law, specialized ownership belongs to the State: "Immovable and movable property that the law provides as specialized State ownership shall not be owned by any organization or individual" (Article 241 of the Civil Code of China, 2020). This is because in China, under the socialist public ownership regime, the ownership of certain property can only belong to the State, and no organization or individual can acquire ownership. Specifically, Article 9 of the 1982 Constitution of China provides: "Natural resources such as mineral resources, water sources, forests, mountains, grasslands, wasteland, tidal flats and so on shall be owned by the State, that is, by the entire people"; Article 10 provides: "Land in cities shall be owned by the State"; Article 12 provides: "The socialist public property is sacred and inviolable. The State protects socialist public property. It is prohibited for any organization or individual to seize or damage State or collective property in any way."

From the perspective of the property rights of minors over land use rights, as mentioned above, under the Labour Code, minors are allowed to participate in labor relations to create material wealth, so they have separate property derived from the salary they receive, and they have rights over that property. Furthermore, Vietnamese civil law provides that a person's separate property includes property given individually and inherited individually. Clause 1 of Article 75 of the Law on Marriage and Family, 2014 provides for the right of a child to have separate property: "A child has the right to have separate property, which includes property inherited individually, property given individually, income from the labor of the child, fruits and income arising from the child's separate property, and other lawful income. Property formed from the child's separate property is also the child's separate property." Vietnamese positive law has very specific provisions on the right of minors to have separate property. However, the shortcoming lies in the fact that while a minor has the right to have separate property, the law provides that the disposal of their property rights must be through their representative.

With regard to separate property that is a minor's land use right, the current Land Law of Viet Nam does not prohibit (nor restrict) an individual from having their name on the land use right certificate, which means that a minor is still allowed to be the owner of property in the form of land use rights and to have their name recorded on the certificate of land use rights. The flexibility of the law has enabled subjects, especially minors with the need and capacity to develop economically from land, to have their rights recognized and protected under the law. For example, an individual under 18 years old may be named in a joint will made by their grandparents to bequeath to them as an inheritance the property right being the land use right. When the grandparents pass away, the will takes legal effect (Article 624 of the Civil Code, 2015), and the individual has the right to carry out the procedure for transfer of ownership of the property being the land use right at the competent State agency. At that time, the certificate of land use rights will be transferred from the name of the grandparents to the name of the person designated in the will.

However, it should be noted that although a minor's name may be recorded on the certificate of land use rights, the minor does not have the right to independently perform civil transactions relating to the land use right, but must act through their legal representative. Specifically, Article 21 of the Civil Code, 2015 provides: (i) A person from full six years old to under fifteen years old, when establishing and performing civil transactions, must also have the consent of their legal representative; (ii) A person from full fifteen years old to under eighteen years old may independently establish and perform certain civil transactions, except for civil transactions relating to immovable property and movable property that must have the consent of their legal representative. The law so provides to ensure the rights and interests of minors in civil transactions and to ensure the transparency and clarity of legal transactions concerning land use rights.

The question arises as to what happens when a minor wishes to perform a civil transaction with respect to land use rights. The law provides that the legal representative, when a person under fifteen years old is named on the certificate of land use rights, has important rights and obligations to protect the interests of the minor in transactions involving land use rights, namely: (i) They have the right to act on behalf of the minor in performing legal transactions relating to land use rights. This includes carrying out transactions such as transfer, lease, or mortgage of the land use right; (ii) Their main responsibility is to protect the lawful rights and interests of the minor with respect to the land use right. This ensures that all activities related to the land are conducted in accordance with the provisions of law.

Regarding the obligations of the legal representative, first, they must perform transactions concerning the land use right in a manner that serves the interests of the minor. This requires the legal representative to evaluate and make decisions based on the long-term interests of the minor, ensuring that their actions in the transaction do not cause disadvantage to the minor. In addition, they bear legal responsibility for acts that violate the law in the process of carrying out transactions involving land use rights. This includes compliance with legal provisions on land transactions, ensuring that all acts of the legal representative are carried out within the limits and content provided by law.

Another question arises: if a civil transaction concerning land use rights is performed by a minor without the consent of their legal representative, how will it be handled? First, civil transactions concerning land use rights carried out by a minor without the consent of their legal representative will be considered invalid. This means that acts such as transfer, lease, or mortgage of land use rights by a minor will have no legal value and will not be protected under the law. Next, the legal representative of the minor has the right and may initiate legal proceedings to reclaim the property right, being the land use right, for the minor. However, the mechanism for protecting the property rights of minors when they perform civil transactions concerning land use rights remains general in nature, therefore it is necessary to add specific provisions in the guiding documents to elaborate the content of the Civil Code.

Third, other property rights of minors. These can be understood to include the right to claim compensation for damage to property, health, life, and other personal rights of minors that are infringed; the right to request payment of a sum of property; the right to claim debts; the right to exploit natural resources; property rights arising from contracts; the right to receive insurance payments; property rights over contributed capital in enterprises; the right to use marine areas allocated for aquaculture; the right to receive maintenance; and other property rights as provided by law. However, the mechanism for protecting other property rights of minors has not been made specific, and is mostly applied generally to individuals as a subject, therefore the law should be adjusted accordingly to ensure the property rights of minors.

3.5 Conclusion

The study of the institution of the property rights of minors in Vietnamese civil law shows that Vietnamese positive law has relatively specific provisions to ensure the property rights of individuals in general, including minors. However, alongside these progressive aspects, there remain certain limitations. Therefore, to build a child-friendly justice system for minors in general, in which the institution of property rights is an important component, is a matter that should be implemented in the coming period, in order to promptly meet the spirit set out in Directive No. 28-CT/TW dated 25 December 2023 of the Politburo.

References

Civil Code. 2015.

Civil Code of China. 2020.

Garner, B. A. (1999). *Black's law dictionary* (7th ed., p. 1232). West Group.

Ho Chi Minh City University of Law. (2019). *Textbook on the law on property, ownership, and inheritance* (revised and supplemented ed.). Hong Duc Publishing House—Viet Nam Lawyers Association.

Law on Children. 2014.

Law on Marriage and Family. 2014.

Nguyen Ngoc Dien. (2005). The need to redefine the concept of property rights in the civil code. *Legislative Studies Journal*, No. 03/2005.

Nguyen Ngoc Dien. (2016). *Textbook on civil law* (Vol. 1). Viet Nam National University Ho Chi Minh City Publishing House.

Nguyen Van Cu & Tran Thi Hue. (2017). *Scientific commentary on the civil code 2015*. People's Public Security Publishing House.

SMH Law School Summaries I, Third Edition, SMH Inc. (1987). *Real Property*, 1.

Part II
Children's Rights in Vietnamese Law and Justice

Chapter 4
Labour Rights of Vietnamese Children: Legal Reforms for a Child-Friendly Justice Approach

Nguyen Hien Phuong and Nguyen Minh Ha

Abstract The labour rights of minors have been protected by Vietnamese law through various mechanisms. However, recent reports on the current situation of juvenile labour indicate that the actual implementation of these mechanisms remains ineffective. Therefore, this study identifies the limitations and root causes of such ineffectiveness and proposes legislative recommendations as well as practical enforcement measures. The objective is to ensure the protection of juvenile labour rights and to contribute to preparing a high quality workforce, serving as a key driver for national economic growth and the development of a civilised society.

4.1 Introduction

Human beings and human rights, including the right to work, are the central focus of development in every nation. Labour is the means for individuals to achieve self development while simultaneously contributing to socio economic development in general. Therefore, the right to work is recognised and protected by law as one of the fundamental human rights. However, scientific research has shown that labour capacity varies according to age, largely depending on psychological, physiological and cognitive characteristics of individuals at specific stages. In particular, minors whose physical and psychological development is not yet complete must be placed under strict management by the state when they participate in the labour market. Such management must go together with appropriate policies and regulations that both respect the labour rights of minors and create a favourable environment for them to fully develop their potential to later assume national responsibilities. Vietnam, in

Article history: Received 02 April 2025; Revised 25 July 2025; Accepted 08 August 2025.

N. H. Phuong
Hanoi Law University, Ha Noi City, Viet Nam
e-mail: hienphuongld@hlu.edu.vn

N. M. Ha (✉)
World Bank Group, Washington, DC, USA

N. Binh An et al. (eds.), *The Future of Child-Friendly Justice and Children's Rights in Vietnam*, https://doi.org/10.1007/978-981-95-3521-7_4

essence, has established a number of policies and regulations to protect juvenile workers. However, in the current context of rapidly advancing science and technology, it is urgently necessary for Vietnam to further improve its legal and policy frameworks to better adapt to ongoing changes.

4.2 Juvenile Labour and the Situation of Juvenile Labour in Vietnam

4.2.1 Definition and Characteristics of Juvenile Labour

The current Vietnamese legal system recognises both terms “children” and “minors”. According to Article 1 of the Law on Children 2016, “a child is a person under 16 years of age”, while under the Civil Code (2015a), “a minor is a person under 18 years of age”. However, Vietnamese labour law does not use the term “child labour” as found in ILO Conventions, but only defines “juvenile labour” as persons under 18 years of age (Clause 1 Article 143 of the Labour Code (2019). Nevertheless, based on the characteristics of juvenile workers and the age threshold used by the ILO to define child labour, it is possible to treat the concept of “juvenile labour” under Vietnamese law and “child labour” under international conventions as equivalent in substance and meaning.

Juvenile labour, meaning persons under 18 years of age engaging in employment, possesses a number of distinctive characteristics. First, they are in a stage of physical and psychological development, making them vulnerable when performing heavy or hazardous work. Therefore, special protection is necessary to ensure their health and overall development. Second, due to lack of experience and occupational skills, they are often only employed in simple jobs such as assisting with agriculture, selling goods or supporting family businesses. This also makes them susceptible to abuse or low wages. Moreover, this group is particularly vulnerable because they lack the ability to protect their own rights and are often unaware of labour law provisions, resulting in a high risk of exploitation in unsafe working conditions.

Additionally, engaging in labour can severely affect their education, leading many to drop out of school. However, if properly managed, suitable employment can help children develop life skills without interfering with schooling. While minors may participate in various forms of work, not all jobs are safe. Furthermore, economic and social factors such as poverty, lack of educational infrastructure or cultural prejudice often push children into early labour, especially in disadvantaged families.

Given these characteristics, juvenile labour must be protected not only in terms of labour rights but also in terms of a safe and healthy working environment. Such an environment must enable minors to cultivate and enhance their capabilities and fully develop their learning potential.

4.2.2 Current Situation of Juvenile Labour in Vietnam

Throughout the process of transforming from a centrally planned economy to a socialist oriented market economy, Vietnam has emerged as one of the prominent examples of economic growth, achieving many notable accomplishments. In 2024, the national economic growth was estimated at over 7 percent of GDP, exceeding the targeted rate of 6 to 6.5 percent of GDP and placing Vietnam among the few countries with high growth rates in both the region and the world (General Statistics Office, 2025a). At the same time, Vietnam is experiencing a period of demographic dividend, with the population aged from 15 to 64 accounting for 67.4 percent of the total population of over 100 million people. This means that for every two people of working age, there is one dependent person. This demographic structure provides favourable conditions for Vietnam to secure sufficient human resources for robust and sustainable development. Children aged from 5 to 17 years old represent a significant demographic, with approximately 21 million individuals, making up around 20.6 percent of the total population (General Statistics Office, 2025b). They are considered the future pillars of the nation and hold great potential if nurtured in a conducive environment.

Like many other countries, Vietnam is undergoing rapid economic development and industrialisation, with the extensive application of advanced science and technology. In the national strategy for socio economic development for the period 2021 to 2030, science, technology and innovation continue to be affirmed as strategic breakthroughs to drive improvements in productivity, quality, efficiency and competitiveness of the economy. This is especially critical in the context of the Fourth Industrial Revolution and the global trend towards digital economy.

Therefore, in order to maintain sustainable growth and create transformative change, in addition to fully utilising the capacity of adult workers, Vietnam must clearly recognise the necessity and importance of preparing a workforce that possesses adequate qualifications and skills to serve as a key driver in the labour market. Among them, minors constitute a strategic labour reserve and must be given special attention.

The current situation of juvenile labour in Vietnam has become a pressing social issue, reflecting significant challenges in protecting the rights of this vulnerable group and ensuring sustainable development. According to the 2023 Labour and Employment Survey Report, there were 731.6 thousand juvenile workers participating in the labour market, of whom 84.6 percent were located in rural areas. This figure not only demonstrates the considerable scale of juvenile labour but also raises questions about the economic and social causes, as well as the inadequacies of the current regulatory and management mechanisms that allow this phenomenon to persist.

In the context of rising labour demand and persistent economic hardship in many regions, early entry into the labour force by minors is often regarded as a temporary solution to support family income. However, such involvement carries serious consequences regarding health, education and long term prospects.

One of the most serious concerns is the high proportion of juvenile workers engaged in hazardous work. The data reveals that 94.3 thousand juvenile workers, accounting for 35.0 percent of the total, are working under conditions that pose risks to their health and development. These jobs frequently involve heavy physical labour, exposure to toxic chemicals or operation in unsafe environments. This situation constitutes a violation of international standards such as ILO Convention No. 182 on the Worst Forms of Child Labour and places juvenile workers at risk of both physical and mental harm.

Specifically, approximately 32.6 thousand juvenile workers, or 12.1 percent, have experienced at least one work related health issue, including injuries, occupational diseases or deterioration of health due to excessive workloads. These harms may have lasting effects, reducing quality of life and future working capacity.

The income level of juvenile workers is also a matter of concern. With an average monthly income of only about three million Vietnamese dong, significantly lower than that of adult workers, juvenile workers are facing severe exploitation of their labour. This level of income is insufficient to meet basic living needs, especially in cases where minors are required to contribute financially to their families. Instead of being invested in education or skill development, juvenile workers are trapped in a cycle of labour to meet short term survival needs. This perpetuates poverty and leads to a vicious cycle in which minors grow into adults without the necessary qualifications and skills to improve their living conditions.

The most serious consequence of juvenile labour is the loss of educational opportunities. When a large portion of time is devoted to labour, minors are unable to participate fully in the educational system, resulting in school dropout or disrupted learning. Research has demonstrated that education is a key factor in breaking the cycle of poverty and enhancing labour market competitiveness. However, juvenile workers who are deprived of access to education are facing significant limitations in terms of future career prospects.

Moreover, lack of education diminishes legal awareness and self protection skills, making juvenile workers more vulnerable to abuse and exploitation in the workplace.

In sum, although Vietnamese law has promulgated specific provisions and policies that aim both to protect the labour rights of minors and to ensure their physical and intellectual development, in practice, such policies and provisions appear to have limited effectiveness and still reveal significant shortcomings in the protection of juvenile labour.

4.3 Legal Study on Juvenile Labour in Vietnam and Key Findings

4.3.1 Current Status of Vietnamese Labour Law on Juvenile Labour

The legal provisions protecting the rights and interests of juvenile labourers are scattered across several legal instruments in Vietnam, including the Law on Children 2016, the Law on Occupational Safety and Hygiene (2015c), the Labour Code (2019), and the Penal Code (2015b). Among these, the Labour Code (2019) and its guiding documents serve as the primary legal basis. Juvenile labour is granted a higher level of protection under the law compared to adult labour, based on the specific characteristics of this group.

Due to their incomplete physical, intellectual and psychological development, juvenile workers are more vulnerable in the workplace, facing risks to health, holistic development and limited capacity to defend their own rights. As such, the legal framework is designed to ensure safety, restrict access to heavy or hazardous work and promote the sustainable development of juvenile workers. These regulations express a legal approach that prioritises protection and applies a flexible regulatory method tailored to the specific needs of juvenile labour, thereby ensuring their rights and comprehensive development within labour relations.

First, Respecting the Right of Minors to Participate in Labour Relations

The right to work is recognised as a fundamental human right under the Constitution of Vietnam and international conventions to which Vietnam is a party. Work is not only a means for individuals to generate material wealth and improve the living standards of themselves and their families, but also serves as a key channel for social interaction, community connection and the construction of shared values.

For minors, participation in labour bears particular significance, as it may contribute to the family economy while also fostering life skills, responsibility and social integration. However, given their incomplete development, juvenile workers must only be involved in suitable labour relations that do not negatively impact their health and development.

Vietnamese law, particularly through the Labour Code (2019) and the Law on Children 2016, shows respect for the labour rights of minors by enabling them to engage in jobs appropriate to their age, health and developmental stage. At the same time, the law imposes necessary restrictions to prevent the exploitation of juvenile labour and to safeguard their rights and ensure a safe and healthy working environment.

Second, Protecting Juvenile Labour through Minimum Standards and Encouragement of Favourable Agreements

Due to their physical and psychological vulnerability, juvenile workers are at greater risk in the workplace compared to adults. Acknowledging this, Vietnamese law establishes a system of minimum standards to protect their rights and interests and limits their labour obligations according to age. For instance, the Labour Code (2019) specifies the types of work that juvenile workers are not permitted to perform, such as heavy, toxic or dangerous jobs, and imposes strict requirements on working hours, rest periods and workplace safety.

Beyond the application of minimum standards, the law encourages employers to enter into more favourable agreements than the statutory requirements. These may include providing a child friendly work environment, flexible working hours or training and skill development programmes. Such agreements not only bring direct benefits to juvenile workers but also enhance the corporate image and social responsibility of businesses.

Importantly, this legal approach does not aim to limit the freedom of contract between the parties, but rather to create a harmonious labour relationship where the interests of juvenile workers are prioritised without disregarding the interests of employers and the goal of sustainable social development.

Third, Balancing the Interests of Juvenile Labour and Employers

The protection of the rights and interests of juvenile workers is a core objective of labour law, but it must be implemented in a way that balances with the legitimate interests of employers. If the legal provisions focus solely on the protection of juvenile workers without considering the concerns of employers, it may create imbalance in labour relations. As a consequence, employers might be reluctant to recruit juvenile labour due to complex legal requirements or high compliance costs, thereby reducing employment opportunities for minors and ultimately harming their interests.

Therefore, Vietnamese labour law is constructed on the principle of balancing the interests of all parties. The legal provisions aim to protect juvenile workers from exploitation and unsafe working conditions, while at the same time facilitating employers in maintaining business productivity. For example, regulations on working hours, rest periods and occupational safety are crafted not only to safeguard the well being of juvenile workers but also to align with the practical realities of labour management in enterprises.

This balance helps maintain a fair labour market in which both workers and employers are protected by law.

Based on the above principles, Vietnam has developed a comprehensive legal framework for the protection of juvenile workers, in line with domestic economic, social and political conditions and international commitments. Legal instruments such as the Law on Children 2016, the Law on Occupational Safety and Hygiene 2015, and especially the Labour Code (2019) have codified provisions on minimum working age, working conditions and protective measures for juvenile labour.

These legal provisions reflect Vietnam's effort to protect children's rights and the rights of young workers, and also demonstrate consistency with international treaties to which Vietnam is a party. Specifically, Vietnam has ratified and implemented the United Nations Convention on the Rights of the Child, ILO Convention No. 138 of 1973 on Minimum Age for Admission to Employment, and ILO Convention No. 182 on the Elimination of the Worst Forms of Child Labour.

These conventions set international standards for the protection of juvenile workers and require member states to establish policies and measures that safeguard the rights of children in the workplace. Adherence to these international commitments not only affirms Vietnam's responsibility within the global community but also contributes to building a progressive system of labour law that supports the sustainable development of the young workforce in the context of international integration.

The legal regulation of juvenile labour in Vietnam covers several key areas

First, employment of juvenile labourers. In principle, juvenile workers may only be employed in jobs suitable to their health conditions, in order to ensure their physical, intellectual and personality development (Clause 1 Article 144 of the Labour Code (2019)). For each age group, the law provides specific limitations on appropriate types of work.

Juvenile workers aged from full 15 years to under 18 years are legally permitted to work in all sectors that are not prohibited by law. According to Article 147 of the Labour Code (2019), the types of work prohibited for this group include heavy, hazardous or dangerous jobs such as carrying loads exceeding physical limits, engaging in the production or trade of addictive substances, or demolition of construction works.

Workers aged from full 13 years to under 15 years are only allowed to perform light work as prescribed by the Minister of Home Affairs[1] (Clause 3 Article 143 of the Labour Code (2019)). In addition, under Clause 3 Article 145 of the Labour Code (2019), employers are not permitted to hire workers under the age of 13 except for certain cultural, artistic, sports or entertainment activities that do not harm the

[1] As of 01 March 2025, the Ministry of Labour, War Invalids and Social Affairs has been merged into the Ministry of Home Affairs. According to Decree No. 25/2025/ND CP issued by the Government, following the merger with the Ministry of Labour, War Invalids and Social Affairs, the Ministry of Home Affairs shall assume state management functions over sectors and areas including labour, wages, social insurance, employment, occupational safety and occupational hygiene.

However, pursuant to Resolution No. 190/2025/QH15, Clause 1 Article 3 provides that: "When restructuring the organisational apparatus of state agencies, the titles of competent agencies and positions as specified in the legal instruments shall be converted to the names of the agencies or positions which assume the respective functions, tasks and powers."

Therefore, in this paper, with respect to matters concerning the management of labour, wages, social insurance, employment, occupational safety and occupational hygiene, the title "Minister of Labour, War Invalids and Social Affairs" shall be converted to "Minister of Home Affairs", and "Ministry of Labour, War Invalids and Social Affairs" shall be replaced with "Ministry of Home Affairs"

.

physical, intellectual or moral development of the child, and only with the consent of the specialised labour authority under the provincial People's Committee.

Circular No. 09/2020/TT BLDTBXH issued by the Ministry of Home Affairs on 12 November 2020 provides detailed guidance on the list of jobs and workplaces where juvenile labour is not allowed, as per the aforementioned legal provisions.

Second, labour contracts involving juvenile workers. Under Clause 4 Article 18 of the Labour Code (2019), a worker aged from full 15 years to under 18 years is entitled to enter into a labour contract with written consent from his or her legal representative. In the case of a worker under 15 years of age, the legal representative must co sign and agree to the contract.

In terms of form, the law requires that a written labour contract must be signed with the worker under 15 years old and his or her legal representative. For workers aged from full 15 years to under 18 years, the labour contract may take either written or electronic form. In addition, a verbal agreement may be used for contracts with a duration of less than one month, in accordance with Article 14 of the Labour Code (2019).

The contents of the labour contract are governed by Article 21 of the Labour Code (2019) and are similar to those applied to adult workers, including information about the parties, the nature of work, workplace, contract duration, wages and other relevant details.

Third, working hours and rest periods of juvenile labourers. Working hours are regulated differently for two age groups: under 15 years of age and from full 15 years to under 18 years. Clause 1 Article 146 of the Labour Code (2019) stipulates that the maximum working time for workers under 15 years old is 4 hours per day and 20 hours per week. They are not allowed to work overtime or at night.

For those aged from full 15 years to under 18 years, Clause 2 Article 146 provides that the maximum working time is 8 hours per day and 40 hours per week. Overtime and night work are permitted for specific jobs such as performing arts, journalism, tutoring and others as prescribed by the Minister of Home Affairs.

Regarding rest periods, the law does not have separate provisions for juvenile workers but applies general regulations applicable to all workers.

Fourth, occupational safety and hygiene for juvenile workers. According to Clause 2 Article 144 of the Labour Code (2019), employers are responsible for ensuring the safety, health and educational conditions for juvenile workers during the employment period. For workers under 15 years of age, employers must obtain a health certificate issued by a competent medical facility, and must organise periodic health examinations at least once every 6 months.

In addition, employers are required to maintain a separate register containing the full name, date of birth, job description and results of each periodic health examination of juvenile workers. This register must be presented upon request by competent state authorities, as prescribed in Clause 3 Article 144 of the Labour Code (2019).

Fifth, wages for juvenile workers. Wages are part of the labour contract and must be agreed upon by both the juvenile worker and his or her legal representative. The wages must be based on labour productivity and job performance, and must not be lower than the minimum wage as prescribed by the Government.

Sixth, labour discipline applicable to juvenile workers. When participating in labour relations, juvenile workers are subject to the same obligations as adult workers. These include compliance with the terms agreed in the labour contract and collective labour agreement, adherence to internal workplace regulations, occupational safety and hygiene requirements, and lawful instructions from the employer.

If a juvenile worker violates these regulations, he or she may be subject to disciplinary measures as provided under labour law. According to Article 124 of the Labour Code (2019), such measures include reprimand, extension of wage increase period (not exceeding 6 months), demotion, or dismissal.

A specific distinction in the disciplinary process for juvenile workers is the requirement for participation of the parent or legal representative. Juvenile workers must be present and have the right to self defence or be represented by a lawyer or labour representative organisation. In the case of a worker under 15 years of age, the legal representative must participate in the disciplinary process (Point c, Clause 1 Article 122 of the Labour Code (2019)).

Seventh, sanctions for violations involving juvenile labour. According to Article 29 Chap. II of Decree No. 12/2022/ND CP, an individual employer may be fined up to 75 million Vietnamese dong for violations involving juvenile labour, such as assigning prohibited jobs or tasks outside the approved list. If the employer is a legal entity, the fine may be doubled.

In more serious cases, the violator may be subject to criminal liability under Article 296 of the Penal Code (2015b).

In summary, Vietnamese labour law has paid special attention to the protection of juvenile workers by establishing specific provisions to safeguard their lawful rights and interests while ensuring their physical and mental development during labour relations (Nguyen, 2023). These regulations are considered relatively complete and coherent, consistent with international conventions to which Vietnam is a party.

They contribute to the prevention of juvenile labour exploitation, the protection of health, and the creation of favourable conditions for the comprehensive development of minors. However, the rapid expansion of the digital economy and the Fourth Industrial Revolution requires that Vietnam further improve its legal framework for regulating labour relations between employers and juvenile workers in line with current realities, including the application of technological advances to the goal of protecting juvenile labour.

4.3.2 Key Findings and Legal Reform Recommendations to Ensure Effective Implementation

First, enhancing legal awareness among juvenile workers through mandatory legal training

One of the prominent issues in protecting juvenile workers is their lack of knowledge regarding labour law regulations. Statistical data shows that 94.3 thousand juvenile workers in Vietnam are currently working in hazardous or dangerous environments that seriously affect their health and holistic development. This number reflects only part of the broader reality of violations by employers, such as assigning prohibited tasks, failing to comply with working hour regulations, or neglecting safety measures.

The root cause of this situation lies in the fact that juvenile workers often lack the necessary legal knowledge to protect their lawful rights and interests in labour relations. To address this, it is necessary to introduce mandatory legal training programmes for juvenile workers before they enter into labour contracts. These programmes should be delivered by state agencies or state established and managed organisations to ensure objectivity, transparency and effectiveness.

The training should cover fundamental regulations on the rights and obligations of workers, safe working conditions, prohibited occupations for juvenile labourers, and procedures for handling violations of rights. Legal training not only helps juvenile workers better understand their rights but also builds the foundation for them to confidently engage in the labour market while reducing the risk of abuse or violations by employers.

Furthermore, the responsibility for organising such training should be assigned to public authorities to ensure uniformity and accessibility, especially for juvenile workers living in remote or disadvantaged areas.

Second, providing training and retraining for juvenile workers with integration of modern technology

Currently, most juvenile workers in Vietnam are engaged in manual and low skill jobs such as agricultural harvesting, manual food packaging or livestock herding. While these jobs may suit the health and developmental level of juvenile workers in the short term, they carry significant risks in the context of the Fourth Industrial Revolution, where automation and machinery increasingly replace human labour in basic tasks.

Low and medium skill workers, including juvenile workers, are projected to be the most affected group, facing high risks of unemployment or exclusion from the labour market even after reaching adulthood. In the long term, limiting juvenile workers to unskilled labour without training or exposure to modern working environments will negatively impact the overall quality of Vietnam's human resources.

This not only hinders their personal development but also reduces the country's competitiveness in the global context, where many nations are investing heavily in high quality and technologically capable workforces.

Therefore, policies on training and retraining juvenile workers must be developed and implemented, focusing on technological skills, creative thinking and professional discipline. Training programmes should combine theory and practice, familiarising young workers with technologies such as automation, artificial intelligence and basic digital tools.

Additionally, the programmes must be designed in line with the age and capacity of juvenile workers and support their physical and intellectual development in a healthy working environment. For example, short term vocational courses or internships can be organised at high tech enterprises, enabling juvenile workers to gain hands on experience and develop practical skills.

These efforts will help prevent future exclusion while building a generation of skilled, disciplined and responsible workers capable of contributing to the sustainable development of the country upon reaching adulthood.

Third, expanding access to vocational education for juvenile workers facing financial barriers.

Many juvenile workers are unable to access vocational education due to financial difficulties. Recently, Vietnam reaffirmed its commitment to education by officially implementing a nationwide policy of full tuition exemption from preschool to the end of public upper secondary education, effective from the academic year 2025 to 2026 (Government, 2025). This policy is highly appreciated and expected to yield positive outcomes, including potential reductions in the number of juvenile workers. However, for minors who lack the ability to study or pass entrance exams for public high schools, it is essential that they have access to vocational education and skills training.

Given Vietnam's current development momentum, the state should adopt support policies for this group by offering tuition exemption or reduction, starting with short term courses in sectors identified as national priorities. The scope of support may then be gradually expanded in accordance with the country's actual conditions.

Fourth, revisiting the legal allowance for juvenile workers to work at night.

Under current law, juvenile workers are permitted to work at night in certain occupations. However, this may adversely affect their health and normal development. From a physiological perspective, working overtime and at night (from 10 pm to 6 am) at this age inevitably impacts their physical and mental growth.

At the same time, this regulation is not fully consistent with ILO Recommendation No. 146, which clearly states: "Overtime for child labourers should be prohibited in order to ensure sufficient time for education, rest and other activities."

Thus, Vietnamese law should consider amending this provision by prohibiting the employment of juvenile workers during night time hours, which should be scientifically reserved for rest and recovery for the next day's labour.

Fifth, standardising disciplinary measures applicable to juvenile workers with a focus on education

Currently, the system of disciplinary measures in Vietnam has not been standardised to reflect the specific characteristics of juvenile workers, a group with unique psychological, physical and developmental traits.

For juvenile workers, the primary objective of disciplinary action should not merely be punishment but rather education and orientation to help them realise their mistakes, learn from experience and improve themselves. Labour discipline, in this context, should be designed as a developmental tool to support young workers in building skills, competence and a sense of responsibility, instead of focusing solely on deterrence or punitive measures.

Due to their psychological sensitivity, juvenile workers may be negatively affected by rigid disciplinary approaches, which may reduce motivation, cause feelings of inferiority or even provoke resistance. In contrast, if disciplinary measures are built on principles of education and support, they can serve as learning opportunities and promote maturity.

Therefore, labour law should research and develop appropriate disciplinary mechanisms tailored to the psychological, physical and working conditions of juvenile workers.

Standardising disciplinary measures based on educational objectives will help build a positive working environment where juvenile workers are encouraged to develop comprehensively. At the same time, it ensures a balance between the rights of workers and employers.

In the long term, these measures will support the formation of a responsible, capable and conscious young workforce ready to meet the demands of the modern labour market.

Sixth, Vietnamese labour law has not yet standardised the rules on material liability of juvenile workers.

Due to the low income level of juvenile workers, in cases where they cause damage to tools or equipment belonging to the employer, they may not have the financial capacity to pay for compensation. In order to protect the legitimate interests of employers while also preventing juvenile workers from being coerced into continued labour "to repay debts", labour law should be revised in accordance with Article 586 of the Civil Code (2015a).

Specifically, the following principle should be introduced: "Where a person under 15 years of age causes damage and still has parents, the parents shall be liable to compensate for the full amount of damage. If the parents do not have sufficient assets for compensation, the child's separate assets shall be used to pay for the remainder." Similarly, "a person aged from full 15 years to under 18 years who causes damage shall compensate using his or her own property. If such property is insufficient, the parents shall be liable for the shortfall using their own assets."

Seventh, administrative sanctions for juvenile labour violations are not strong enough and criminal provisions remain incomplete.

Currently, the maximum administrative fine is 75 million Vietnamese dong for individuals and 150 million dong for organisations based on the Decree no. 22/2022/ND-CP. As for criminal sanctions, violators may face imprisonment of up to 12 years if they use persons under 16 years of age for heavy, hazardous or toxic jobs.

Violators may also be subject to monetary fines from ten million to 50 million Vietnamese dong and be banned from practicing certain professions for a period from one to five years.

However, current criminal law does not mention sanctions for violations against workers aged from 16 to under 18 years. Therefore, to strengthen deterrence and create real economic pressure on violators, the law should both increase administrative sanctions and expand criminal liability provisions to cover not only those under 16 years of age but also the 16 to under 18 age group.

This would help maximise the effectiveness of prevention and eradication of violations in the use of juvenile labour.

Eighth, Vietnam has yet to establish specialised support mechanisms for juvenile workers

Vietnam has achieved certain progress in child protection through mechanisms such as the national child protection hotline 111 and the Child Online Protection Network (VN-COP) (Ministry of Information and Communications, 2021). However, no specialised organisation currently exists to support juvenile workers, who are particularly vulnerable in labour relations due to their weaker physical and intellectual capacity compared to employers.

The absence of support mechanisms makes it difficult for juvenile workers to protect their rights and increases their risk of being exploited or facing legal violations.

Therefore, it is necessary to establish juvenile labour support centres at the local level, particularly in areas with high rates of juvenile labour. These centres should be assigned specific functions including: (i) assisting in job placement and connecting suitable employment opportunities; (ii) receiving and handling reports of employer violations; (iii) providing legal education, knowledge dissemination and psychological counselling; (iv) acting as an intermediary in resolving labour disputes. This solution would not only help juvenile workers defend their rights but also contribute to building a fair and safe working environment.

One major cause of juvenile labour violations lies in the ineffective inspection and enforcement system. The traditional mechanisms of labour inspection and enforcement have shown limitations, especially in the context of the digital economy. New types of jobs such as telesales, social media content moderation or simple data entry now pose emerging challenges.

These jobs often require juvenile workers to work long hours (10 to 12 hours per day) under high pressure, causing serious harm to physical and mental health. Yet such harms are difficult to observe and violations are easily concealed.

To address this, it is necessary to apply technological advancements and artificial intelligence in monitoring and management. For example, AI systems can be deployed to analyse data from online working platforms and detect irregularities such as excessive working hours or job assignments unsuitable for the worker's age.

This approach would improve violation detection and enforcement, placing pressure on employers to comply with the law, and thereby reducing exploitation and occupational burnout.

Finally, the absence of diversified reporting channels limits public monitoring of violations involving juvenile labour

Experience from traffic enforcement shows that the implementation of reporting tools such as the VNeTraffic application, iHanoi, hotlines, and official Zalo channels of traffic police units has proven effective.

According to statistics from the Traffic Police Department, in just over two weeks following the implementation of the Decree 168, there was a noticeable reduction in all three criteria: number of accidents, number of deaths, and number of injuries (ANTV, 2025).

Learning from this model, labour law should develop diversified reporting channels such as mobile apps, hotlines or integration into widely used platforms like Zalo.

The information handling process must be accurate, timely and legally compliant. Community participation through such channels would enhance monitoring and increase pressure on employers to obey the law, thereby reducing violations against the rights of juvenile workers.

4.4 Conclusion

This paper has examined the current state of Vietnamese labour law regarding juvenile workers and identified key areas for improvement, accompanied by reform proposals.

In addition to amending and supplementing existing policies, Vietnam must pay special attention to the development of new legal provisions that respond to the modern transformation brought about by digital technology in the current era.

Through these proposals, Vietnam will be able to better protect the labour rights of juvenile workers and establish mechanisms that shield them from exploitation, thereby contributing to the fulfilment of the developmental goals of a socialist oriented market economy.

References

ANTV. (2025). "Traffic Situation Improves after Decree 168 Comes into Effect," *Public Security Television Portal*. Retrieved March 03, 2025, from https://antv.gov.vn/xa-hoi-4/tinh-hinh-giao-thong-chuyen-bien-tich-cuc-sau-khi-nghi-dinh-168-co-hieu-luc-7C1C2D410.html

General Statistics Office. (2025a). Report on the Socio Economic Situation in Q4 and Year 2024. Retrieved March 03, 2025, from https://www.gso.gov.vn/bai-top/2025/01/bao-cao-tinh-hinh-kinh-te-xa-hoi-quy-iv-va-nam-2024/

General Statistics Office. (2025b). Press Release on the Results of the 2024 Mid Term Population and Housing Survey. Retrieved March 03, 2025, from https://www.gso.gov.vn/du-lieu-va-so-lieu-thong-ke/2025/01/thong-cao-bao-chi-ket-qua-dieu-tra-dan-so-va-nha-o-giua-ky-nam-2024/

General Statistics Office. (2025c). "The Status of Child Labour in Vietnam in 2023—Key Findings," *Tạp chí Con số Sự kiện*. Retrieved March 03, 2025, from https://consosukien.vn/tre-em-tham-gia-lao-dong-va-lao-dong-tre-em-cua-viet-nam-nam-2023-nhung-phat-hien-chinh.htm

Government. (2022). Decree No. 12/2022/ND CP dated 17 January 2022 on administrative sanctions in the field of labour, social insurance and Vietnamese workers working abroad under contracts.

Government. (2025). "Politburo Approves Free Tuition for Public School Students from Preschool to End of High School," *Government Electronic Portal*. Retrieved March 03, 2025, from https://baochinhphu.vn/bo-chinh-tri-quyet-dinh-mien-hoc-phi-cho-hoc-sinh-pho-thong-cong-lap-102250228180111544.htm

International Conventions of ILO and the United Nations.
Ministry of Information and Communications. (2021). Decision No. 88/QD BTTTT on the Code of Conduct for Child Protection Online.
National Assembly. (2015a). Civil Code.
National Assembly. (2015b). Penal Code.
National Assembly. (2015c). Law on Occupational Safety and Hygiene.
National Assembly. (2019). Labour Code.
Nguyen Binh An. (2023). The role of hard law and soft law in developing CSR. In N. B. An & P. T. Anh (Eds.), *Laws on corporate social responsibility and the developmental trend in Vietnam*. Springer. https://doi.org/10.1007/978-981-19-9255-1_1

Chapter 5
Eliminating Child Labour in Vietnam: Legal Framework and Policy Solutions

Nguyen Binh An

Abstract The chapter has provided an in depth analysis of child labor in Vietnam, focusing on the current situation, relevant international standards, and the national legal framework. While Vietnam has achieved notable progress, evidenced by a consistent decline in child labor rates since 2012, the phenomenon persists, particularly in informal sectors such as agriculture, household enterprises, and craft villages. International standards from the CRC, ILO Conventions 138 and 182, have been relatively comprehensively domesticated into Vietnamese law. Nevertheless, persistent challenges remain, including the absence of early warning mechanisms, a lack of harmonization across various laws, and unclear delineation of responsibilities among local authorities and businesses. This chapter puts forth several key proposals, encompassing the codification of the concept of "labor vulnerable children," the establishment of community based early detection and intervention mechanisms, enhanced corporate accountability, the extension of compulsory education through lower secondary school, the integration of financial support, and ensuring child participation in policy formulation.

5.1 Eliminating Child Labor as an Essential Step in Protecting Children's Rights and Fostering Child Friendly Justice

The involvement of children in labor remains a pervasive and deeply concerning issue in many nations, including Vietnam. This phenomenon is not merely a reflection of societal challenges but represents a grave infringement upon the fundamental rights of children, rights that have been recognized and committed to protection by both international and national law (Phillips & Sakamoto, 2012). When children are compelled to work, it not only indicates conditions of poverty or social inequality but,

Article History: Received 20 April 2025; Revised 23 July 2025; Accepted 26 August 2025.

N. B. An (✉)
Doctor of Laws, University of Finance - Marketing, Ho Chi Minh City, Viet Nam
e-mail: an.luatsu@gmail.com

N. Binh An et al. (eds.), *The Future of Child-Friendly Justice and Children's Rights in Vietnam*, https://doi.org/10.1007/978-981-95-3521-7_5

more profoundly, signifies a deprivation of their right to holistic physical and psychological development, their right to access education, and their right to protection from all forms of exploitation and abuse (Basu, 2003).

From a children's rights perspective, every individual is entitled to the right to education and to mature in a safe environment, free from labor exploitation or impediments to comprehensive development. This right has been robustly affirmed in the 1989 United Nations Convention on the Rights of the Child (CRC), the most significant international legal instrument concerning children, which Vietnam ratified in 1990. Furthermore, the foundational conventions of the International Labor Organization (ILO), particularly Convention No. 138 on the Minimum Age for Admission to Employment and Convention No. 182 on the Worst Forms of Child Labor, have established a firm legal bedrock, requiring member states to undertake clear and concrete efforts to protect children from forced, hazardous, and age inappropriate labor.

On a global scale, the elimination of child labor has also been identified as one of the critical targets of the 2030 Sustainable Development Goals (SDGs), to which Vietnam has committed, specifically under Target 8.7. Accordingly, Vietnam has pledged to adopt effective measures to end all forms of child labor by 2025 (Ministry of Labour, War Invalids and Social Affairs, 2018). These international commitments necessitate that Vietnam implements decisive, synchronized, and systematic measures to ensure the feasibility and effectiveness of child labor elimination in practice.

Despite considerable legislative and institutional progress in recent years, child labor remains prevalent in Vietnam, particularly in informal economic sectors and disadvantaged mountainous and rural areas. This presents an urgent demand for the national legal and policy system to continue refining protective, oversight, and intervention mechanisms, aligning with local realities and international standards.

Given the issues outlined, the elimination of child labor is not merely a humanitarian objective but a fundamental requirement for building a child friendly justice system that ensures comprehensive legal protection and fosters equal developmental opportunities, fully harnessing children's potential. This leads to a guiding research question for the entire content of this chapter: "*What legal framework and policy solutions need to be perfected to ensure the effective elimination of child labor in Vietnam, meeting international commitments and promoting the full realization of children's rights in practice?*"

5.2 The Reality of Child Labor in Vietnam: Scope, Nature, and Consequences

Vietnam has developed a relatively comprehensive legal framework aimed at protecting children's rights. Nevertheless, in practice, child labor persists in many areas, particularly in economically disadvantaged regions. While the number of child laborers in Vietnam has shown a declining trend, this remains a pressing issue. The first National Child Labor Survey in 2012 recorded approximately 1.75 million children, representing 9.6% of the population aged 5 to 17, engaged in child labor (Ha Thi, 2020). Thanks to intervention efforts, this figure has significantly decreased; by 2018, the child labor rate fell to 5.4%, equivalent to over one million children (Agriculture and Environment Newspaper, 2021), and by 2023, it was further reduced to 3.5%, corresponding to over 700,000 children (Thuy Hien, 2025). The reduction reflects significant strides, yet the hundreds of thousands of Vietnamese children still working prematurely indicate a serious violation of their fundamental rights to life, education, and development.

Child labor in Vietnam exhibits several noteworthy characteristics. Firstly, this phenomenon is predominantly concentrated in rural and remote areas, where economic conditions remain challenging and the enforcement of child protection laws is less effective. Statistics reveal that over 84% of child laborers reside in rural areas, often working within small scale household economic models. These children are primarily engaged in agriculture; although its proportion has shown a decreasing trend, agriculture still accounted for approximately 53.6% of the total child labor force in 2018. The remaining proportion is distributed across industrial, construction, and service sectors, including traditional craft villages and urban domestic work. The majority of child laborers fall within the 15 to 17 year old age group, representing older adolescents. However, a significant proportion, exceeding 18%, of child laborers are in the 5 to 12 year old group, an age highly vulnerable to exploitation. The fact that children are forced into labor at such a tender age serves as a grave warning, necessitating decisive measures to completely eradicate this situation for younger children.

Furthermore, child labor in Vietnam primarily occurs in the informal sector and takes the form of uncontracted labor. Over 43% of child laborers assist their own families without receiving wages. The tasks they undertake are often arduous and demanding, ranging from farming, animal husbandry, and fishing to working in craft workshops, construction sites, or small scale trading. Many children are compelled to work excessive hours beyond legal limits. For instance, survey results indicate that approximately 20% of child laborers work over 40 hours per week, far exceeding what is appropriate for their physical well being. This implies that children bear adult workloads in environments posing occupational safety risks, directly impacting their current health and future development (Trần Quý Long, 2022).

The consequences of child labor are profound and long lasting, affecting multiple dimensions of a child's life. Foremost among these is the undeniable impact on education: child laborers are frequently forced to drop out of school prematurely, thereby forfeiting opportunities for learning and intellectual development. It is estimated that up to half of child laborers in Vietnam do not attend school, and a staggering 1.4% of these have never attended school at all. This disruption or denial of the right to education renders them illiterate or skill deprived, effectively closing off pathways for life transformation. Concurrently, arduous labor from a young age severely impairs children's physical and mental health. Many children work in hazardous or toxic environments, making them susceptible to occupational diseases or accidents. The ILO has consistently warned that child labor deprives children of their childhood, potential, and dignity, while adversely affecting their physical and mental development (Thuy Ngoc, 2014). Beyond physical debilitation, child laborers also suffer psychological trauma due to premature work pressure, potentially leading to anxiety, low self esteem, and even entanglement in social ills. These experiences leave negative imprints on a child's personality and psyche throughout their later life.

More alarmingly, child labor functions as a critical link in the vicious cycle of poverty. Impoverished families compel their children to work for survival, and the consequence is that these very children grow up lacking knowledge and skills, struggling to secure stable employment and decent income, thus perpetuating poverty across generations. As international organizations have recognized, child labor not only deprives children of current educational opportunities but also perpetuates intergenerational poverty and lack of opportunity. The reality in Vietnam indicates that the majority of child laborers originate from low income households with uneducated parents; consequently, these children lack opportunities for future development and decent employment, leading many to fall into a cycle of poverty and backwardness in adulthood. This vicious cycle is both a cause and a consequence of child labor: poverty leads to early labor for children, and this early labor, in turn, sustainably reproduces poverty (Gia Doan & To Sa, 2024).

5.3 International Standards and Current Vietnamese Law on Child Labor Elimination

5.3.1 International Standards

The United Nations Convention on the Rights of the Child (CRC) establishes a comprehensive framework for children's rights, including the right to be protected from economic exploitation and from work that is hazardous or interferes with their education, health, or development. Article 32 of the CRC requires state parties to enact legislative, administrative, social, and educational measures to realize this right. Such measures must stipulate a minimum age for employment, set limits on working hours and conditions appropriate for children, and impose adequate penalties for violations (United Nations General Assembly, 1989).

Alongside these legally binding obligations, a rights based approach guides the formulation of policies for child labor elimination. This implies that all policy decisions must prioritize the best interests of the child (Alston, 1994). The best interests principle, enshrined in Article 3 of the CRC, demands that when considering any measure related to children, the state must ensure that the decision yields maximum welfare for the children, safeguarding their long term holistic development. Furthermore, the principle of nondiscrimination requires that child labor elimination policies must encompass all groups of children, ensuring no child is left behind due to ethnicity, gender, economic circumstances, or place of residence. Empirical evidence shows that child labor is often highly concentrated in poor communities, ethnic minority regions, or remote rural areas; thus, the state must pay particular attention to these vulnerable groups, ensuring they receive equitable access to support programs. Moreover, children's right to participate (Article 12 CRC) emphasizes that children have the right to have their views heard in matters concerning them. Applied to the policy domain, policymakers must create opportunities for children's voices, especially those who have experienced early labor, to be reflected in the formulation and implementation of child labor elimination programs. This rights based approach not only adheres to international standards but also renders policies more humane and effective by directly addressing children's needs and rights.

Complementing the CRC, two fundamental conventions of the International Labor Organization (ILO) provide specialized standards on child labor. ILO Convention No. 138 concerning the Minimum Age for Admission to Employment (1973) requires each nation to commit to pursuing a national policy designed to ensure the effective abolition of child labor and to progressively raise the minimum age for admission to employment or work to a level consistent with the fullest physical and mental development of young persons. Under Convention 138, the minimum age for work must not be below the age for completing compulsory schooling, and in no case less than 15 years. Concurrently, hazardous or dangerous work, or work that is likely to harm the health, safety, or morals of young persons, must be prohibited for children under 18 years of age.

ILO Convention No. 182 concerning the Prohibition and Immediate Action for the Elimination of the Worst Forms of Child Labor (1999) mandates that states "take immediate and effective measures to secure the prohibition and elimination of the worst forms of child labor." The worst forms are defined to include: all forms of slavery or practices similar to slavery (sale and trafficking of children, forced or compulsory labor), the use of children in prostitution or pornography, the use of children for illicit activities (such as drug trafficking), and work which, by its nature or the circumstances in which it is carried out, is likely to harm the health, safety, or morals of children.

5.3.2 *Achievements, Limitations, and Shortcomings of Current Vietnamese Law on Child Labor Elimination*

5.3.2.1 Achievements

Vietnam's early ratification of international treaties on child labor elimination demonstrates its strong commitment to protecting children's rights. Notably, Vietnam was the first country in Asia and the second globally to ratify the CRC in 1989. Concurrently, Vietnam also ratified two fundamental International Labor Organization (ILO) Conventions directly related to child labor: Convention No. 138 (1973) concerning the Minimum Age for Admission to Employment and Convention No. 182 (1999) concerning the Prohibition and Immediate Action for the Elimination of the Worst Forms of Child Labor (Nguyen et al., 2024). These international commitments establish legal obligations and policy directions for Vietnam in its efforts to abolish child labor. Based on these international commitments, Vietnam's legal system has progressively domesticated many crucial provisions of these conventions. It can be affirmed that Vietnam currently possesses a fairly comprehensive legal framework for preventing and reducing child labor, one that is consistent with international law (Gia Doan & To Sa, 2024).

The Labor Code of 2019, effective from 2021, dedicates Chap. XI to regulating the employment of minors, stipulating the general minimum working age as 15 years old. This provision aligns with ILO Convention 138 and reflects the domestication of ILO Convention 182's requirements for identifying and prohibiting hazardous forms of child labor. The 2019 Labor Code has classified and set forth specific regulations for minor workers based on age and job nature. Individuals aged 15 to under 18 are permitted to work but must adhere to limitations on job types and conditions. Specifically, Article 147 of the 2019 Labor Code prohibits the employment of individuals in this age group in hazardous or harmful jobs or workplaces, including strenuous carrying, working with chemicals or explosives, underground or underwater work, construction sites, or at gambling establishments, bars, or dance clubs. This law also strictly prohibits any work that could harm the physical, intellectual, or moral development of minors.

For labor involving children under 15, the 2019 Labor Code provides a narrow exception. Individuals aged 13 to under 15 may perform light work according to a list stipulated by the Ministry of Labor, Invalids and Social Affairs. The employment of children aged 13 to 14 must comply with strict conditions: a labor contract must be signed with the child's legal representative, working hours must not interfere with schooling, safe working conditions must be ensured, and regular health examinations must be provided. Children under 13 are only permitted to participate in artistic, athletic, or sports activities that do not harm their development and must have the consent of the provincial labor management authority. These regulations accurately reflect the spirit of Convention 138, simultaneously respecting the right of young children to participate in certain appropriate activities while preventing the risk of labor exploitation.

Regarding working hours, the 2019 Labor Code establishes stringent protective limits for minor workers. Individuals under 15 years old may not work more than 4 hours per day and 20 hours per week. Those aged 15 to under 18 may work a maximum of 8 hours per day and 40 hours per week. The law strictly prohibits the use of minors for overtime or night work, with very limited exceptions prescribed by law, consistent with their health and specific characteristics. These limits aim to ensure that children have sufficient time for rest and study, aligning with international recommendations that children should not be overworked to the detriment of their education and development.

In addition to the Labor Code, the 2016 Law on Children, enacted to replace the previous Law on Protection, Care, and Education of Children, expanded the legal framework for protecting children's rights in line with the CRC. Although it defines children as individuals under 16 years old, narrower than the international definition of under 18 years old, this Law still plays a crucial role in preventing child labor. A notable achievement is that the Law on Children for the first time explicitly recognizes children's right to protection from labor exploitation. Specifically, Article 26 of this law stipulates that children have the right to protection in all forms to prevent forced labor; they must not be compelled to work underage, beyond prescribed hours, or in arduous, hazardous, or dangerous jobs. This clearly affirms that illegal child labor constitutes an infringement of children's rights. The Law on Children also emphasizes the responsibility of families, communities, and authorities in detecting and preventing instances of child labor exploitation. Acts of harming or exploiting children, including labor exploitation, are categorized as absolutely prohibited acts.

Parallel to direct prohibitions on child labor, the current Law on Education, amended in 2019, plays a pivotal role in indirectly eliminating child labor by extending the duration of children's schooling. The 2019 Law on Education ensures that all children complete primary education; concurrently, the state continues its policy of universalizing lower secondary education. Although lower secondary education is not yet legally compulsory but rather universal, in practice, the vast majority of Vietnamese children complete grade 9, which is approximately 14 to 15 years old. Gradually completing the compulsory education roadmap to higher ages is also an important direction to ensure that children do not enter the labor market prematurely.

To strictly address violations, Vietnam's Penal Code of 2015 introduced offenses related to illegal child labor. For instance, Article 296 of the Penal Code criminalizes individuals who exploit children in strenuous or dangerous work or violate labor regulations concerning individuals under 16 years old. This provides a strong deterrent legal basis aimed at progressively eliminating child labor exploitation (Nguyễn Thị Kim Thanh, 2024).

5.3.2.2 Limitations and Shortcomings

Despite achieving considerable progress, the current legal framework and practical enforcement in Vietnam regarding child labor prevention continue to exhibit several limitations that necessitate redress.

Firstly, a lack of harmonization and consistency across various legal instruments, including the Labor Code, the Law on Children, the Law on Education, and the Penal Code, remains a significant challenge. This inconsistency is most apparent in the definition of a child's age. The Law on Children 2016 defines a child as an individual under 16 years old, whereas most international standards, such as the United Nations Convention on the Rights of the Child and ILO Convention 182, consider individuals under 18 as children. This discrepancy occasionally leads to practical difficulties in protection. The age group from 16 to under 18, while no longer classified as "children" under the Law on Children 2016, are not yet adults but fall under the category of "minors" and thus require protection. While labor law addresses this group, the terminological inconsistency within the legal system affects the criminalization of violations. The current Penal Code only prosecutes illegal labor involving individuals under 16, omitting the 16 to 17 age group. This partly stems from the Penal Code's attempt to align its age threshold with the Law on Children, yet it contradicts the spirit of protecting minors under 18 as per labor law. This overlap creates a legal loophole (Ha Thi, 2020). For instance, a 17 year old compelled to work in a hazardous environment might not be considered a "child" victim under the Law on Children, thus failing to trigger specific protective mechanisms. Simultaneously, the exploitation of that individual might not be criminally prosecuted under Article 296 of the current Penal Code.

Secondly, there is a dearth of effective early warning and detection mechanisms at the community level, particularly within the informal economic sector. Although the provisions of the Labor Code and related guiding documents are increasingly comprehensive, they primarily focus on regulating formal labor relationships characterized by clear contracts between employers and employees. Conversely, a substantial number of children engage in work such as farming, family based craft production, or domestic help, which are typically not considered formal labor and thus often fall outside the strict management or oversight of competent authorities. Current labor inspection institutions are only effective within formal enterprises, operating with a limited number of inspectors and a highly restricted scope of intervention, especially in household settings or remote areas (Agriculture and Environment Newspaper, 2021). This means that child laborers in these localities are frequently overlooked and do not receive timely protection from authorities. This reality was previously acknowledged when the Ministry of Labor, Invalids and Social Affairs issued Circular 09/2020, effective March 15, 2021, aiming to expand the scope of management and enhance oversight of child labor in cooperative groups, cooperatives, and households. However, these regulations have only addressed the behavioral aspect of concluding labor contracts with minors and clarifying guardians' responsibilities in case of violations, while the establishment of an early warning mechanism to prevent illegal child labor from the outset has not been adequately addressed. Local realities reveal that many parents and small scale production owners are not fully aware of their obligation to declare, contract, or notify authorities about the employment of child labor. This further exacerbates the risk of children working in uncontrolled conditions, making the protection of their legitimate rights highly challenging.

Thirdly, there is a lack of independent and effective monitoring mechanisms to ensure children's rights. The Law on Children 2016 stipulates general principles regarding the right to be protected from child labor, while also defining the responsibilities of families, the state, schools, and society in ensuring this right. However, this Law lacks independent and effective monitoring mechanisms to ensure these rights are fully realized. For instance, the Law on Children assigns responsibilities to numerous agencies, including the National Assembly, the Government, various ministries, and local authorities, but interagency coordination in child protection remains inadequate, leading to low effectiveness in preventing and addressing child labor cases. Meanwhile, the Labor Code and its subsidiary regulations specifically define the responsibilities of employers and labor inspectors regarding the unlawful employment of children. This fragmentation risks each party focusing only on its narrow scope. For example, the labor sector inspects businesses, the education sector encourages students to attend school, and the child protection sector supports children in special circumstances. A case of child labor may not receive timely intervention if it falls into the gaps between these functions. For instance, if a 14 year old drops out of school to become a domestic helper, the school might consider it a child protection issue, local authorities might attribute it to family economics, and labor inspectors typically do not investigate households employing domestic helpers.

Fourthly, current administrative penalties lack the necessary deterrent effect. According to the Department of Child Protection and Care, many cases of child labor exploitation are only subject to administrative fines. This leads to the recurrence of such tragic situations. Indeed, the maximum fine for illegal employment of minors under current regulations is merely around 75 million VND (approximately 3000 USD). This amount is disproportionate to the profits gained by those exploiting children through meager wages. Due to the profitability of illegal child labor, employers are often willing to employ various tactics to evade authorities rather than voluntarily comply. The consequence of inadequate deterrence is that many cases continue without appropriate punishment (Nguyễn Thị Kim Thanh, 2024). A prime example occurred in a "child labor neighborhood" in Binh Tan District, Ho Chi Minh City. Reporters discovered dozens of children under 15 working relentlessly in family run garment facilities. Upon notification of an inspection, the facility owners immediately dispersed all child laborers to evade prosecution. All the children were either sent back to their hometowns or hidden before the inspection team arrived. As a result, the "child labor rescue" inspection found deserted premises, failing to catch violations in flagrante delicto (Phu Nu Online, 2017). Only after strong media outcry was the case further investigated. A representative from the Department of Children admitted that these facilities showed signs of criminal offense under the Penal Code concerning the crime of child labor exploitation. However, until that point, most similar cases had only resulted in very light administrative penalties and rarely in criminal prosecution, leading to insufficient deterrence.

Fifthly, child laborers often lack information regarding their rights and complaint mechanisms. Many children, due to limited education and early withdrawal from school, are unaware of how the law protects them or where to seek assistance. They virtually have no voice in labor relations, often passively accepting arrangements made by adults. Their limited awareness of their own rights results in very few child labor cases being reported or complained about in a timely manner. The national hotline for child protection, 111, is a free support channel for exploited children; however, child laborers' ability to independently access this channel is very low. Victims often have to rely on detection by neighbors, teachers, the press, or authorities. Child laborers typically lack effective complaint mechanisms: they do not know about or dare to use channels like child protection hotlines, and they fear retaliation or harbor feelings of shame. Their voices are largely absent from the processing procedures, creating a significant barrier to accessing justice.

Sixthly, local authorities and businesses have not fully exercised their roles in preventing and reducing child labor. At the grassroots level, many commune/ward authorities remain passive regarding child labor. This is partly due to a mindset that views it as a private family matter, and partly due to a lack of guidance and intervention resources. Ineffective interagency coordination means many localities lack clear mechanisms to address cases of children working outside of school. In cases where children from other localities are brought in for "underground" labor, such as the group of ethnic minority children from Quang Nam lured to work on farms in Lam Dong in a 2015 incident, both the sending and receiving authorities struggled with management (Vân Anh, 2015). Only when severe consequences occur, such as child abuse or accidents, do agencies become involved, often too late. Coordination between grassroots authorities and labor inspectors and police is often loose, leading to a failure to strictly prosecute those illegally employing child labor.

Regarding businesses, their responsibility in preventing child labor is also not clearly defined or fully implemented. While major industry associations often commit to not employing child labor, supply chain oversight remains lax. Head of chain businesses rarely fully inspect all subcontractors or household producers working for them (An, 2023a). Particularly in small scale businesses or cooperatives, the role and obligation to prevent child labor are not adequately understood. Some large businesses in the supply chain commit to adhering to international labor standards, but subcontractors or small processing facilities easily exploit child labor to reduce costs. The corporate social responsibility of actively detecting and eliminating child labor has not been fully realized. Many businesses only act under legal pressure or from international partners, rather than voluntarily considering it a moral and legal obligation (An, 2023b). Without independent inspection and auditing mechanisms, businesses can deny responsibility for indirect child labor in their production chains.

5.3.3 Recommendations and Solutions for Improving Current Vietnamese Law on Child Labor Elimination

Firstly, to effectively address the issue of child labor, the initial imperative is to clearly codify the concept of "labor vulnerable children" and subsequently develop specialized policies based on this definition. This concept should not merely describe the general situation of children engaged in labor; rather, it must aim to specifically identify and protect high risk groups within the community, such as children belonging to ethnic minority groups, children with disabilities, or children from impoverished families. According to research by Ruck et al. (2016), a clear definition of vulnerable children will enable legislators and policymakers to construct protection mechanisms tailored to specific child groups, rather than relying on generic solutions that often prove ineffective in practice. This implies that policy formulation must be grounded in concrete and profound empirical evidence, as well as quantitative and qualitative studies, to respond most effectively to these target groups (Bourdillon & Myers, 2022).

Currently, Vietnamese law lists some groups of children requiring special protection, but lacks a specific definition for "labor vulnerable children." Codifying this concept will establish a legal basis for early prevention measures and specialized support for at risk children. International practice, particularly ILO Convention No. 182, emphasizes the importance of identifying particularly vulnerable child groups and addressing their specific needs as an essential element for eliminating child labor. Therefore, adding a definition of "labor vulnerable children" to the Law on Children or the Labor Code is necessary to delineate the target population and design early, specialized intervention policies for this group.

Secondly, it is essential to design an early detection and timely intervention system at the community level through educational institutions, healthcare facilities, and the social protection system. Experience demonstrates that relying solely on legal sanctions is insufficient; enforcing regulations such as compulsory education or prohibitions on child labor faces numerous challenges where resources are limited. Poverty and the weaknesses of local institutions, such as schools or basic social services, still compel many children to work for survival. Therefore, the proactive role of the community in detecting children who show signs of dropping out to work or being exploited must be fostered.

According to Edmonds (2016), this system needs to be established on a systematic interagency cooperation framework, wherein teachers, healthcare workers, and social workers play crucial roles in the early detection of signs that children are engaging in excessive or age inappropriate labor. Recent studies underscore the role of teachers in early detection of cases where children frequently miss school, indicating a risk of falling into illegal labor, thereby creating a timely feedback mechanism to local authorities and child protection agencies (De Silva & Sumarto, 2015).

Specifically, schools can monitor student attendance for early warnings of abnormal truancy. Local healthcare services, upon admitting children with labor related accidents or severe malnutrition, should coordinate information sharing. Child protection officers and social workers at the local level should regularly review and visit impoverished households with children to provide timely support. The model of collaboration between schools and community based social services has been effectively piloted by UNICEF in several locations. For example, in Serbia, UNICEF supported projects have established cooperation mechanisms between schools with high dropout rates and local social work centers, mobilizing social workers for early intervention. This approach helps prevent students from dropping out to work in a timely manner, thereby preventing child labor at the grassroots level (Edmonds, 2006).

Integrating such a community monitoring system into the legal framework will create a proactive prevention foundation. The law needs to clearly define the responsibilities of each local entity, including schools, health clinics, and commune/ward authorities, in reporting and addressing detected cases of child labor or high risk children. Concurrently, interagency intervention procedures should be developed, for instance: truant children will receive counseling and support to return to school; their families will receive livelihood assistance; and suspected exploitation cases must be investigated and addressed. This close coordination mechanism will create a robust social safety net directly within communities, ensuring that no child falls through the "safety net" of the law.

Thirdly, enhance consultation with and listening to children's opinions during the law and policy making process. A core principle that Vietnamese law and policy must particularly prioritize is ensuring consultation with and listening to children's views when developing laws and policies that directly affect them. According to Nylund's (2019) research on children's rights, children are the ones who best understand their own circumstances and needs. Therefore, consulting with them not only demonstrates respect for children's right to participate but also increases the effectiveness and practicality of enacted policies. The voices of children—those directly affected—need to be heard seriously when formulating policies on education, labor, and social protection. According to Article 12 of the United Nations Convention on the Rights of the Child, it not only requires listening to children in individual cases but also demands that states consult with children during the process of developing laws and policies that affect them. In other words, children have the right to speak out on issues concerning them at a macro level, and the state has a responsibility to create conditions for that voice to be reflected in policy.

To implement this principle, Vietnam should establish systemic mechanisms for child consultation. This requires legislative and executive bodies to engage in genuine forms of consultation with children, including child forums, extensive opinion surveys, and social media activities to make it easy for children to participate and clearly and comfortably express their aspirations. For example, before enacting policies on child labor prevention, the drafting agency could organize consultations and workshops to gather children's opinions, especially from those who have experienced labor or are at risk, through schools, youth organizations, or community groups. The National Assembly and People's Councils at all levels, when debating child related laws, should also consider children's voices, possibly through reports from Children's Councils or by organizing mock sessions with child participation.

This will not only demonstrate respect for children's right to be heard under international human rights law but also help ensure that enacted policies are more realistic and feasible. Children, with their unique experiences and perspectives, can contribute creative ideas to solve the problem of child labor in a humane and effective way. More importantly, consulting with and involving children in the policy making process will raise their own awareness of their rights and responsibilities. When children are encouraged to express their views, they will better understand the value of education and the harms of early labor, thereby becoming positive agents of change in their communities. In the long term, shaping a generation of rights conscious children will contribute to building a society that does not tolerate child labor, consistent with the human rights goals that Vietnam and the world are striving towards.

Fourthly, extend compulsory education through lower secondary school, coupled with specific financial support programs for impoverished children. Education is not only a fundamental right of children but also the most effective means of removing children from the labor market. Numerous international studies have affirmed the strong correlation between keeping children within the compulsory education system and reducing the incidence of early child labor (Basu, 2003). Extending compulsory schooling to approximately 15 to 16 years of age also aligns with international standards, as the International Labor Organization (ILO) recommends that the minimum working age should not be lower than the age of completion of compulsory education. When children remain in school longer, their risk of premature labor decreases, while their educational attainment increases, providing them with better employment opportunities in adulthood.

However, for compulsory education to be truly effective, economic barriers for impoverished children must be removed. Poverty remains the primary cause of early child labor, as families need income or cannot afford schooling costs. Therefore, the government needs to combine the expansion of compulsory education with direct financial support for disadvantaged families whose children attend school. These support programs should not merely be cash transfers but could also include policies for reducing tuition fees, providing free textbooks and learning materials, or school lunch programs, to alleviate the economic burden on families. When the economic burden is eased, parents will be motivated to keep their children in school rather than sending them to work early. Additionally, investment is needed to enhance the quality of lower secondary education, ensuring schools are appealing and beneficial so that children and families clearly perceive the long term benefits of education over premature work. Universal and meaningful education, coupled with economic support, will create a strong shield protecting children from being drawn into the cycle of early labor.

Fifthly, enhance corporate accountability, particularly for businesses operating within supply chains and the informal sector. Experience has demonstrated that child labor often occurs in production stages that are not strictly controlled, where social responsibility and legal obligations are not concretized and rigorously enforced (Phillips & Sakamoto, 2012). Currently, the majority of child labor is concentrated in the agricultural sector and informal activities. Global statistics indicate that the agricultural sector accounts for approximately 70% of total child labor worldwide, equivalent to 112 million children, due to the seasonal nature of the work and the perception of child labor as cheap manpower. Similarly, in craft villages, small scale production facilities, or self employed households, children are vulnerable to labor abuse that is difficult to detect. Insufficient law enforcement in these areas exacerbates the problem of child labor. Therefore, in addition to the responsibilities of regulatory agencies, businesses and employers must be more proactive in committing to zero tolerance for child labor.

Globally, the legal trend is shifting from voluntary to mandatory corporate social responsibility. Many countries have enacted laws requiring businesses to conduct human rights due diligence in their supply chains to eliminate forced labor and child labor. For example, Canada recently passed the Fighting Forced Labor and Child Labor in Supply Chains Act, effective January 1, 2024, which prohibits the import of goods produced by child labor (Canada, 2024). This law compels large companies to publicly report the measures they have taken to prevent and mitigate child labor risks in their manufacturing and import operations, with significant penalties for noncompliance. Many experts also advocate for mandatory human rights due diligence legislation that requires businesses not only to report but also to take concrete action to prevent abuses, failing which they would face civil legal liability. These developments indicate that corporate accountability is becoming an international legal norm in child rights protection.

For Vietnam, strengthening corporate responsibility should be achieved through both incentives and legal obligations. Regulations in labor law and child law must be enhanced to compel businesses, particularly those involved in international supply chains, to rigorously ensure that child labor is not utilized at any stage of production. Sanctions against businesses that unlawfully employ child labor must also be effectively strengthened, for example, by increasing administrative fines or even pursuing criminal liability in severe cases, including for individual business households or small production facilities. Furthermore, promoting certification models for child labor free products in export industries, such as textiles and agricultural goods, will create market pressure for businesses to comply. Businesses should also be obligated to periodically report on child labor within their supply chains, fostering transparency and subjecting themselves to societal oversight. The application of international standards, such as those from the International Labor Organization (ILO), is also considered an effective measure for businesses to raise awareness and commit to not using child labor. These efforts, combined with enhanced awareness and livelihood support for child labor households, will progressively reduce child labor in the informal sector.

5.4 Conclusion

The chapter's analysis demonstrates that, despite significant improvements to Vietnam's existing legal framework, considerable limitations persist that must be addressed to thoroughly eliminate child labor. Recent legal and policy advancements underscore Vietnam's commendable efforts in tackling this issue; however, the practical implementation of regulations continues to face substantial challenges, particularly at the community level and within the informal sector.

In the author's view, reinforcing the responsibility and oversight role of local authorities, coupled with clearer accountability from businesses, is essential to ensure the genuine effectiveness of enacted legal policies. Additionally, strengthening direct financial support mechanisms for disadvantaged children and expanding the compulsory education system are pivotal factors in mitigating and preventing child labor.

Future research should delve deeper into assessing the practical efficacy of current policies at the community level, with particular emphasis on the role and active participation of social organizations, as well as developing independent monitoring mechanisms to enhance child protection from the risks of illegal labor.

References

Agriculture and Environment Newspaper. (2021). *Ngăn ngừa và giảm thiểu lao động trẻ em trong nông nghiệp|Preventing and Reducing Child Labor in Agriculture.* https://nongnghiepmoitruong.vn/ngan-ngua-va-giam-thieu-lao-dong-tre-em-trong-nong-nghiep-d312652.html

Alston, P. (Ed.). (1994). *The best interests of the child: Reconciling culture and human rights.* Oxford University Press.

An, N. B. (2023a). Analytical facts of corporate social responsibility for enforcement of labor rights. In N. B. An & P. T. Anh (Eds.), *Laws on corporate social responsibility and the developmental trend in Vietnam* (pp. 41–56). Springer Nature Singapore. https://doi.org/10.1007/978-981-19-9255-1_4

An, N. B. (2023b). *Global supply chain: The role of disclosure and due diligence related to soft and hard law*, 030038. https://doi.org/10.1063/5.0164871

Basu, K. (2003). The global child labor problem: What do we know and what can we do? *The World Bank Economic Review, 17*(2), 147–173. https://doi.org/10.1093/wber/lhg021

Bourdillon, M., & Myers, W. (2022). Illusions in the protection of working children. In N. Howard & S. Okyere (Eds.), *International child protection* (pp. 77–100). Springer International Publishing. https://doi.org/10.1007/978-3-030-78763-9_4

Canada, H. (2024, May 31). *Fighting against forced labour and child labour in Supply Chains Act: 2023 to 2024 Report: Health Canada* [Transparency - other]. https://www.canada.ca/en/health-canada/corporate/transparency/corporate-management-reporting/supply-chains/fighting-forced-child-labour-act-2023-2024.html

De Silva, I., & Sumarto, S. (2015). How do educational transfers affect child labour supply and expenditures? Evidence from Indonesia of impact and flypaper effects. *Oxford Development Studies, 43*(4), 483–507. https://doi.org/10.1080/13600818.2015.1032232

Edmonds, E. V. (2006). Child labor and schooling responses to anticipated income in South Africa. *Journal of Development Economics, 81*(2), 386–414. https://doi.org/10.1016/j.jdeveco.2005.05.001

Edmonds, E. V. (2016). *Economic Growth and Child Labor in Low Income Economies. 3.* https://g2lm-lic.iza.org/wp-content/uploads/2017/06/glmlic_sp003.pdf

Gia Doan & To Sa. (2024). *Việt Nam là quốc gia hình mẫu, tiên phong trong ngăn chặn lao động trẻ em|Vietnam is a model country, a pioneer in preventing child labor.* Báo điện tử Dân Trí. https://dantri.com.vn/lao-dong-viec-lam/viet-nam-la-quoc-gia-hinh-mau-tien-phong-trong-ngan-chan-lao-dong-tre-em-20241225233936279.htm

Ha Thi. (2020). *Giảm 2% tỷ lệ lao động trẻ em, chưa hết lo|2% reduction in child labor rate, still no end to worries.* BÁO PHỤ NỮ THỦ ĐÔ-CƠ QUAN NGÔN LUẬN CỦA HỘI LIÊN HIỆP PHỤ NỮ TP HÀ NỘI. https://baophunuthudo.vn/article/91045/166/giam-2-ty-le-lao-dong-tre-em-chua-het-lo/

Ministry of Labour, War Invalids and Social Affairs. (2018). *Bảo vệ trẻ em khỏi các hình thức lao động nặng nhọc, nguy hiểm|Protecting children from hazardous and arduous labour.* https://molisa.gov.vn/baiviet/27915

Nguyễn Thị Kim Thanh. (2024). PHÁP LUẬT VỀ LAO ĐỘNG TRẺ EM Ở VIỆT NAM HIỆN NAY-THỰC TRẠNG VÀ GIẢI PHÁP HOÀN THIỆN|Child labor law in vietnam today-current situation and solutions for improvement. *Tạp chí Khoa học Kiểm sát, 01*, 38–45.

Nguyen, H., Pham, V., Ngo, H. Q., Huynh, A., Nguyen, B., & Machado, J. (2024). Intelligent search system for resume and labor law. *PeerJ Computer Science, 10*, e1786. https://doi.org/10.7717/peerj-cs.1786

Nylund, A. (2019). Childrens right to participate in decision-making in Norway: Paternalism and autonomy. In T. Haugli, A. Nylund, R. Sigurdsen, & L. R. L. Bendiksen (Eds.), *Childrens constitutional rights in the Nordic countries* (pp. 201–224). Brill|Nijhoff. https://doi.org/10.1163/9789004382817_012

Phillips, N., & Sakamoto, L. (2012). Global production networks, chronic poverty and 'slave labour' in Brazil. *Studies in Comparative International Development, 47*(3), 287–315. https://doi.org/10.1007/s12116-012-9101-z

Phu Nu Online. (2017, May 8). *Bóc lột lao động trẻ em vẫn diễn ra từng ngày: Nhiều dấu hỏi quanh cuộc giải cứu bất thành|Child labor exploitation still happens every day: Many questions surrounding the failed rescue.* https://www.phunuonline.com.vn/boc-lot-lao-dong-tre-em-van-dien-ra-tung-ngay-nhieu-dau-hoi-quanh-cuoc-giai-cuu-bat-thanh-a19752.html

Ruck, M. D., Peterson-Badali, M., & Freeman, M. (Eds.). (2016). *Handbook of childrens rights: Global and multidisciplinary perspectives* (0th ed.). Routledge. https://doi.org/10.4324/9781315766300

Thuy Hien. (2025). *Công bố kết quả điều tra về lao động trẻ em Việt Nam|Announcing the results of the investigation on child labor in Vietnam.* https://baotintuc.vn/xa-hoi/cong-bo-ket-qua-dieu-tra-ve-lao-dong-tre-em-viet-nam-20250123131712132.htm

Thuy Ngoc. (2014). *Tỷ lệ lao động trẻ em tại VN thấp hơn thế giới|Child labor rate in Vietnam is lower than the world.* Báo Công Thương. https://congthuong.vn/ty-le-lao-dong-tre-em-tai-vn-thap-hon-the-gioi-704.html

Trần Quý Long. (2022). *Quan điểm của Lao động trẻ em và mối liên hệ với các yếu tố nhân khẩu học—Xã hội|Perspectives on Child Labor and its Relationship to Socio-Demographic Factors.* https://vjol.info.vn/index.php/khxhvn/article/view/76169/64865

United Nations General Assembly. (1989). *Convention on the Rights of the Child.* https://www.ohchr.org/en/instruments-mechanisms/instruments/convention-rights-child

Vân Anh. (2015, August 7). *Quảng Nam: Giải cứu 7 học sinh bị dụ đưa đi bóc sức lao động|Quang Nam: Rescuing 7 students who were lured into forced labor.* Báo Pháp Luật Việt Nam. https://baophapluat.vn/quang-nam-giai-cuu-7-hoc-sinh-bi-du-dua-di-boc-suc-lao-dong-post201465.html

Chapter 6
Children's Rights in the Business Field—Some Theoretical and Legal Issues in Vietnam

Ut Ha Thi

Abstract The chapter examines the theoretical and legal underpinnings of children's rights within the business context in Vietnam, drawing on the country's international commitments and the extent to which these have been incorporated into domestic law. It underscores Vietnam's legal achievements in safeguarding against child labor, protecting child consumers, and addressing violations stemming from business practices that infringe upon children's rights. Simultaneously, the chapter identifies persistent challenges in enforcing relevant laws, including illegal child labor, deceptive or inappropriate advertising, harmful products and services, and unsafe working environments. In response, it proposes measures to strengthen the legal framework and enhance corporate social responsibility, thereby advancing the protection of children's rights in business activities in Vietnam.

6.1 Overview of Children's Rights in Vietnamese Law

Children are considered the joy of the family and the future of the nation. Accordingly, Vietnam consistently regards the care and development of children as a paramount national policy. With this orientation, Vietnam has been among the leading countries in implementing children's rights. Children maintain daily interactions with businesses, both within and outside the workplace. They may be young workers, children of workers, consumers, or members of communities where enterprises operate. As one of the most vulnerable groups in society, children are exposed to potential violations of their rights through business activities if proper compliance and oversight are lacking. Issues such as illegal child labor, inappropriate advertising, harmful products, and unsafe working environments seriously threaten children's holistic development, both physically and mentally.

Article History: Received 10 April 2025; Revised 18 July 2025; Accepted 17 August 2025.

H. T. Ut (✉)
Comparative Law Institute, Hanoi Law University, Ha Noi City, Viet Nam
e-mail: hathiut@hlu.edu.vn

N. Binh An et al. (eds.), *The Future of Child-Friendly Justice and Children's Rights in Vietnam*, https://doi.org/10.1007/978-981-95-3521-7_6

Pursuant to the 1989 United Nations Convention on the Rights of the Child (CRC), children's rights are categorized into four principal groups: the right to survival, the right to development, the right to protection, and the right to participation. Vietnam was the second country in the world and the first in Asia to ratify the CRC in 1990. Over the past 35 years, Vietnam has endeavored to establish a domestic legal framework aligned with the provisions of the CRC and other international treaties to which it is a party. These provisions have been internalized into domestic legal instruments to ensure the implementation of international commitments. From the 1992 Constitution and the 1994 Law on Children to the 2013 Constitution, the 2016 Law on Children, the 2019 Labor Code, the 2020 Enterprise Law, the 2005 Commercial Law, the 2010 Law on Consumer Protection, and the 2012 Law on Advertising, domestic regulations have become increasingly comprehensive in promoting children's rights in general and in the business context in particular.

Protecting children's rights in business entails measures, policies, and actions undertaken by enterprises and other business entities to ensure that children's rights are respected, protected, and fulfilled in all business operations. This protection yields numerous benefits for businesses. First, safeguarding children's rights helps enterprises build a positive and trustworthy public image, thereby enhancing their reputation. Second, investors and business partners increasingly favor companies with robust child protection policies, thereby enhancing competitiveness. Third, promoting children's rights within business contributes to a healthy work environment, motivates employees, and supports the sustainable development of communities.

6.2 Legal Regulations on Protecting Children's Rights in the Business Sector

6.2.1 Child Labor Protection

Vietnam has ratified ILO Convention No. 182 on the prohibition and immediate action for the elimination of the worst forms of child labor, and ILO Convention No. 138 on the minimum age for employment. Vietnamese labor laws have delineated the permissible circumstances and conditions under which minors may be employed in certain sectors, while strictly prohibiting the illegal use of child labor. According to Article 143 of the 2019 Labor Code, individuals aged 15 and older may only be employed under safe and non-hazardous conditions. Clause 2 of Article 6 expressly prohibits the exploitation of child labor. The principles governing the employment of minors in business activities and establishments are set forth in Article 144 of the 2016 Law on Children. These include: minors may only perform work appropriate to their health, ensuring their physical, mental, and personality development; employers must provide care in terms of labor conditions, health, and education throughout the employment period; parental or guardian consent is mandatory; and employers must maintain a separate logbook recording full names, dates of birth, current work assignments, results of periodic health examinations, and present this information upon request by competent state authorities. These provisions collectively satisfy the safety and protection principles applicable to child labor.

Minors are permitted to engage in certain types of work, specifically as follows:

First, individuals aged 15 to under 18 are prohibited from performing the tasks or working in the environments specified in Article 147 of the 2019 Labor Code and Appendices III and IV of Circular No. 09/2020 dated November 12, 2020, which detail and guide the implementation of several provisions of the Labor Code concerning minor workers.

Second, individuals aged 13 to under 15 may only engage in light work as listed by the Minister of Labor, Invalids, and Social Affairs in Appendix II of Circular No. 09/2020. These are light tasks that help children acquire vocational skills, develop their personalities, and earn income to support themselves and their families.

Third, individuals under 13 may only perform the tasks specified in Clause 3, Article 145 of the 2019 Labor Code, namely artistic and athletic activities that do not harm their physical, mental, or personality development, and such employment must be approved by the specialized labor agency under the provincial People's Committee. This regulation constitutes a critical legal basis for employing individuals under 13, reflecting the State's strict oversight and ensuring the legitimate rights and interests of these children within labor relations.

Regarding working hours and rest periods, the regulations are as follows: for individuals under 15, working hours must not exceed 4 h per day and 20 h per week; overtime and night work are prohibited. For individuals aged 15 to under 18, the limit is 8 h per day and 40 h per week. This group may engage in overtime and night work only for certain occupations listed by the Minister of Labor, Invalids, and Social Affairs, as set forth in Appendix V. However, Recommendation No. 146 accompanying ILO Convention No. 138 prohibits overtime for child laborers to ensure adequate time for education, rest, and other activities. Therefore, the current Vietnamese regulations on overtime and night work for individuals aged 15 to under 18 are inconsistent with ILO standards (Giao & Ha, 2017).

With respect to conditions for employing minors, Articles 144 and 145 of the 2019 Labor Code must be followed. In addition to the general provisions, specific requirements include: obtaining parental or guardian consent; maintaining a separate logbook; recording full name, date of birth, current job, and results of periodic health examinations; and providing this information upon request by competent authorities. For individuals under 15, a written contract must be executed between the employer, the minor, and the minor's legal representative; a health certificate from a competent medical facility confirming the minor's fitness for the job must be obtained; periodic health check-ups must be conducted at least every 6 months; and safe, hygienic working conditions suitable for the minor's health must be ensured. For individuals aged 13 to under 15, only the jobs listed in Clause 3, Article 143 of the 2019 Labor Code may be assigned. For individuals under 13, employment is permissible only when the conditions set out in Clause 3, Article 145 of the 2019 Labor Code are met. While these provisions are detailed and explicit, in practice, many labor relationships involving minors lack formal written contracts as required by the 2019 Labor Code. Instead, verbal agreements are prevalent, complicating the resolution of related legal issues.

Periodic health examinations and occupational disease treatment are regulated in Article 21 of the 2015 Law on Occupational Safety and Hygiene, which mandates that minor and elderly workers receive health check-ups at least once every 6 months. For children who are dependents of workers, Decree No. 145 dated December 14, 2020, guiding the implementation of the Labor Code regarding working conditions and labor relations, includes numerous provisions on establishing facilities for breast-feeding, milk storage for female workers, child-rearing, and organizing nurseries and kindergartens where large numbers of workers are employed. Additionally, Clause 1, Article 2 of the 2014 Law on Social Insurance recognizes children under 15 as subjects of compulsory social insurance. Collectively, these legal provisions form a comprehensive and detailed legal framework that serves as a critical basis for the practical regulation of child labor.

6.2.2 Protecting Children as Consumers

Vietnamese law provides explicit provisions for the protection of children as consumers in advertising and commercial activities. Clause 4, Article 12 of the 2016 Law on Children establishes that children have the right to be protected from all forms of harmful information and communication. Similarly, Clause 3, Article 8 of the 2012 Law on Advertising prohibits advertising content that negatively affects the healthy development of children or that uses children's images and voices without the consent of their parents. In addition, Article 6a of the 2023 Law on Consumer Protection identifies children as a vulnerable consumer group that must be afforded special protection mechanisms.

Prohibited acts in advertising that safeguard children's rights are delineated in Clause 14, Article 8 of the 2012 Law on Advertising, which prohibits advertisements that cause children to think, speak, or act contrary to morality and customs or that adversely affect their health, safety, or normal development. Advertising content containing provocative, violent, frightening, obscene, or unethical elements; references to drugs, stimulants, or abuse of women and children; or unapproved games is also prohibited. With respect to advertising nutritional products for children, Article 23 of Decree 37/2006/ND-CP on trade promotion stipulates that commercial advertising of goods that are nutritional products for children must comply with the law on the business and use of such products. Advertisements may not exploit children's lack of knowledge or experience by including content that undermines their trust in family and society, directly encourages them to pressure parents to purchase the advertised products, persuades them that using such products provides advantages over non-use, or fosters attitudes or behaviors contrary to morality, customs, or traditions, with negative impacts on health, safety, or normal development.

In practice, serious violations have occurred. For instance, in August 2021, Rance Pharma International Pharmaceutical Joint Stock Company and Hacofood Group Pharmaceutical Nutrition Joint Stock Company (Ha Dong, Hanoi) were discovered producing and distributing counterfeit powdered milk and nutritional supplements. These products, which included items marketed for individuals with diabetes, kidney disease, premature infants, and pregnant women, falsely claimed to contain ingredients such as bird's nest extract, cordyceps, and walnut powder. Investigations revealed that the products did not contain the advertised substances and were manufactured with substituted additives. Over four years, the companies produced more than 570 types of powdered milk under different brand names, generating nearly 500 billion VND in revenue. Several of these products were promoted by celebrities and endorsed by experts, misleading consumers and resulting in widespread use by infants under three years old and elderly patients post-surgery. The case, prosecuted in April 2025, sparked public outrage and underscored the urgent need for stricter regulations governing the advertising of children's products, especially nutritional goods for young children and vulnerable groups, as well as more severe sanctions against producers and distributors of counterfeit goods (Tue My, 2025).

The field of cinema also provides safeguards. Article 9 of the 2022 Cinema Law prohibits content that violates the lawful rights and interests of children and minors. Article 19, Clause 3, further mandates that film screenings must ensure adequate ratios of Vietnamese films, appropriate time slots for children's films, and sufficient broadcast time for children's programming on domestic television channels. Dissemination of films online must incorporate technical measures and guidance enabling parents or guardians to manage children's viewing and report violations. Likewise, Decree 144/2020/ND-CP on performing arts requires that artistic activities maintain content consistent with national traditions and culture and remain age-appropriate, with specific compliance obligations for events involving children.

In the digital environment, the Ministry of Information and Communications issued Decision No. 88/QD-BTTTT, promulgating the "Code of Conduct for Child Protection in the Online Environment." This Code obligates businesses to monitor and verify children's ages and usage frequency, implement protective measures, and restrict online gaming time for children under 18 in accordance with child protection law.

Tourism law and policy also integrate child protection. Communication campaigns have been organized to raise awareness of child abuse prevention in the tourism sector, instructing businesses to publicize the National Child Protection Hotline (111) for reporting abuse (Hoang, 2023). In the context of the rapid expansion of digital media, children have become a primary target of advertising campaigns on platforms such as YouTube, TikTok, and online games. Yet, the absence of an effective monitoring mechanism for child-directed advertising has raised serious concerns. Many advertisements employ cartoon characters, popular icons, and persuasive language to attract children, despite the lack of specific legal standards for advertising content aimed at them. While Article 8, Clause 3 of the 2012 Law on Advertising prohibits advertising harmful to children and the 2016 Law on Children guarantees protection from harmful information, enforcement in the online environment remains limited due to insufficient personnel and technical tools. Compounding this issue, many parents are unaware of the risks posed by uncontrolled advertising, leading to weak supervision. Therefore, it is essential to develop more specialized regulations on advertising directed at children, promote parental media literacy, and strengthen corporate social responsibility to ensure that advertising is safe and appropriate for young audiences.

6.2.3 Legal Liability of Enterprises Violating Children's Rights

When enterprises violate regulations on children's rights, they may be subject to administrative sanctions under Decree No. 12/2022/ND-CP, civil liability pursuant to the 2015 Civil Code, and criminal liability under the 2015 Penal Code.

With respect to administrative liability, Article 29 of Decree No. 12/2022/ND-CP of the Government, dated January 17, 2022, provides that administrative sanctions in the field of labor and social insurance apply to violations involving underage workers. Employers who violate Clause 1 of Article 29 are subject to a fine ranging from VND 1,000,000 to VND 2,000,000. Those who violate Clause 2 of Article 29 face fines ranging from VND 20,000,000 to VND 25,000,000.

Decree No. 119/2020/ND-CP prescribes administrative sanctions in the field of press and publishing, including acts such as disseminating information that adversely affects the physical or mental development of children or failing to ensure adequate content, timing, and duration of programs for children. Decree No. 130/2021/ND-CP on social protection and child assistance imposes fines ranging from VND 5,000,000 to VND 50,000,000 for violations involving the provision of cultural, informational, and communication products or services harmful to children's healthy development, depending on the specific conduct defined in Article 30.

Decree No. 38/2021/ND-CP sets out administrative sanctions in the fields of culture and advertising. For instance, Point e, Clause 4, Article 8 prohibits disseminating films to children under 16 outside the hours of 8:00 a.m. to 10:00 p.m. Point c, Clause 4, Article 34 prohibits advertisements that induce children to think, speak, or act contrary to morality and customs or that adversely affect their health, safety, or normal development. Point d, Clause 2, Article 50 prohibits advertisements for pharmaceuticals that fail to provide contraindication or dosage information for children.

With respect to criminal liability, employers who unlawfully employ minors may be prosecuted under Article 296 of the 2015 Penal Code (as amended in 2017). Specifically, Clause 1 provides for penalties ranging from fines of VND 30,000,000 to VND 200,000,000, non-custodial reform for up to two years, or imprisonment from three months to three years. Clause 2 prescribes imprisonment of three to seven years for aggravated circumstances, while Clause 3 imposes imprisonment of five to twelve years for especially serious violations.

6.2.4 *Responsible Business Practices and Children's Rights in Viet Nam*

The Children's Rights and Business Principles (CRBP) were jointly developed by UNICEF, the UN Global Compact, and Save the Children in consultation with businesses and stakeholders. These principles call upon enterprises to respect and support children's rights across all business activities. The ten principles emphasize, among other commitments: respecting children's rights as part of corporate human rights obligations; eliminating child labor in all business operations and relationships; creating decent work opportunities for young workers, parents, and caregivers; ensuring the safety and protection of children in all business activities and premises; guaranteeing the safety of products and services and leveraging them to advance children's rights; adopting advertising and marketing practices that respect children's rights; addressing environmental and land use issues in a manner that protects children; ensuring that security arrangements respect children's rights; protecting children affected by emergencies; and strengthening community and government efforts to fulfill children's rights (UNICEF and UN Global Compact, 2012). This framework guides enterprises in integrating child rights into business operations.

Since 2017, UNICEF Vietnam has collaborated with the Vietnam Chamber of Commerce and Industry (VCCI) to implement the CRBP program, aiming to generate broad impact within the business community. The program prioritizes sectors such as garment, footwear, ICT, and tourism, which pose significant risks to children, and undertakes initiatives including evidence-building, capacity-building workshops, policy advocacy, and specialized training. For example, the 2019 "Good Business Practice Forum," co-organized by VCCI and UNICEF, brought together more than 100 enterprises to share family-friendly policies, promote breastfeeding, and prevent child labor (UNICEF Vietnam, 2019). In May 2023, the "Responsible Business for a Sustainable Future" forum highlighted the role of children's rights in ESG strategies, urging enterprises to incorporate child protection measures into internal policies and supply chains (Linh, 2023). These initiatives not only raised awareness but also facilitated concrete measures, such as supporting factories in adopting maternity leave and childcare policies, preparing a Practical Guide for state agencies to enforce child rights protections, and promoting supply chain compliance.

A 2021 survey conducted by VCCI with UNICEF support on the implementation of children's rights by small and medium-sized enterprises (SMEs) in Vietnam revealed that SMEs exporting to international markets are more motivated to advance children's rights. In particular, textile and footwear enterprises demonstrate higher levels of compliance due to the stringent requirements imposed by importers. The survey found that 23.5% of textile and footwear SMEs are required to integrate child rights into business operations, compared with 8.3% in tourism and travel and 5.2% in supply chain enterprises. However, only 2% of SMEs in the textile and footwear sector reported receiving training on child rights, while tourism and travel SMEs benefited more from NGO support (8.6%). Notably, 39% of textile and footwear enterprises provided lactation rooms for breastfeeding workers compared to an average of 27% across other sectors, and one-third of them offered housing subsidies for migrant workers compared with only 14% in tourism and travel. These figures demonstrate that participation in global supply chains significantly influences compliance with child rights principles.

Several corporate initiatives have also contributed to protecting children's rights. For example, the "Strengthening Capacity and Promoting Child Protection Practices in Coffee Production" project in Dak Lak province (2020–2023), funded by Lavazza Group Italy and Save the Children Italy, sought to improve children's well-being in coffee-producing communities (Kim, 2022). In addition, tourism enterprises have joined the Tuoi Tho Project, a program under the Project Childhood Prevention Pillar, aimed at preventing child sexual exploitation in tourism through six targeted actions to enhance children's safety and sustainable development.

Vietnamese law incorporates provisions to safeguard children's right to a safe and healthy environment. Clause 13, Article 6 of the Law on Children prohibits the establishment of polluting or hazardous production sites near educational, medical, cultural, or recreational facilities for children. Clause 14 prohibits the misuse of infrastructure intended for children's learning, recreation, and protection services. Clause 3, Article 4 of the Law on Environmental Protection also affirms that environmental protection must be linked to social security, children's rights, gender equality, and the right of all individuals to live in a clean environment.

Despite these measures, implementation largely depends on voluntary corporate initiatives. Binding legal regulations and systematic monitoring remain limited, and awareness of the CRBP is inconsistent across enterprises. To ensure effective implementation, Vietnam must establish clearer legal mechanisms, integrate child rights indicators into ESG assessments, and strengthen collaboration between the state, enterprises, and international organizations.

6.3 Recommendations for Improving Vietnamese Laws on Protecting Children's Rights in Business

6.3.1 Improving Laws on Protecting Children's Rights in Business

The Vietnamese legal system currently contains relatively comprehensive provisions on the prevention and prohibition of illegal child labor. Children under the age of 15 are generally not permitted to work, except in limited cases involving light work under strict safety conditions. Nevertheless, in practice, the use of child labor remains prevalent, particularly in rural and remote areas and in informal production establishments such as garment, footwear, and handicraft workshops. Many children work under unsafe conditions, seriously impairing their health, education, and overall development. The main causes include ineffective inspection and supervision, limited public awareness, and economic pressures faced by impoverished households. Although the law prohibits child labor, gaps in enforcement persist.

Firstly, Vietnamese law has not provided a clear definition of child labor. The Law on Children defines a child as a person under 16 years old. The 2019 Labor Code, however, regulates juvenile workers as persons under 18 years old and establishes the minimum working age as 15, except as otherwise provided in Section 11.1, Chapter 11. Thus, the concept of juvenile workers encompasses child labor. Vietnam's current minimum working age is therefore consistent with ILO Convention No. 138. Secondly, the law lacks sufficient specificity, particularly in defining what constitutes "light work" or a "safe environment" suitable for workers under 15 (Article 143, Labor Code 2019), leading to inconsistent interpretation and potential abuse. Thirdly, monitoring and enforcement mechanisms remain ineffective: the labor inspection force is limited, violations are mostly detected through denunciations, and child labor often occurs in informal sectors that are difficult to regulate. Fourthly, sanctions remain too lenient to deter violations. In addition, the lack of inter-agency coordination between the Ministry of Labor, Invalids, and Social Affairs, the police, and the education sector further reduces the effectiveness of child protection efforts. These challenges require continued improvement of the legal framework and stronger enforcement to ensure the protection of children's rights in the field of labor.

A notable inconsistency exists between the Law on Children and the Labor Code. Article 1 of the 2016 Law on Children defines children as under 16 years old, while the 2019 Labor Code permits employment from the age of 15. Consequently, enterprises may face legal uncertainty when employing workers aged 15 to under 16. To avoid risk, many businesses prefer hiring workers from 16 to under 18, even though Circular No. 09/2020 provides detailed guidance on employing 15-year-old workers. This "blind spot" between the two laws unintentionally creates vulnerability for enterprises subject to inspection under the Law on Children.

Furthermore, a 2021 survey on the implementation of children's rights in nearly 300 small and medium-sized enterprises conducted by VCCI with UNICEF support revealed that Vietnam has only ratified 15 of 178 ILO technical conventions. Several important conventions remain unratified, including the Convention on the Protection of Wages, the Convention on Migration for Employment, the Convention on Paid Educational Leave, the Convention on Workers with Family Responsibilities, and the Convention on Maternity Protection. To fully implement commitments under free trade agreements and ensure compliance with international labor standards, Vietnam must close these legal gaps and strengthen the role of children's rights in business.

6.3.2 Developing a Corporate Code of Conduct to Protect Children's Rights

In the context of international economic integration, the need to improve legal provisions on responsible business principles with respect to children's rights is increasingly urgent. At present, the regulatory framework remains fragmented and lacks explicit requirements for enterprises to integrate child rights protections throughout their value chains. Certain violations, such as the exploitation of child labor in the informal sector, the misuse of children's images online, and the advertising of age-inappropriate products, remain inadequately regulated and lack clear enforcement mechanisms.

Accordingly, it is necessary to develop a corporate Code of Conduct on children's rights consistent with the United Nations Guiding Principles on Business and Human Rights. This should be accompanied by supplementary regulations on corporate accountability, including mandatory reporting obligations on respect for children's rights. The law should also establish independent monitoring and inspection mechanisms, strengthen sanctions, and impose obligations to remedy harm and provide compensation in cases of violations. Completing the legal framework along these lines not only strengthens the protection of vulnerable groups but also enhances corporate social responsibility, thereby fostering a sustainable and humane business environment aligned with international standards.

6.3.3 Developing Advertising Monitoring Tools for Children

An essential measure for protecting children's rights in business is the development of effective tools to monitor advertising directed at children. Such tools should ensure that advertising content does not adversely affect children's awareness, behavior, or mental health. Monitoring must cover both traditional and online advertising, given the growing influence of digital platforms that often expose children to covert or misleading content.

It is also necessary to establish an early-warning system to receive reports of violations from parents, schools, and community actors, thereby enabling the prompt handling of cases involving the exploitation of children's images or the advertising of products unsuitable for their age.

6.4 Conclusion

In conclusion, protecting children's rights in the business sector is both a legal obligation and an essential social responsibility, reflecting enterprises' commitment to sustainable and humane development. Vietnamese law has gradually evolved to include provisions prohibiting illegal child labor, regulating advertising, protecting children's images and personal information, and imposing penalties for violations. However, enforcement challenges remain, as certain violations have become increasingly sophisticated while monitoring and detection mechanisms remain inconsistent and lack specialized tools.

To ensure that children's rights are fully respected in business operations, it is necessary to continue reviewing and amending legal provisions in line with the context of digital transformation, encourage enterprises to adopt corporate social responsibility standards that incorporate children's rights, and develop monitoring mechanisms to promptly address violations. Equally important is raising awareness among communities, families, and businesses themselves. Only through the strict enforcement of these principles can children's rights be effectively safeguarded, thereby contributing to the creation of a safe, fair, and sustainable business environment.

References

Giao, V. C., & Ha, N. H. (2017). Prevention and elimination of child labor in international law and Vietnamese law. *Journal of Law* (11).

Hoang, L. T. (2023, March). Solutions to prevent and combat sexual abuse of children in tourism activities. *Democracy and Law Journal* (1), 376.

Kim, B. (2022, November 18). *Promoting child protection practices in coffee production in Dak Lak.* Dien Dan Dan Sinh. https://dantri.com.vn/doi-song/thuc-day-thuc-hanh-bao-ve-tre-em-trong-san-xuat-ca-phe-tai-dak-lak-20221118101844141.htm

Linh, D. (2023). *Responsible business for the sustainable future of Vietnam's young generation.* VietnamPlus. https://www.vietnamplus.vn/kinh-doanh-co-trach-nhiem-vi-tuong-lai-ben-vung-the-he-tre-viet-nam/

Ministry of Information and Communications. (n.d.). *Decision no. 88/QD-BTTTT on the code of conduct for the protection of children in cyberspace.*

Ministry of Information and Communications. (n.d.). *Program for the prevention of sexual abuse of children in tourism activities.*

Tue My. (2025). *Fake milk, fake functional foods targeting the elderly and children.* VnEconomy. https://vneconomy.vn/sua-gia-thuc-pham-chuc-nang-gia-nham-vao-nguoi-gia-tre-nho.htm

Unicef Vietnam. (n.d.). *Responsible business for children.* https://www.unicef.org/vietnam/responsible-business-children/

Unicef Vietnam. (2019). *UNICEF, VCCI and businesses share promising family-friendly workplace policies and practices to promote child rights.* https://www.unicef.org/vietnam/press-releases/unicef-vcci-and-businesses-share-promising-family-friendly-workplace-policies/

UNICEF, & UN Global Compact. (2012). *Children's rights and business principles.*

Chapter 7
Advancing Child-Friendly CSR: Protecting Minor Workers Under Vietnam's Labor Law

Nguyen Thi Bich

Abstract In contemporary discourse, sustainable development has unequivocally emerged as a global vision and mission. Within this overarching framework, Corporate Social Responsibility (CSR) plays a pivotal role, serving as a foundational pillar in constructing corporate brand value and fostering client trust. A fundamental tenet of CSR involves ensuring the fulfillment of legal responsibility, often termed legal compliance, particularly with respect to underage laborers. This demographic represents a distinct and vulnerable segment of the workforce, warranting significant attention from the International Labor Organization and most nations. Notably, Vietnam holds the distinction of being the first country in Asia and the second globally to ratify the United Nations Convention on the Rights of the Child in 1990. Furthermore, Vietnam has demonstrated an ongoing commitment to addressing underage labor through the establishment of comprehensive legal frameworks, policies, and institutional support mechanisms. This article provides a foundational overview of CSR as it pertains to underage labor, undertaking a thorough analysis, comparative examination, and critical commentary on the prevailing provisions of Vietnamese labor law from the vantage point of protecting underage laborers. Building upon this analysis, the author identifies and proposes concrete strategies to enhance the implementation of CSR concerning underage labor within Vietnamese enterprises in the forthcoming period.

Article History: Received 14 April 2025; Revised 29 July 2025; Accepted 19 August 2025.

N. T. Bich (✉)
Labor Law Department, Faculty of Civil Law, Ho Chi Minh City University of Law, Ho Chi Minh City, Viet Nam
e-mail: ntbich@hcmulaw.edu.vn

N. Binh An et al. (eds.), *The Future of Child-Friendly Justice and Children's Rights in Vietnam*, https://doi.org/10.1007/978-981-95-3521-7_7

7.1 General Overview of "Corporate Social Responsibility" and "Underage Labor"

7.1.1 The Concept of "Corporate Social Responsibility"

CSR is a concept that has been extensively examined by numerous scholars globally. For instance, Keith Davis (1973) defined it as: "Corporate social responsibility is the firm's consideration of and response to issues beyond the narrow economic, technical, and legal requirements of the firm." Similarly, researcher Archie Carroll (1999) posited that: "Corporate social responsibility encompasses the economic, legal, ethical, and discretionary (philanthropic) expectations that society has of organizations at a given point in time." Rupp (2011) asserted that: "CSR represents organizational activities and policies within a specific context, taking into account stakeholder expectations while simultaneously striving for economic, social, and environmental performance."

Currently, a significant authoritative guide on CSR is the ISO 26000:2010 standard, published by the International Organization for Standardization in November 2010. Building upon the ISO 26000:2010 standard, Vietnam promulgated the TCVN ISO 26000:2013 standard, which was drafted by the National Technical Subcommittee TCVN/TC01/SC1 on Social Responsibility, proposed by the Directorate for Standards, Metrology and Quality, and announced by the Ministry of Science and Technology. According to this standard, the concept of CSR is defined as: "The responsibility of an organization for the impacts of its decisions and activities on society and the environment, through transparent and ethical behavior that contributes to sustainable development, including health and the welfare of society; takes into account the expectations of stakeholders; is in compliance with applicable law and consistent with international norms of behavior; and is integrated throughout the organization and practiced in its relationships."

Thus, CSR can be understood as a fundamental business principle voluntarily adopted by enterprises, whereby they operate not solely for profit maximization but also commit to fulfilling their obligations, thereby contributing to and fostering sustainable development for the common good and the benefit of society.

7.1.2 The Concept of Underage Labor

The International Labor Organization's Convention No. 138 concerning Minimum Age for Admission to Employment stipulates that the minimum age "shall not be less than the age of completion of compulsory schooling and, in any case, shall not be less than 15 years" (Article 2, Paragraph 3). It further allows that "a Member whose economy and educational facilities are insufficiently developed may, after consultation with the organizations of employers and workers concerned, if such organizations exist, initially specify a minimum age of 14 years" (Article 2, Paragraph

4). Moreover, "the minimum age for admission to any type of employment or work which by its nature or the circumstances in which it is carried out is likely to jeopardize the health, safety or morals of young persons shall not be less than 18 years" (Article 3, Paragraph 1). The Convention also permits, "after consultation with the organizations of employers and workers concerned, if such organizations exist, the admission of persons from 16 years of age to employment or work where they are fully protected, where they receive adequate specific instruction or vocational training in the relevant branch of activity" (Article 3, Paragraph 3).

In the context of current Vietnamese labor law, the concept of underage labor is established based on the definition of a minor as per Clause 1, Article 21, the 2015 Civil Code. Accordingly, an underage laborer is defined as an employee under 18 years of age (Clause 1, Article 143, the 2019 Labor Code). This cohort constitutes a vulnerable group of laborers due to their incompletely developed physical and psychological attributes, necessitating protection under both international and national law. From the perspective of protecting underage laborers, ensuring their rights is achieved through the comprehensive activities of competent state agencies, enterprises, and other social organizations and individuals, with the objective of preventing and safeguarding against risks that may infringe upon the legitimate rights and interests of underage laborers.

7.1.3 The Role of Corporate Social Responsibility in Protecting Underage Labor

The early entry of underage individuals into the workforce often deprives them of educational opportunities, compels them to leave school prematurely, or necessitates a challenging combination of schooling and employment. This precarious situation renders them particularly susceptible to adverse impacts on their health, well being, and personal development. Consequently, the legal framework consistently affords a heightened degree of protection to underage laborers compared to their adult counterparts.

Firstly, a corporation's adherence to legal regulations concerning underage labor significantly enhances its international market standing and reputation (An, 2023b). A study by the International Labor Organization (ILO) (2020) revealed that numerous foreign clients, particularly prominent brands such as Adidas and Nike, may mandate their suppliers to implement child labor prevention measures that exceed statutory requirements.

Furthermore, the ILO's (2022) analysis demonstrated that enterprises, especially those exporting seafood to major markets like the European Union, the United States, Japan, South Korea, and China, must not only satisfy technical, food safety, traceability, and labeling prerequisites but also fulfill stringent demands related to labor practices and social responsibility. These often include explicit prohibitions against the use of child labor, forced labor, and discrimination, as clearly articulated in various social responsibility standards, voluntary sustainability standards, or specific market and client stipulations. Examples encompass the SA8000 standard, the Business Social Compliance Initiative (BSCI) standard, and SMETA.

Secondly, a firm's commitment to legal compliance regarding underage labor offers several distinct advantages. It enables the enterprise to (i) avoid legal costs and repercussions; (ii) exhibit transparency during governmental inspections, as well as in public awareness campaigns and initiatives launched by the state or consumers; and (iii) cultivate collaborative, rather than adversarial, relationships with public authorities. Phan Thi Thu Hien (2023) observed that many Vietnamese enterprises still operate under the misconception that "CSR is exclusively for large, multinational corporations," or even that "CSR is a luxury of developed nations, unsuitable for developing countries." This perspective is entirely incongruous with current global development trends. Voluntarily integrating CSR commitments into business decisions simultaneously exemplifies corporate business ethics and contributes to the establishment of sustainable values, benefiting not only the enterprise but also the broader community and society (An, 2023c).

Thirdly, the exercise of social responsibility toward underage labor holds profound significance in advancing the policies and directives of the Party and State aimed at eradicating child labor and its worst forms, thereby aligning with fundamental international labor standards on child labor elimination. In an expansive and multinational business environment, beyond merely seeking profits from international trade through new Free Trade Agreements (FTAs) such as the Comprehensive and Progressive Agreement for Trans Pacific Partnership (CPTPP) and the European Union Vietnam Free Trade Agreement (EVFTA), Vietnamese enterprises—particularly foreign invested enterprises, export oriented enterprises, export processing firms, and those involved in manufacturing, trade, services, or consultancy, or engaging in supply and investment with foreign partners—are also obligated to adhere to commitments regarding the implementation of international labor standards on child labor eradication.

7.2 Methodology

Theoretical Framework

Ho Viet Tien and Ho Thi Van Anh (2018) observe that Corporate Social Responsibility is typically examined through three distinct lenses: (1) the Institutional Approach, (2) the Organizational Approach, and (3) the Individual Approach. To achieve the research objective regarding corporate social responsibility toward underage labor, this author adopts the Organizational Approach as the foundational theoretical model for this inquiry. Building upon these theoretical underpinnings and applying them to the scope of this investigation, the author will first meticulously define CSR and the concept of underage labor as articulated under Vietnamese law. Subsequently, this study will scrutinize the existing legal provisions governing the employment of underage laborers. Consistent with the findings of Pisani et al. (2017) at the institutional level, the primary subjects of consideration are typically business ethics. This analytical framework will guide the author's subsequent exploration of corporate business ethics, leading to an empirical assessment. The author will leverage the aforementioned theoretical constructs to analyze and critically evaluate Vietnamese legal provisions and their practical application within enterprises, highlighting both achievements and persistent limitations from the perspective of corporate business ethics. Ultimately, the author will propose a series of recommendations aimed at enhancing the efficacy of CSR implementation for the protection of underage laborers.

Research Methodology

Pisani et al. (2017) note that during the 1985–2005 period, CSR research was predominantly theoretical, whereas empirical research saw a substantial increase only during the 2006–2015 period. Studies commonly employ either quantitative or qualitative methods, with a relatively limited number of studies utilizing mixed methodologies. The institutional level tends to favor theoretical methods, while the organizational and individual levels primarily select empirical methods (quantitative, qualitative, and other approaches) for CSR research. Based on this established framework, the author's research methodology for this paper is fundamentally rooted in a theoretical approach. Additionally, several supplementary methods, including comparative analysis, critical analysis, and commentary, will be synergistically employed.

7.3 Current Labor Law on Corporate Social Responsibility in Protecting Underage Labor

According to the 2023 National Child Population Survey, a collaborative effort by the General Statistics Office, the ILO, and the Ministry of Labor, Invalids, and Social Affairs, individuals aged 5 to 17 total 20.6 million, constituting 20.6% of the national population.

CLASSIFICATION BY RESIDENTIAL AREA

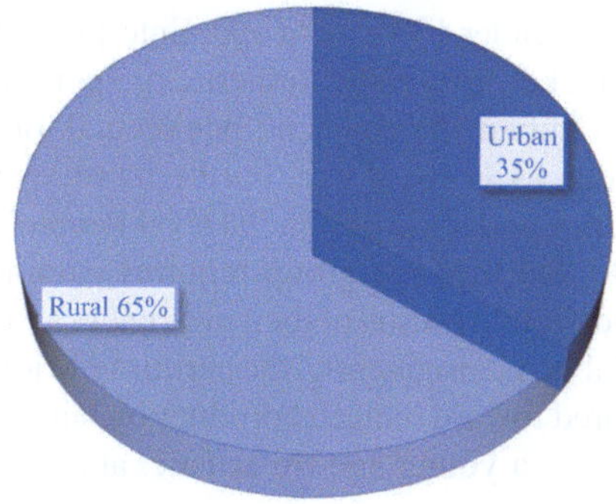

Of this demographic, 35.0% reside in urban areas, while 65.0% live in rural areas.

Nationally, 96.4% of children aged 5 to 17 are "attending school." Specifically, 94.8% of children are "only attending school," 1.6% are "both attending school and participating in labor," 2% are "only participating in labor," and 1.6% are "neither attending school nor participating in labor."

These statistics underscore the persistent reality of child labor, despite the critical need for these children to acquire knowledge and skills rather than engage in employment. To effectively safeguard these vulnerable individuals when they are compelled to work, the author will now delineate the specific responsibilities of enterprises toward underage laborers, as follows.

7.3.1 Conditions for Recruitment and Labor Contract Conclusion with Underage Laborers

Given the unique characteristics of underage individuals, not all enterprises are permitted to recruit or employ them. Rather, specific jobs and workplaces must align with legal stipulations. These are detailed below:

- Recruitment of laborers under 13 years of age: Enterprises may only employ individuals in this age bracket for artistic, athletic, or sports related work, provided such activities do not impair the physical, intellectual, or personal development of the individual under 13 years of age. Furthermore, explicit consent from the specialized labor agency under the provincial level People's Committee is mandatory. It is undeniable that this age group requires paramount attention to their health, education, and the cultivation of their awareness and moral character, rather than engagement in labor. Consequently, the permissible jobs for this demographic are not primarily geared toward material production but rather focus on nurturing their innate talents from a young age (in artistic, athletic, and sports fields). To ensure stringent management and oversight of employment for this age group, the law mandates that enterprises obtain permission from competent state agencies, as outlined in Articles 5, 6, and 7 of Circular No. 09/2020/TT BLDTBXH.

- Recruitment of laborers aged 13 to under 15 years: Enterprises are authorized to employ individuals in this category exclusively for light work, as enumerated in Article 8 of Circular No. 09/2020/TT BLDTBXH. This list includes: performing arts; sports athletes; software programming; traditional crafts such as ceramic glazing, oyster shell sawing, do paper making, conical hat making, conical hat decorating, mat weaving, drum making, brocade weaving, brocade embroidery, rice noodle making, vermicelli making, bean sprout cultivation, rice cracker making, silk weaving, lotus thread spinning, lacquer painting, incense rolling, and votive paper making (excluding stages involving harmful chemicals like raw lacquer, cleaning agents, coloring agents, scenting agents, or those creating curling ash); fine handicraft arts such as embroidery, artistic carpentry, horn comb making, folk painting (e.g., Dong Ho painting, Hang Trong painting), to he figurine molding, wood carving, silk painting, picking up clam and oyster shells for artistic decoration, polishing artistic paintings, stringing prayer beads and beading, polishing artistic jewelry, making dolls, creating greeting cards from artistic paper for decorative purposes, making paper models, paper boxes, paper bags; weaving and crafting household items or handicrafts from natural materials like rattan, bamboo, nipa palm, coconut, banana, water hyacinth, jute, sedge, cinnamon, fern, straw, and conical hat leaves; wrapping spring rolls, candies, and cakes (excluding the operation or use of packaging machinery, equipment, or tools); silkworm rearing; weeding clean vegetable gardens; harvesting seasonal clean vegetables and fruits; pasturing livestock on farms; assisting in untangling fishing nets, weaving fishing nets, drying aquatic products; and cutting threads, sewing buttons, making buttonholes, and packaging handmade textile products.
- Recruitment of laborers aged 15 to under 18 years: Enterprises may employ individuals in this age group for all types of work, with the explicit exception of prohibited jobs or workplaces. Specifically, prohibited jobs include: carrying, lifting, or moving heavy objects beyond the physical capacity of the underage individual; producing or trading alcohol, beer, tobacco, psychotropic substances, or other addictive substances; producing, using, or transporting chemicals, gases, or explosives; maintaining or servicing equipment and machinery; demolishing construction works; melting, blowing, casting, rolling, stamping, or welding metals; deep sea diving or offshore fishing; and other work causing harm to the physical, intellectual, or moral development of underage individuals, as detailed in Annex III of Circular 09/2020/TT BLDTBXH. Concurrently, employment is prohibited in the following locations: underwater, underground, in caves, or in tunnels; construction sites; livestock slaughterhouses; casinos, bars, dance halls, karaoke rooms, hotels, motels, saunas, massage parlors; lottery business outlets, and electronic game service establishments; and other workplaces causing harm to the physical, intellectual, or moral development of underage individuals, as detailed in Annex IV of Circular 09/2020/TT BLDTBXH.

Therefore, to effectively fulfill their social responsibility toward underage laborers, enterprises must first thoroughly understand their operational domain and the types of jobs for which they employ labor, in order to accurately determine the recruitment entitlements for each underage age group. A clear understanding of their rights and obligations from the recruitment stage will enable enterprises to uphold their commitment to eliminating child labor and mitigate potential risks during employment. However, practical challenges persist in the recruitment of underage laborers. For instance, a 2021 survey on the implementation of children's rights by Small and Medium Enterprises (SMEs) in Vietnam, conducted by the Vietnam Chamber of Commerce and Industry (VCCI) and UNICEF, revealed that a large percentage of enterprises have age verification procedures prior to recruitment (82.3%) and disseminate these regulations to relevant stakeholders (73.8%). Yet, only 53.9% of enterprises have clear regulations stipulating a minimum working age of 15 years. This rate is higher in textile, garment, and footwear enterprises compared to tourism, travel, and supply chain enterprises. Fewer enterprises have impact assessment processes (43.5%) or monitor remediation of child labor issues (36.5%). Overall, according to VCCI and UNICEF (2021), enterprises and supply chains often lack clear policies and regulations regarding the minimum working age.

Furthermore, enterprises must be thoroughly acquainted with the procedural requirements for employing each group of underage laborers. Specifically, when employing underage individuals, enterprises must obtain the consent of their parents or guardians. For laborers under 15 years of age, the enterprise must conclude a written labor contract with both the underage individual and their legal representative. This requirement stems from their incomplete physical and psychological development, necessitating the involvement of a legal representative in decisions regarding their participation in labor. This point aligns with the consensus on minors' participation in transactions, as stipulated in Article 21, Clause 4 of the 2015 Civil Code. However, in the author's view, the aforementioned written labor contract requirement applies only to individuals under 15 years of age and does not encompass those aged 15 to under 18. Although this latter group possesses more developed awareness than those under 15, in practice, they constitute a larger proportion of the working population than the under 15 group and are commonly employed through oral labor contracts. The absence of a written labor contract can create opportunities for enterprises to obscure their obligations, potentially failing to safeguard the rights of underage laborers and increasing the likelihood of exploitation. In the event of disputes, it also becomes more challenging to ascertain the rights and obligations stipulated in the labor contract for the protection of underage laborers.

To ensure effective recruitment practices, in addition to establishing standardized recruitment procedures, employers must train recruitment personnel in age verification techniques and interview methodologies to gather information and authenticate applicant ages. Employers must ensure that recruitment staff possess comprehensive knowledge of regulations pertaining to the working age of minors, thereby enabling accurate adherence to the enterprise's recruitment policy commitments.

7.3.2 Working Conditions for Underage Laborers

Firstly, ensuring appropriate working hours and rest periods for underage laborers is paramount. Pursuant to Article 146 of the 2019 Labor Code, individuals aged 15 to under 18 may not work more than eight hours per day and 40 h per week. For laborers under 15 years of age, the limits are further reduced to no more than four hours per day and 20 h per week. This reduction in working hours for those under 15, compared to the 15 to under 18 age group, is entirely judicious, as the younger demographic necessitates a greater emphasis on their health and education over their labor involvement. Regarding overtime, laborers aged 15 to under 18 are permitted to work overtime and at night in certain occupations and jobs as stipulated by the Ministry of Labor, Invalids, and Social Affairs. Conversely, individuals under 15 years of age are strictly prohibited from working overtime or at night, and their working hours must be scheduled so as not to interfere with their schooling. Concerning rest periods, underage laborers are entitled to rest rights when participating in employment relationships. Specifically, they are granted breaks during working hours in accordance with Article 109 of the 2019 Labor Code, an annual leave of 14 working days for jobs under normal conditions as per Article 113, Clause 1, Point b of the 2019 Labor Code, and other forms of leave such as holidays, weekly rest days, personal leave, and agreed upon leave with the employer, similar to adult laborers. The current absence of specific, tailored provisions for this particular vulnerable group represents a significant inadequacy, as ensuring appropriate working and rest times for underage laborers is critically important. Only by safeguarding their working hours, overtime, and rest can their holistic development during their minor years be assured.

Consequently, when enterprises ensure adequate working and rest periods, it provides these young individuals with time for study, cultivation, and enhancement of their knowledge and cultural understanding, as well as opportunities to participate in other social activities that foster comprehensive physical, intellectual, and personal development. According to VCCI and UNICEF (2021), over 50% of enterprises implement supportive monitoring policies to ensure assigned tasks are not beyond the capacity and ability of underage laborers. These policies include, but are not limited to: assigning personnel to supervise and support young laborers; providing vocational training or internship opportunities for young laborers and students; conducting training or guidance for young laborers to develop their skills; educating young laborers about their rights; offering accommodation for young laborers on par with standards for other employees; permitting flexible working hours; and providing scholarships. The integration of these policies with regulated working and rest periods enables underage laborers to enhance their professional qualifications, skills, and awareness, thereby equipping them for skilled employment upon reaching adulthood.

Despite these efforts, current practical implementation still reveals numerous shortcomings in controlling the employment of underage laborers. For example, the explosive growth of e commerce platforms has seen widespread participation of underage laborers in online sales activities, such as livestream advertising and sales, often involving overtime or night work. However, this sector remains inadequately regulated to ensure proper working hours for this demographic. A study by the General Statistics Office, ILO, and the Ministry of Labor, Invalids, and Social Affairs (2023) indicated that, on average, child laborers work 37.5 h per week. As their age increases, so does their average working time. A concerning 65.9% of child laborers work more hours than legally permitted. Of children working excessive hours, 75% are from rural areas and 61.6% are boys. While child laborers primarily work during the day or on weekends, approximately 50.1 thousand children (18.6% of total child laborers) are compelled to work at night, defined as between 10:00 PM and 6:00 AM the following day.

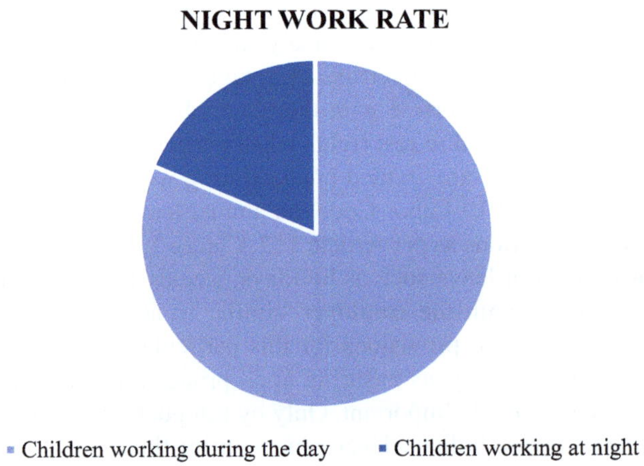

Night work for children directly impacts their health and full developmental opportunities. Furthermore, specific regulations are needed regarding daily overtime limits and rest periods for underage laborers to protect their rights, prevent the abuse of their labor, and ensure their healthy development.

Secondly, ensuring healthcare for underage laborers is a critical obligation. Pursuant to Article 147 of the 2019 Labor Code and Circular 09/2020/BLDTBXH, enterprises are prohibited from employing minors in heavy, hazardous, or dangerous work, or in workplaces or jobs that adversely affect their moral character. Furthermore, during the management and employment of underage laborers, enterprises must maintain a separate monitoring log, meticulously recording their full name, date of birth, current job, and the results of periodic health examinations, and must present this log when requested by competent state agencies. Regarding healthcare, enterprises are obligated to arrange health examinations for underage laborers at least once every six months and bear all associated costs. They must also regularly inspect and monitor workplaces to ensure the safety of minors. Consistent healthcare facilitates the timely detection and treatment of any illnesses that underage laborers may unfortunately contract. Should an underage laborer's health no longer be suitable for their job, the enterprise must inform the individual, and in cases of those under 15 years of age, their legal representative must also be notified concurrently. Beyond these regulations, the State also mandates responsibilities for relevant organizations and competent agencies, such as trade unions and state inspectors, in overseeing and managing labor safety and hygiene, particularly concerning underage laborers. A survey by the General Statistics Office (2023) revealed that nearly 94.3 thousand children nationwide (35.0%) are engaged in work that poses harm to themselves. Child laborers in urban areas face a 1.5 times higher risk of performing such work compared to those in rural areas, at 47.9% and 31.9% respectively. Approximately 12 out of every 100 child laborers experience at least one health issue due to their participation in labor. This alarming reality underscores the persistent inadequacies and limited effectiveness of current monitoring efforts regarding compliance in the employment of underage laborers.

Thirdly, guaranteeing the right to wages for underage laborers is essential. Under current regulations, there are no specific provisions for the wages of underage laborers; rather, general wage provisions applicable to adult laborers are uniformly applied. The 2019 Labor Code stipulates a minimum wage for laborers generally, without specific provisions for underage laborers. In stark contrast, Dr. Pham Thi Hai Diu's research (2024), referencing Korean law, highlights very specific regulations concerning wage payment methods, payment in special circumstances such as dismissal, payment during work stoppages, and in emergency situations for underage laborers. Under Korean law, employers must pay wages directly, in cash, and in full to working minors, at least once a month on a fixed day (Article 43). If a working minor resigns or their employment relationship is terminated due to dismissal, all outstanding wages, severance pay, and other monies must be settled within 14 days from the termination date (Article 36). Employers are prohibited from paying wages to the parents of underage laborers (Article 68). If a working child is unable to work due to reasons attributable to the employer, they are entitled to 70% of their average wage (Article 46). In the event of an emergency, such as illness or accident, where a working minor requests immediate payment for work already performed prior to the request to cover related expenses, the employer must disburse wages before the regular pay date (Article 45).

The study by the General Statistics Office, ILO, and the Ministry of Labor, Invalids, and Social Affairs (2023) indicated that the average income of child laborers is approximately 3.0 million VND per person per month, which is less than half the average income of laborers aged 15 and above (7.1 million VND per person per month). This demonstrates that despite their early entry into the workforce, their income is very low, making it challenging to secure a livelihood. Moreover, in many instances, their wages are not received directly but through their parents. Furthermore, in unfortunate emergency situations such as illness or accidents, there is currently no mechanism to ensure that they receive immediate wage payments.

Fourthly, ensuring the right of underage laborers to provide feedback is crucial. According to Clause 2, Article 12, Circular 09/2020/TT BLDTBXH, enterprises are responsible for soliciting feedback from underage individuals on matters related to their rights and interests. However, this provision is generic and lacks specific enforcement mechanisms, rendering its feasibility low. There is an urgent need to supplement this with specific regulations on regular dialogue with underage laborers to ascertain their thoughts and attitudes when working at a non adult age.

7.3.3 Sanctions for Unlawful Employment of Underage Laborers

Enterprises that violate regulations concerning the employment of underage laborers may face legal liability in both administrative and criminal domains. Specifically:

- Monetary fines ranging from VND 1,000,000 to VND 2,000,000 may be imposed on enterprises that fail to maintain a separate monitoring log, or maintain one that lacks complete required information, when employing underage laborers, or fail to produce such a log when requested by competent state authorities.
- Monetary fines ranging from VND 20,000,000 to VND 25,000,000 may be levied against enterprises committing any of the following offenses: employing an underage laborer without the consent of the minor's parents or guardian; employing an individual under 15 years of age without a written labor contract between the employer and the minor's legal representative; arranging working hours that interfere with the schooling of an individual under 15 years of age; lacking a health certificate from a competent medical facility verifying the fitness for work of an individual under 15 years of age; failing to conduct periodic health examinations at least once every six months, or failing to ensure working conditions, safety, and occupational hygiene appropriate for the age group; employing an underage laborer beyond the stipulated working hours; employing an individual under 15 years of age for overtime or night work; or employing an individual aged 15 to under 18 years for overtime or night work in occupations or jobs not permitted by law.
- Monetary fines ranging from VND 50,000,000 to VND 75,000,000 may be imposed on enterprises committing any of the following offenses: employing an individual aged 13 to under 15 years in work outside the legally permitted list; employing an individual under 13 years of age in work outside the legally permitted list, or employing an individual under 13 years of age in legally permitted work without the consent of a competent authority; or employing a laborer aged 15 to under 18 years in prohibited jobs or at prohibited workplaces, provided the severity does not warrant criminal prosecution.
- In the criminal domain: Vietnamese law provides a relatively comprehensive mechanism to eliminate egregious forms of child exploitation, such as forced labor, prostitution, illegal activities, and heavy or hazardous work. Enterprises employing laborers under 16 years of age in heavy, hazardous, or toxic work, as designated by the State, under the circumstances outlined in Article 296 of the Criminal Code, are subject to penalties ranging from monetary fines to non custodial reform or imprisonment.

Overall, these penalties are designed to be sufficiently specific and possess a deterrent and educational effect, encouraging enterprises to enhance their legal compliance and mitigate legal risks associated with employing underage laborers.

7.4 Suggestions for Promoting Corporate Social Responsibility in Protecting Underage Labor

To effectively promote the implementation of corporate social responsibility when employing underage laborers, the author proposes a synchronized approach incorporating several key solutions:

Firstly, supplementing regulations on the conclusion of written labor contracts for individuals aged 15 to under 18 years. Oral labor contracts, even for durations under one month, can easily lead to the infringement of rights for this vulnerable group due to a lack of transparency and difficulties in management, inspection, and verification of compliance regarding underage labor. Mandating written labor contracts for this age group would provide a stronger basis for oversight and management. Furthermore, a written contract would empower underage laborers with a clear understanding of their entitlements, enabling them to better protect themselves in cases of employer violations.

Secondly, clarifying and supplementing regulations regarding working hours. Specifically, there is a need to introduce separate provisions limiting the number of night working hours per workday for underage laborers. In this regard, Vietnam could consider referencing Article 9 of the European Union's Directive 94/33/EC concerning night work. Additionally, it is crucial to supplement regulations limiting overtime, drawing inspiration from Article 5 of Finland's Young Workers' Act, which caps overtime at no more than 80 h per year, in addition to daily or normal working hours. Moreover, to ensure the holistic development of this labor group, additional provisions should be introduced regarding reasonable compensatory rest periods for underage laborers, beyond any overtime remuneration. Fundamentally, underage laborers should prioritize health care over financial gain (An, 2023a). Therefore, when they are required to work overtime, they expend additional physical effort and should be granted compensatory rest to restore their energy, enabling their physical, intellectual, and personal development after extended working hours.

Thirdly, introducing specific regulations concerning wages and protecting the right to wages for underage laborers. As analyzed in Section 7.3, Vietnam could draw upon the experience of South Korea, particularly Article 45 of the Korean Labor Standards Act regarding emergency payments, to add provisions for wage payments in certain special circumstances, thereby safeguarding the wage rights of this particular labor group. For example, in cases of illness, disease, or accident, underage laborers should have the right to request immediate payment for work already performed prior to the request, to cover associated expenses.

Fourthly, supplementing specific regulations on dialogue with underage laborers in the presence of their parents or guardians. While this demographic may constitute a relatively small proportion within enterprises, they are particularly vulnerable due to their physical characteristics. Mandating enterprises to enhance dialogue with underage laborers, with their parents or guardians present, is a measure that would effectively promote greater corporate social responsibility in protecting underage laborers, as well as mitigate unnecessary conflicts and disputes. Furthermore, the Government should organize additional tripartite consultations to contribute positively to promoting sustainable and long term programs for the prevention and responsible employment of underage laborers. At the national level, governments, employers' and workers' organizations participate in national tripartite policy dialogue and may request support for the establishment and operation of national steering committees on underage labor, for the development of bilateral declarations by social partners, and, where appropriate, for their local structures.

Fifthly, strengthening the role of trade unions. Despite existing labor law provisions ensuring working conditions for underage laborers, the majority of laborers in this age group require guidance and support from trade union organizations. Decision No. 782/QD TTg, dated May 27, 2021, approving the "Program for Prevention and Reduction of Child Labor in Violation of Law for the Period 2021–2025, with Orientation to 2030," explicitly assigns responsibility to the Vietnam General Confederation of Labor to "organize communication, education, and legal and policy counseling on child labor for cadres, union members, underage individuals, and children engaged in labor." According to the Charter of the Vietnam General Confederation of Labor, the Women's Affairs Committee serves as the focal point for representing and addressing issues directly related to female laborers and children. It also advises and assists the corresponding level of the trade union executive committee in developing legal policies related to female laborers, gender equality, women's development, family affairs, and children. Grassroots trade union organizations can participate in numerous activities aimed at preventing and reducing underage labor, including: 1. Investigating the situation of underage laborers; 2. Advocating for enterprises not to employ underage laborers through the signing and implementation of Collective Bargaining Agreements; and 3. Monitoring the enforcement of policies, laws, and commitments concerning underage labor.

Sixthly, enterprises need to proactively develop action plans to prevent and mitigate risks to protect underage laborers. This includes: regularly and thoroughly reviewing labor recruitment processes; assessing the situation within the enterprise and throughout its supply chain. Enterprises should proactively scrutinize their supply chains, partners, and clients to ascertain whether underage laborers are employed and the level of compliance with relevant labor laws. They should also formulate and issue formal commitments regarding the employment of underage laborers; expand and integrate other policies to enhance the capacity and awareness of underage laborers, such as assigning personnel to supervise and support young laborers; providing training or guidance for young laborers to develop their skills; educating young laborers about their rights; offering accommodation for young laborers on par with standards for other employees; permitting flexible working hours; and providing scholarships. Enterprises might also consider developing their own Code of Conduct on underage labor for both the enterprise itself and its supply chain. Such a Code would comprise a set of corporate commitments declaring their stance on underage labor prevention, outlining regulations, recruitment procedures, and merchandise procurement procedures with commercial partners, incorporating standards for scrutinizing compliance with underage labor employment practices.

In addition, enterprises must establish effective internal complaint and grievance resolution mechanisms specifically for issues related to underage labor. These mechanisms should clearly stipulate timeframes for receiving and responding to suggestions from underage laborers, outline transparent processing methods, and define clear sanctions for failing to ensure full and legitimate rights for underage laborers.

Seventhly, intensifying communication efforts, intrinsically linking the elimination of underage labor with poverty eradication and hunger alleviation, and implementing measures to enhance the quality of legal compliance enforcement. Referencing the experiences of several countries, as highlighted in Truong Thi Ngoc Lan's research (2019), provides valuable insights. For instance, in 2002, the government of Bangladesh declared that primary school children would receive scholarships. School fees were also subsidized to enable children from impoverished families to attend school. These two initiatives jointly aimed to incentivize students to remain in school rather than enter the workforce. According to Karen Tietgen (2003), the Primary Education Stipend Project (PESP) in Bangladesh sought to increase educational participation—enrollment, attendance, retention, and achievement—among primary school aged children from poor households across Bangladesh by providing direct cash payments to targeted families. Eligible households with students received 100 Taka (approximately 1.76 USD) per month for one student (with a maximum of 1200 Taka annually) and 125 Taka per month for more than one student (with a maximum of 1500 Taka annually).

India also developed an anti child labor movement known as Rugmark. RUGMARK emerged in 1995, spurred by the threat of boycotts of Indian carpets from importing nations such as Germany, the United States, and the United Kingdom, due to concerns about child labor. This organization was the outcome of collaboration among carpet manufacturers, exporters, NGOs, and international organizations, dedicated to eliminating illegal child labor in the carpet manufacturing industry. Each product manufactured is affixed with the Rugmark label, assuring consumers that no child labor was employed during its production. In Brazil, the government enacted legislation protecting children under 18 from hazardous work, imposing fines and imprisonment sentences ranging from 4 to 12 years for cases of forced labor. Furthermore, the Brazilian government integrated provisions into its Labor Code concerning mobile inspection units, tasked with inspecting forced labor issues, including forced child labor in remote areas. Currently, over 100 labor inspectors are part of this unit. To address cases of forced labor, this unit can prosecute facility owners and issue on site fines. Specifically, Article 149 of the Brazilian Penal Code prohibits forced labor, with penalties of two to eight years imprisonment and a fine. The penalty increases by half if the crime is committed against a child or an underage individual (Article 149, Paragraph 2).

Through these examples, Vietnam can learn from the experiences of the aforementioned nations to improve the situation of underage labor employment. Strategies could include: fully exempting tuition fees for children (as concluded by the Politburo in Official Letter No. 13594 CV/VPTW dated March 1, 2025, from the Central Party Office, which needs to be promptly formalized in legal normative documents) combined with awarding scholarships to children from impoverished or disadvantaged households; implementing public awareness campaigns promoting a zero tolerance approach to child labor, particularly in rural, mountainous, and difficult regions; and strengthening inspection, supervision, and timely enforcement actions against violations.

7.5 Conclusion

In the emerging global landscape, adherence to business principles that safeguard the rights of underage laborers is an indispensable prerequisite for enterprises to integrate into regional and global economies. When enterprises fail to conduct business responsibly by protecting the rights of underage laborers, their goods cannot be exported to certain member states that demand compliance with such principles. Therefore, actively promoting the full and clear implementation of corporate social responsibility to protect and ensure the proper employment of underage laborers plays a crucial role. This commitment contributes significantly to building sustainable development values for the common good of the community and society.

References

An, N.B. (2023a). The Role of Hard Law and Soft Law in Developing CSR. In N. B. An & P. T. Anh (Eds.), *Laws on Corporate Social Responsibility and the Developmental Trend in Vietnam*. Springer. https://doi.org/10.1007/978-981-19-9255-1_1

An, N. B. (2023b). Analytical Facts of Corporate Social Responsibility for Enforcement of Labor Rights. In N. B. An & P. T. Anh (Eds.), *Laws on Corporate Social Responsibility and the Developmental Trend in Vietnam*. Springer. https://doi.org/10.1007/978-981-19-9255-1_4

An, N. B. (2023c, September 12). An Evaluation of the Global Supply Chain Codes of Conduct Concerning Soft Law Regulations of Labour. *AIP Conference Proceeding, 2827*(1), 030039. https://doi.org/10.1063/5.0164872

Brazilian Penal Code. https://www.fairlabor.org/wp-content/uploads/2023/08/08.21.2023-Issue-Brief-Forced-Labor-in-Brazil-English-1.pdf

Carroll, A. B. (1999). Corporate Social Responsibility: Evolution of a Definitional Construct. *Business & Society, 38*(3), 268–295.

Circular No. 09/2020/TT BLDTBXH dated November 12, 2020, Issued by the Ministry of Labor, Invalids, and Social Affairs, Detailing and Guiding the Implementation of Certain Articles of the Labor Code Concerning Underage Labor.

Civil Code 2015.

Council Directive 94/33/EC of June 22, 1994, on the Protection of Young People at Work. https://eurlex.europa.eu/eli/dir/1994/33/oj/eng. Accessed January 8, 2025.

Davis, K. (1973). The Case for and Against Business Assumption of Social Responsibilities. *Academy of Management Journal, 16*(312), 323.

General Statistics Office, ILO & Ministry of Labor, Invalids, and Social Affairs. (2023). Summary Information on Key Findings on Children in Labor and Child Labor in Vietnam.

ILO Convention No. 138 on Minimum Age for Admission to Employment, 1973 (Vietnam Acceded on June 24, 2003).

International Labor Organization. (2020). Guidelines for Enterprises on Preventing and Reducing Child Labor.

International Labor Organization. (2022). Practical Guidance Document on Preventing Child Labor in Fisheries Supply Chains.

Korean Labor Standards Act. https://elaw.klri.re.kr/eng_service/lawView.do?hseq=25437&lang=ENG

Labor Code 2019.

Law on Occupational Safety and Health 2015.

National Law on Hazardous Child Labor—Brazil. https://www.ilo.org/sites/default/files/2025-02/2014%20Compendium%20of%20hazardous%20child%20labour%20lists%20-%20Brazil.pdf.

Pham, T. H. D. (2024). Regulations of the International Labor Organization and Some Countries on Underage Labor, Judicial Academy. http://hvta.toaan.gov.vn/portal/page/portal/hvta/27676686/27677461?pers_id=28346379&folder_id=&item_id=313412040&p_details=1

Phan, T. T. H. (2023). Enhancing Corporate Social Responsibility to Promote Sustainable Development, Foreign Trade University. https://www.tapchicongsan.org.vn/web/guest/kinh-te/-/2018/827496/nang-cao-trach-nhiem-xa-hoi-cua-doanh-nghiep-nham-thuc-day-phat-trien-ben-vung.aspx. Accessed April 2, 2025.

Pisani, N., Kourula, A., Kolk, A., & Meijer, R. (2017). How Global is International CSR Research? Insights and Recommendations from a Systematic Review. *Journal of World Business, 52*(5), 591–614.

RUGMARK Organization. https://rugmarkindia.de/.

Rupp, D. E. (2011). An Employee Centered Model of Organizational Justice and Social Responsibility. *Organizational Psychology Review, 1*(1), 72–94.

Tien, H. V., & Anh, H. T. V. (2018). Corporate Social Responsibility: Research Trends. *Asian Economic and Business Studies Journal* (12), 25–36.

Tietjen, K. (2003). Bangladesh Primary Education Stipend Project: A Descriptive Analysis. https://documents1.worldbank.org/curated/en/715271468741642014/pdf/282570PAPER0BangladeshStipend.pdf.

Tran, H. H. (2018). Summary Report of Ministerial Level Science and Technology Project, Corporate Social Responsibility in Labor Relations from a Legal Perspective, Ho Chi Minh City University of Law.

Truong, T. N. L. (2019). *Eliminating Child Labor: Experiences from Some Countries and Reference Value for Vietnam.* https://www.quanlynhanuoc.vn/2019/09/25/xoa-bo-lao-dong-tre-em-kinh-nghiem-o-mot-so-quoc-gia-va-gia-tri-tham-khao-cho-viet-nam/. Accessed May 19, 2025.

VCCI & UNICEF. (2021). Report on the Survey of Children's Rights Implementation by Small and Medium Enterprises, Within the Framework of the Project "Promoting Children's Rights and Business Principles in Enterprises in Vietnam".

Chapter 8
Corporate Social Responsibility and the Protection of Children from Labor Exploitation in Vietnam's Textile Supply Chain

Nguyen Binh An

Abstract This chapter meticulously analyzes the pivotal role and inherent limitations of Corporate Social Responsibility (CSR) in safeguarding children from labor exploitation within Vietnam's textile and garment supply chains. The discussion commences by identifying the significant economic contributions of the textile and garment industry, concurrently highlighting the pervasive reality of child labor in informal processing facilities, household enterprises, and craft villages. These entities often operate with minimal oversight and largely remain beyond the effective reach of the current legal framework. While Vietnam has commendably domesticated international child labor standards through the Labor Code 2019, the Law on Children 2016, and various ILO conventions, enforcement remains constrained. The author posits that CSR, being predominantly voluntary, is frequently adopted by enterprises as a performative measure to placate international pressure, rather than stemming from an intrinsic commitment. Consequently, tools such as social audits, codes of conduct, and CSR reports often prove lacking in substantive efficacy. This chapter advocates for a transformative shift from voluntary CSR to mandatory legal obligations within the textile and garment sector. Furthermore, it proposes bolstering supply chain transparency, imposing stringent penalties on enterprises found to utilize facilities employing children, establishing child friendly grievance mechanisms, and integrating "child sensitive justice" principles into CSR practices. The author underscores the imperative for a synchronized integration of hard law, market pressure, and independent oversight mechanisms to genuinely protect children's rights and foster sustainable development within Vietnam's textile and garment industry.

Article History: Received 10 April 2025; Revised 25 July 2025; Accepted 15 August 2025.

N. B. An (✉)
University of Finance - Marketing, Ho Chi Minh City, Viet Nam
e-mail: an.luatsu@gmail.com

N. Binh An et al. (eds.), *The Future of Child-Friendly Justice and Children's Rights in Vietnam*, https://doi.org/10.1007/978-981-95-3521-7_8

The textile and garment industry occupies a critical position within Vietnam's economy. This is vividly evidenced by its export turnover reaching an impressive 37.6 billion USD in 2022, constituting approximately 10% of the nation's total export value (Ministry of Industry & Trade, 2023). Leveraging its competitive advantage in human resources and deep integration through free trade agreements such as the EVFTA and CPTPP, Vietnam's textile and garment sector has increasingly become an integral component of global supply chains. However, this escalating engagement simultaneously imposes increasingly rigorous demands concerning CSR compliance and the protection of human rights, particularly the rights of child laborers.

Concomitant with this economic expansion, the persistent issue of child labor in informal processing zones, satellite workshops, and household enterprises endures. The International Labor Organization has reported the widespread prevalence of child labor in Vietnam's small scale establishments and family run production units. In these settings, legal regulations and oversight mechanisms prove challenging to effectively implement. These children are frequently compelled to work under precarious conditions, lacking adequate safety and hygiene provisions, while simultaneously enduring intense pressure regarding working hours and productivity demands (Better Work Vietnam, 2020).

Within the context of globalization, CSR has emerged as a valuable instrument for safeguarding the rights of workers, including child laborers (An, 2023a). New generation free trade agreements, such as the EVFTA and CPTPP, impose stringent requirements regarding corporate social responsibility, particularly in the elimination of forced labor and child labor from global supply chains. Practical implementation of CSR in Vietnam reveals that many enterprises within the garment sector have not demonstrated a full and genuine commitment. Their efforts largely remain superficial and responsive to pressures emanating from international partners and foreign consumer markets (Cao Dinh Lanh & Dong Thi Huyen Nga, 2022).

Based on this observed reality, this chapter posits the scientific hypothesis that the substantive and effective implementation of corporate social responsibility within Vietnam's garment industry possesses the potential to significantly mitigate child labor exploitation. The research objective is to elucidate the actual role and efficacy of CSR in protecting children's rights from labor exploitation within the textile and garment supply chain. To achieve this objective, the study employs an empirical legal analysis methodology, integrating assessments of practical reports from international organizations, exemplary cases within Vietnam, and comparative international experiences. From this comprehensive examination, pertinent evaluations and reform proposals tailored to Vietnam's current context are presented.

8.1 Legal Framework on Child Labor and CSR in Vietnam

8.1.1 *Labor Code 2019*

The Labor Code 2019 has established a rigorous legal framework aimed at protecting underage workers, defined as individuals under 18 years of age, thereby preventing labor exploitation.

Clause 1, Article 3 of the Labor Code 2019 stipulates the minimum working age as 15 years. Nevertheless, the law permits exceptions for the employment of individuals under 15 years, particularly in artistic and athletic fields, provided specific conditions are met and official approval is secured from competent authorities. Pursuant to this framework, individuals aged 13 to under 15 are legally permitted to engage only in light work, as specifically enumerated in a catalog promulgated by the Ministry of Labor, Invalids and Social Affairs. Employers are strictly permitted to recruit and employ individuals under the age of 13 solely for artistic, athletic, or sports related endeavors, provided such activities do not compromise the physical, intellectual, or personal development of the minor. This employment is contingent upon securing the explicit consent of the specialized labor agency operating under the provincial level People's Committee. Enterprises are authorized to employ laborers aged 15 to under 18, subject to rigorous adherence to regulations governing the nature of the work and the working environment.

Accordingly, underage laborers are expressly prohibited from undertaking the following tasks: carrying, lifting, or moving heavy objects exceeding their individual physical capacity; engaging in the production or trade of alcohol, spirits, beer, tobacco, psychotropic substances, or other addictive substances; manufacturing, utilizing, or transporting chemicals, gases, or explosives; performing maintenance or servicing on equipment and machinery; demolishing construction works; melting, blowing, casting, rolling, stamping, or welding metals; and deep sea diving or offshore fishing. Furthermore, any work identified as detrimental to the physical, intellectual, and personal development of underage individuals, as specified in Annex III of Circular 09/2020/TT BLDTBXH, is unequivocally forbidden.

Concurrently, underage laborers are also precluded from working in the following locations: underwater, underground, in caves, or in tunnels; construction sites; animal slaughterhouses; casinos, bars, dance halls, karaoke rooms, hotels, motels, saunas, and massage parlors; lottery business outlets, and electronic game service establishments. Other locations deemed injurious to the physical, intellectual, and personal development of underage individuals, as delineated in Annex IV of Circular 09/2020/TT BLDTBXH, are similarly prohibited. These stringent regulations are meticulously designed to safeguard the safety and holistic development of underage laborers.

The stipulations concerning working hours for underage laborers are clearly delineated in Article 146 of the 2019 Labor Code. Specifically, laborers aged 15 to under 18 are permitted to work a maximum of 08 h per day and 40 h per week. For the demographic of laborers under 15 years of age, the maximum working time is more stringently limited to just 04 h per day and 20 h per week.

Furthermore, when employing laborers under 15 years of age, employers must strictly adhere to supplementary conditions. These encompass the execution of a written labor contract with the child's legal representative, the assignment of work that does not impede the child's educational pursuits, the conduct of periodic health examinations for the child, and the prerequisite of obtaining authorization from the local labor management authority if employing individuals under 13 years of age.

8.1.2 The 2016 Law on Children, The 2015 Penal Code (Amended 2017), and The 2024 Law on Juvenile Justice

While the Labor Code of 2019 primarily regulates working conditions, the Law on Children of 2016 establishes a comprehensive legal framework pertaining to children's rights, including the fundamental right to protection from labor exploitation.

Under the Law on Children of 2016, a child is formally defined as an individual under 16 years of age. This stands in contrast to the concept of "underage person" (below 18 years of age) as defined in the Labor Code of 2019. Notwithstanding this definitional distinction in age, both statutes converge upon the overarching objective of safeguarding children from prohibited forms of labor and exploitation. The Law on Children prohibits all acts that harm and exploit children in any form. Article 6 of this Law explicitly enumerates prohibited behaviors such as abandoning, abusing, exploiting the labor of children, and any other actions that negatively impact their development. This clearly demonstrates Vietnamese law's commitment to protecting children from arduous and hazardous work, while simultaneously classifying child labor exploitation as a grave violation of children's rights. For instance, compelling children to work in sectors like construction or mineral extraction is not only prohibited but also subject to severe penalties. The law further underscores that the responsibility for child protection extends beyond the family to include schools, the community, and state agencies. The State encourages compulsory education and implements policies to support children in difficult circumstances, such as providing scholarships or financial aid to impoverished families, thereby preventing children from entering the workforce prematurely. These concerted efforts aim to address the root causes of child labor, ensuring that children receive education and develop within a safe environment.

Furthermore, Article 296 of the Criminal Code specifically criminalizes "Violations of Regulations on Employing Laborers Under 16 Years of Age." The penalties for this offense can extend to up to 12 years of imprisonment if children are coerced into performing arduous, hazardous, or dangerous work as per the prohibited list. This punitive framework reflects Vietnam's resolute determination to deter and stringently prosecute acts of child exploitation.

Additionally, Vietnam's judicial system is progressively enhancing its capacity to better support children. In line with this, the Law on Juvenile Justice has been officially enacted and is projected to take effect from January 1, 2026. This Law clarifies regulations concerning the responsibilities and participation of various organizations at all stages of the juvenile justice process, with particular emphasis on the reintegration phase into the community. The Law strongly upholds the principle of "ensuring the participation of agencies, organizations, individuals, and families" in the reintegration process. The law emphasizes the principle of "ensuring the participation of agencies, organizations, individuals, and families" in the reintegration process. This implicitly underscores the role of society as a whole, including businesses, in supporting underage individuals. Specifically, "other agencies, organizations, and individuals" are entrusted with the responsibility to assist underage individuals in community reintegration, which includes vocational training and employment support once they reach the legal working age. Furthermore, the Law explicitly prohibits "businesses, organizations, and individuals from discriminating against or stigmatizing underage laborers aged 15 or older" solely because they have previously undergone educational measures at a reform school or served a prison sentence.

8.1.3 The Regulatory Landscape of Corporate Social Responsibility in Vietnamese Law

The legal framework governing CSR in Vietnam is articulated across a multiplicity of legislative instruments and pertinent policies, encompassing the Law on Enterprises, alongside regulations pertaining to labor, environmental protection, and consumer rights (Nguyen et al., 2024). While the precise term "social responsibility" has not been afforded a formally unified definition within Vietnamese statutes, extant law demonstrably integrates numerous legal imperatives compelling enterprises to fulfill obligations towards both employees and society at large. These obligations, fundamentally, constitute the core tenets of CSR (An, 2023c).

The Law on Enterprises 2020, as amended and supplemented in 2025, has meticulously delineated the obligations of enterprises towards their employees, the community, and the environment. Article 8 of this Law explicitly sets forth the general duties enterprises must observe, prominently emphasizing the assurance of legal rights and interests for employees in accordance with labor law. Enterprises are strictly prohibited from engaging in discrimination, insulting the honor or dignity of employees, or utilizing forced labor and child labor. Furthermore, enterprises are mandated to support and facilitate employee access to education, enhance vocational skills, and comprehensively fulfill insurance entitlements. This stipulation directly binds enterprises to the responsibility of excluding child labor from their production and business operations, viewing this exclusion as an integral component of their legal compliance and business ethics. Vietnamese enterprise law upholds the principle that enterprises must not solely pursue profit but are also obligated to adhere to legal and ethical standards concerning their employees and society. The diligent fulfillment of these fundamental legal obligations, such as lawful wage payments, social insurance contributions, ensuring occupational safety, respecting working hour limitations, and refraining from employing children, constitutes the bedrock upon which enterprises can genuinely demonstrate their social responsibility (Nguyen et al., 2018).

In addition to the Law on Enterprises, various policies and guidelines issued by the Government and relevant ministries and agencies also serve to promote CSR within the business community. The Ministry of Labor Invalids and Social Affairs, now the Ministry of Home Affairs, has promulgated programs and plans designed to encourage enterprises to effectively discharge their responsibilities towards employees, with particular emphasis on issues such as occupational safety, employee welfare, and the non utilization of child labor. For instance, the Government approved the National Program on Prevention and Reduction of Child Labor (for the period 2016 to 2020 and continued with the period 2021 to 2025), spearheaded by the Ministry of Labor Invalids and Social Affairs in collaboration with the ILO and UNICEF (ILO Vietnam, 2021). This program not only raises societal awareness concerning the detrimental effects of child labor but also solicits active enterprise participation in committing to the non employment of unlawful child labor and providing support to at risk children. Moreover, the Ministry of Labor Invalids and Social Affairs, alongside various organizations, has disseminated numerous CSR practical guidelines for enterprises, integrating child rights provisions into business codes of conduct. These concerted efforts demonstrate Vietnam's progressive establishment of a responsible business culture, wherein mandatory compliance with labor law and the non employment of child labor are paramount requirements, simultaneously serving as a benchmark for corporate ethics. As one report cogently observed, in Vietnam, "the implementation of CSR must first commence with legal compliance," given that legal adherence represents the foundational level of corporate social responsibility (Nguyen Thi Yen, 2021).

8.1.4 Vietnam's International Commitments on Child Labor and Corporate Social Responsibility

Vietnam's robust commitment to international labor norms is exemplified by its membership in the ILO and its ratification of seven of the eight fundamental ILO conventions. These include Convention 138 concerning Minimum Age for Admission to Employment and Convention 182 concerning the Prohibition and Immediate Action for the Elimination of the Worst Forms of Child Labor. The principles enshrined in these conventions have been meticulously integrated into Vietnamese domestic law through the Labor Code 2019 and the Law on Children 2016, thereby demonstrating a concerted effort to prevent child labor in accordance with global standards. Illustratively, regulations strictly prohibiting the employment of children in sectors such as garment manufacturing or mineral extraction are rigorously enforced.

Furthermore, Vietnam's engagement with significant trade agreements, such as the European Union Vietnam Free Trade Agreement (EVFTA), underscores its obligation to uphold labor rights, particularly the imperative of child labor elimination. The EVFTA incorporates a monitoring mechanism that assists in ensuring Vietnam's adherence to these commitments, simultaneously elevating its international standing (Navasartian, 2020). Similarly, the Comprehensive and Progressive Agreement for Trans Pacific Partnership (CPTPP) also imposes analogous requirements, thereby incentivizing ongoing legal reforms in the realm of labor law.

Increasingly, Vietnamese enterprises, particularly those engaged in export-oriented sectors, are adopting international standards such as SA8000 and ISO 26000. This trend actively contributes to transforming prevailing perceptions within the business community regarding child labor (Tam Nhi et al., 2021). The pursuit of SA8000 certification by numerous textile, footwear, electronics, and timber enterprises in Vietnam demonstrates their commitment to adhering to international labor standards and eliminating child labor from their production lines to penetrate discerning export markets. Concurrently, the proliferation of voluntary CSR standards such as SA8000, BSCI, and WRAP creates competitive pressure compelling domestic enterprises to elevate their social responsibility, thereby contributing to the widespread adoption of a "say no to child labor" culture within the business community (Nguyen Thi Kim Phung, 2022).

8.2 Manifestations of Child Labor Exploitation in Vietnam's Textile Supply Chain

8.2.1 The Reality of Informal Child Labor

The prevalence of child labor within Vietnam's textile and garment industry predominantly occurs in the informal sector, particularly within household enterprises, satellite processing facilities, and traditional craft villages. Many children engage in garment work at home or in family owned craft workshops, often under the guise of "helping the family" or "learning a trade." In reality, this often masks labor exploitation. Statistics indicate that over 40% of child laborers in Vietnam work directly within household enterprises and receive no remuneration (Thuy Hien, 2025). These young individuals are frequently compelled to work extended hours under arduous conditions, blurring the critical distinction between "learning traditional crafts" and "child labor utilization," especially in traditional garment craft villages. Empirical evidence reveals that many traditional craft villages exploit family children as a cheap and easily manageable labor force. This phenomenon leads to a significant proportion of rural children leaving school prematurely to engage in labor. National survey data indicates that approximately 84% of child laborers are concentrated in rural areas, with nearly half engaged in agriculture and about 40.5% working as domestic helpers within households (informal labor, without contracts). This demographic is particularly susceptible to being overlooked as it largely falls outside the direct purview of labor law and receives virtually no oversight from trade unions or labor inspectors (Thuy Trang, 2022).

Concrete instances serve to illustrate this persistent issue. For example, the egregious case of the owner of a bánh xèo eatery in Yen Trung Commune, Yen Phong District, Bac Ninh Province, who subjected two child employees to brutal abuse and beatings over an extended period (Thanh Hương, 2020). Similarly, several garment processing villages on the outskirts of cities have been exposed by the press for employing children excessively under the pretext of vocational training. In one garment processing workshop in Ho Chi Minh City, reporters discovered children working overnight in a toxic environment. However, upon inspection by authorities, the owner had swiftly relocated the workshop, leaving local authorities "unaware" (Phu Nu Online, 2017). These cases underscore the clandestine and elusive nature of child labor within the garment supply chain, particularly in the satellite processing and household enterprise segments.

8.2.2 *Pressures from Global Supply Chains*

A significant contributing factor to the exploitation of child labor within the textile and garment industry is the intense competitive pressure emanating from global supply chains (An, 2023b). Vietnam presently hosts approximately 6000 textile and garment enterprises, of which around 2500 are exclusively dedicated to export production. Major fashion brands from the United States, the European Union, and Japan frequently demand low processing costs and expedited delivery timelines, compelling domestic contractors to relentlessly cut expenses and meet stringent deadlines. Within large scale garment factories (Tier 1 suppliers), while the overt employment of underage labor is rare due to concerns about violating international standards (Better Work Vietnam compliance reports indicate no detected instances of children under 15 years in monitored factories), productivity pressures nevertheless exert considerable strain on adult workers. These individuals are often compelled to undertake continuous overtime and work extended hours to fulfill the production quotas imposed by commissioning parties.

However, at lower tiers of the supply chain (smaller Tier 2 and Tier 3 facilities), meeting orders with low prices and short delivery times can only be achieved by hiring the most inexpensive labor possible, which regrettably includes child labor. Research indicates that large garment companies frequently subcontract orders to smaller processing workshops and satellite household enterprises. These processing facilities, in turn, further disperse work to home based tailors (artisanal home workers), a practice that is exceedingly difficult to monitor. This situation engenders a "grey area" within supply chain management: children may participate in family based production (e.g., assisting with sewing, thread cutting, or artisanal embroidery) for garment orders without detection during official inspections. One garment business owner conceded that numerous private sewing workshops specializing in "black market" processing "exploit child labor, finding them both easy to exploit and manage, requiring no contracts or insurance contributions, thereby yielding substantial profits" (International, 2019). Thus, the pressure for price reductions and rapid delivery from end clients in the supply chain has indirectly incentivized downstream processing stages to utilize child labor as a cost reduction measure.

Organizations such as the ILO, UNICEF, and numerous journalistic entities have conducted investigations illuminating this egregious issue. Since 2012, the United States Department of Labor (USDOL) has listed garment products from Vietnam on its list of goods produced by child or forced labor. Consequently, Vietnam's textile and garment industry faces increasing scrutiny from the international community regarding child labor. In a rapid assessment report conducted by Anti Slavery International, experts cautioned that while children are rarely observed in large factories, the utilization of children at lower production tiers may be far more severe (International, 2019). This report, citing ILO MOLISA sources, indicated that nearly 50,000 workers in Vietnam's garment industry were under 18 years of age, with a disconcerting 1.2% of this demographic being merely 5 to 11 years old. The majority of these young children work in unregistered workshops (family owned or "underground" sewing establishments). Moreover, a local organization once rescued children working in "fourth floor sewing workshops" a term referring to small scale, end of chain processing facilities. These children were forced to work under deplorable, slavery like conditions: confined within workshops, sleeping beside sewing machines, receiving no wages, and having their phones confiscated to sever external contact. They were often trafficked from rural to urban areas under the guise of "apprenticeships," with some as young as 10 years old being deceived into working to the point of exhaustion. Although the number of rescue operations has decreased in recent years, experts contend that it is likely recruitment networks for children have shifted to more sophisticated operations rather than genuinely reducing in scale. These investigative findings reveal the persistent existence of "blind spots" within Vietnam's textile and garment supply chain, where children are unlawfully exploited and remain difficult to detect through conventional inspection systems alone.

8.3 The Role and Limits of Corporate Social Responsibility

8.3.1 Voluntary Versus Mandatory CSR

CSR, traditionally conceived, is regarded as a voluntary commitment on the part of enterprises to adhere to ethical standards for human welfare and sustainable development. Given the intrinsic distinction between ethical norms and legal precepts, CSR does not conventionally fall within the ambit of mandatory legal dictates but rather belongs to the category of "soft law," signifying voluntary, flexible commitments not formally promulgated by the State. This inherent characteristic has fueled scholarly debate regarding whether CSR possesses a legally binding nature for enterprises (An, 2023d).

Under the traditional paradigm, enterprises were deemed to have fulfilled their minimum social responsibility by merely demonstrating full compliance with existing law; conversely, non compliance with legal provisions was equated with a fundamental breach of CSR. However, contemporary perspectives contend that CSR transcends minimal legal obligations, encompassing both the ethical and philanthropic responsibilities that society expects of enterprises (Carroll, 2016).

In recent decades, numerous nations have commenced a transition from entirely voluntary CSR frameworks to the establishment of legally mandated CSR requirements. For instance, some countries now compel enterprises to publicly disclose CSR reports or to undertake mandatory social due diligence. French law, enacted in 2017, obliges large corporations to devise and implement monitoring plans aimed at identifying risks and preventing severe human rights violations within their supply chains (Li-Wen Lin, 2020). India has even codified a legal obligation for corporations to contribute 2% of their profits to CSR activities.

Nonetheless, on a global scale, the voluntary CSR model continues to predominate. A systematic review conducted in 2023 indicated that voluntary CSR remains widely adopted across many nations, including developing countries, even in contexts where mandatory CSR legislation exists (Putri et al., 2023). This is largely attributable to the fact that "hard law" is often insufficient to ensure enterprises comprehensively implement every facet of CSR. Practical experience demonstrates that a harmonious amalgamation of both approaches, encompassing adherence to mandatory legal requirements alongside proactive, voluntary elevation of ethical responsibility, will facilitate stable enterprise development and a balanced consideration of stakeholder interests.

In Vietnam, CSR is primarily incentivized as a voluntary undertaking. However, the pressures of international integration are progressively transforming CSR into a de facto mandatory requirement. Particularly within the context of implementing new generation free trade agreements such as the EVFTA, adherence to labor and environmental standards is increasingly considered a prerequisite for market access to demanding jurisdictions. Empirical evidence corroborates that "CSR is no longer a voluntary element but has become a mandatory requirement for businesses, especially when exporting to the European Union" (Bảo Trung, 2024). This suggests a blurring of the line between voluntary and mandatory CSR: many CSR standards once considered voluntary are now evolving into legal conditions or conditions imposed by global supply chains. Despite this trend, current Vietnamese law (such as the Law on Enterprises and Labor Law) does not contain separate provisions specifically defining a general "CSR obligation"; social requirements are primarily embedded within specialized legislation (labor, environment, etc.). Consequently, the actual implementation of CSR largely hinges on enterprises' self awareness and pressure from partners and the community, rather than specific legal sanctions.

8.3.2 Social Audits and Perfunctory Ethical Commitments as Current CSR Implementations by Major Brands

Multinational corporations and prominent brands typically implement CSR programs through the promulgation of ethical codes of conduct and the conduct of social audits within their supply chains. On a formalistic level, nearly all large companies possess codes prohibiting child labor, commit to safeguarding worker rights, and conduct periodic assessments at their own factories and those of their contractors. However, numerous studies and investigative reports reveal that these mechanisms sometimes serve merely as perfunctory responses rather than substantive efforts.

For instance, an investigation by The New York Times (2023) into food supply chains in the United States uncovered that private auditing firms frequently provide merely "a veneer of compliance for global corporations," thereby enabling businesses to exaggerate the rigor of their supply chain oversight. Many auditors confessed to perfunctory work: conducting overly brief surveys, departing factories prematurely, or neglecting to inspect workshops where children might be employed. Assessments primarily based on documentation rather than direct worker interviews often fail to detect child labor, particularly when children are coached to misrepresent their age or utilize falsified documents (Hannah Dreier, 2023).

The ethical commitments articulated by large enterprises also sometimes lack effective enforcement mechanisms. Research published in the University of New South Wales Law Journal notes that corporate declarations and codes of conduct often lack concrete actions and enforcement provisions, thus amounting to "mere statements on websites…with little practical meaning." Many companies issue grand pronouncements about refraining from child labor, yet their monitoring largely relies on self reporting or outsourced audits, which are prone to overlooking violations (Boersma, 2017). Indeed, some companies exploit the public announcement of CSR commitments as a public relations tool rather than genuinely improving labor conditions. Researchers emphasize that self regulatory efforts such as codes of conduct, supplier audits, and charitable donations, if not fundamentally integrated with systemic changes in supply chain governance, yield highly limited efficacy. In other words, "image polishing" CSR risks creating an illusion of ethical conduct, while severe human rights issues persist in the shadows of global supply chains.

8.3.3 Limitations of CSR in Detecting and Eliminating Child Labor

The majority of child labor persists within the informal economic sector or in deeply embedded tiers of the supply chain, realms often beyond the effective reach of conventional CSR audit activities. Scholars consistently emphasize that corporate codes of conduct and social activities exert influence over only a minuscule proportion of child laborers situated within formal supply chains, given that the preponderance of child laborers operate within the informal sector or the "shadow economy" (Boersma, 2017). These children may be employed in diminutive processing workshops, household enterprises, or small scale farms, locations infrequently accessed by auditors. Consequently, even multinational corporations genuinely committed to CSR face formidable challenges in ensuring the complete absence of child labor across their entire multifaceted supply chains.

Furthermore, CSR primarily relies on the principle of voluntary compliance and lacks robust enforcement mechanisms. Measures of sanction, such as the termination of contracts or cancellation of orders, are purportedly implemented when suppliers violate regulations, for example, through the employment of children. However, the repercussions of such actions possess the inherent capacity to exacerbate the circumstances of children, potentially leading to a loss of income or compelling them into more perilous informal labor. Concurrently, inspection resources are frequently insufficient to facilitate the timely detection of deeply concealed violations. Experience within the United States has demonstrably illustrated that even in developed nations, private audits cannot fully substitute the indispensable role of state inspection in scrutinizing child labor (Hannah Dreier, 2023).

A number of scholarly investigations have also documented the long term limitations of CSR. Barrientos et al. (2011) observed that corporate codes of conduct can mitigate child labor within direct supply tiers (principal factories and Tier 1 contractors). Nevertheless, this impact proves unsustainable in lower supply tiers where oversight is inherently more lax, resulting in the recurring phenomenon of child labor when continuous monitoring is absent. This implies that sole reliance on the voluntary endeavors of enterprises cannot effectively eradicate the pervasive issue of child labor, a problem profoundly entrenched and inextricably linked to complex socioeconomic factors such as poverty, educational deprivation, and the demand for inexpensive labor.

Therefore, while CSR constitutes a critical instrument, it is unequivocally insufficient in its solitary capacity to comprehensively resolve the problem of child labor. The egregious exploitation of child labor emanates from systemic root causes, necessitating a multifaceted approach that incorporates a robust legal framework, stringent state enforcement, authentic CSR initiatives, and independent oversight from civil society organizations. Should CSR remain merely a voluntary mechanism, devoid of effective monitoring and meaningful sanctions, its capacity to genuinely safeguard vulnerable populations such as children will remain severely constrained.

8.3.4 "Child-Friendly Business Justice"

The concept of "child friendly justice in the business environment" refers to the establishment of a system of justice and grievance mechanisms where the rights and interests of children are maximally protected when implicated in corporate activities. In essence, this constitutes an extension of the "child friendly justice" principle (traditionally applied within criminal and civil justice systems) to the domain of business and human rights.

Consistent with the principles enshrined in the United Nations Convention on the Rights of the Child (CRC) and General Comment No. 16 (2013) of the UN Committee on the Rights of the Child, States bear a legal obligation to ensure that the private sector respects children's rights, refrains from impeding their exercise, and actively contributes to their promotion (UNICEF Viet Nam, 2015). This encompasses the State's responsibility to require enterprises to establish child friendly grievance and remedy mechanisms. Accordingly, enterprises must provide, support, and facilitate children's access to both judicial and non judicial remedial and compensatory mechanisms for business related child rights violations.

In practice, "child friendly justice in business" necessitates that enterprise level grievance mechanisms are designed to be appropriate for children. UNICEF recommends that companies develop child friendly grievance and feedback mechanisms, ensuring they are accessible, transparent, and safe, so that any child, or their family, affected by business operations can voice concerns and receive adequate resolution. For instance, within agricultural supply chains, enterprises can collaborate with local nongovernmental organizations to establish hotlines or dedicated grievance mailboxes for child laborers. Such mechanisms must consider the unique characteristics of children: using simple language, ensuring identity confidentiality, protecting whistleblowers from retaliation, and providing support from guardians or social experts. Concurrently, the State and independent organizations must assume an oversight role, ensuring that children genuinely receive justice when their rights are violated by enterprises (UNICEF, 2012). For example, the State could mandate that all enterprises above a certain scale establish channels for receiving child labor grievances and periodically report on resolution outcomes. Labor inspection agencies also require "child friendly" procedures when engaging with children, such as during the collection of testimony in child labor investigations, where psychological professionals should be present to avoid causing emotional distress to the children.

8.4 Policy and Legal Reform Proposals

8.4.1 Proposing Mandatory CSR in the Textile and Garment Industry

To address the aforementioned challenges, the international trend is shifting from voluntary CSR to legal mandates, aiming to ensure corporate transparency and accountability, and to harmonize economic interests with sustainable development. For instance, the European Union has enacted Directive 2014/95/EU, obliging large companies to disclose non financial information concerning environmental and social matters. The United States has also integrated CSR requirements into legislation such as Sarbanes Oxley and Dodd Frank to enhance transparency. Notably, India stands as the pioneering nation to legislate CSR obligations: India's Companies Act 2013 stipulates that large scale enterprises must allocate at least 2% of their net profits to social activities. Such "codification" of CSR demonstrates that social commitment has become a legal requirement in numerous countries, establishing a framework that compels the private sector to participate in sustainable development and accrue long term benefits such as brand reputation and investor confidence.

In the context of international integration, numerous new generation trade agreements, such as the Comprehensive and Progressive Agreement for Trans Pacific Partnership (CPTPP) and the European Union Vietnam Free Trade Agreement (EVFTA), mandate Vietnam's adherence to stringent standards concerning labor rights, environmental protection, and governance transparency. Consequently, the legal codification of CSR obligations within the textile and garment industry becomes not merely expedient, but imperative. This proactive measure is crucial for fostering a level playing field, thereby mitigating the risk of a "race to the bottom" in labor standards. Legislative provisions can unequivocally delineate minimum responsibilities related to fundamental worker rights, ensuring safe working conditions, and, most critically, enforcing an absolute prohibition on child labor throughout the entire textile and garment supply chain. International experience consistently demonstrates that, notwithstanding initial concerns regarding compliance costs, the practical implementation of CSR ultimately enhances corporate reputation and yields sustained long term benefits, concurrently contributing more effectively to broader societal development (Bonnie G. Buchanan et al., 2018).

8.4.2 Enhancing Supply Chain Transparency

Illustrative examples include the California Transparency in Supply Chains Act (2010) in the United States and the United Kingdom's Modern Slavery Act (2015), which compel large companies to report annually on the measures and mechanisms implemented to ensure the absence of forced or child labor within their supply chains. Similarly, the EU requires enterprises to assess and report on human rights risks in their business operations and supply chains (Millar et al., 2022).

Vietnam should draw upon these experiences to enhance supply chain transparency and, consequently, the accountability of textile and garment enterprises regarding child labor. Legislation could require enterprises to periodically disclose information pertaining to all stages of production, ranging from principal factories to satellite processing facilities, accompanied by explicit commitments to comply with child labor standards. According to experts, the pressure of public disclosure will incentivize enterprises to proactively eliminate child labor from their supply chains to mitigate reputational risks and legal sanctions. In practice, importers in the EU and US markets are increasingly imposing stringent requirements for supply chain transparency related to child rights (Millar et al., 2022). For instance, the EU is developing the Corporate Sustainability Due Diligence Directive (CSDDD), which will compel enterprises to scrutinize and report on environmental and social risks throughout their supply chains. Should Vietnam promptly enact supply chain transparency legislation, its textile and garment enterprises will gain an advantageous position in meeting these international requirements, preserving export markets, and concurrently better protecting children's rights domestically (Dũng Hiếu, 2024).

8.4.3 Mechanism for Penalizing Enterprises Utilizing Subcontractors Employing Children

The establishment of a joint liability penalty mechanism is essential to comprehensively address responsibility across the entire production chain. This mechanism would stipulate that if any segment of the supply chain engages in child labor, the lead enterprise at the apex of that chain must also bear accountability (Hai Nhi, 2024). Such a mechanism could encompass administrative sanctions, such as substantial fines or revocation of business licenses; civil remedies, including compensation for victims; and even criminal penalties for managers if intent or systematic recidivism can be demonstrably proven.

International experience provides compelling precedents for this punitive approach. France's Duty of Vigilance Law of 2017 (Loi de Vigilance) mandates that large French companies establish monitoring plans to prevent human rights violations within their own operations and those of their business partners (RESPECT, 2017). Significantly, should a company fail to implement its monitoring plan or if severe, preventable consequences ensue, the court possesses the authority to impose fines up to 10 million Euros, escalating to 30 million Euros if the violation causes actual harm to victims. This rigorous approach sends a powerful message that disregarding supply chain oversight responsibilities will incur substantial costs. Similarly, the Netherlands enacted a Duty of Care Law in 2019, compelling enterprises to verify and prevent child labor in the production chains of goods sold in the Netherlands, with non compliance incurring administrative and criminal penalties (Millar et al., 2022).

For such a penalty mechanism to be truly effective, Vietnamese law must incorporate provisions for the joint liability of contracting companies for violations occurring at processing workshops. This must be complemented by a proactive inspection and investigation system designed to detect instances of "circumvention," such as when lead enterprises subcontract work to household units or informal facilities. Experts underscore that only with robust enforcement mechanisms and stringent sanctions will child labor prohibition laws genuinely translate into tangible impact. A strong penalty framework will also incentivize enterprises to proactively select legally compliant partners and consistently audit their supply chains.

8.4.4 Developing a Child Sensitive Grievance System

Beyond preventative and punitive measures, a crucial element involves ensuring access to justice for children who have been, or are currently being, exploited in labor. At present, young children often face immense difficulty in independently voicing their concerns or lodging complaints due to age related barriers, limited awareness, and apprehension, particularly when the perpetrators of exploitation are their employers or even their own parents. Therefore, it is imperative to establish child sensitive grievance mechanisms to enable these children, or their guardians, to safely and empathetically report violations and seek redress. UNICEF emphasizes that child friendly grievance mechanisms will reinforce an enterprise's commitment to respecting children's rights and provide communication channels to help businesses improve their operations and relationships (UNICEF, 2024).

For instance, enterprises could establish hotlines or secure mailboxes specifically for child laborers (or for workers who detect child abuse) to receive reports. This mechanism must guarantee anonymity, protect whistleblowers, and incorporate a rapid processing procedure involving child psychology experts and child protection organizations. An effective grievance system must be tailored to the psychological and circumstantial realities of children. This means that every step in the process, from receiving information and verification to victim support, must be designed to be child friendly and easily accessible. Research indicates that enterprises need to train their personnel and collaborate with civil society organizations to operate such grievance mechanisms, ensuring that children are heard and receive timely support.

A child sensitive grievance mechanism will contribute to the early detection of child labor cases and provide immediate remedial measures, such as returning children to school, psychological counseling, and financial support for their families. While the benefits are clear, there are currently very few practical examples of children directly participating in corporate grievance mechanisms. Therefore, Vietnam could pioneer the piloting of this model within the textile and garment industry, under the oversight of state agencies and child protection organizations, to then scale up if successful. From a legal perspective, the State could issue guidelines or mandatory regulations for large enterprises to establish mechanisms for receiving and resolving child related grievances. This approach also concretizes Principle 5 of the United Nations Guiding Principles on Business and Human Rights (2011) concerning the assurance of effective grievance mechanisms at the enterprise level. A child friendly grievance mechanism will enhance corporate accountability, while simultaneously empowering children with a safe and respected means to claim their rights.

8.4.5 Connecting CSR with Child Friendly Justice

According to international standards, when children come into contact with the law, there must be a "child friendly justice" system that respects children's rights and vulnerabilities, incorporating specialized procedures to support them. In the context of CSR, this concept of child friendly justice applies to addressing corporate related child rights violations: from initial inspection and investigation to judicial proceedings or out of court settlements, every step should be designed to minimize psychological pressure on the child and encourage their participation in protecting their interests (UNICEF, 2024). For example, if a violation, such as illegal child employment, is brought before a court, the court should employ discreet procedures, with a child psychologist supporting the child's testimony. Alternatively, if addressed through a corporate grievance mechanism, children should be permitted to present information in a supportive environment, free from intimidation by the violating party.

Connecting CSR with child friendly justice implies that when implementing the aforementioned policies (supply chain transparency, grievance mechanisms, penalties for violations), the State must simultaneously refine specific procedural regulations for children. This includes, for instance, adding provisions that child victims of labor exploitation receive free legal aid, have their identities protected, and are provided with a guardian or legal representative throughout the legal process.

8.5 Conclusion

Despite Vietnam's existing legal provisions on child labor and established mechanisms designed to safeguard children from exploitation, the efficacy of their practical enforcement remains constrained. The principal contributing factors to this limitation stem from a dearth of specific sanctions for CSR infractions and inadequate early detection mechanisms within supply chains. While voluntary CSR initiatives undertaken by enterprises are commendable, they risk becoming merely perfunctory in the absence of sufficiently robust enforcement pressures. Concomitantly, should Vietnam elect to enact mandatory legal regulations concerning CSR, such as human rights reporting or due diligence requirements, it must simultaneously implement preventative measures to preclude their superficial application.

Consequently, advancing towards the establishment of a "child friendly justice framework" from an enterprise perspective would represent a resolute stride toward ensuring justice for these vulnerable individuals. Nevertheless, this endeavor poses substantial questions regarding the requisite resources and political commitment necessary to codify these principles. Existing legal limitations and lacunae pertaining to corporate responsibility for children's rights demand more profound scholarly inquiry. Through such rigorous examination, Vietnam can refine its legal system, not merely to enhance the protection of children but also to align with the sustainable development objectives of enterprises in this era of global integration.

References

An, N. B. (2023a). Analytical Facts of Corporate Social Responsibility for Enforcement of Labor Rights. In N. B. An & P. T. Anh (Eds.), *Laws on Corporate Social Responsibility and the Developmental Trend in Vietnam* (pp. 41–56). Springer Nature. https://doi.org/10.1007/978-981-19-9255-1_4

An, N. B. (2023b). *Global Supply Chain: The Role of Disclosure and Due Diligence Related to Soft and Hard Law*. 030038. https://doi.org/10.1063/5.0164871

An, N. B. (2023c). Mitigation of CSR Issues and the Shadow of Hard and Soft Law. In N. B. An & P. T. Anh (Eds.), *Laws on Corporate Social Responsibility and the Developmental Trend in Vietnam* (pp. 13–25). Springer Nature. https://doi.org/10.1007/978-981-19-9255-1_2

An, N. B. (2023d). The Role of Hard Law and Soft Law in Developing CSR. In N. B. An & P. T. Anh (Eds.), *Laws on Corporate Social Responsibility and the Developmental Trend in Vietnam* (pp. 1–12). Springer Nature. https://doi.org/10.1007/978-981-19-9255-1_1

Bảo Trung. (2024). *Thúc đẩy trách nhiệm xã hội của doanh nghiệp trong thực hiện EVFTA | Promoting CSR in Implementing EVFTA*. https://moit.gov.vn/tin-tuc/bao-chi-voi-nguoi-dan/thuc-day-trach-nhiem-xa-hoi-cua-doanh-nghiep-trong-thuc-hien-evfta.html

Barrientos, S., Gereffi, G., & Rossi, A. (2011). Economic and Social Upgrading in Global Production Networks: A New Paradigm for a Changing World. *International Labour Review, 150*(3–4), 319–340. https://doi.org/10.1111/j.1564-913X.2011.00119.x

Better Work Vietnam. (2020). *Better Work Vietnam Annual Report 2020: An Industry and Compliance Review*. Better Work. https://betterwork.org/reports-and-publications/better-work-vietnam-annual-report-2020-an-industry-and-compliance-review/

Boersma, M. (2017). Changing Approaches to Child Labour in Global Supply Chains: Exploring the Influence of Multi-Stakeholder Partnerships and the United Nations Guiding Principles on Business and Human Rights. *University of New South Wales Law Journal*, *40*(3). https://doi.org/10.53637/WKMT2453

Buchanan, B. G., Cao, C. X., & Chen, C. (2018, September 26). *How Corporate Social Responsibility and Influential Institutional Ownership Affect Firm Value*. CLS Blue Sky Blog. https://clsbluesky.law.columbia.edu/2018/09/26/how-corporate-social-responsibility-and-influential-institutional-ownership-affect-firm-value/

Cao Dinh Lanh & Dong Thi Huyen Nga. (2022). Thực Thi Trách Nhiệm Xã Hội Của Doanh Nghiệp Tại Việt Nam: Thách Thức Và Một Số Gợi Mở | Implementing Corporate Social Responsibility in Vietnam: Challenges and Some Suggestions. *Tạp chí Luật học*, *7*, 122–134.

Carroll, A. B. (2016). Carroll's Pyramid of CSR: Taking Another Look. *International Journal of Corporate Social Responsibility, 1*(1), 3. https://doi.org/10.1186/s40991-016-0004-6

Dũng Hiếu. (2024, March 18). *Hoàn thiện "khoảng trống" pháp lý về quyền trẻ em để tham gia sâu hơn vào chuỗi cung ứng | Closing the Legal "Gap" on Children's Rights to Engage More Deeply in the Supply Chain*. Nhịp sống kinh tế Việt Nam & Thế giới. https://vneconomy.vn/hoan-thien-khoang-trong-phap-ly-ve-quyen-tre-em-de-tham-gia-sau-hon-vao-chuoi-cung-ung.htm

Hai Nhi. (2024, November 27). *Bàn cách kiểm soát tình trạng lao động trẻ em, đáp ứng chuỗi cung ứng của EU | Discussing Ways to Control Child Labor and Meet EU Supply Chains*. Báo Pháp Luật TP. Hồ Chí Minh. https://plo.vn/share821961.html

Hannah Dreier. (2023). *USA: Private Auditors Fail to Detect Child Labour in Supply Chains of Major Supermarkets & Renowned Food Brands*. Business & Human Rights Resource Centre. https://www.business-humanrights.org/en/latest-news/usa-private-auditors-fail-to-detect-child-labour-in-the-food-supply-chains-of-major-us-companies-incl-cos-responses-non-responses/

ILO Vietnam. (2021, December 1). *Viet Nam Launches Second Programme of Action Plan to Tackle Child Labour | International Labour Organization*. https://www.ilo.org/resource/news/viet-nam-launches-second-programme-action-plan-tackle-child-labour

International, A.-S. (2019, March 29). *Sitting on Pins and Needles*. Anti-Slavery International. https://www.antislavery.org/latest/sitting-on-pins-and-needles/

Li-Wen Lin. (2020, November 18). *Mandatory Corporate Social Responsibility Legislation around the World: Emergent Varieties and National Experiences | Oxford Law Blogs*. https://blogs.law.ox.ac.uk/business-law-blog/blog/2020/11/mandatory-corporate-social-responsibility-legislation-around-world

Millar, H., Dandurand, Y., & Chan, M. (2022). *Supply Chains Transparency and Due Diligence Legislation to Prevent Child and Forced Labour*.

Ministry of Industry and Trade. (2023). *Vietnam Import-Export Report 2022*. Hong Duc Publisher. https://trungtamwto.vn/file/22356/bao-cao-xuat-nhap-khau-viet-nam-nam-2022.pdf

Navasartian, A. (2020). EU-Vietnam Free Trade Agreement: Insights on the Substantial and Procedural Guarantees for Labour Protection in Vietnam. *European Papers—A Journal on Law and Integration, 5*(1), 561–571. https://doi.org/10.15166/2499-8249/344

Nguyen, H., Pham, V., Ngo, H. Q., Huynh, A., Nguyen, B., & Machado, J. (2024). Intelligent Search System for Resume and Labor Law. *PeerJ Computer Science, 10*, Article e1786. https://doi.org/10.7717/peerj-cs.1786

Nguyen, M., Bensemann, J., & Kelly, S. (2018). Corporate Social Responsibility (CSR) in Vietnam: A Conceptual Framework. *International Journal of Corporate Social Responsibility, 3*(1), 9. https://doi.org/10.1186/s40991-018-0032-5

Nguyen Thi Kim Phung. (2022, February). Nâng cao ý thức thực hiện trách nhiệm xã hội của doanh nghiệp Việt Nam | Raising Awareness on Corporate Social Responsibility among Vietnamese Enterprises. In *Tạp chí Tài chính*. https://tapchitaichinh.vn/nang-cao-y-thuc-thuc-hien-trach-nhiem-xa-hoi-cua-doanh-nghiep-viet-nam.html

Nguyen Thi Yen. (2021, January). Trách nhiệm xã hội của doanh nghiệp theo quy định tại Luật Doanh nghiệp Việt Nam | Corporate Social Responsibility under the Vietnamese Law on Enterprises. In *Tạp chí Công Thương*. https://tapchicongthuong.vn/trach-nhiem-xa-hoi-cua-doanh-nghiep-theo-quy-dinh-tai-luat-doanh-nghiep-viet-nam-78506.htm

Phu Nu Online. (2017, May 8). *Bóc lột lao động trẻ em vẫn diễn ra từng ngày: Nhiều dấu hỏi quanh cuộc giải cứu bất thành | Child Labor Exploitation Still Happens Every Day: Many Questions Surrounding the Failed Rescue*. https://www.phunuonline.com.vn/boc-lot-lao-dong-tre-em-van-dien-ra-tung-ngay-nhieu-dau-hoi-quanh-cuoc-giai-cuu-bat-thanh-a19752.html

Putri, C. N. T., Masse, F. A. U., & Kesuma, S. A. (2023). The Implementation of Mandatory or Voluntary for Corporate Social Responsibility: A Systematic Literature Review. *Journal of Entrepreneurship*, 1–14. https://doi.org/10.56943/joe.v2i3.337

RESPECT. (2017). *French Corporate Duty of Vigilance Law* (English Translation). https://respect.international/french-corporate-duty-of-vigilance-law-english-translation/

Tam Nhi N., Thi Ngoc Tuyet B., Yen Nhi Q., Tu Van Ha T., & Thi Thanh Xuan P. (2021). Trách nhiệm xã hội của doanh nghiệp đối với người lao động: Nghiên cứu tình huống tại khu chế xuất Tân Thuận | Corporate Social Responsibility toward Workers: A Case Study in the Tan Thuan Export Processing Zone. *Tạp chí Nghiên cứu Tài chính—Marketing, 56*. https://doi.org/10.52932/jfm.vi56.126

Thanh Hương. (2020, November 26). *Bóc lột sức lao động, ngược đãi trẻ em: Đừng để thành chuyện đã rồi | Exploitation of Labor, Child Abuse: Don't Let It Become a Fait Accompli*. VOV.VN. https://vov.vn/xa-hoi/boc-lot-suc-lao-dong-nguoc-dai-tre-em-dung-de-thanh-chuyen-da-roi-820138.vov

Thuy Hien. (2025). *Công bố kết quả điều tra về lao động trẻ em Việt Nam | Announcing the Results of the Investigation on Child Labor in Vietnam*. https://baotintuc.vn/xa-hoi/cong-bo-ket-qua-dieu-tra-ve-lao-dong-tre-em-viet-nam-20250123131712132.htm

Thuy Trang. (2022, July 9). *Khó khăn trong phát hiện vi phạm sử dụng lao động trẻ em | Difficulty in Detecting Child Labor Violations*. https://laodong.vn/cong-doan/kho-khan-trong-phat-hien-vi-pham-su-dung-lao-dong-tre-em-1066048.ldo

UNICEF. (2012). *Children's Rights and Business Principles | UNICEF Child Rights and Business*. https://www.unicef.org/childrightsandbusiness/documents/childrens-rights-and-business-principles

UNICEF. (2024, June 11). *UNICEF Paper: Operational-Level Grievance Mechanisms Fit for Children.* ALNAP. https://alnap.org/help-library/resources/unicef-paper-operational-level-grievance-mechanisms-fit-for-children/

UNICEF Viet Nam. (2015, January 1). *Obligations and Actions on Children's Rights and Business | UNICEF Viet Nam.* https://www.unicef.org/vietnam/reports/obligations-and-actions-childrens-rights-and-business

Part III
Child-Friendly Justice in Judicial and Administrative Processes

Chapter 9 Child-Friendly Administrative Justice for Children in Conflict with the Law in Vietnam

Ha Thi Phuong Nguyen

Abstract Depending on the nature and seriousness of a violation of law, citizens in general, including children, are subject to corresponding legal liability as prescribed in legal normative documents. Among the current types of legal liability is administrative liability (Le Minh Toan, 2019). Within the scope of this article, the author focuses on certain theoretical and legal issues concerning child-friendly administrative justice, or in other words, the protection of children's rights when they bear administrative liability in Vietnam, particularly in cases of administrative sanctioning. On that basis, the article identifies several shortcomings in the relevant legal provisions and proposes solutions for improvement, aiming to ensure greater effectiveness in protecting children's rights in general and in the context of administrative sanctioning in particular in Vietnam in the coming period.

9.1 Introduction

Vietnam ratified the 1989 Convention on the Rights of the Child in 1990, becoming one of the first States to do so. Since then, Vietnam has consistently regarded the protection, care, and education of children as an important task, thereby promoting the better realization of children's fundamental rights. Clause 1 Article 37 of the 2013 Constitution affirms: "Children shall be protected, cared for, and educated by the State, family, and society; and shall be allowed to participate in matters concerning children." The 2016 Law on Children concretizes this policy by stipulating twenty-three groups of specific rights, covering almost all four categories of rights under the grouping in the 1989 Convention on the Rights of the Child. These include the right to be protected in legal proceedings and in the handling of administrative violations. In order to ensure the best protection of children's rights in cases involving

Article history: Received 03 April 2025; Revised 22 July 2025; Accepted 13 August 2025.

H. T. P. Nguyen (✉)
Da Lat University, Lam Dong Province, Viet Nam
e-mail: hantp@dlu.edu.vn

N. Binh An et al. (eds.), *The Future of Child-Friendly Justice and Children's Rights in Vietnam*, https://doi.org/10.1007/978-981-95-3521-7_9

violations of law in general and administrative sanctioning in particular, the legal system in Vietnam has undergone significant improvements in recent years, reflecting the commitment to child-friendly justice in the administrative domain. However, certain limitations remain and need to be addressed promptly.

9.2 Overview of the Protection of Children's Rights in Administrative Sanctioning

Today, the protection and promotion of human rights is not the responsibility of any single individual or specific community but is the common cause of all progressive humanity (Nguyen Thi Viet Huong & Le Thi Hong Nhung, 2011), with particular importance attached to the protection and promotion of children's rights. The 1989 Convention on the Rights of the Child, adopted by the United Nations General Assembly on 20 November 1989 and entering into force on 2 September 1990, is considered the most comprehensive and complete legal instrument for protecting the rights of children worldwide. The Convention also provides for the establishment of the Committee on the Rights of the Child to monitor its implementation. In addition, the General Assembly adopted three Optional Protocols: the 2000 Optional Protocol on the involvement of children in armed conflict, the 2000 Optional Protocol on the sale of children, child prostitution and child pornography, and the 2011 Optional Protocol on a communications procedure enabling children to submit complaints concerning violations of their rights under the Convention. Vietnam officially ratified the Convention on 28 February 1990 and acceded to the first two Optional Protocols in December 2001 (Vo Khanh Kinh & Le Mai Thanh, 2014). Since then, Vietnam has consistently recognized children as vital to the nation's future. Under the Convention, a child is defined as any person under the age of eighteen, whereas in Vietnam Article 1 of the 2016 Law on Children defines a child as a person under the age of sixteen.

Human rights in general, including children's rights, are approached in many ways and are multi-faceted in nature. According to a United Nations document, approximately fifty definitions of human rights have been published (United Nations, 1994). Each definition addresses the issue from a specific perspective, identifying certain attributes, yet none encompasses all aspects of human rights; in practice, there are hundreds of interpretations of the concept (Vietnam National University, 2015). Thus, definitions of human rights largely depend on the subjective approach of each individual. At the international level, the Office of the High Commissioner for Human Rights often cites the following: "Human rights are universal legal guarantees that protect individuals and groups against actions and omissions that interfere with fundamental freedoms, entitlements, and human dignity" (OHCHR, 2006). This definition is widely referenced in scholarly research.

In Vietnam, definitions of human rights are likewise diverse, as provided by various agencies, organizations, and researchers. In the author's view, the most comprehensive definition is as follows: "Human rights are the ability to exercise the natural and objective entitlements of a human being, both as an individual and as a member of society, guaranteed by national policies and laws as well as international legal agreements on human values in material, cultural, and spiritual relations, and in the needs for freedom and development" (Chu Hong Thanh, 1997).

Accordingly, human rights in general are fundamental values that must be respected and protected by both national law and international legal agreements under all circumstances. Children's rights are likewise inherent needs and interests of children that are recognized, respected, and protected. Based on the 1989 Convention, children's rights are classified into four groups: the right to survival, the right to development, the right to protection, and the right to participation. Their contents are as follows (Nguyen Linh Giang, 2011):

First, the right to survival is based on the recognition that children are physically and mentally underdeveloped and thus highly vulnerable, warranting priority protection of life.

Second, the right to development emphasizes healthy physical and mental growth, aiming to improve children's quality of life and to ensure their full developmental potential.

Third, the right to protection safeguards children against discrimination, exploitation, abuse, and torture, and is especially relevant in circumstances such as abandonment, unlawful conduct, refugee status, or armed conflict.

Fourth, the right to participation recognizes children as rights-holders who may take part in decision-making processes concerning matters that affect their lives.

Protection of children in conflict with the law falls within the third category under the 1989 Convention. In Vietnam, Clause 1 Article 4 of the 2016 Law on Children defines child protection as the implementation of appropriate measures to ensure a safe and healthy life for children; to prevent, stop, and handle acts of child abuse; and to assist children in special difficult circumstances. The Law sets out twenty-three groups of rights in Sect. 2.1, including the right to protection in legal proceedings and in the handling of administrative violations. Article 30 specifies: "Children have the right to be protected in the course of legal proceedings and administrative sanctioning; to have the right to legal defence and self-defence; to have their legitimate rights and interests protected; to receive legal aid; to present their opinions; not to be unlawfully deprived of liberty; and not to be subjected to torture, coercion, corporal punishment, humiliation, infringement of bodily integrity, psychological pressure, or other forms of abuse."

The right to protection in administrative sanctioning, as addressed in this article, belongs to the third category of rights under the 1989 Convention. Vietnam has complied with Article 2(1) of the Convention, which provides: "States Parties shall respect and ensure the rights set forth in the present Convention to each child within their jurisdiction".

To concretize this, in addition to the 2016 Law on Children, Article 8 of Decree No. 56/2017/ND-CP of 9 May 2017 detailing certain provisions of the Law on Children defines children in conflict with the law as including:

(1) Children subject to administrative measures of education in communes, wards, or townships, or to reform school placement; or to substitute administrative measures of family-based management.
(2) Children without a stable place of residence subject to administrative measures of education in communes, wards, or townships, in child protection service establishments, or in social assistance establishments.
(3) Children subject to judicial measures of education in communes, wards, or townships, or to reform school placement; or to criminal penalties of non-custodial reform or fixed-term imprisonment, including suspended sentences.
(4) Children who have completed fixed-term imprisonment or reform school placement.

In addition, Clause 3 Article 2 of the 2012 Law on Handling of Administrative Violations (as amended in 2020) stipulates that administrative measures apply to individuals who violate laws on security, order, and social safety but whose acts are not criminal offences, including education in communes, wards, or townships; reform school placement; placement in compulsory education establishments; and placement in compulsory rehabilitation establishments. Since "children" are defined as those under sixteen, only education in communes, wards, or townships and reform school placement may be applied. Articles 94 and 96 of the 2012 Law (as amended in 2020) provide that placement in compulsory education establishments and compulsory rehabilitation establishments applies only to persons aged eighteen and over (Nguyen Canh Hop, 2015).

The protection of children's rights in administrative sanctioning in Vietnam consists of implementing appropriate measures to safeguard children during the application of education in communes, wards, or townships and reform school placement for violations of laws on security, order, and social safety that do not constitute criminal offences.

9.3 Provisions of Vietnamese Law on the Protection of Children's Rights in Administrative Sanctioning

9.3.1 Provisions of Law on Administrative Sanctioning Measures Applicable to Children

9.3.1.1 The Measure of Education in Communes, Wards, or Townships

Clause 1 Article 89 of the 2012 Law on Handling of Administrative Violations (as amended in 2020) provides: "The measure of education in communes, wards, or townships is an administrative sanctioning measure applicable to the subjects specified in Article 90 of this Law, aiming to educate and manage them at their place of residence in cases where it is deemed unnecessary to isolate them from the community." This indicates that the measure of education in communes, wards, or townships has a nature distinct from the remaining measures. The measures of placement in reform schools, compulsory education establishments, or compulsory rehabilitation establishments, by their very names, carry the connotation of special administrative coercion. The special nature of such administrative coercion lies in the isolation of the violator from the community (Ho Chi Minh City University of Law, 2017; Lai Son Tung, 2022). In contrast, the measure of education in communes, wards, or townships does not isolate the person subject to its application from the community. Therefore, it is regarded as the least severe coercive measure among the administrative sanctioning measures (Nguyen Van Tung & Nguyen Van Nhat, 2021). Its objective is to harness the influence of the local community to directly participate in educating and rehabilitating the violator so that they may soon repent, correct their wrongdoing, and become a good citizen (Nguyen Thanh Ha, 2021).

Specific provisions on the application of the measure of education in communes, wards, or townships to children are as follows:

Firstly, regarding the subjects and statute of limitations for application.

Article 90 of the 2012 Law on Handling of Administrative Violations (as amended in 2020) and Clause 2 Article 5 of Decree No. 120/2021/ND-CP dated 24 December 2021 stipulate the subjects and statute of limitations in the case of children as follows:

(a) Children aged from twelve to under fourteen years who commit acts indicative of a very serious criminal offence committed intentionally under the Penal Code, with a statute of limitations of one year from the date of the act.
(b) Children aged from fourteen to under sixteen years who commit acts indicative of a serious criminal offence committed intentionally under the Penal Code, with a statute of limitations of six months from the date of the act.
(c) Children aged from fourteen to under sixteen years who have twice been administratively sanctioned and are recorded in an administrative violation record for the third time within six months for one of the acts of disturbing public order, theft of property, gambling, fraud, or illegal racing, with a statute of limitations of six months from the date of the last act.
(d) Children aged from fourteen years and above who have twice been administratively sanctioned and are recorded in an administrative violation record for the third time within six months for the act of illegal use of narcotics, with a statute of limitations of three months from the date of the last act.

Secondly, regarding the competence for application.

Clause 1 Article 105 of the 2012 Law on Handling of Administrative Violations (as amended in 2020) and Points a Clause 1 and Clause 2 Article 7 of Decree No. 120/2021/ND-CP provide that:

(a) In cases where the child has a place of residence, the Chairperson of the People's Committee of the commune where the child resides shall have the competence to apply the measure.

(b) In cases where the child has no stable place of residence and has been admitted to a social protection centre or a child support establishment, the Chairperson of the People's Committee of the commune where such centre or establishment is located shall have the competence to apply the measure.

Thirdly, regarding the procedures for application.

(a) Preparation of the application dossier. Clause 1 Article 97 of the 2012 Law on Handling of Administrative Violations (as amended in 2020) prescribes that the Chief of the Commune Police where the child resides or where the child commits the violation, either ex officio or upon the request of the Chairperson of the commune-level Vietnam Fatherland Front Committee or the representative of a grassroots agency, organization, or residential unit, shall prepare the dossier proposing the application of the measure.

   In cases where the violation is detected, investigated, and handled by a higher-level police authority but does not warrant criminal prosecution, Clause 2 Article 97 of the Law stipulates that the handling police authority shall verify, collect evidence, and prepare the dossier proposing the application of the measure of education in communes, wards, or townships.

(b) Decision on application. Clauses 1 and 2 Article 98 of the 2012 Law (as amended in 2020) and Clause 3 Article 22 of Decree No. 120/2021/ND-CP provide that within seven working days from the date of receipt of the dossier, the Chairperson of the commune-level People's Committee shall convene and preside over a consultation meeting with the participation of the Chief of Commune Police, the judicial–civil status officer, representatives of the Vietnam Fatherland Front, relevant political–social organizations, and representatives of the local community. The child proposed for the application of the measure, their lawful representative, parents, or guardian must be invited to attend and express their opinions.

   Within two working days from the conclusion of the consultation meeting, the Chairperson of the commune-level People's Committee shall consider and issue the decision on the application of the measure. Depending on the circumstances, the Chairperson may assign the child to an agency, organization, or family for management and education; or, if the child has no stable place of residence, to a social protection centre or a child support establishment.

(c) Implementation of the decision. Articles 29 to 35 of Decree No. 120/2021/ND-CP provide detailed rules on the implementation of the measure, including the designation of persons directly assisting the child, as well as the preparation of an education and management plan. Pursuant to Clause 1 Article 108 of the 2012 Law (as amended in 2020), the decision applying the measure of education in communes, wards, or townships shall lapse after six months from the date it takes legal effect.

9.3.1.2 The Measure of Placement in Reform Schools

Clause 1 Article 91 of the 2012 Law on Handling of Administrative Violations (as amended in 2020) stipulates: "The measure of placement in reform schools is an administrative sanctioning measure applied to persons whose violations are prescribed in the Law on Handling of Administrative Violations (as amended in 2020), including children, with the aim of enabling them to study general education, vocational training, engage in labour, and participate in daily activities under the management and education of the school."

As previously analysed, the measure of placement in reform schools is one of the administrative sanctioning measures characterised by special administrative coercion through the isolation of the violator from the community. Its primary purpose is to remove minors, including children in conflict with the law, from their social environment for a fixed period so that they may receive general education, vocational training, engage in labour, and live under the management and education of the reform school. This objective stems from the best interests of the minor, providing an environment conducive to correcting their misconduct. Therefore, although this measure is coercive in nature and restricts personal liberty, it also embodies a profound humanitarian character (Nguyen Canh Hop, 2015).

The specific provisions on the application of the measure of placement in reform schools to children are as follows:

Firstly, regarding the subjects of application.

Article 92 of the 2012 Law on Handling of Administrative Violations (as amended in 2020) prescribes the subjects in the case of children as follows:

(a) Children aged from twelve to under fourteen years who commit acts showing signs of a particularly serious criminal offence under the Penal Code.
(b) Children aged from fourteen to under sixteen years who commit acts showing signs of a very serious criminal offence or a particularly serious criminal offence under the Penal Code, except for the offences prescribed in Clause 2 Article 12 of the 2015 Penal Code (as amended in 2017).
(c) Children aged from fourteen to under sixteen years who commit one of the acts prescribed in Clauses 2 and 3 Article 90 of the 2012 Law on Handling of Administrative Violations (as amended in 2020) and have previously been subject to the measure of education in communes, wards, or townships.

Secondly, regarding the duration of application.

Clause 1 Article 91 of the 2012 Law on Handling of Administrative Violations (as amended in 2020) provides that the duration of placement in a reform school ranges from six months to twenty-four months.

Thirdly, regarding the competence for application.

Article 100 of the 2012 Law on Handling of Administrative Violations (as amended in 2020) prescribes that the People's Court of the district where the person proposed for application committed the violation has the competence to decide on the application of the measure of placement in a reform school.

Fourthly, regarding the procedures for application

(a) Preparation of the application dossier. For children in conflict with the law who have a stable place of residence, Point a Clause 1 Article 99 of the 2012 Law (as amended in 2020) stipulates that the Chairperson of the commune-level People's Committee where the child resides shall prepare the dossier proposing the application of the measure of placement in a reform school.

For children in conflict with the law who do not have a stable place of residence, Point b Clause 1 Article 99 of the same Law stipulates that the Chairperson of the commune-level People's Committee where the child committed the violation shall prepare the dossier proposing the application of the measure of placement in a reform school.

In cases where the violation is detected, investigated, and handled by a higher-level police authority, but does not warrant criminal prosecution and falls within the scope of Article 92 of the Law, Clause 2 Article 99 stipulates that the handling police authority shall verify, collect evidence, and prepare the dossier proposing the application of the measure of placement in a reform school.

(b) Decision on application. Clause 3 Article 99 and Clause 1 Article 100 of the 2012 Law (as amended in 2020) provide that once the preparation of the dossier has been completed, the preparing authority must notify the parents or lawful representative of the child in writing. These persons have the right to read the dossier and take necessary notes within three working days from receipt of the notice.

Within one working day from the expiry of the time limit for reading the dossier, the head of the competent police authority shall decide on the transfer of the dossier to the district-level People's Court where the child committed the violation for a decision on the application of the measure of placement in a reform school.

(c) Implementation of the decision. Article 107 of the 2012 Law (as amended in 2020) provides that within three days from the date the decision takes legal effect, the district-level People's Court must send the decision to the agency that prepared the dossier, or to the competent police authority, the commune-level People's Committee where the child resides, and other relevant agencies for enforcement in accordance with the law; the decision must also be sent to the parents or lawful representative of the child.

Similar to the decision applying the measure of education in communes, wards, or townships, the decision on the application of the measure of placement in a reform school expires after six months from the date it takes legal effect, as prescribed in Clause 1 Article 108 of the 2012 Law (as amended in 2020).

9.3.2 *Provisions of Law on the Protection of Children's Rights in Administrative Sanctioning*

9.3.2.1 General Provisions

Protection requirements

Article 70 of the 2016 Law on Children prescribes the general requirements for protecting children in administrative sanctioning as follows:

Firstly, to ensure that children are treated fairly, equally, and with respect, in a manner appropriate to their age and maturity.

Secondly, to give priority to the prompt resolution of cases involving children in order to minimise harm to their physical and mental well-being.

Thirdly, to ensure the support of parents, guardians, or other lawful representatives for children throughout the administrative sanctioning process in order to protect their lawful rights and interests.

Fourthly, to require that persons with competence to impose administrative sanctions, lawyers, and legal aid providers possess the necessary knowledge of child psychology and educational science, and to use language that is friendly and understandable to children.

Fifthly, to guarantee the child's right to legal defence and legal aid.

Sixthly, to take proactive measures to prevent and deter unlawful acts and reoffending by children through timely support and intervention to address the causes and conditions of violations, thereby enabling the child to recover and reintegrate into the community.

Seventhly, to ensure the timely provision of preventive, supportive, and intervention measures that are safe, continuous, adequate, flexible, and appropriate to the needs, circumstances, age, and psychological and physiological characteristics of each child, based on consideration and respect for the child's opinions, aspirations, emotions, and attitudes.

Eighthly, to ensure close and timely coordination among agencies, organisations, child protection service establishments, families, and educational institutions with the administrative sanctioning authorities.

Ninthly, to give priority to preventive, supportive, and intervention measures, or the measure of education in communes, wards, or townships, or substitute administrative measures for children in conflict with the law; coercive measures and restrictions on liberty may be applied only after other preventive and educational measures are deemed inappropriate.

Tenthly, to guarantee the confidentiality of the child's private life and to take necessary measures to limit the child's appearance before the public during proceedings.

These general requirements for protecting children's rights in administrative sanctioning under Vietnamese law are consistent with the undertaking set out in Clause 1 Article 37 of the 1989 Convention on the Rights of the Child, which provides: "Every child deprived of liberty shall have the right to prompt access to legal and other appropriate assistance, as well as the right to challenge the legality of the deprivation of liberty before a court or other competent, independent, and impartial authority, and to a prompt decision on any such action."

Protection measures

Clause 1 Article 71 of the 2016 Law on Children provides that, in addition to the general requirements for protecting children in administrative sanctioning, where a child in conflict with the law is subject to the measure of education in communes, wards, or townships, or has completed the measure of placement in a reform school, the following protection measures shall be applied to address the causes and conditions of the violation, support recovery, and prevent reoffending:

Firstly, protection measures at the level of support (specifically prescribed at Points c and d Clause 2 Article 49 of the 2016 Law on Children).

Secondly, protection measures at the level of intervention (specifically prescribed at Points a and e Clause 2 Article 50 of the 2016 Law on Children).

Thirdly, family reunification where the child has no stable place of residence.

Fourthly, application of substitute care where the child has no parents, cannot be identified as having parents, cannot live with parents, or has no identified place of residence during the period of implementation of the decision on education in communes, wards, or townships or a substitute administrative measure imposed by a competent authority.

Fifthly, support for the family in supervising, managing, and educating the child.

Sixthly, other protective measures deemed necessary.

9.3.2.2 Specific Provisions

Rights of children subject to the measure of education in communes, wards, or townships

Clause 1 Article 36 of Decree No. 120/2021/ND-CP provides that during the period of implementation of the measure of education in communes, wards, or townships, children shall have the following rights:

Firstly, to work, study, and live in their place of residence, and to be guided in carrying out the procedures for temporary absence declaration, and for permanent or temporary residence registration.

Secondly, to be facilitated in seeking employment; and, in cases of special difficulty, to be considered for support in obtaining loans from social policy banks, social funds, charitable funds, or humanitarian funds in the locality.

Thirdly, to participate in educational or vocational training programmes, and in locally organised counselling and life skills development programmes appropriate to their circumstances.

Fourthly, to express their wishes and recommendations to the Chairperson of the commune-level People's Committee, the Chief of Commune Police, social organisations, schools, and the assigned support person.

Fifthly, to be absent from their place of residence or to change their place of residence in accordance with the law.

Sixthly, to lodge complaints or initiate lawsuits against the decision to apply the measure of education in communes, wards, or townships, and against other administrative acts occurring during the execution of such decision.

Rights of children subject to the measure of placement in reform schools

Decree No. 140/2021/ND-CP of 31 December 2021 on the regimes applicable to the measures of placement in reform schools and compulsory education establishments, as prescribed in Articles 17 to 26, provides that during the period of implementation of the measure of placement in a reform school, children shall enjoy the following regimes to ensure their rights:

Firstly, the regime of food, clothing, and daily living supplies.

Secondly, the regime of accommodation.

Thirdly, the regime of medical care.

Fourthly, the regime of general education, vocational training, and labour.

Fifthly, the regime of cultural activities, arts, and recreational activities.

Sixthly, the regime of commendation and discipline.

Seventhly, the regime of visits from relatives, communication, and receipt of money or gifts.

Eighthly, the regime applicable in the event of death, bereavement, or special hardship.

Through all of the above provisions on the rights of children in the application of the measures of education in communes, wards, or townships, and placement in reform schools, it is evident that Vietnam has complied with the undertaking set out in Clause 2 Article 3 of the 1989 Convention on the Rights of the Child, namely: "In all actions concerning children, whether undertaken by public or private social welfare institutions, courts of law, administrative authorities, or legislative bodies, the best interests of the child shall be a primary consideration."

9.4 Certain Shortcomings and Recommendations for Improving Vietnamese Law on the Protection of Children's Rights in Administrative Sanctioning

Overall, the provisions of Vietnamese law on the administrative sanctioning of children and the protection of children's rights in this process have made a significant contribution to ensuring the full range of rights for children—a group particularly vulnerable when committing acts that violate laws on security, order, and social safety but do not constitute criminal offences. These provisions have thereby contributed to ensuring child-friendly administrative justice for children in conflict with the law in Vietnam in recent years. Nevertheless, practical application still reveals shortcomings that require legislative improvement. In the author's view, the main shortcomings and corresponding proposals are as follows:

Firstly, Article 1 of the 2016 Law on Children defines "children" as persons under 16 years of age, while the 1989 Convention on the Rights of the Child defines a child as any person under 18 years of age. Thus, although Vietnam was among the first States to ratify the 1989 Convention, the age definition in Vietnamese law remains inconsistent with the Convention. Under current Vietnamese law, persons aged from 16 to under 18 are not considered children but "youth", since Article 1 of the 2020 Law on Youth provides: "Youth are Vietnamese citizens from full 16 years to 30 years of age." In reality, the trend of smaller family sizes and the continuing parental protection over children mean that at age 16, most have yet to achieve full physical and mental maturity. This age group is particularly susceptible to temptation, abuse, labour exploitation, and especially to violations of laws on security, order, and social safety.

Although Article 11 of the 2020 Law on Youth stipulates: "The international treaty on the rights of the child shall apply to youth aged from full 16 years to under 18 years," in order to better protect this group and align with the 1989 Convention, the definition of a child in Vietnamese law should be adjusted to include persons under 18 years of age.

Secondly, also concerning age, Articles 90 and 92 of the 2012 Law on Handling of Administrative Violations (as amended in 2020) provide that children from 12 years of age may be subject to administrative measures. This has two specific limitations: (a) children at 12 years of age are too young to be subjected to any State-imposed sanction (Phi Manh Long & Dang Duc Duy, 2024); and (b) Clause 2 Article 12 of the 2015 Penal Code (as amended in 2017) sets the minimum age of criminal liability in Vietnam at 14 years.

Therefore, the current provision allowing the application of administrative measures from the age of 12 is inconsistent with both the physical and mental development of children and the minimum age of criminal liability under the Penal Code. This should be revised to ensure consistency and appropriateness.

Thirdly, Clause 1 Article 98 of the 2012 Law on Handling of Administrative Violations (as amended in 2020) and Clause 3 Article 22 of Decree No. 120/2021/ND-CP provide that the consultation meeting to decide on the application of the measure of education in communes, wards, or townships shall invite the child concerned, their parents or guardians, and their lawful representative (if any). These invitees are allowed to "express their opinions" at the meeting.

However, in the author's view, merely allowing "expression of opinions" does not fully ensure the child's right to protection. In practice in Vietnam, speaking at a meeting is not equivalent to exercising the right to adversarial argument in judicial proceedings. The law is also unclear as to whether lawyers may participate as lawful representatives of the child. As a result, the presentation of arguments, responses, and legal reasoning to protect the lawful rights and interests of the child may be inadequately guaranteed.

It is therefore recommended that the law replace the right to "express opinions" with the right to present arguments, respond, and give views on evidence, documents, and applicable law. The law should also explicitly allow lawyers to participate as lawful representatives of the child. This improvement would better implement Article 12 of the 1989 Convention and General Comment No. 12 of the UN Committee on the Rights of the Child on the right of the child to be heard in all matters affecting them.

Fourthly, Clause 1 Article 36 of Decree No. 120/2021/ND-CP grants children under the measure of education in communes, wards, or townships the right to be "facilitated in seeking employment" and "considered for loan support from social policy banks, social funds, charitable funds, or humanitarian funds in the locality." This is inappropriate for children under 15 years of age, as this is the minimum legal working age under Clause 1 Article 3 of the 2019 Labour Code. Constitutionally, Article 35 of the 2013 Constitution prohibits discrimination, forced labour, and the employment of persons below the minimum working age (Hoang Minh Khoi, 2014). Furthermore, the provision on loan support is vague and not practically feasible without more specific regulation.

It is therefore necessary to add the phrase "in accordance with the Labour Code" to the provision on facilitating employment, and to specify the conditions and procedures for loan support for children.

Fifthly, also in Clause 1 Article 36 of Decree No. 120/2021/ND-CP, children have the right to initiate lawsuits against decisions applying the measure of education in communes, wards, or townships and against other administrative acts during execution of the decision. However, for decisions applying the measure of placement in reform schools, the child has no such right. These cases are excluded from administrative complaints within the jurisdiction of the courts under Point b Clause 1 Article 30 of the 2015 Law on Administrative Procedure (as amended in 2019) (Ho Chi Minh City University of Law, 2024). Moreover, the child has no right of appeal comparable to procedural decisions of the court, but only the rights to complaint, petition, or protest under Clause 1 Article 31 of the 2022 Ordinance on the procedures for considering and deciding on the application of administrative handling measures at the People's Court.

Therefore, it is recommended that the law be amended to grant children subject to the measure of placement in reform schools the right to appeal the decision through their lawful representatives, in order to maximise the protection of their rights.

9.5 Conclusion

In Vietnam there is a well-known saying, "Children today, the world tomorrow," which is also the title of a song by composer Le May. Although concise, this phrase reflects the special status of children as the future human resources and decisive factors for national development (Lai Son Tung, 2024). It also fully conveys our responsibility to protect children so that they may live safely and healthily, and to prevent, stop, and handle acts of child abuse while assisting children in special difficult circumstances. With twenty-three groups of rights specifically identified in the 2016 Law on Children, Vietnam has demonstrated particular concern for this group in many aspects. Nevertheless, in the author's view, children in conflict with the law, especially in the domain of security, order, and social safety, who are subject to administrative measures, are in need of special protection through various means, including legal safeguards, to help them recover promptly, avoid reoffending, and become good citizens for their families and for society.

References

Chu, H. T. (1997). *Human Rights and International Law on Human Rights* (p. 23). National Political Publishing House.

Ho Chi Minh City University of Law. (2024). *Textbook on Vietnamese Administrative Procedure Law* (pp. 116–119). Hong Duc Publishing House.

Ho Chi Minh City University of Law, Nguyen, C. H. (Chief Ed.). (2017). *Textbook on Vietnamese Administrative Law* (p. 313). Hong Duc Publishing House.

Hoang, M. K. (2014, August). The 2013 Constitution and the Protection of Children's Rights. *Legislative Studies Journal* 15(271). https://www.nghiencuuphapluat.vn/hien-phap-nam-2013-voi-viec-bao-ve-quyen-cua-tre-em/. (Accessed 26 June 2025).

Lai, S. T. (2022). The Measure of Education in Communes, Wards, or Townships—Practical Difficulties and Directions for Improvement. *Procuracy Science Journal,* (2), 26–31.

Lai, S. T. (2024, August). Protecting and Promoting Children's Rights—Current Situation and Solutions. *Democracy and Law Journal, 411*(2). https://danchuphapluat.vn/bao-ve-va-thuc-day-quyen-tre-em-thuc-trang-va-giai-phap-3299.html. (Accessed 26 June 2025).

Le, M. T. (2019). *General Law for Universities, Colleges, and Secondary Schools* (pp. 99–100). National Political Publishing House—Truth.

Long, P. M., & Dang, D. H. (2024). *Some Recommendations for Improving the Measure of Education in Communes, Wards, or Townships.* https://tapchitoaan.vn/mot-so-kien-nghi-hoan-thien-bien-phap-xu-ly-hanh-chinh-giao-duc-tai-xa-phuong-thi-tran10600.html. (Accessed 26 June 2025).

Nguyen, C. H. (Chief Ed.). (2015). *Scientific Commentary on the 2012 Law on Handling of Administrative Violations* (pp. 514–604). Vietnam National University—Ho Chi Minh City Publishing House.

Nguyen, L. G. (2011). *International Conventions on Human Rights* (pp. 45–46). Social Sciences Publishing House.

Nguyen, T. H. (2021, June). Subjects and Conditions for Applying the Measure of Education in Communes, Wards, or Townships. *Democracy and Law Journal,* (Special Issue), 11.

Nguyen, T. V. H., & Nhung, L. T. H. (2011). *Human Rights Education for State Officials and the Entire Population—A Mechanism to Ensure Human Rights in Vietnam Today* (p. 277). Vietnam Social Sciences Publishing House.

Nguyen, V. T., & Nguyen, V. N. (2021). The Measure of Education in Communes, Wards, or Townships under Vietnamese Law. *Democracy and Law Journal,* (10), 54.

OHCHR. (2006). *Frequently Asked Questions on a Human Rights-based Approach to Development Cooperation* (p. 1). New York and Geneva.

United Nations. (1994). *Human Rights: Questions and Answers* (p. 4). Geneva.

Vietnam National University, Hanoi. (2015). *Textbook on Theory and Law on Human Rights* (p. 28). National Political Publishing House.

Vinh, V. K., & Thanh, L. M. (Chief Eds.). (2014). *International Law on Human Rights* (pp. 95–97). Social Sciences Publishing House.

Chapter 10
Lawyer Skills in Guaranteeing Fair Trial Rights for Juvenile Drug Offenders in Vietnam

Luong Van Tuan and Nguyen The Vinh

Abstract This chapter examines the specialised questioning skills of lawyers in first-instance criminal trials involving juvenile drug offenders in Vietnam, a particularly vulnerable group within the justice system. Against the backdrop of rising drug use and decreasing age of users, the chapter situates lawyer questioning within the broader framework of international standards, notably General Comment No. 10 of the UNCRC, and relevant Vietnamese legal provisions, including the Law on Juvenile Justice 2024. Through analysis of courtroom practices, the chapter identifies the unique psychological and procedural considerations required when working with juvenile defendants who are drug addicts, as well as with other minors participating as victims or witnesses. Detailed scenarios illustrate both ineffective and effective questioning techniques, emphasising the importance of friendly interaction, age-appropriate communication, and avoidance of stigmatising or sensitive terminology. The study further explores direct and supplementary questioning strategies, the creation of a comfortable courtroom atmosphere, and the lawyer's role in enabling truthful and coherent testimony. Recommendations to the State include reform of legal education, incorporation of juvenile-friendly justice into professional training for lawyers, judges, and procurators, and the potential establishment of specialised juvenile drug courts. The chapter argues that enhancing lawyer skills in this area not only improves the fairness and effectiveness of trials but also reflects the humanitarian and human rights values essential to a civilised justice system, contributing to the reintegration of juvenile offenders and the prevention of recidivism.

Article history: Received 29 April 2025; Revised 12 July 2025; Accepted 15 August 2025.

L. Van Tuan (✉)
Judicial Academy, Ministry of Justice, Ha Noi City, Viet Nam
e-mail: luongtuan.lawyer@gmail.com

N. T. Vinh
Member of the Standing Committee, Head of Party Development Committee, Party Committee of Hai Son Commune, Quang Ninh Province, Viet Nam
e-mail: nguyenthevinh.phd@gmail.com

N. Binh An et al. (eds.), *The Future of Child-Friendly Justice and Children's Rights in Vietnam*, https://doi.org/10.1007/978-981-95-3521-7_10

10.1 Introduction

Ensuring the right to a fair trial for juvenile offenders, especially in cases involving narcotic substances, remains a significant challenge within the criminal justice system of any country, including Vietnam. From the practical experience in adjudicating drug-related cases, juvenile offenders often face a high risk of being subjected to criminal proceedings that fail to adequately ensure their procedural rights and the guarantees of a child-friendly justice process. This situation raises concerns of violating the principle of fairness as affirmed in General Comment No. 10 of the United Nations Committee on the Rights of the Child—UNCRC (2007, 4), which states: "States parties must take all necessary measures to ensure that all children in conflict with the law are treated equally. Particular attention should be paid to actual discrimination and disparities which may result from the absence of consistent policy and which may affect vulnerable groups of children."

According to PV (2024), "the total number of illegal drug users, drug addicts, and individuals under post-rehabilitation management in Vietnam as of October 2024 is nearly 230,000. The age of drug users tends to decrease, with the 12 to 30 age group accounting for 44.6%." TTXVN (2024) further reports that "according to the Drug Crime Investigation Police Department—C04, the age of initial drug use is decreasing, with around 60% of first-time users aged between 15 and 25, including many between 13 and 15 years old." As stated by Nguyễn Hiền and Quang Huy (2022), "according to statistics from the Ministry of Public Security as of 31 December 2021, there were 743 individuals aged from 12 to under 18 addicted to narcotics." In a specific province, according to vksnd.gialai.gov.vn (2022), "in the first six months of 2022 alone, Gia Lai province recorded 434 drug addicts and 737 illegal drug users; among them, 18 individuals were aged from 16 to under 18."

Due to the fact that these individuals have not yet reached full maturity both biologically and socially, coupled with the social stigma, public condemnation, and even rejection from family and peers related to their drug use behaviors, juveniles who are drug addicts (hereinafter referred to as drug-addicted children) face significant vulnerability when brought before a court. Therefore, they require special protection. Participation in a trial involving drug-addicted children demands that defense lawyers possess the necessary skills to protect their lawful rights and interests. In particular, questioning is an indispensable activity for lawyers in clarifying the substance of the case. This paper focuses on the questioning skills of lawyers. In order for the child to participate in the questioning process naturally and comfortably, and to provide honest answers without being affected by feelings of fear, anxiety, or shame, lawyers must apply questioning techniques that are appropriate to the age and psychological development of the child. The aim is not only to contribute to the effectiveness of the criminal proceedings, but also, as (Vu Thi Quyen, 2022) emphasizes, "to protect the child from the hardships of the justice process, guide them to take responsibility for their acts, and more importantly, to create a chance for them to avoid similar violations in the future and grow into responsible individuals."

In the context where drug use is increasingly becoming prevalent among younger populations, ensuring fair trials for drug-addicted children in order to safeguard their human rights has become an urgent requirement. With their professional skills, in-depth knowledge of the law and the psychology of minors, and the capacity to flexibly apply legal provisions and international standards, lawyers are expected to be among the legal professions that can effectively safeguard the rights of drug-addicted children in criminal proceedings. To undertake this study, the paper employs an integrated set of commonly used scientific research methods, including legal analysis, statistical data, case study analysis, documentary research on juvenile justice, children's rights, and the role of lawyers in criminal trials, and generalisation. The combination of these methods enables a comprehensive, scholarly, and practical perspective on the role and skills of lawyers in questioning activities at trial, in order to ensure the right to a fair trial for juvenile drug offenders in Vietnam, aligned with international standards.

10.2 Subjects to Be Questioned in the Trial of Juvenile Drug Addicts

Drug addiction is caused by various factors, among which the following five are considered the most prominent, according to fortbehavioral com (2022): peer pressure, social media, cultural and social influences, curiosity, and the desire to be oneself. According to Holovanova and Okhrimenko (2024), a comprehensive study conducted by experts in psychology, sociology, and medicine using methods such as bibliographic semantics, questionnaire surveys, comparative and psychological diagnostics, system analysis and generalization, and mathematical statistics in the article "Motivational factors in the formation of adolescent drug involvement" has pointed out that strong motivational orientations may contribute to the emergence of addictive behavior in drug-addicted juveniles (aged 18–23 years old). Specifically: (1) the search for positive emotions and new sensations (65.4%, where "clearly expressed motivation" predominated significantly); (2) pseudo cultural motivation (influence from the micro social environment) (55.8% "clearly expressed" and 34.6% "situationally expressed"); (3) deviant behavioral motivation such as the desire to escape from boredom, apathy, and inner emptiness (51.9% "clearly expressed" and 25.0% "situational"); (4) pleasure seeking motivation (desire to achieve physical and psychological pleasure from drug effects) (48.1% "clearly expressed" and 28.8% "situational"). According to the National Institute on Drug Abuse (2020), curiosity and social pressure are two significant factors. In this regard, adolescents are particularly at risk because peer pressure can be very strong. Adolescence is a stage of development where the presence of risk factors, such as peers using drugs, can easily lead to substance abuse.

When referring to drug addicts in general, public perception often associates this group with criminal conduct (such as illegal trading, possession, or use of narcotics), while rarely recognizing them as victims (of drug production and trafficking networks). Therefore, when confronting individuals with drug addiction, people often react harshly, forming an exclusionary attitude toward them. However, in-depth studies, especially those focusing on minors, have shown that juvenile drug addicts are in fact victims of drug problems. Under the influence of biological and environmental factors, juveniles do not have sufficient knowledge or skills to resist the temptations of narcotics or the traps set by illegal drug manufacturers and dealers. The above research has shown that most adolescents begin using drugs due to "the search for positive emotions and new sensations" (65.4%, with "clearly expressed motivation" prevailing). Curiosity and the desire to explore new feelings are natural parts of human development, both biologically and socially, yet without adequate life knowledge and experience, adolescents are more vulnerable to distorted experiences involving narcotics.

Therefore, even when regarded from the legal viewpoint as offenders (due to the illegal use of narcotics leading to addiction, or committing other crimes afterward), they remain victims of drug-related issues. In this article, the addicted juvenile is identified as a victim of the drug problem, and this requires lawyers to have a deep sense of empathy. The behavior of drug use that leads to addiction is not the subject of research, and even subsequent criminal acts committed by the addicted juvenile such as disturbing public order or even committing homicide are also not the target of analysis. This study only takes the image of addicted juveniles who commit other crimes as a background to illustrate and analyze the questioning skills of lawyers during their trials. In such trials, there may already be or may additionally appear other juveniles participating in the capacity of victims, related parties, or witnesses. Some of these individuals may also be drug addicts. The aim here is to further clarify the professional skills required when working with juveniles in general and drug-addicted children in particular.

When participating in a trial involving a drug-addicted child, the lawyer, acting as the legal representative protecting the rights and lawful interests of the accused, must not treat them as an ordinary client but should clearly recognize that they are a special group requiring special protection through a friendly working method. Based on the belief that "children are the future of the world" or "youth are the pillars of the nation," the protection of this group when they are addicted to drugs and being prosecuted for criminal offenses has a significant meaning for safeguarding the nation's future. Whether the lawyer is defending the addicted child as the accused, the victim, or another party, or dealing with juvenile witnesses, participation in trials of drug-addicted children demands professional skills that ensure friendliness toward minors. This means the lawyer must apply a working method that is sensitive to age and developmental psychology so that the juvenile does not feel or at least reduces fear, shyness, or hesitation when appearing in the first instance court and responding to questions posed by the lawyer.

The purpose of questioning by the lawyer in the first instance trial of a drug-addicted juvenile will depend on which party the lawyer represents. Specifically:

(1) In case the lawyer defends the accused:

The lawyer may choose to conduct the defence under two main directions, namely pleading for acquittal or requesting mitigation of criminal liability. The lawyer conducts questioning of the accused in order to clarify the inconsistencies and contradictions in the incriminating evidence, for example the contradictions among the testimonies of witnesses or inconsistencies between the statement of the victim and the indictment regarding the acts of the accused. The lawyer may also ask questions to expose serious procedural violations during the investigation process conducted by the investigating officer.

Questioning the juvenile accused who is a drug addict also serves the purpose of clarifying the reasonableness of exculpatory evidence such as proving that the accused did not commit the act as alleged in the indictment, that the act was committed under inducement or coercion, or to prove absence of intent or existence of an alibi. The questioning may also aim to demonstrate that the accused is not yet mature and therefore lacked full awareness of the consequences caused by his or her conduct.

In order to argue for leniency, the lawyer, through questioning, should clarify the causes, conditions, context, motives and purposes of the crime in a way favourable to the accused. It is also necessary to point out the mitigating circumstances and personal characteristics of the juvenile drug-addicted accused, such as the fact that he or she was not the mastermind, the organiser, or the instigator, but merely an accomplice or an accessory. The lawyer may also question to show that the accused did not have determination to commit the crime to the end.

Moreover, questioning should also highlight the mitigating factors and positive personal background of the juvenile offender so that the accused may be entitled to clemency under the law, for example if he or she has good records in study or community participation.

Through the process of questioning, the lawyer also helps the accused juvenile drug addict to become aware that the act he or she committed was a violation of law, an infringement upon the lawful rights and interests of the victim or other parties. At the same time, the accused will be made to understand that legal consequences must be borne under the law.

(2) In case the lawyer protects the victim or another related party:

The lawyer questions in order to clarify the criminal act in the event the accused juvenile drug addict denies the crime. The questioning may also help to clarify the criminal liability of the accused, which may serve as a basis for increasing the degree of criminal liability. The questions by the lawyer should also clarify the damages caused by the criminal act, including physical, psychological, and material damage suffered by the victim or related parties. The lawyer shall demonstrate that the compensation claims are grounded and supported by evidence, and that the accused must bear the responsibility for compensation.

(3) Besides the accused and the victim, the trial may also involve other juveniles such as witnesses.

When questioning a juvenile witness, the lawyer not only serves to protect the interests of his or her client, but also to clarify the facts of the case. Therefore, whether the lawyer represents the accused, the victim or another party, he or she must still apply the necessary and specialised skills when working with juvenile witnesses, so that these individuals can remain calm, confident, and answer the lawyer's questions naturally and truthfully about what they have seen, heard, or known.

The above requirement, and whether lawyers can meet it, is crucial to prevent the juvenile witness from feeling scared, hesitant, or panicked to the point they answer vaguely or provide inaccurate affirmation or denial that distorts the facts. This could cause the case to stray far from the true nature of the legal event. The purpose of questioning a juvenile witness in a trial is to uncover the "story" they experienced.

According to the Child Witness Institute—Judicial Academy (2023a, 2023b), it can be stated that "The main purpose of presenting evidence is to deliver the testimony of the witness in a chronological way so that the parties at trial can understand the story from the witness's point of view." Also, according to the same Institute, "The questioner does not only guide the testimony to include the legal elements of the offence, but also presents the story that happened in order to observe the full picture."

Achieving these purposes is very meaningful in a first-instance trial of drug-addicted juveniles, who are extremely vulnerable to what can be called dual trauma—meaning accumulated suffering: as minors they are immature in psychology and physiology, as drug addicts they are shunned by peers, condemned by society, criticised by their families, placed in detention, and frequently face powerful investigating bodies and procedural actors. This creates fear in them and makes them easily withdrawn, more likely to answer questions of procedural persons including lawyers without considering what is true or false, only wishing that the trial finishes quickly.

Therefore, having questioning skills means knowing how to ask appropriately. This will help both the lawyer and the trial panel to approach the truth of the case. It ensures that everyone can see clearly what really happened, why it happened, and how to resolve it accordingly.

10.3 Requirements of Questioning Skills for Lawyers in Trials Involving Juvenile Drug Addicts

In order to achieve the goal of approaching the truth of the case and protecting the lawful rights and interests of the client, the lawyer, before conducting questioning, needs to apply several essential measures such as initiating interaction with the person to be questioned, creating an opportunity for them to tell their story freely, then proceeding to necessary questions, and finally ending the questioning process. Therefore, before starting the questioning activity, the lawyer should make subtle observations about the child's expressions and behaviour. According to Pham Thi Bich Hao (2023):

> When questioning children, it is necessary to ask clear questions that help them provide accurate answers. Words should be simple and easy to understand, preferably the kind of vocabulary normally used by grandparents or parents at home. Attention should be paid to children who show signs such as clinging to their parents, avoiding eye contact with

strangers, or crying when facing unfamiliar people. Appropriate methods should be applied from the very beginning in order to make the child feel safe and comfortable to speak, share and express their thoughts, which allows the lawyer to collect essential evidence.

– *Skill of the Lawyer in Creating Interaction with Juvenile Drug Addicts*

Before conducting the questioning in the procedural process, the lawyer should begin by building interaction with the juvenile subject in the case. This is to initiate the process in such a way that the minor feels comfortable, relaxed, and ready to cooperate. This process may take only a few minutes and involves the application of age-appropriate and delicate communication techniques. The purpose is to help the minor overcome the initial psychological barriers when facing a courtroom full of people, many of whom are in positions of authority and may be accusing or judging them, and who may impose adverse judicial measures if they are not satisfied with the responses.

Thus, creating interaction through simple and everyday questions will help the juvenile feel that the questions are easy to answer and will quickly reduce fear and hesitation, allowing the minor to actively engage in the questioning process.

In reality, in most trials involving juvenile offenders at the Family and Juvenile Court in Vietnam in recent years, those who conduct proceedings or participate in proceedings often do not have prior interaction with the juvenile being questioned, or if they do, it is not done in an appropriate way. As a result, the minor may not feel sufficiently comfortable to respond. Usually, with only a few cold and indifferent questions, the trial panel, the procurator, and other procedural participants begin what becomes a harsh interrogation, forcing the minor to recount details of the legal event they were involved in.

For instance, in one case involving a juvenile defendant, the lawyer protecting the victim questioned a 14-year-old defendant as follows (Situation 1):

Lawyer for the victim	You are already 14 years old, right?
Defendant	(No answer, looking down)
Guardian of the defendant	Sir, I believe that has already been established. He has told the investigation agency that he is 14
Lawyer for the victim	Yes, but I still want to ask him again to confirm that. Is it correct that you are 14?
Defendant	Yes
Lawyer for the victim	I heard that you have not been attending school regularly recently, is that true?
Defendant	Yes
Lawyer for the victim	What do you know about marijuana? How many times have you used it?
Defendant	(Fidgeting with shirt, looking down, no answer)
Guardian of the defendant	Sir, the child has stated to the investigation agency that he used it five times

(continued)

(continued)

Lawyer for the victim	Was it five times or more? And with whom did you use it?

From the questioning activity above, several strengths and weaknesses can be observed:

(1) Although the lawyer used a more familiar term like "you" instead of calling the child "the defendant," which is a friendly gesture, overall the interaction was still insufficient and not age-appropriate; (2) When the lawyer asked about the age of the defendant, the minor was confused, not knowing the purpose of the question, and therefore remained silent, which is a natural defensive reaction; (3) The guardian answering on behalf of the minor reinforced the child's passive position, encouraging him to rely on previous statements and avoid direct engagement; (4) The lawyer's insistence on asking about age may have given the impression that the child was not being trusted, leading to increased anxiety and fear; (5) Asking about school attendance may have triggered feelings of compounded guilt. The child was already struggling with drug use, which is disapproved of by family, school, and society, and now also felt accused of violating school discipline. This may have made him retreat further; (6) The question "What do you know about marijuana?" is conceptually difficult. Even for adults, this kind of question can be confusing. For a 14-year-old, this question is even harder and leads naturally to hesitation and silence. The guardian answering on behalf of the child gives the impression that the guardian already knows everything and can speak for the child, further reinforcing the child's passivity and reluctance to communicate with the lawyer and others.

With questioning techniques like these, it is difficult to achieve the goal of accessing the factual truth of the legal event. In fact, the truth may be distorted. The lawyer in this case did not initiate the necessary interaction with the juvenile defendant, and therefore failed to create a friendly, comfortable, and controllable environment for effective questioning.

Also participating in the questioning during the trial, the lawyer protecting the rights and interests of the juvenile defendant proceeded as follows (Situation 2):

The lawyer defending the juvenile accused	You should feel confident and relaxed. You do not need to worry or be afraid when I and the other uncles and aunties here ask you a few questions, okay? I see that you are fidgeting with your shirt. Are you worried about something?
Defendant	No, I am fine
The lawyer defending the juvenile accused	Good. Do you have an older brother or sister, Nam?
Defendant	I have a younger sibling
The lawyer defending the juvenile accused	Oh, so you are the elder brother. Is your sibling a boy or a girl?
Defendant	A younger sister

(continued)

(continued)

The lawyer defending the juvenile accused	What is your sister's name? I bet she likes to play with her big brother a lot, right?
Defendant	Her name is Lan. Sometimes she clings to me playfully
The lawyer defending the juvenile accused	How old is your sister? What grade is she in, Nam?
Defendant	She is five. She is in senior kindergarten
The lawyer defending the juvenile accused	Oh, so she is still very young and must be very cute. What is the name of her school?
Defendant	It is Smile Kid Kindergarten
The lawyer defending the juvenile accused	I know that school. My child also studies there And which school do you attend?
Defendant	Nguyen Hue Primary School
The lawyer defending the juvenile accused	Ah, now I remember. You told me that before, but I forgot. I am sorry. What is your favourite subject at school?
Defendant	I like physical education the most
The lawyer defending the juvenile accused	Good. Which sport do you play?
Defendant	I signed up for basketball
The lawyer defending the juvenile accused	Excellent. I also like that sport because it promotes teamwork and you get to stretch and jump high a lot How many people are in your basketball team?
Defendant	Each team has three or five players. My team has five
The lawyer defending the juvenile accused	Good. Thank you for sharing all that with me. When we have time, I hope we can talk more about your basketball team and your teammates. I believe there are many interesting things we can exchange about that. For now, I and everyone here really want to hear from you about what happened that day with you and your friends. Please believe that I am always here with you, I trust you, and I am ready to listen to whatever you want to share

This dialogue shows that the lawyer protecting the rights of the accused juvenile in the trial of a drug-addicted child: (1) engaged in friendly interaction through very simple, everyday, natural, and easy-to-answer questions, which are appropriate to the psychological characteristics of the age group; (2) did not begin by leading the child into legal declarations about guilt, but rather created a comfortable and trusting atmosphere for the child to begin recounting the story of their own experience. This makes it easier for the child to describe the legal event in detail, which may be essential for the court to consider the facts and decide issues related to the rights of the child and other persons; (3) from the beginning, the lawyer calmed the juvenile accused upon noticing signs of temporary psychological disturbance, demonstrating careful observation and an empathetic attitude; (4) asked about the accused's younger sister, her age, personality, and school. These are questions that are almost certain to be easy for the juvenile to answer correctly, creating confidence; (5) when the lawyer asked about the name of the accused's school and pretended to forget, then apologized, this served as a subtle gesture. It signalled to the juvenile that adults too can make mistakes, not just the accused. This may increase the juvenile's sense of trust in the lawyer; (6) the story about basketball and the promise of continuing to share more about the sport and the team completely won the goodwill of the accused; (7) the lawyer's subtlety is also shown by the fact that during this entire warm-up interaction, there was no mention of marijuana or the act of drug use. Therefore, the accused did not feel scrutinized or judged about the violation and was more willing to start telling the story of what they had experienced.

- *The Lawyer's Skill in Creating the Opportunity for the Juvenile to Tell the Story in the Most Natural Way*

The appropriate interaction created a friendly atmosphere and gained the goodwill of the juvenile accused. This helped the court and the lawyer to move into a new phase—the phase where the person who experienced the event recounts what happened, with natural details, without psychological pressure from the presence of many people. This is an ideal condition for a trial that needs to collect evidence from the testimony of the accused, the victim, and others involved. Taking a little time to build friendly interaction allows the juvenile to recall the incident and narrate it in the order in which it occurred. Ideally, the child will describe the incident clearly and coherently, but in reality, there will be moments when the story is fragmented, disordered, or lengthy. This is inevitable, as the child is still at an age not fully developed in every aspect and is speaking in front of many people. Therefore, the lawyer's effort in friendly interaction must continue to support the child in focusing on the necessary core of the event. When observing that the child shows signs such as hesitation, nervousness, or shortness of breath, the lawyer should respond with continued friendly engagement. For example, asking caring questions such as "Are you feeling okay?" or "Would you like to take a short break to feel more comfortable?" can be very helpful.

- *Direct Questioning Skills of the Lawyer on Issues of Interest that the Drug-addicted Child Defendant Has Not Yet Mentioned or Has Mentioned but Without Clarity*

When narrating, the storyteller may have a tendency to focus only on a particular individual that they are concerned about or have the strongest impression of, while there may be other persons whose conduct is also relevant and in which the lawyer has a strong interest to clarify necessary matters. At that point, the lawyer should help the storyteller focus on the important issues by asking specific questions, but it is necessary to avoid making them feel abrupt. Therefore, the lawyer should use questions for pausing and shifting direction such as "Thank you for talking in detail about A, now can you tell me what happened with B?" or "Would you mind if I ask what you and C were doing at that time? May I ask you a few other questions?". Such technical questions not only reassure the psychology of the person telling the story but also help them to arrange the events in the order they occurred and to respond to the lawyer's purpose.

Even when the drug-addicted child defendant is given the opportunity to narrate the event, the information they provide can sometimes be too lengthy and scattered or too brief, which may prevent the listener from determining clearly the circumstances of the legal event. Therefore, the lawyer may need to ask further questions to clarify the necessary details. However, the lawyer must continue to help the minor overcome the barriers of social knowledge, language, or the ability to express in words what they have experienced, by telling them about the difficulty the lawyer is facing, for example "Nam, please note that I was not present at the place where the incident you experienced took place, so it is quite difficult for me to understand it fully, right? Can you kindly tell me this particular matter that you have mentioned?". The lawyer must also pay attention to assessing whether the person answering the question has answered correctly and has actually understood the question. If there is doubt about the quality of the question, the lawyer may say "If my question is difficult for you to understand, please tell me so I can ask it in another way, is that okay? Thank you for helping me."

To make the questioning most effective, the lawyer should use varied types of questions, which can be in the form of open-ended or closed-ended, in order to collect as much necessary information as possible. However, when seeing that the storyteller appears to be going off track or lacking focus, the lawyer can assist them by suggesting the matter to be clarified. For example, an open-ended question could be "Nam, can you tell me what D was doing at that time? You said D went into the room, so after that what did D and you do?". A closed-ended example could be "As you just said, after D entered the room, D gave you a small package or a bag." With such specific open and closed questions, the lawyer can collect a significant amount of necessary information to serve the defence work in the trial.

This questioning technique shows that the lawyer avoids mentioning sensitive words with a drug-addicted child defendant or any minor participating in the first-instance trial of a drug-addicted child, such as narcotics, marijuana, methamphetamine, smoking, inhaling, injecting, and so on, which can make them feel shy or guilty. This approach ensures they will narrate in the most specific, detailed, and truthful way possible what they have experienced and what the lawyer needs to ask. Using terms like "package" or "bag" also avoids mentioning what substance is inside, which might cause unease or embarrassment for the minor. Of course, in a trial for a prohibited substance such as narcotics, the investigating body has already determined through assessment what was inside the package or bag, so there is no need to use sensitive words in questioning the minor.

- *Interaction Skills of the Lawyer with the Drug-Addicted Child Defendant to Conclude the Questioning*

After the drug-addicted child defendant has narrated their story and answered all the supplementary questions from the lawyer, the lawyer may conclude their part of the questioning. However, this does not mean that the questioning has ended, since other lawyers and other procedural actors may continue. To help the child defendant continue answering subsequent questions from others, before ending their questioning the lawyer should continue friendly interaction by thanking them and explaining what will happen next, for example "Thank you, I have finished asking about the matters I was concerned with. I really appreciate your cooperation. Now, the lawyer for the victim and the other parties may ask you some questions about matters they are concerned about, but only to confirm that they have understood your story. Is that okay, Nam? Would you like to rest for a while before continuing?". Ending the questioning with friendly interaction helps the minor to feel more comfortable before working with other lawyers or procedural actors. It also creates conditions for the next lawyer to interact more effectively with the minor. The next lawyer or procedural actor, regardless of whose interests they are protecting, should also continue to apply friendly measures with the minor to achieve effective questioning and ensure that the person answering works in a child-friendly judicial environment, a friendly trial.

As seen in the questioning table from Situation 1, it reflects the current common practice that during participation in trials, lawyers have not yet applied child-friendly justice for minors. From the objective of participating in a trial to protect the rights and interests of their client and the constant desire to control evidence sources, especially from testimony at trial, lawyers often want to ask leading questions on details favourable to their client and do not want to spend much time listening to a narrative that might be unfavourable. As a result, lawyers and even other procedural actors often skip the friendly interaction and the opportunity for the minor to give a truthful account of the event, or they do not ask questions suited to the psychology of the age group. In contrast, the trial panel aims to approach the most truthful version of events, so friendly interaction and the opportunity for minors such as the defendant, the victim, or the witness in a trial of a drug-addicted child to tell the story are important. The trial panel should clearly express its view that lawyers and other procedural actors must apply age-appropriate friendly skills so that this group experiences the trial with the most positive feelings, and so that psychological impacts on their testimony are minimised. This ensures that the court's judgment is on the right person and the right matter, guarantees the rights of minors in criminal proceedings, and also supports their reintegration into the community afterward, preventing unnecessary psychological harm that could have long-term social consequences.

10.4 Some Recommendations for the State of Vietnam

In absorbing the international standards set out in General Comment No. 10 of the UNCRC, it is important to promote the application of appropriate judicial measures for children in conflict with the law, including the right to a fair trial, with legal assistance from a lawyer or other persons possessing the necessary skills and experience. The Law on Juvenile Justice No. 59/2024/QH15, adopted by the National Assembly of the Socialist Republic of Vietnam and to take effect on 01 January 2026, provides for the assurance of child-friendly procedures for minors. The National Assembly of Vietnam (2024) stipulates: "Procedures involving minors must be simple, friendly, and appropriate to the psychology, age, level of maturity, and cognitive capacity of the minor" (Article 6). This constitutes an important legal basis to guarantee the rights of minors in legal proceedings. However, to ensure that this law truly meets the objective of protecting the rights of minors in legal proceedings, apart from ensuring facilities that meet international standards, the State of Vietnam should continue to promote the following measures:

- In the long term, it is necessary to (1) train legal professionals with in-depth understanding of procedures involving minors, and an understanding of the psychology of minors in each different age group. Specifically, juvenile justice should be included in the curriculum of legal training at all levels (college, university, postgraduate). It should also be considered in other training programs such as Social Work, Psychology, and Youth Work to ensure a team of professionals who are knowledgeable in juvenile justice and in procedural processes that guarantee their basic rights under the law and in conformity with international standards. In professional legal training (lawyer, judge, procurator), all training institutions should include juvenile-friendly justice as a compulsory subject; (2) review the law training curricula and both theoretical and practical materials of law education and legal profession training, in order to supplement an adequate amount of knowledge and skills on juvenile-friendly justice. Currently, in the High-Quality Lawyer Training Program of the Judicial Academy (2023a, 2023b, pp. 26–27) and in the Lawyer Training Program by Credit System of the Judicial Academy (2023a, 2023b, pp. 31–32), there is an elective Module 10 on Skills for Participation in Handling Cases Involving Persons Under 18. However, there is still no specific textbook for this subject. In Sect. 2.5 on Skills for Detecting Procedural Violations by the Investigator and Making Requests and Proposals, in the textbook on Skills of the Lawyer in Handling Criminal Cases (Compulsory Training), only a brief reference is made to ordinary questioning skills in all cases without presenting the specific questioning skills needed for minors:

  > For a person in custody or a suspect under 18 years of age, the lawyer must ask clearly whether they have a guardian, whether the guardian was present during the interrogation, and whether the guardian signed the interrogation minutes, since according to the Criminal Procedure Code, when interrogating a minor from full 14 to under 16 years of age, or a person with a physical or mental disability, the representative must be present and has the right to sign the minutes. (Judicial Academy, 2020, p. 81)

  In the textbook on Skills of Judges, Procurators, and Lawyers in Handling Criminal Cases (Elective Training) of the Judicial Academy (2019), there is still no discussion of the skills of these judicial and auxiliary judicial positions when working with minors. In the undergraduate law curriculum of the Vietnam Women's Academy (2021, p. 4), there is a subject on Law on the Rights of the Child, but it is placed among elective supplementary subjects. The fact that courses related to minors are placed as electives in both theoretical and professional legal training demonstrates that there has not yet been a proper recognition of the role of juvenile-friendly justice; (3) conduct research on the juvenile drug court model with a view to establishing a specialised court for this group, due to the benefits it brings, namely "promoting the development of socially friendly skills and capacities… providing a wide range of services at reasonable costs to participants and creating opportunities to engage with external agencies… involving both the family and the juvenile in the adjudication process in the drug court" (Deborah Koetzle Shaffer, 2006, pp. 32–35); (4) in addition to enhancing the effectiveness of juvenile-friendly justice, it is necessary to research and issue legal normative documents aimed at improving the awareness and commitment to compliance of lawyers (and other judicial positions) regarding medical treatment for drug-addicted children during and after proceedings, as recommended by ncjfcj.org (2019): "NCJFCJ recommends that juvenile court judges, family judges, lawyers, and stakeholders comply with the Department of Justice's guidance on ensuring appropriate access to and use of prescribed MAT." Implementing this effectively is itself a step toward the beginning of juvenile-friendly justice; (5) alongside promoting juvenile-friendly justice, research and evaluation activities should be strengthened to assess the effectiveness of the Program on Prevention and Control of Drug Use Among Youth to 2030 under Decision No. 140/QD-TTg of 2024 by the Prime Minister; the suitability of Ordinance No. 01/2022/UBTVQH15 on the procedures for the People's Court to consider and decide on sending drug addicts from full 12 to under 18 years of age to compulsory rehabilitation facilities; the standard practices of adjudication by Family and Juvenile Courts, so as to draw lessons and develop appropriate solutions, considering this as "testing a relatively effective strategy to improve the capacity of juvenile drug courts (JDC) to reduce adolescent substance use and criminal behaviour by integrating components of evidence-based treatment into their existing services" (Henggeler et al., 2012).

These long-term measures embody the principle to "identify appropriate steps to create across the country a range of educational and alternative measures at the stages of investigation, prosecution, adjudication, and enforcement, in order to prevent reoffending and promote the reintegration into society of children who have committed offences" (Crights, 2011, p. 794).

- In the immediate term, it is necessary to provide short-term training or capacity building on juvenile-friendly knowledge and skills for judicial officers of the Court, the Procuracy, investigators of the Investigation Agency, civil status–judicial officers of the commune-level People's Committee, and social work officials, in a way that approaches international standards.
- It is also necessary to further promote the equipping of knowledge and skills on juvenile-friendly justice in the current lawyer profession through short-term courses to improve their ability to work effectively with minors in trials. This task should be carried out by the Ministry of Justice or the Vietnam Bar Federation as part of the annual lawyer training program.

10.5 Conclusion

The questioning skills of the lawyer in the first-instance trial of a drug-addicted child defendant are a form of specialised skills applied to one of the most vulnerable groups in society, which is children. Addressing this skill is an elevation of the role of lawyer questioning in cases involving minors. Minors are inherently vulnerable, and for children who are drug addicts, their vulnerability is even greater due to heavier pressures from the stigma of family, friends, and the community. Therefore, in the context of the increasing number and the decreasing age of drug addicts, this is a group that requires special attention from the State and society, with the objective that caring for children means caring for the future of the country and of the world, and limiting negative consequences in the future. At the same time, emphasising the questioning skills of the lawyer in the first-instance trial of a drug-addicted child defendant is also a demonstration of the humanitarian and humane spirit of a civilised society that always pays attention to human rights, and is an indicator of the effectiveness of the protection of the rights of the child in the sphere of criminal justice.

References

Child Witness Institute—Judicial Academy. (2023). *Strengthening Access to Justice for Child Victims of Abuse, Advanced Module* (p. 78).

fortbehavioral-com. (2022). https://fortbehavioral-com.translate.goog/addiction-recovery-blog/5-causes-teen-drug-use/?_x_tr_sl=en&_x_tr_tl=vi&_x_tr_hl=vi&_x_tr_pto=sc. Accessed 01 May 2025.

Holovanova, I. A., & Okhrimenko, I. M. (2024). *Motivational Factors in the Formation of Youth Drug Addiction.* https://womab.com.ua/en/smb-2024-01/10068. Accessed 5 June 2025.

Human Rights Research Centre (Crights). (2011). *Introduction to International Instruments on Human Rights.* Labour and Social Publishing House.

https://fortbehavioral-com.translate.goog/addiction-recovery-blog/5-causes-teen-drug-use/?_x_tr_sl=en&_x_tr_tl=vi&_x_tr_hl=vi&_x_tr_pto=sc. Download 5 January 2025.

Judicial Academy. (2019). Textbook on Skills of Judges, Procurators, and Lawyers in Handling Criminal Cases (Elective Training).

Judicial Academy. (2020). Textbook on Skills of Lawyers in Handling Criminal Cases (Compulsory Training).

Judicial Academy. (2023a). Decision No. 885/QD-HVTP dated 11 May 2023 of the Director of the Judicial Academy on the Issuance of the Detailed Curriculum for the High-Quality Lawyer Training Programme by Credit System.

Judicial Academy. (2023b). Decision No. 79/QD-HVTP dated 27 January 2023 of the Director of the Judicial Academy on the Issuance of the Detailed Curriculum for the Lawyer Training Programme by Credit System.

National institute on drug abuse. (2020). *Drug Misuse and Addiction.* https://nida-nih-gov.translate.goog/publications/drugs-brains-behavior-science-addiction/drug-misuse-addiction?_x_tr_sl=en&_x_tr_tl=vi&_x_tr_hl=vi&_x_tr_pto=sc. Accessed 25 June 2025.

National Assembly of Vietnam. (2000, 2008, 2021). *Law on Prevention and Control of Narcotics.*

National Assembly of Vietnam. (2024). Law on Juvenile Justice 2024.

Nguyễn, H., & Quang, H. (2022). https://vov.vn/emagazine/cai-nghien-tre-tu-12-den-duoi-18-tuoi-tram-be-kho-khan-943268.vov#:~:text=%C3%94ng%20Tr%E1%BA%A7n%20Ng%E1%BB%8Dc%20T%C3%BAy%3A%20Theo,ma%20t%C3%BAy%20l%C3%A0%20743%20em

ncjfcj.org. (2019). *Resolution on Access to Medication-Assisted Treatment (MAT) for Adolescents and Adults in the Juvenile and Family Justice System.* https://ncjfcj.org/wp-content/uploads/2019/12/NCJFCJ_MATResolution_10-2019_finalApproved_508Compl.pdf. Accessed 02 July 2025.

PV. (2024). https://congan.com.vn/vu-an/phong-chong-ma-tuy/nguoi-su-dung-ma-tuy-co-xu-huong-tre-hoa-tu-12-30-tuoi-chiem-den-446_170232.html. Accessed 08 May 2025.

Pham, T. B. H. (2023). *Skills of Lawyers When Interacting with Children as Victims in Criminal Cases*. https://lsvn.vn/ky-nang-cua-luat-su-khi-tiep-xuc-voi-tre-em-la-bi-hai-trong-vu-an-hinh-su-1675858747-a127559.html. Accessed 19 May 2025.

Quyen, V. T. (2022). *Juveniles Charged in Criminal Proceedings Under International Law and Vietnamese Law*. https://tapchitoaan.vn/nguoi-chua-thanh-nien-bi-buoc-toi-trong-to-tung-hinh-su-theo-phap-luat-quoc-te-va-phap-luat-viet-nam6935.html. Accessed 29 June 2025.

Standing Committee of the National Assembly. (2022). Ordinance No. 01/2022/UBTVQH15 on the Procedures for the People's Court to Consider and Decide on Sending Drug Addicts from Full 12 to Under 18 Years Old to Compulsory Rehabilitation Facilities.

Shaffer, D. K. (2006). *Reconsidering Drug Court Effectiveness: A Meta-Analytic Review*. https://etd.ohiolink.edu/acprod/odb_etd/ws/send_file/send?accession=ucin1152549096&disposition=inline

Scott, W. H., McCart, M. R., Cunningham, P. B., & Chapman, J. E. (2012). *Enhancing the Effectiveness of Juvenile drug Courts by Integrating Evidence-Based Practices*. https://pubmed-ncbi-nlm-nih-gov.translate.goog/22309470/. Accessed 02 July 2025.

TTXVN. (2024). *Report of the Police: The Age of Drug Users in Vietnam is Increasingly Younger*. https://tuoitre.vn/bao-cao-cua-cong-an-do-tuoi-su-dung-ma-tuy-tai-viet-nam-ngay-cang-tre-hon-20241015202252309.htm. Accessed 01 May 2025.

UNCRC. (2007). *General Comment No. 10 Children's Rights in Juvenile Justice*. https://www.right-to-education.org/sites/right-to-education.org/files/resource-attachments/CRC_General_Comment_10.pdf. Accessed 02 July 2025.

Vietnam Women's Academy. (2021). Decision No. 651A/QD-HVPNVN dated 27 September 2021 on the Approval and Issuance of the Undergraduate Law Programme.

vksnd.gialai.gov.vn. (2022). https://vksnd.gialai.gov.vn/Nghien-cuu-Trao-doi/nghien-ma-tuy-o-lua-tuoi-thanh-thieu-nien-la-tai-hoa-cua-xa-hoi-hien-dai-va-can-co-giai-phap-de-phong-ngua-2224.html. Accessed 08 May 2025.

Chapter 11
Child-Friendly Justice for Child Victims in First-Instance Criminal Proceedings in Vietnam

Hieu Thi Ngoc Tran

Abstract The protection of child victims' rights in criminal proceedings in general, and in the first-instance stage in particular, is a matter of significant importance in both legal theory and practice. Vietnamese law provides certain provisions to ensure the rights of child victims; however, there remain shortcomings in the legal framework and difficulties in implementation. Based on an analysis of the legal regulations on child-friendly justice for child victims in first-instance criminal proceedings and their application in practice, this article proposes solutions to improve the law and strengthen its enforcement, thereby ensuring the best possible protection for child victims in first-instance criminal proceedings.

11.1 Introduction

In recent years, Viet Nam's legal system has made positive progress in protecting the rights of children, especially those who are victims in criminal cases. Children, due to their specific psychological and physical characteristics, are highly vulnerable and require special safeguards during criminal proceedings, particularly at the first-instance stage where public adversarial hearings are conducted, and the judgment is rendered. Vietnamese criminal procedure law includes numerous provisions to protect the rights of child victims in this stage. The enactment of the 2024 Juvenile Justice Law is of particular significance in building a child-friendly, humane justice system adapted to the psychological and developmental characteristics of children. Nevertheless, practical application still faces challenges that require attention and improvement. The pressing issue is how to ensure that the provisions on child-friendly justice for child victims are effectively enforced, securing their full rights in

Article history: Received 18 April 2025; Revised 19 July 2025; Accepted 22 August 2025.

H. T. N. Tran (✉)
Tra Vinh University, Vinh Long Province, Viet Nam
e-mail: ttnhieu@tvu.edu.vn

N. Binh An et al. (eds.), *The Future of Child-Friendly Justice and Children's Rights in Vietnam*, https://doi.org/10.1007/978-981-95-3521-7_11

first-instance criminal proceedings while addressing the existing legal gaps in their protection.

11.2 Theoretical Basis of Child-Friendly Justice for Child Victims in First-Instance Criminal Proceedings

11.2.1 Concept and Characteristics of Child Victims in First-Instance Criminal Proceedings

11.2.1.1 Concept of Child Victims

A first-instance criminal trial is "the central stage of the proceedings, where the court's independence and objectivity are exercised through a public and fair adjudication of the criminal case for the first time before the law" (Nguyen Ngoc Chi, 2020). At this stage, the court has the authority to adjudicate, evaluate evidence publicly, and clarify the objective truth of the case, thereby "establishing social justice at the first point where the case is brought before the public with the participation of the parties on an equal footing" (Tran, 2018). This is a decisive stage in criminal procedure, demonstrating most clearly the court's role in resolving a case in an objective and lawful manner while protecting the fundamental rights of citizens. Proper, strict, and humane conduct of first-instance criminal trials forms the foundation for public trust in the criminal justice system.

According to Article 62(1) of the Criminal Procedure Code 2015 (amended 2021), "A victim is an individual who has suffered direct physical, mental, or property damage, or an agency or organization that has suffered property damage or harm to its reputation due to a crime or a threat of crime." A victim is thus a procedural participant with specific rights and obligations, including the right to present testimony, request protection of their lawful interests, claim compensation for damages, and participate in procedural activities.

Determining the status of a child victim is not only a technical legal matter but also reflects a deeper theoretical approach to human rights protection, particularly for vulnerable groups. From a legal science perspective, scholars have examined this concept from multiple angles to clarify procedural standing and the special protection needs of children. For example, "Children who are victims in criminal proceedings should be regarded not only as individuals who have suffered harm but as the focal point of protective mechanisms in the process of restoring justice. Procedural design must prioritize humanitarian and psychological considerations while avoiding secondary victimization" (Nguyen Ngoc Anh, 2021). Another view asserts that "The rights of child victims must be based on a rights-based approach, ensuring their participation in proceedings in safe conditions with adequate legal, psychological, and counseling support" (Nguyen Thi Phuong Hoa, 2020).

From an international perspective, UNICEF warns that "The justice systems of many countries are not designed to align with the socio-psychological development of child victims, resulting in risks of serious mental harm and even re-victimization during proceedings" (UNICEF, 2018). The United Nations has also developed several international reference standards, such as the 1989 Convention on the Rights of the Child, the 1985 Beijing Rules, and the 2010 Guidelines on Child-Friendly Justice.

Consistent with the 1989 Convention on the Rights of the Child, to which Viet Nam is a State Party, "a child means every human being below the age of eighteen years unless under the law applicable to the child, majority is attained earlier" (United Nations, 1989, Article 1). Article 21(1) of the Civil Code 2015 defines a minor as a person under eighteen years of age, while Article 1 of the 2016 Law on Children defines children as persons under sixteen years of age. In Vietnamese criminal procedure practice, friendly procedures, lawful representation, and special protective measures are applied to minors who are victims of crimes affecting their dignity, honor, health, or life. Thus, *a child victim may be understood as a person under eighteen years of age who has suffered harm caused by a criminal act and who is entitled to special procedural protection adapted to their age, psychological condition, and cognitive capacity.*

11.2.1.2 Characteristics of Child Victims in First-Instance Criminal Proceedings

In criminal proceedings, child victims are a special category requiring attention and protection through dedicated legal mechanisms. Their main characteristics include:

Firstly, when participating as victims, children often have difficulties in recalling, remembering, and narrating events. Due to incomplete psychological and physiological development, they may struggle to remember details accurately and to present them clearly, coherently, and consistently. With limited life experience, when harmed by crime, children "are more severely traumatized, more easily collapse, and lose orientation more quickly than adults" (Le Lan Chi, 2022).

Secondly, they are easily influenced by their surroundings. Children may be swayed by adults' words and actions when giving testimony and may have difficulty maintaining their stance or expressing their views. Particularly when entering the criminal justice process, they may not fully understand their rights and obligations as procedural participants, nor be aware enough to assert those rights.

Thirdly, courts must apply special procedural measures in cases involving child victims. For cases of sexual abuse, violence, or incidents that significantly affect the dignity, honor, and development of children, the court must hold closed hearings to protect the child's identity and avoid psychological harm. Restrictions on media coverage, recording, broadcasting, or detailed reporting of the child's testimony are strictly enforced.

Fourthly, child victims receive special protection during proceedings. When conducting procedural activities involving child victims, competent authorities must ensure that all their lawful rights and interests are protected. For example, the court may summon a child victim to participate in the trial if necessary, but should arrange a child-friendly courtroom (if available) or a separate room with a screen, indirect audio or video link to prevent direct confrontation with the defendant. The presence of a lawful representative or a legal advocate for the child must be ensured throughout the trial.

Fifthly, psychological or expert support must be provided when necessary. During proceedings, child victims may be assisted by social workers, psychologists, or child protection officers to safeguard their rights and avoid unnecessary pressure.

11.2.2 Theoretical Foundations of Child-Friendly Justice

Children are a distinctive group in society whose physical, mental, and legal cognitive development remains incomplete. When participating in first-instance criminal proceedings as victims, they require access to a justice system appropriate to their age and psychological condition. From this need, the concept of "child-friendly justice" emerged and has gained increasing prominence in criminal justice reform. UNICEF and UNODC define child-friendly justice as a justice system that "ensures children are treated with respect, fairness, and without discrimination; safeguards the best interests of the child in all stages of proceedings; guarantees appropriate participation of children in legal processes; and minimizes the potential negative impact of the justice system on them" (UNODC & UNICEF, 2015). Child-friendly justice not only embodies humanitarian values but also serves as a foundation for building a fair legal system adapted to the developmental characteristics of children.

The theoretical basis of child-friendly justice for children is reflected in the following core principles: (1) Ensuring the best interests of the child. Every judicial decision concerning children must give primary consideration to their physical, mental, and social development (United Nations, 1989, Article 3). (2) Ensuring the right to participate. Children have the right to be heard and to express their views on matters affecting them, in a manner consistent with their age and maturity (United Nations, 1989, Article 12). Child-friendly justice facilitates a safe and voluntary environment for such participation. (3) Non-discrimination. All children must be treated equally in accessing and participating in criminal proceedings, without discrimination based on gender, ethnicity, religion, family circumstances, health status, or any other characteristic (United Nations, 1989, Article 2). Guaranteeing equality before the law for all citizens, and for child victims in particular, constitutes "the respect for, protection of, and assurance of the equal rights of the prosecuting and defending parties by competent procedural authorities, in which the presiding judge plays a decisive role in establishing the basis for lawful judgments in the interest of justice" (Hoang Hung Hai, 2015). (4) Protection of privacy and dignity. The justice system must respect and protect the privacy of children, ensuring that procedural measures do not compromise their honor, dignity, or future (United Nations, 1989, Article 16). (5) Child-friendly and fair procedures. A fair and child-friendly justice system is not limited to determining right or wrong but is also a place where children feel respected, supported, and genuinely protected. This includes support from judicial officers trained in child matters, a trial environment adapted for children, and the use of understandable language (Council of Europe, 2010).

In Viet Nam, these principles are reflected through child protection policies and codified in the Law on Children, the Criminal Procedure Code, and the Juvenile Justice Law. Child-friendly justice is no longer only a theoretical concept but has become a normative standard in modern legal reform. Building a justice system that protects the best interests of children reflects not only legal responsibility but also ethical and humanitarian values within a rule-of-law state. This principle is rooted in the respect for the human rights of children, who possess full legal and personal rights and must be protected throughout the criminal process as any adult would be. The Convention on the Rights of the Child affirms that "In all actions concerning children, whether undertaken by public or private social welfare institutions, courts of law, administrative authorities, or legislative bodies, the best interests of the child shall be a primary consideration" (United Nations, 1989, Article 3). In first-instance criminal proceedings involving child victims, any judicial decision affecting them must assess what is best for their comprehensive physical, mental, moral, and social development; prioritize their rights to life, protection, and to be heard; and avoid any action, procedure, or decision that could cause them harm.

11.3 Vietnamese Legal Provisions on Protecting the Rights of Child Victims in First-Instance Criminal Proceedings

11.3.1 The Right to Have a Lawful Representative in Proceedings

Vietnamese law provides specific regulations on the lawful representation of child victims. Article 9 of the 2024 Juvenile Justice Law expressly affirms the right of persons under eighteen years of age to have a lawful representative in criminal proceedings: "A minor is guaranteed the presence of a representative during the settlement of the matter or case." Furthermore, Clause 1 of Article 3 of Joint Circular No. 06/2018/TTLT-VKSNDTC-TANDTC-BCA-BTP-BLĐTBXH stipulates: "The representative of a participant in proceedings who is under eighteen years of age must be a person aged eighteen or older, with full legal capacity and civil act capacity, and must meet the conditions for representation as prescribed in Articles 134, 135, and 136 of the Civil Code. The representative is determined in the following order: biological or adoptive parents; guardian; person appointed by the court."

Accordingly, when children participate in first-instance criminal proceedings, they have the right to a lawful representative—a "substitute voice"—who protects their lawful rights and interests, makes requests, presents arguments, and responds in court on their behalf. Having a lawful representative in proceedings not only ensures procedural compliance but also safeguards the full protection of the child victim's rights, preventing them from facing the pressures and prejudices of the courtroom alone. This also aligns with international legal principles, which require that "every child involved in judicial proceedings is provided the opportunity to be heard, either directly or through a representative or an appropriate body" (United Nations, 1989, Article 12). Additionally, the lawful representative offers psychological and emotional support, aiding in the recovery of the child's personality and in healing physical and mental harm after the criminal act (Le Lan Chi, 2022).

Comparative studies of criminal procedure laws in other jurisdictions reveal a similar approach to guaranteeing the right of child victims to have a lawful representative, consistent with the principles of the 1989 Convention on the Rights of the Child. For example, in the United Kingdom, a child victim may be assigned a special supporter or guardian to ensure their voice is heard in a safe and appropriate environment (UK Government, 1999). In China, the 2018 amendment to the Criminal Procedure Law requires procedural authorities in cases involving child victims to notify the lawful guardian and, if the guardian is unsuitable, to appoint another lawful representative (Standing Committee of the National People's Congress, 2018).

11.3.2 The Right to the Protection of Honor, Dignity, and Confidentiality of Information

Child victims are often involved in crimes such as sexual abuse, domestic violence, school violence, or kidnapping—acts associated with profound physical and psychological harm. The public nature of a trial not only harms the individual but may also reopen psychological wounds within the community. Vietnamese law currently contains detailed provisions to protect the honor, dignity, and confidentiality of information of children when participating in proceedings, as these rights are considered among the "fundamental human rights, reflecting the state of human existence in which each individual is legally guaranteed inviolability of life, health, honor, dignity, and personal liberty" (Trinh Tien Viet, 2015).

Accordingly, Article 5 of the 2015 Criminal Procedure Code stipulates the holding of closed trials to protect the rights of children in general and child victims in particular: "The court shall conduct trials in public, except where it is necessary to keep State secrets, preserve fine customs and traditions… or to protect persons under eighteen years of age…," and Clause 2 Article 13 of the 2024 Juvenile Justice Law states: "The court shall conduct a closed trial in criminal cases involving minors who have been sexually abused or in other special cases where it is necessary to protect minors."

A "closed trial" should not be understood simply as barring the public from attending the hearing but must also ensure measures such as restricting audio and video recording; prohibiting the media from disclosing the child's real identity; and limiting those allowed in the courtroom. However, in practice, there are trials that, despite being held in closed session, still allow personal information to leak to the media, affecting participants in proceedings in general and the rights of child victims in particular.

In addition, Clause 1 Article 13 of the 2024 Juvenile Justice Law provides: "The personal secrets of minors must be respected and protected throughout the process of receiving and handling reports of crimes, initiation of proceedings, investigation, prosecution, trial, diversion, execution of judgments, and reintegration into the community." Clause 11 Article 6 of the 2016 Law on Children prohibits: "Disclosing or revealing information about the private life or personal secrets of children without the consent of the child from the age of seven and above and of the child's parents or guardian." Clauses 5 and 9 of the 2016 Law on the Press also prohibit: "Disclosing information belonging to the category of State secrets, personal privacy, or other secrets as prescribed by law; providing information that affects the normal physical and mental development of children."

Children must have their identities protected throughout the proceedings, not only in law but also by the media and on social networks. These provisions ensure that the honor, dignity, and personal information of child victims are not violated during proceedings.

The legal provisions of some countries also reflect a humanitarian, child-centered approach in modern justice systems. U.S. law protects the identities of child victims by sealing records and using initials or pseudonyms in procedural documents (U.S. Department of Justice, 2020). The Child Protection Law and the Criminal Procedure Law of China both clearly stipulate the confidentiality of personal information and prohibit the media from disclosing the names, images, and addresses of child victims (Standing Committee of the National People's Congress, 2020).

11.3.3 The Right to Psychological Support and Legal Counseling

Children appearing in court often experience "secondary victimization," meaning a second wave of trauma caused by the procedural process, such as being repeatedly questioned or being compelled to give testimony in front of the defendant. Therefore, a child-friendly justice system must provide mechanisms for psychological support. Article 6 of the 2024 Juvenile Justice Law stipulates that procedures for minors must be friendly: "Procedures for minors must be simple, friendly, and suited to the psychology, age, maturity, and cognitive ability of the minor." Article 30 of the 2016 Law on Children also provides that children are entitled to consultation when participating in proceedings: "Children have the right to be protected during proceedings and in the handling of administrative violations; the right to defense and self-defense; the right to have their lawful rights and interests protected; the right to legal aid; the right to present their opinions; the right not to be unlawfully deprived of liberty; the right not to be tortured, coerced, subjected to corporal punishment, insulted in honor and dignity, assaulted physically, subjected to psychological pressure, or subjected to other forms of abuse."

Accordingly, child victims are able to access support services such as psychological counseling and free legal aid throughout the proceedings.

Not only in Viet Nam, the full protection of the mental and legal rights of children in proceedings is a global endeavor. In the United Kingdom, child victims have the right to special measures in a friendly environment, such as the provision of psychological support staff, legal representatives, the use of screens, and the use of recorded testimony (Ministry of Justice, 2020). In China, the Child Protection Law requires procedural authorities to coordinate with community service centers to provide legal advice and psychological care for child victims (Standing Committee of the National People's Congress, 2020).

11.3.4 The Right to Be Tried in a Friendly Environment Appropriate to Age

This is one of the rights of children to access justice, provided for in many international and national legal instruments. A friendly environment is one in which children feel safe, heard, and respected. For child victims, such an environment helps them avoid re-traumatization and promotes the ability to give truthful and accurate testimony. UNODC & UNICEF recommend that in trial environments involving child victims, attention should be given to: "No direct confrontation with the defendant; a separate room for giving testimony via camera; and avoiding the use of complex legal terminology" (UNODC & UNICEF, 2015).

In Viet Nam, the "child-friendly courtroom" model has been implemented since 2017 under the "Enhancing Access to Justice and Protecting the Rights of Children" project carried out by the Supreme People's Court in cooperation with UNICEF Viet Nam, the Ministry of Justice, and the Ministry of Labour, Invalids and Social Affairs. In addition, provisions ensuring the right to be tried in a friendly, age-appropriate environment have been emphasized. Specifically, Article 414 of the 2015 Criminal Procedure Code sets out the principles for conducting proceedings for persons under eighteen years of age, requiring "procedures to be friendly, appropriate to the psychology, age, maturity, and cognitive ability of persons under eighteen years of age," and obliging the court to apply measures to ensure the best interests of the child victim.

Child victims have the right to express their views and present their wishes in a safe space without psychological intimidation. The method of questioning must be age-appropriate and may use friendly interview techniques. At the same time, Article 159 of the 2024 Juvenile Justice Law specifies detailed procedures to best ensure the right to be tried in a friendly environment, requiring the following in cases involving child victims: (1) Limit the summoning of child victims to the trial if it does not affect the resolution of the case. The presiding judge should use their statements in the case file or apply other alternative measures to adjudicate the case. (2) The presiding judge may decide to conduct an online hearing under the law so that the child victim participates from a remote location. (3) Where the child victim participates in the hearing, arrange for them to sit in a separate room and use electronic devices; if a separate room is not available, arrange seating in the courtroom with a partition separating them from the defendant. (4) During the trial, the following must be ensured: First, when questioning, questions must be short, simple, and easy to understand, using language appropriate to the child's age, gender, cognitive ability, and maturity, and avoiding asking about multiple issues at once. Questioning must take into account their family circumstances, psychological state, health, and other specific characteristics. Second, if necessary, diagrams, anatomical models, electronic devices, or other tools may be used to help the child answer questions. The child victim must not be asked to point to parts of their own body. Third, questions that are aggressive, threatening, humiliating, or insulting to the child victim must not be asked. Fourth, the child victim should be given the opportunity to become familiar with and understand the trial process and procedures in advance.

Like Viet Nam, many countries maintain their international commitments to building a friendly and humane justice system for children. In the United Kingdom, child victims are tried in a friendly environment with the support of special measures such as separate rooms for testimony, video recording, the use of simple language, and avoiding direct confrontation with the defendant (Ministry of Justice, 2020). Under China's criminal procedure law, when taking statements from child victims, procedural authorities must assign officers familiar with child psychology and prioritize friendly methods, such as taking statements in places familiar to the child and recording them to avoid repeated questioning (Standing Committee of the National People's Congress, 2020).

11.4 Practical Application of Legal Provisions on Protecting the Rights of Child Victims in First-Instance Criminal Proceedings in Viet Nam

11.4.1 Achievements in the Practical Application of Law

Based on legal provisions ensuring the rights of child victims in first-instance criminal proceedings, practice in recent years shows that many localities have recorded positive results in implementing these provisions, thereby protecting the legitimate rights and interests of child victims in the best possible way. The achievements can be summarized as follows:

First, People's Courts at all levels have gradually adopted child-friendly trial models, in which separate hearings and closed trials in criminal cases involving child victims are increasingly applied. To concretize the policies and guidelines of the Party and the laws of the State, and to institutionalize the provisions of the Constitution on the protection, care, and education of children in general and of child victims in particular, the Family and Juvenile Court model was piloted at the High People's Court in Ho Chi Minh City (28 May 2015) and the High People's Court in Ha Noi (1 June 2015), and then gradually expanded to several provincial People's Courts nationwide. By the end of 2022, the Supreme People's Court had established 40 Family and Juvenile Courts at 38 provincial People's Courts, 2 High People's Courts, and set up the Division for Supervision of Labour, Family, and Juvenile Affairs at the Supreme People's Court (Division III) (Do Thi Hong Van, 2023). This also demonstrates Viet Nam's commitment to respecting international recommendations on ensuring children's rights in criminal proceedings. Accordingly, in cases involving child victims, the courtroom is arranged on a single level, with a roundtable layout, blue-colored walls, and office-style tables and chairs. Child victims participating in proceedings sit next to their lawful representative and their legal counsel. "The courtroom is arranged in this way to reduce tension, prevent psychological stress, and suit the age of minors, in accordance with the 'child-friendly procedure' principle stipulated in the Criminal Procedure Code" (Do Viet, 2023).

Second, in criminal proceedings involving persons under eighteen in general and in first-instance trials with child victims in particular, procedural authorities consistently respect the dignity and protect the personal information of children. The confidentiality of child victims' identities is strictly maintained. The media and judgments involved encode all information relating to the child's real name, image, or identifying details. According to the Supreme People's Court, from July 2020 to June 2023, courts received 7,064 cases involving 7,677 defendants accused of child abuse crimes; 6,755 cases involving 7,318 defendants were resolved and tried, accounting for 95.63% of cases and 95.32% of defendants (PVH, 2023). Some particularly serious cases of abuse against persons under eighteen were promptly and lawfully tried with seriousness and in compliance with the law (Anh Phuong, 2024).

Third, in first-instance criminal trials, child victims are always guaranteed procedural rights such as being informed of their rights through a guardian, lawyer, or social worker. In some trials, children are provided with illustrated diagrams explaining the trial process so that they better understand their role in the case. They may also present their views via recorded video in a private setting to ensure accuracy without causing panic or fear.

Fifth, in recent years, legal and psychological support for child victims in criminal cases in Viet Nam has made significant progress. In many localities, legal aid centers have actively coordinated with procedural authorities and social organizations to promptly support abused children. Organizations such as Hagar International in Viet Nam "are pioneers in assisting those who have experienced violence, abuse, and trafficking, directly providing victims with psychological, medical, cultural, and educational support" (Nguyen Huy, 2023), especially child victims of sexual abuse. Recently, Hagar has made efforts to provide rights and legal counseling to children and their families; prevent re-traumatization before, during, and after their participation in medical and legal procedures and their return to school; and foster trust in justice through meetings between families and local authorities (Nguyen Huy, 2023).

The practical application of law in protecting the rights of child victims in first-instance criminal trials in Viet Nam has progressively improved toward friendliness, humanity, and compliance with international standards. Trial practice has recorded many positive changes, such as the establishment of Family and Juvenile Courts with child-friendly courtrooms, ensuring respect for the dignity, honor, and privacy of child victims, and strengthening legal and psychological support for them.

11.4.2 Limitations and Obstacles

Although the practical application of the law to protect the rights of child victims in first-instance criminal trials has achieved positive results and the legal framework has made considerable progress, implementation still faces some limitations and obstacles that need to be addressed and improved:

First, ensuring the right to have a lawful representative for child victims in first-instance criminal trials in some localities still encounters difficulties. The lawful representative is often the child's parent, but when participating in proceedings, they may not receive thorough guidance on their role in court, or their legal awareness may not be strong enough to fulfill their procedural responsibilities effectively. This significantly affects the protection of the lawful rights and interests of child victims during the trial.

Second, although regulations on organizing child-friendly trials have been issued, their implementation remains slow and has only been carried out in certain localities. As a result, there is a lack of uniformity and consistency, and the best lawful rights and interests of child victims in first-instance criminal trials are not always ensured.

Third, there is a lack of standardized post-trial intervention procedures for persons under eighteen in general and for child victims in particular. At present, most child protection and support processes focus heavily on procedural stages such as investigation, prosecution, and trial. However, after the trial and the pronouncement of the judgment, support for child victims remains very limited. They are at risk of falling into depression, becoming socially isolated, or experiencing re-traumatization due to being "abandoned" after proceedings. The withdrawal of procedural agencies means that child victims in criminal cases are no longer protected within a continuous system. The reasons include the absence of a legal mechanism, a lack of post-trial interagency procedures, and insufficient stable budgets and long-term policies.

Fourth, the lack of specialized professionals in proceedings involving children remains a significant obstacle. For those conducting proceedings, although the law sets out some general competency and responsibility standards, these remain at the level of broad principles without specific and detailed mandatory professional standards or a dedicated training system for procedural officers in areas such as developmental psychology, child-appropriate communication, and questioning methods that avoid causing fear, panic, or trauma. In addition, the team of experts providing procedural support to children is still lacking and not strictly regulated, with little stability or coordination. Psychologists, social workers, and special education experts are not officially integrated into the procedural process; therefore, their participation remains voluntary, lacking binding obligations, which reduces their accountability.

11.5 Recommendations and Solutions for Ensuring Protection

Children are a special group that must be given specific protection when participating in legal proceedings, especially when they take part in first-instance criminal trials as victims. The correct application of legal provisions to protect the rights of child victims in first-instance proceedings not only concretizes the requirements of national law but also fulfills Viet Nam's international commitments. Although the promulgation of the Law on Juvenile Justice in 2024 marks a significant step forward, ensuring the law's effective integration into social life requires synchronized implementation mechanisms, from infrastructure to personnel and procedural frameworks. Therefore, research and proposals for solutions are both necessary and urgent.

First, continue to improve the law and issue detailed guidance on the implementation of provisions related to guaranteeing the rights of child victims in general and of child victims in first-instance proceedings in particular. This should focus on amending and supplementing legal provisions toward concretizing the standards and responsibilities of procedural actors in relation to child victims. In addition, guidance documents for the implementation of the Law on Juvenile Justice 2024 should be promulgated to ensure effective and uniform law enforcement.

Second, provide training and enhance the professional capacity and ethical standards of procedural officers and experts. Organize professional training courses on trial work involving children. Gradually build and improve a specialized cadre for child-related matters in procedural agencies. Accordingly, it is recommended to supplement provisions on the establishment of specialized child units within each procedural authority, composed of individuals trained in child-friendly proceedings, including knowledge of children's psychological development by age group, training in non-leading interview techniques, and familiarity with procedures for supporting child victims. Strengthen the involvement of protectors and support personnel by formalizing the role of expert support, referencing effective models from other jurisdictions.

Third, strengthen monitoring and evaluation of the practical enforcement of laws protecting the rights of child victims in first-instance criminal proceedings by establishing independent and specialized monitoring mechanisms, while enhancing the role of community and media oversight.

Fourth, invest in developing infrastructure to support child-friendly trials in criminal proceedings. Gradually complete the construction of separate courtrooms for cases involving child victims that meet international standards in localities across the country. Increase the availability of technological devices to facilitate child-friendly proceedings, enabling child victims to participate indirectly yet effectively.

This should be included in the medium- and long-term plans of the Government, the Ministry of Justice, the Ministry of Public Security, and the Supreme People's Court for investment in juvenile justice infrastructure.

Fifth, raise public awareness of the law in protecting the rights of child victims. Disseminate basic legal knowledge to children by organizing legal education programs in schools with diverse, active, and accessible content and methods. Provide free legal counseling to parents, guardians, and lawful representatives by establishing free legal counseling hotlines operating continuously and regularly, expanding the network of grassroots law clubs, and organizing periodic community legal awareness events with the participation of legal experts. Strengthen mass media communication to spread societal awareness.

Sixth, establish coordination mechanisms between agencies and units to develop standardized post-trial intervention procedures for child victims, ensuring their rights, recovery, and reintegration.

11.6 Conclusion

Children are a vulnerable group, easily harmed both physically and mentally when participating in criminal proceedings, especially as victims. Protecting the rights of child victims in first-instance criminal trials is the responsibility of procedural actors and society as a whole. Therefore, it is necessary to implement a coordinated set of solutions, including improving the law and issuing implementation guidelines, providing in-depth training for judicial officers and procedural support experts, investing in infrastructure, raising community awareness, and developing standardized post-trial intervention procedures. These measures aim to ensure the substantive and effective protection of the rights of child victims, moving toward a civilized and humane justice system that places human beings at the center of development.

Acknowledgements We acknowledge the support of time and facilities from Tra Vinh University (TVU) for this study.

References

Council of Europe. (2010). *Guidelines of the Committee of Ministers of the Council of Europe on Child-Friendly Justice*. Strasbourg Council of Europe Publishing.

Do, T. H. V. (2023). *Some Difficulties and Obstacles in the Operation of the Family and Juvenile Court*. https://tapchitoaan.vn/mot-so-kho-khan-vuong-mac-trong-hoat-dong-cua-toa-gia-dinh-va-nguoi-chua-thanh-nien9163.html?. [Accessed 02 May 2025].

Do, V. (2023). *Friendly Courtrooms a Humanitarian Mark in the Process of Judicial Reform*. https://congly.vn/phong-xet-xu-than-thien-dau-an-nhan-van-trong-tien-trinh-cai-cach-tu-phap-394336.html. [Accessed 02 May 2025].

Hai, H. H. (2015). *Ensuring Citizens' Right to Equality in Criminal Trials*(p. 21). People's Army Publishing House.

Le, L. C. (2022). *Ensuring the Rights of Victims and Certain Vulnerable Groups in Criminal Justice from Legal Provisions to the Activities of Legal Practitioners* (p. 231). National Political Publishing House Truth.

Ministry of Justice. (2020). *Achieving Best Evidence in Criminal Proceedings Guidance on Interviewing Victims and Witnesses and Guidance on Using Special Measures.* https://www.gov.uk/government/publications/achieving-best-evidence-in-criminal-proceedings

Nguyen, N. A. (2021). *Juvenile Criminal Justice in Vietnam From Theory to Practice.* Judicial Publishing House.

Nguyen, N. C. (2020). *Scientific Commentary on the Criminal Procedure Code 2015* (Vol. 2, p. 115). National Political Publishing House Truth.

Nguyen, T. P. H. (2020). Rights-Based Approach in Developing Child Protection Policies in Criminal Procedure in Vietnam. *State and Law Review,* (4), 15–25.

Nguyen, H. (2023). *Challenges and Solutions in Supporting Children Who Have Experienced Sexual Abuse.* https://donghanhviet.vn/thach-thuc-va-giai-phap-trong-cong-tac-ho-tro-tre-em-trai-qua-xam-hai-tinh-duc/?. [Accessed 02 May 2025].

PVH. (2023). *100% of Child Sexual Abuse Cases Brought to Trial Within the Statutory Time Limit.* https://phunuvietnam.vn/100-vu-an-xam-hai-tre-em-duoc-dua-ra-xet-xu-trong-thoi-han-luat-dinh-20231106091213264.htm. [Accessed 02 May 2025].

Phương, A. (2024). *Number of Child Sexual Abuse Cases in 2023 Increased by 9.2% Compared to 2022.* https://www.sggp.org.vn/so-vu-xam-hai-tre-em-nam-2023-tang-92-so-voi-nam-2022-post739042.html?. [Accessed 02 May 2025].

Standing Committee of the National People's Congress. (2018). *Criminal Procedure Law of the People's Republic of China (Amended 2018).* https://fyjjxy.zuel.edu.cn/_upload/article/files/02/15/0647e4ff43bf99ae7be0a48c4f07/4eab8abe-a78b-4487-bf63-cf19e1a4569e.pdf

Standing Committee of the National People's Congress. (2020). *Law of the People's Republic of China on the Protection of Minors (Revised 2020).* http://www.npc.gov.cn/npc/index.html

Tran, V. B. (2018). *Textbook on Criminal Procedure Law of Vietnam* (p. 78). People's Public Security Publishing House.

Trinh, T. V. (Chief Ed.) (2015). *Protecting Personal Freedom and Security through Vietnamese Criminal Law* (p. 43). Judicial Publishing House.

UK Government. (1999). *Youth Justice and Criminal Evidence Act 1999.* https://www.legislation.gov.uk/ukpga/1999/23/contents

UNICEF. (2018). *Child-Friendly Justice Perspectives and Experiences of Children Involved in Judicial Proceedings as Victims, Witnesses or Parties in Nine EU Member States.* UNICEF Publications. https://www.unicef.org

UNODC & UNICEF. (2015). *Justice in Matters Involving Child Victims and Witnesses of Crime Model Law and Related Commentary.* United Nations Publications.

United Nations. (1989). *Convention on the Rights of the Child.* https://www.ohchr.org/en/instruments-mechanisms/instruments/convention-rights-child

U.S. Department of Justice. (2020). *Child Victims and Witnesses Support Materials Protecting Children's Identities in Criminal Proceedings.* https://www.justice.gov/opa/video/united-states-files-civil-forfeiture-complaint-against-225m-cryptocurrency-investment

Chapter 12
The Model of Child-Friendly Trial Under Vietnamese Criminal Procedure Law

Pham Minh Trang

Abstract Ensuring access to justice for children, including defendants, victims, and witnesses, has increasingly become a matter of significant concern and priority for many countries, including Vietnam. This chapter aims to provide a comprehensive analysis of the development of a child-friendly trial model that upholds the best interests of the child. It examines the current legal framework and the practical implementation of this model in Vietnam. Based on this analysis, the chapter offers recommendations to enhance the effectiveness of child friendly trial practices, thereby contributing to a child sensitive justice system and strengthening the protection of children's rights in Vietnam.

12.1 Introduction

Although Vietnamese law contains specific provisions concerning children, the criminal justice system as a whole remains primarily designed for adults. The formalistic and often intimidating nature of criminal proceedings can hinder children's ability to participate fully and effectively. Therefore, to ensure that children are adequately served and protected, the justice system must adapt its trial procedures to be more child friendly. The child-friendly trial model is a progressive judicial approach designed to maximize the protection of children's legal rights and interests when they are involved in criminal proceedings. Its central objective is to minimize psychological harm and to ensure a safe, effective, and age appropriate environment for children participating in the justice process.

Article history: Received 11 April 2025; Revised 11 July 2025; Accepted 11 August 2025.

P. M. Trang (✉)
Hanoi Law University, Ha Noi City, Viet Nam
e-mail: trangpm@hlu.edu.vn

N. Binh An et al. (eds.), *The Future of Child-Friendly Justice and Children's Rights in Vietnam*, https://doi.org/10.1007/978-981-95-3521-7_12

12.2 Rationale and Significance of Developing a Child-Friendly Trial Model for Children Provided in Vietnamese Criminal Procedure Law

The development of a child-friendly trial model in criminal proceedings is grounded in theoretical, scientific, political, and legal foundations, as outlined below.

Theoretical basis: The theoretical basis for developing a child-friendly trial model in criminal proceedings primarily stems from the theoretical foundation for establishing a specialized juvenile justice system. Global theoretical studies on juvenile justice identify two fundamental models that have influenced the emergence and development of specialized courts and special trial procedures for this group: the welfare model and the justice model. These models are grounded in two philosophies of handling juvenile offenders, namely the welfare philosophy and the justice philosophy (Đào & Trần, 2022, p. 8).

According to Nguyễn (1999), "*Philosophy is the deepest and most general viewpoint of humans on existential and social issues*" (p. 1707). The philosophy of dealing with juvenile offenders encompasses core ideologies or viewpoints held by legal scholars in general, criminologists and criminal law experts in particular, legislators, and practitioners working within the juvenile justice system. These philosophies form part of the foundation for the formation and development of juvenile justice models (Đào, 2024, p. 17). *First*, regarding the welfare model, this model is grounded in the welfare philosophy, which considers the State the guardian of juveniles and therefore responsible for their welfare. The philosophy emphasizes rehabilitation as the core principle of the criminal justice system concerning juveniles. Accordingly, the development of criminal laws and law enforcement institutions concerning juveniles aims primarily at their rehabilitation (Dammer & Albanese, 2014, p. 286). Under this model, the organization and conduct of trials display distinct characteristics that embody a child-friendly approach. Notably, trials are conducted behind closed doors, which minimizes public criticism and helps juveniles maintain calmness and a balanced mindset when confronting their mistakes; and at the same time, this mechanism protects their reputation for the future. Furthermore, the role of the judge in these trials exemplifies the welfare model (UNICEF Việt Nam & Viện Khoa học xét xử Tòa án nhân dân Tối cao, 2012, p. 83). Rather than exercising state power harshly, the judge assumes a parental role, bridging the gap of estrangement and engaging closely to listen to the child's voice. Đào and Trần (2022) argue that "*to effectively implement the welfare model, maintaining a balance between firmness and leniency, advancement and retreat when engaging with juveniles is one of the critical skills judges must possess during trials*" (p. 9). *Second,* regarding the justice model: This model is founded on the philosophy of justice, which on one hand emphasizes the protection of society through principles of prevention and appropriate handling of juvenile offenders, considering them capable of being held responsible for their actions; on the other hand, it stresses the right to defense and legal safeguards for juveniles. According to Reid and Bromwich (2019, pp. 70–72), this philosophy seeks to balance society's need for protection with the individual interests of the offender.

The guiding principle of the justice philosophy is that any restriction on a juvenile's liberty must be limited by procedural safeguards and based on the highest possible consensus among parties. Therefore, the justice model is characterized by fair procedural processes and judicial accountability, valuing the process over the outcome, and focusing on ensuring the procedural rights of juveniles. Thus, each model and philosophy embodies certain ideas about juvenile criminal justice. In Vietnam, the welfare and justice philosophies are combined to build the juvenile justice system as well as to operate child-friendly trials oriented toward the best interests of children.

Scientific basis: Numerous scientific studies have demonstrated that the human brain does not fully develop until approximately 20–25 years of age (Arain et al., 2013). Due to this biological characteristic, children—who are still in the process of development—are limited in terms of psychological and emotional maturity, and therefore possess a reduced capacity for self-regulation and self-protection. Moreover, because of their age, children are more vulnerable to psychological and physical harm and face a higher risk of losing or having limited opportunities for full personal and physical development when they come into contact with the criminal justice system as offenders, compared to adult counterparts (Vũ, 2020, pp. 19–20). Given these vulnerabilities, Trương (2019, p. 568) asserts that the United Nations Convention on the Rights of the Child as well as Vietnam's criminal law recognize juvenile offenders as a particularly vulnerable group. They must not be judged by the same standards applied to adults and should be subject to specialized criminal policies—ones that not only hold them accountable but also ensure the protection of their lawful rights and interests.

Political basis: Since the early years of the twenty-first century, the vision for a specialized justice system that safeguards the rights and legitimate interests of all individuals, especially children, has been recognized and prioritized by the Politburo of the Communist Party of Vietnam. This vision was affirmed in Resolution No. 08-NQ/TW, dated January 2, 2002, titled "On a Number of Key Tasks for Judicial Work in the Coming Period". The Resolution emphasized the need to study the establishment of family and juvenile courts and required that all trials ensure equality before the law, as well as uphold the principles of democracy and objectivity. These directions reflect the Party and State's concern for vulnerable groups in society and lay the political groundwork for developing a child-friendly trial model. Subsequently, Resolution No. 49-NQ/TW, dated June 2, 2005, on "Judicial Reform Strategy to 2020", outlined directions and tasks for improving judicial procedures to ensure coherence, democracy, transparency, and the protection of human rights. The Resolution emphasized the importance of improving criminal policy and judicial procedures while promoting crime prevention and rehabilitation in the treatment of offenders. Although it did not specifically mention the development of a child-friendly trial model, Resolution No. 49-NQ/TW addressed several key aspects of judicial proceedings and human rights protection, issues that directly support the research and development of mechanisms to respect and uphold the rights of children in legal processes. More recently, the Party Committee of the Supreme People's Court has developed the Judicial Reform Project of the People's Court to 2030, with a Vision to 2045, aligned with the objectives set out at the 13th National Congress of the Communist Party of Vietnam (2021). This reform strategy provides an important political foundation for improving legal regulations concerning children and for institutionalizing the child-friendly trial model within Vietnam's judicial system. Thus, it is evident that the establishment of a child-friendly trial model in Vietnam has a solid political foundation. It is a key objective receiving strong attention from the Communist Party of Vietnam, especially in the context of ongoing integration and globalization.

Legal basis: The child-friendly trial model in criminal proceedings, as a component of the broader juvenile justice system for individuals under the age of 18, has been developed and implemented within a comprehensive legal framework that spans both international and national legal foundations. At the international level, the United Nations Convention on the Rights of the Child (UNCRC) has become a foundational legal standard for the formulation of legislation relating to children in Vietnam. Article 3 of the UNCRC emphasizes that: "*In all actions concerning children, whether undertaken by public or private social welfare institutions, courts of law, administrative authorities or legislative bodies, the best interests of the child shall be a primary consideration.*" This principle obliges State Parties not only to comply with international legal standards and to respect, protect, and fulfill children's fundamental rights but also to establish specialized courts and develop child-friendly, non-discriminatory, and age-appropriate judicial procedures (Hoàng, 2021, p. 84). In addition to the UNCRC, other international legal instruments, such as: the United Nations Standard Minimum Rules for the Administration of Juvenile Justice (the Beijing Rules), adopted by UN General Assembly Resolution 40/33 on 29 November 1985; and the United Nations Guidelines for the Prevention of Juvenile Delinquency (the Riyadh Guidelines), adopted by UN General Assembly Resolution 45/112 on 14 December 1990, etc. also urge member states to develop juvenile justice systems that are compatible with children's needs and minimize the adverse psychological impacts of criminal proceedings on child development. From the perspective of Vietnamese domestic law, the 2013 Constitution affirms in Article 37 that: "*Children shall be protected, cared for, and educated by the State, family, and society; and shall be allowed to participate in decisions relating to children.*" Building on this constitutional foundation, a number of key legal instruments such as the Criminal Code, Criminal Procedure Code, Law on the Organization of the People's Courts, Law on Children, and the Law on Juvenile Justice, among others—provide specific legal provisions governing the handling of criminal cases involving children. These laws are further supported by subordinate legal documents detailing child participation in criminal proceedings, with a particular emphasis on safeguarding their rights and adapting judicial processes to their age and developmental needs.

In summary, the development of a child-friendly trial model in criminal proceedings represents a harmonious integration of international commitments, domestic legal provisions, and the humanistic policies of the Party and the State. It is grounded in a comprehensive foundation of theory, politics, science, and law, all aiming toward the paramount goal of safeguarding the best interests of the child. This model contributes to the realization of children's rights as enshrined in the United Nations Convention on the Rights of the Child; enhances the quality of adjudication in cases involving children in particular, and improves the overall effectiveness and fairness of court proceedings in general. It also helps strengthen the judicial capacity of judges and other justice officials; ensures that children feel respected, protected, and confident in the legal system; and provides flexibility in the design of trial procedures—thereby aligning with the broader objectives of judicial reform currently underway in Vietnam.

12.3 Concept, Characteristics, and Requirements of the Child-Friendly Trial Model in Criminal Proceedings

Most legal systems worldwide contain specific procedural provisions for children participating in legal proceedings. This approach is commonly referred to as "child-friendly justice" or "child-sensitive justice." In essence, these concepts refer to legal proceedings that ensure a safe and supportive environment, where questioning methods during both investigation and trial are adapted to the child's age and stage of development (Cao & Nguyễn, 2015). The primary objective is to protect children from physical and psychological harm and to enable their participation in legal proceedings in a manner that is safe, age-appropriate, and sensitive to their mental and emotional development.

The fundamental features of the child-friendly trial model in criminal proceedings are reflected in the following aspects:

First, trials are conducted by specialized courts. According to Phạm Minh Trang (2017), many countries have established specialized courts to handle cases involving families in general and children in particular, such as Thailand, the Philippines, Japan, the United States, New Zealand, and Australia. Courtrooms are specifically designed so that the space is less formal and intimidating than conventional courtrooms. Bright colors may be used, and furniture may be arranged in a more approachable manner, such as round or U-shaped tables, to create a sense of closeness and reduce stress for the child. The traditional defendant's dock is avoided; a child defendant under the age of 18 is seated next to their legal representative (parent or guardian) and defense lawyer, fostering a sense of protection and support. Additionally, courts may include functional rooms such as a separate waiting room for children, or a child-sensitive interview room equipped with toys, books, and visual materials to help children feel relaxed and emotionally stable before and during proceedings. Mobile court sessions may also be organized in familiar settings such as schools or social protection centers.

Second, judicial personnel must be specifically trained and experienced in handling cases involving children. In accordance with Rule 6 of the United Nations Standard Minimum Rules for the Administration of Juvenile Justice (the Beijing Rules), decision-makers must possess special qualifications or receive targeted training to carry out their duties with discernment and in accordance with their roles and responsibilities. In addition to judges and prosecutors, the trial panel may include lay assessors such as teachers, youth union officials, or individuals with expertise in child psychology. These participants should be well trained in child psychology, possess effective and empathetic communication skills, and be equipped to respond appropriately based on the child's age and level of maturity. Furthermore, all professionals involved in the proceedings are expected to demonstrate an attitude of care, respect, and non-discrimination, consistently prioritizing the best interests of the child.

Third, the presence of the child's guardian or legal representative must be ensured during the trial. The United Nations Convention on the Rights of the Child (UNCRC) affirms that throughout the judicial process, children have the right to be accompanied by their parents, except where such presence is deemed contrary to the child's best interests. Similarly, the Beijing Rules stipulate that parents or guardians must be permitted to participate in proceedings and may be required by competent authorities to attend hearings to ensure the child's interests are protected. However, their participation may be restricted if the competent authority finds valid reasons to believe that exclusion is necessary to serve the best interests of the juvenile.

Fourth, the trial must ensure the child's right to legal assistance and the right to express their views and opinions. Given children's developmental characteristics and limited legal understanding, they are generally unable to defend themselves adequately against criminal charges or procedural decisions. It is therefore essential to guarantee their right to be represented by a defense lawyer or legal representative to protect their rights and interests. While defense lawyers and legal representatives may act on the child's behalf, judicial authorities remain obligated to ensure that the child has the opportunity to be heard, regardless of whether they are a victim, witness, or defendant.

Fifth, the trial must safeguard the child's right to privacy and the confidentiality of personal information. This requirement is grounded in international legal standards. For example, Article 40(2)(b)(vii) of the United Nations Convention on the Rights of the Child (1989) provides that "Every child alleged as or accused of having infringed the penal law has the right to have his or her privacy fully respected at all stages of the proceedings." Similarly, Article 8 of the Beijing Rules (1985) emphasizes that the juvenile's right to privacy must be respected at all stages of the proceedings to avoid unnecessary harm caused by excessive public exposure or stigmatization. Accordingly, criminal cases involving children are often conducted in closed court to protect the child's privacy, dignity, and reputation, and to prevent social discrimination. This practice also facilitates the reintegration of children into the community and supports their normal development after undergoing judicial procedures or even after serving a sentence (Đỗ, 2023). Moreover, protecting a child's privacy is particularly important in safeguarding the personality, dignity, safety, and well-being of child victims, as public disclosure of their identity can result in severe and long-lasting consequences (Nguyễn, 2018).

Based on the characteristics outlined above, the concept can be drawn as follows: *The child-friendly trial model in criminal proceedings is a trial conducted by a specialized court, involving judicial personnel who are professionally trained and experienced in handling cases involving children, with the presence of a guardian or legal representative, ensuring the child's right to legal assistance, the right to express views and opinions, and the right to privacy and confidentiality of personal information. The ultimate aim of this model is to protect the best interests and legal rights of children participating in criminal proceedings.*

The implementation of this model in practice must meet several strict requirements, including: ensuring the best interests of the child; non-discrimination against children; promoting cooperation, autonomy, and accountability among all parties involved in the proceedings; treating children with respect and dignity; Resolving cases in a timely and efficient manner without unnecessary delay… Only by fulfilling these requirements can the benefits of establishing and applying the child-friendly trial model in criminal proceedings be fully realized.

In conclusion, the child-friendly trial model is not merely about modifying the physical courtroom environment; rather, it represents a comprehensive transformation in philosophy, procedural design, and judicial approach. Its goal is to humanize the criminal justice process, minimize harmful impacts, and fully safeguard the rights of children involved in the system.

12.4 Vietnamese Law and the Practical Implementation of the Child-Friendly Trial Model in Criminal Proceedings

12.4.1 Vietnamese Legal Framework for the Child-Friendly Trial Model in Criminal Proceedings

The child-friendly trial model in Vietnamese criminal proceedings has been developed and implemented within a comprehensive legal framework that spans from the Constitution to major statutes such as the Penal Code, the Criminal Procedure Code, the Law on the Organization of the People's Courts, the Law on Children, and the Law on Juvenile Justice, along with relevant subordinate legal documents.

First and foremost, the 2013 Constitution establishes the foundation for the protection of fundamental human rights, including the rights of children. This constitutional framework guides the development of specialized legislation such as the Law on Children (2016), which affirms the principle of ensuring the best interests of the child in all activities, including legal proceedings (Article 5); the Penal Code (2015, as amended in 2017 and 2025), which emphasizes that the handling of juvenile offenders under 18 years of age must prioritize their best interests and focus primarily on education and rehabilitation, helping them correct mistakes and reintegrate into society. Such handling must be based on the child's age, capacity for legal awareness, and the circumstances of the offense (Article 91); the Criminal Procedure Code (2015, as amended in 2025), which devotes Chapter XXVIII specifically to criminal procedures for persons under the age of 18; and the Law on the Organization of the People's Courts (2014, amended in 2024 and 2025), which contains provisions for establishing the Family and Juvenile Court as part of the organizational structure of provincial- and district-level People's Courts.

Among these legal instruments, the Law on Juvenile Justice, adopted by the 15th National Assembly at its 8th session on November 30, 2024, and scheduled to take effect on January 1, 2026, constitutes a breakthrough in legislative development. It fully institutionalizes the Party's policy on developing a child-friendly justice system and protecting children, while aligning with international standards and United Nations guidelines on juvenile justice. The law seeks to establish a more appropriate and humane approach to the treatment of juveniles in conflict with the law. According to the Supreme People's Court (2025), one of its key objectives is to create child-friendly procedures tailored to the juvenile's age, psychological development, maturity level, cognitive capacity, and best interests. The law sets out 16 progressive and humanistic principles specific to the protection of juveniles within the criminal justice system. Notably, Article 6 affirms the principle of ensuring child-friendly procedures: "Procedures for juveniles must be simple, friendly, and appropriate to their psychology, age, level of maturity, and cognitive ability."

The Law on Juvenile Justice provides for two separate procedural models for juveniles involved in criminal proceedings:

(1) Child-friendly trial procedures for juveniles who are denounced, recommended for prosecution, held in urgent circumstances, or formally charged, as regulated in Section IV, Chapter VII (Article 151):

- –Criminal cases involving juveniles as defendants shall be adjudicated by the Family and Juvenile Court. In courts where a Family and Juvenile Court has not yet been established, such cases shall be heard by judges specified under Clause 1, Article 29 of the Law on Juvenile Justice.
- –Trials involving juvenile defendants must be conducted in child-friendly courtrooms.
- –Hearings must follow child-friendly procedures, including: The presiding judge wears administrative judicial attire (rather than a traditional courtroom robe); The prosecutor wears appropriate civilian attire instead of the formal uniform of the People's Procuracy; Handcuffs or other coercive measures must not be applied unless the juvenile shows resistance, disrupts courtroom order, or engages in other negative behaviors; Examination and argumentation must be conducted in a manner appropriate to the juvenile's age, gender, level of cognitive development, and maturity; Questions should be short, simple, and easy to understand; Multiple issues should not be asked in a single question.
- –In special cases where the protection of the juvenile is necessary, the court may hold a closed hearing, but the judgment must still be pronounced publicly. When delivering the verdict, the panel of judges shall read aloud the decision section of the judgment.

(2) Child-friendly procedures for juvenile victims and witnesses, as stipulated in Chapter VIII of the Law on Juvenile Justice:

–Proceedings involving juvenile victims and witnesses must be conducted in an environment that ensures their safety and protection, including their life, health, dignity, honor, property, personal privacy, and other legal rights and interests (Clause 1, Article 153).
–Authorities and officials responsible for legal proceedings must adopt appropriate measures to reduce anxiety and stress for juvenile victims and witnesses participating in the process (Clause 2, Article 153).
–The summoning of juvenile victims and witnesses to appear in court should be limited, provided it does not affect the resolution of the case. The presiding judge may rely on their previous statements in the case file or use other alternative methods. The judge may also decide to conduct online hearings, in accordance with the law, enabling juvenile victims and witnesses to attend remotely from a designated location (Clause 1, Article 159).
–If juvenile victims or witnesses are required to participate in court proceedings, they should be placed in a separate room (isolation room) and connected via electronic devices. If a separate room is not available, they must be seated in a designated area within the courtroom that is physically separated from the defendant (Clause 2, Article 159).
–During the hearing, the following procedural safeguards must be observed (Clause 3, Article 159): (a) When questioning juveniles, questions must be short, simple, age-appropriate, and easy to understand, taking into account the juvenile's age, gender, maturity, and cognitive capacity. Only one issue should be raised at a time. Examiners must consider the juvenile's family background, mental and physical condition, and other relevant personal characteristics; (b) Where necessary, the court may use visual aids such as diagrams, body charts, electronic devices, or other tools to help juveniles answer questions. However, they must not be asked to point to parts of their own body, particularly in cases of sexual abuse; (c) Questions must not be aggressive, threatening, shaming, or offensive to the juvenile victims or witnesses.
–Juvenile victims and witnesses must be given the opportunity to familiarize themselves with court procedures and environments before participating in the proceedings (Clause 4, Article 159).

In addition to the provisions outlined above, the Law on Juvenile Justice also introduces regulations concerning the specialization of juvenile justice practitioners, the design and arrangement of child-friendly courtrooms, the involvement of social workers, the participation of legal representatives and support persons in proceedings, as well as the confidentiality of information and the adoption of rehabilitative and supportive measures for juvenile victims.

Beyond the Constitution and primary legislation, various subordinate legal instruments also contain direct or indirect provisions relevant to the model of child-friendly courts. Notable examples include: Circular No. 01/2017/TT-TANDTC of the Supreme People's Court, dated July 28, 2017, providing guidelines on courtroom arrangements; Circular No. 02/2017/TT-TANDTC of the Supreme People's Court, dated July 28, 2017, promulgating regulations on the organization of court hearings; Circular No. 02/2018/TT-TANDTC of the Supreme People's Court, dated September 21, 2018, providing detailed rules on the adjudication of criminal cases involving participants under 18 years of age within the jurisdiction of the Family and Juvenile Court; and Joint Circular No. 06/2018/TTLT-VKSNDTC-TANDTC-BCA-BTP-BLĐTBXH, dated December 21, 2018, jointly issued by the Supreme People's Procuracy, the Supreme People's Court, the Ministry of Public Security, the Ministry of Justice, and the Ministry of Labour, Invalids and Social Affairs, on inter-agency coordination in implementing certain provisions of the Criminal Procedure Code relating to procedures for individuals under 18 years of age.

12.4.2 Practical Implementation of the Child-Friendly Trial Model in Criminal Proceedings in Vietnam

According to Báo điện tử Pháp luật thành phố Hồ Chí Minh (2024), as of mid-2024, Vietnam had established 41 Family and Juvenile Courts. The creation of these specialized courts represents a significant milestone in Vietnam's efforts to develop a judicial system that is responsive to and respectful of the rights and needs of children. This progress reflects the country's commitment to building a legal framework consistent with international standards on child protection and juvenile justice. From the practical implementation of the child-friendly trial model in criminal proceedings, several notable observations can be identified as follows:

Firstly, the legal instruments governing the establishment and operation of the Family and Juvenile Courts in Vietnam are, in many respects, aligned with international standards and best practices on juvenile justice. These include provisions on courtroom design and physical facilities to create a child-friendly trial environment, measures to enhance privacy protection and children's participatory rights during proceedings, and capacity-building for judges and other judicial officials involved in child-related cases. Nevertheless, certain provisions remain inconsistent with international norms and best practices. For instance, the Law on Children (2016) defines a "child" as a person under 16 years of age, thereby excluding minors aged 16 to under 18 from full procedural protections and support measures during proceedings. Moreover, although the legal framework for the Family and Juvenile Courts is relatively comprehensive, the relevant provisions are dispersed across various legal instruments, and the criteria for establishing specialized courts are not clearly defined, leading to inconsistent interpretations (Australian Aid, European Union, and UNICEF, 2024, p. 71). These shortcomings have contributed to slow, inconsistent, and at times hesitant implementation of the child-friendly trial model in practice.

Secondly, the operations of the Family and Juvenile Courts have contributed to the initial application of child-sensitive procedures and to ensuring that the best interests of minors are considered in judicial decisions and judgments. However, while the majority of cases involving children are adjudicated by district-level People's Courts, Family and Juvenile Courts have primarily been established at the provincial level. By the end of 2022, the Supreme People's Court had established 40 Family and Juvenile Courts within 38 provincial-level courts and two high-level courts, as well as created the Division of Labor, Family, and Juvenile Affairs (Division III) under the Supreme People's Court (Đỗ, 2023). This situation has limited children's access to child-friendly trial mechanisms, particularly access to alternatives to administrative sanctions and criminal prosecution, such as diversion measures, for minors.

Thirdly, under Article 25 of the Criminal Procedure Code 2015 (as amended in 2025), courts may conduct closed hearings to protect minors who are defendants or victims; however, the judgment must still be announced publicly. Because this provision is discretionary rather than mandatory, public trials remain possible in cases involving minors. The participation of large audiences, including members of the media, may inadvertently result in the disclosure of minors' personal information and expose them to psychological distress, such as anxiety, fear, or shame, thereby potentially compromising the accuracy and reliability of their testimony.

Fourthly, Vietnam has implemented notable initiatives to strengthen the professional capacity of judicial actors in juvenile justice, particularly through targeted training programs for judges assigned to Family and Juvenile Courts. Nevertheless, the current training framework lacks uniformity in both content and delivery. There is no requirement for mandatory certification for judges serving in specialized juvenile courts, and judicial officers continue to express a need for additional training in areas such as child developmental psychology, education, gender sensitivity, and child-appropriate procedural practices.

Fifthly, in terms of the broader personnel structure, the absence of dedicated officers within investigative bodies and procuracies presents significant challenges to ensuring that minors receive consistent and timely access to child-friendly justice at all stages of criminal proceedings. Defense counsel, whether chosen by the minor or appointed by the court, often practice across multiple legal domains, which may limit their ability to provide specialized and effective legal support tailored to the needs of minors. Furthermore, the participation of professionals such as psychologists and social workers remains limited in practice. At present, there is no formalized legal or procedural framework defining the role of social workers in criminal trials involving minors, nor any guidance on how they should perform support functions within the courtroom.

Sixthly, Official Dispatch No. 13/TANDTC-PC dated 24 February 2020, issued by the Supreme People's Court, sets out recommendations on the provision of appropriate equipment and facilities for Family and Juvenile Courts, including the establishment of child-friendly courtrooms and functional support spaces. These measures are intended to create a courtroom environment that is psychologically safe and conducive to the effective participation of minors. However, such infrastructural arrangements are not mandated as prerequisites for the establishment of specialized juvenile courts. As noted in a 2024 study conducted by Australian Aid, the European Union, and UNICEF (pp. 66–67), many local jurisdictions still face significant difficulties in allocating space and securing resources necessary to establish child-sensitive courtrooms and ancillary facilities. Accordingly, there is an urgent need for practical and context-appropriate guidelines to support the creation of child-friendly trial environments, particularly in areas lacking dedicated infrastructure and specialized equipment.

Thus, although Vietnam has established a relatively comprehensive legal framework that aligns with relevant international commitments for the organization and operation of the child-friendly trial model, its practical implementation continues to face significant challenges and limitations. Nevertheless, with the sustained attention and support of the Party, the State, and relevant authorities, together with the recent promulgation of the Law on Juvenile Justice, there is a strong expectation that the model will continue to improve and operate more effectively. Such progress will contribute to the development of a more humane justice system and provide stronger safeguards for the rights of children in the adjudication of criminal cases.

12.5 Recommendations for Enhancing the Effectiveness of the Child-Friendly Trial Model in Criminal Proceedings in Vietnam

Based on an analysis of the current legal framework and the practical implementation of the child-friendly trial model, the author proposes several recommendations to improve the criminal justice system for juveniles in general, and the operation of child-friendly trials in particular. This section also offers practical solutions aimed at improving the effectiveness of law enforcement and the implementation of this model in real-world judicial practice.

First, competent authorities should conduct a comprehensive review and refinement of policies and legal provisions relating to the child-friendly trial model. For instance, guidelines should be issued to address challenges in the establishment and operation of Family and Juvenile Courts, including conditions for their establishment and instructions on child-friendly courtroom design. At the same time, Vietnam should amend the Law on Children (2016) to unify the definition of a "child" as a person under 18 years of age. This change would broaden the scope of protection and access to child-friendly justice for those aged 16 to under 18. Any legislative amendments should align with the objectives set forth in Decision No. 23/QĐ-TTg dated January 7, 2021, approving the National Program of Action for Children for the period 2021–2030, and National Assembly Resolution No. 121/2020/QH14 dated June 19, 2020, on enhancing the effectiveness of policies and laws on child abuse prevention. These include ensuring child-friendly adjudication, continuing the establishment of Family and Juvenile Courts under the Law on the Organization of the People's Courts, resolving more than 90 percent of child abuse cases, and strengthening judicial training on handling such cases (Article 2.4).

Second, the establishment of Family and Juvenile Courts at provincial and regional People's Courts should be actively promoted, particularly at the first-instance level. In local courts that are not yet eligible to establish specialized divisions, judges with expertise in family and juvenile matters should be appointed. Given limited human and financial resources, a judge may be concurrently assigned to multiple specializations. In localities where only Civil or Criminal Courts can be established, it is still feasible to designate judges specializing in family and juvenile matters within those divisions. While such judges may also handle other types of cases, all proceedings involving minors should be assigned to them.

Third, it is essential to strengthen the capacity of judges in adjudicating cases involving children. In a child-friendly justice system, modern courtrooms or costly facilities are not the sole determinants of effectiveness. More importantly, the manner in which judges and other professionals interact with children plays a decisive role. Simple adjustments in attitude, approach, and communication can make courtroom procedures significantly more child-friendly. Such adjustments include demonstrating patience and empathy, encouraging children's participation in proceedings while ensuring their understanding, being firm yet non-punitive with juvenile defendants, addressing children by their given names, avoiding expressions of surprise, disgust, doubt, or strong emotional reactions to their statements, using plain and simple language, avoiding legal jargon, complex sentence structures, and confusing questions, and treating all children equally without assumptions based on background, gender, ethnicity, or socio-economic status. To equip judges of Family and Juvenile Courts, specialized judges, and those handling juvenile-related cases with appropriate knowledge and skills, it is necessary to incorporate a juvenile justice module into judicial training programs, particularly for judges. In parallel, regular training, certification, and refresher courses for judges, court clerks, and judicial examiners should be organized, with an emphasis on social knowledge and child-friendly interaction skills.

Fourth, it is essential to strengthen the participation and professional capacity of supporting personnel involved in the child-friendly trial model. To this end, the specialization of personnel within adjudicative bodies and related institutions must be reinforced. In the long term, Vietnam should develop a cadre of dedicated investigators and prosecutors with the necessary expertise to handle juvenile-related cases, based on an assessment of organizational structures and existing staffing capacities. At the same time, legal aid centers and bar associations should adopt a more specialized approach to ensure effective legal assistance for children. In particular, establishing a well-trained team of social workers to support adjudicating agencies in handling juvenile cases is of paramount importance. Consideration may also be given to developing a network of professional or semi-professional social workers, including through the mobilization of part-time collaborators such as child, population, and family workers currently being piloted in certain provinces.

Fifth, greater attention should be given to the investment in and renovation of child-friendly courtrooms. Simple adjustments to courtroom settings can significantly reduce children's anxiety and encourage their meaningful participation in legal proceedings. Where feasible, a private and quiet space should be provided for children and their caregivers to rest while waiting. Courtroom personnel may wear less formal attire instead of official judicial uniforms; trials should be conducted in closed sessions where appropriate; furniture can be rearranged so that all participants sit around a single table at the same floor level; and the distance between the child and those needing to hear their testimony should be minimized, as children often experience challenges in vocal expression and may feel stress when required to repeat themselves. Children should be allowed to sit next to a parent or guardian and to remain seated when speaking in court, rather than being required to stand. Given the budgetary and infrastructural limitations of many courthouses, practical guidelines should be issued for creating a child-friendly trial environment in the absence of dedicated courtrooms or specialized equipment. For example, proceedings involving minors could be scheduled at different times from adult criminal trials. Moreover, the use of multi-functional rooms, rather than multiple separate spaces, should be encouraged to optimize available resources.

Sixth, courts and relevant authorities must strengthen their awareness of and commitment to protecting the privacy rights of children. The disclosure of a child's identity can cause shame, stigmatization, and significantly hinder the child's recovery and reintegration process. Therefore, the law should mandate closed hearings in criminal cases involving persons under 18 years of age, whether they are defendants or victims. During proceedings, courts must ensure that children's names and identifying details are not disclosed to the public or the media. All case files involving children must be kept strictly confidential, and full names should not be used in court verdicts or written judgments. At the same time, public awareness of the importance of safeguarding children's personal information in legal proceedings should be strengthened. Clear and strict sanctions should be imposed for the unauthorized disclosure of identifying information concerning child defendants or victims, creating a deterrent effect and reinforcing the accountability of responsible individuals, organizations, and state agencies.

Seventh, while the implementation of child-friendly trials must be grounded in legal regulations, it should also allow a degree of flexibility to ensure appropriateness in individual cases and uphold the best interests of the child. For example, child victims may be permitted to testify from a separate room equipped with audio-visual links to the courtroom to avoid direct confrontation with the accused; examination durations may be moderated, and breaks introduced to prevent fatigue or psychological stress; and cases involving children should be prioritized for prompt resolution to minimize negative effects on the child's mental well-being and daily life. Such procedural flexibility is essential to address the diverse circumstances encountered in practice, as well as to incorporate feedback and adapt to challenges that arise in the operation of Family and Juvenile Courts. This need for adaptability is also reflected in broader judicial reform strategies and the National Action Program for Children.

Eighth, the judicial sector should establish clearer and more comprehensive regulations to guide effective coordination among judicial authorities, including the police, the procuracy, and the courts, and other stakeholders such as social organizations, schools, families, and relevant professionals including psychologists, healthcare providers, and social workers, to provide holistic support for children. Personnel from sectors such as labor, health, education, psychology, and civil society organizations should be mobilized to contribute to child-sensitive judicial assistance. Children and their families should also receive legal guidance, psychological support, and post-trial follow-up to ensure their stable recovery and reintegration. Furthermore, relevant ministries, agencies, and organizations should regularly convene inter-agency meetings and international conferences on child-friendly justice to promote consistency and effectiveness in the application of relevant regulations by judicial authorities and social actors, thereby ensuring better protection of children's rights (Cao & Nguyễn, 2015). In addition, for the purposes of legal dissemination, public education, and raising community awareness about the child-friendly trial model and the protection of children's rights during legal proceedings—while safeguarding their privacy—the author recommends that organizations such as the Youth Union, the Women's Union, and the Bar Association collaborate to organize mock child-friendly trials. These mock proceedings can serve as an effective tool for education and advocacy.

12.6 Conclusion

The child-friendly trial model in criminal proceedings represents an intersection of justice, psychology, education, and social welfare, aiming to create a more humane justice system centered on the rights and interests of children. It constitutes a significant step toward implementing the United Nations Convention on the Rights of the Child and advancing ongoing judicial reform efforts in Vietnam. Although the practical implementation of the model has faced several challenges and limitations, it has nonetheless demonstrated its value and relevance in both general and criminal litigation. With continued political commitment, progressive legal refinement, and growing institutional awareness, this model is expected to be further expanded and improved in Vietnam in the coming years.

References

Party Resolutions and Legal Documents

Bộ Chính trị. (2002, 02 tháng 01). *Nghị quyết số 08-NQ/TW về Một số nhiệm vụ trọng tâm công tác tư pháp trong thời gian tới* [Resolution No. 08-NQ/TW on Key Tasks of Judicial Work in the Coming Period].

Bộ Chính trị. (2005, 02 tháng 6). *Nghị quyết số 49-NQ/TW về "Chiến lược cải cách tư pháp đến năm 2020"* [Resolution No. 49-NQ/TW on the "Judicial Reform Strategy to 2020"].

Ban cán sự Đảng Tòa án nhân dân tối cao. (n.d.). *Đề án Cải cách tư pháp tại Tòa án nhân dân đến năm 2030, định hướng đến năm 2045* [Project on Judicial Reform in the People's Courts to 2030, with Orientation to 2045].

Đại hội đồng Liên Hợp Quốc. (1985, 29 tháng 11). *Các quy tắc tối thiểu của Liên hợp quốc về quản lý tư pháp đối với người chưa thành niên (Quy tắc Bắc Kinh)* [United Nations Standard Minimum Rules for the Administration of Juvenile Justice (The Beijing Rules)] (Nghị quyết 40/33).

Đại hội đồng Liên Hợp Quốc. (1990, 14 tháng 12). *Các hướng dẫn của Liên hợp quốc về phòng ngừa phạm pháp ở người chưa thành niên (Hướng dẫn Ri-át)* [United Nations Guidelines for the Prevention of Juvenile Delinquency (The Riyadh Guidelines)] (Nghị quyết 45/12).

Liên Hợp Quốc. (1989). *Công ước về Quyền trẻ em* [Convention on the Rights of the Child].

Quốc hội. (2013, 28 tháng 11). *Hiến pháp nước Cộng hòa xã hội chủ nghĩa Việt Nam* [Constitution of the Socialist Republic of Vietnam].

Quốc hội. (2014, 24 tháng 11). *Luật số 62/2014/QH13: Luật Tổ chức Tòa án nhân dân* [Law on Organization of People's Courts].

Quốc hội. (2015a, 27 tháng 11). *Bộ luật Hình sự số 100/2015/QH13* [Criminal Code No. 100/2015/QH13].

Quốc hội. (2015b, 27 tháng 11). *Bộ luật Tố tụng hình sự số 101/2015/QH13* [Criminal Procedure Code].

Quốc hội. (2016, 05 tháng 4). *Luật số 102/2016/QH13: Luật Trẻ em* [Law on Children].

Quốc hội. (2017, 20 tháng 6). *Luật số 12/2017/QH14: Luật sửa đổi, bổ sung một số điều của Bộ luật Hình sự số 100/2015/QH13* [Law Amending and Supplementing Certain Articles of the Criminal Code No. 100/2015/QH13].

Quốc hội. (2020, 19 tháng 6). *Nghị quyết số 121/2020/QH14 về tiếp tục tăng cường hiệu lực, hiệu quả việc thực hiện chính sách, pháp luật về phòng, chống xâm hại trẻ em* [Resolution No. 121/2020/QH14 on Strengthening the Effectiveness and Efficiency of the Implementation of Laws and Policies on Child Protection from Abuse].

Quốc hội. (2024a, 24 tháng 6). *Luật số 34/2024/QH15: Luật Tổ chức Tòa án nhân dân* [Law on Organization of People's Courts].

Quốc hội. (2024b, 30 tháng 11). *Luật số 59/2024/QH15: Luật Tư pháp người chưa thành niên* [Law on Juvenile Justice].

Quốc hội. (2025a, 25 tháng 6). *Luật số 86/2025/QH15: Luật sửa đổi, bổ sung một số điều của Bộ luật Hình sự* [Law Amending and Supplementing Certain Articles of the Criminal Code].

Quốc hội. (2025b, 27 tháng 6). *Luật số 99/2025/QH15: Luật sửa đổi, bổ sung một số điều của Bộ luật Tố tụng hình sự* [Law Amending and Supplementing Certain Articles of the Criminal Procedure Code].

Quốc hội. (2025c, 24 tháng 6). *Luật số 81/2025/QH15: Luật sửa đổi, bổ sung một số điều của Luật Tổ chức Tòa án nhân dân* [Law Amending and Supplementing Certain Articles of the Law on Organization of People's Courts].

Tòa án nhân dân tối cao. (2017a, 28 tháng 7). *Thông tư số 01/2017/TT-TANDTC quy định về phòng xử án* [Circular No. 01/2017/TT-TANDTC on Courtroom Regulations].

Tòa án nhân dân tối cao. (2017b, 28 tháng 7). *Thông tư số 02/2017/TT-TANDTC ban hành Quy chế tổ chức phiên tòa* [Circular No. 02/2017/TT-TANDTC Issuing the Regulations on Trial Proceedings].

Tòa án nhân dân tối cao. (2018, 21 tháng 9). *Thông tư số 02/2018/TT-TANDTC quy định chi tiết việc xét xử vụ án hình sự có người tham gia tố tụng là người dưới 18 tuổi thuộc thẩm quyền của Tòa Gia đình và người chưa thành niên* [Circular No. 02/2018/TT-TANDTC on Guidelines for Adjudicating Criminal Cases Involving Persons Under 18 Years of Age within the Jurisdiction of Family and Juvenile Courts].

Tòa án nhân dân tối cao. (2020, 24 tháng 02). *Công văn số 13/TANDTC-PC về việc hướng dẫn bố trí trang thiết bị cần thiết cho Tòa Gia đình và người chưa thành niên* [Official Dispatch No. 13/TANDTC-PC on Equipment Requirements for Family and Juvenile Courts].

Thủ tướng Chính phủ. (2021, 07 tháng 01). *Quyết định số 23/QĐ-TTg phê duyệt Chương trình hành động quốc gia vì trẻ em giai đoạn 2021–2030* [Decision No. 23/QĐ-TTg on Approval of the National Program of Action for Children for the Period 2021–2030].

Viện kiểm sát nhân dân tối cao, Tòa án nhân dân tối cao, Bộ Công an, Bộ Tư pháp, Bộ Lao động – Thương binh và xã hội. (2018, 21 tháng 12). *Thông tư liên tịch số 06/2018/TTLT-VKSNDTC-TANDTC-BCA-BTP-BLĐTBXH về phối hợp thực hiện một số quy định của Bộ luật Tố tụng hình sự về thủ tục tố tụng đối với người dưới 18 tuổi* [Joint Circular No. 06/2018/TTLT-VKSNDTC-TANDTC-BCA-BTP-BLĐTBXH on Coordination in Implementing Certain Provisions of the Criminal Procedure Code Regarding Juvenile Proceedings].

Academic and Research Publications

Arain, M., Haque, M., Johal, L., Mathur, P., Nel, W., Rais, A., Sandhu, R., & Sharma, S. (2013). Maturation of the adolescent brain. *Neuropsychiatric Disease and Treatment, 9*, 449–461. https://doi.org/10.2147/NDT.S39776

Australian Aid, Liên minh châu Âu, & UNICEF. (2024). *Nghiên cứu đánh giá tiến trình hình thành và hoạt động của Tòa Gia đình và người chưa thành niên tại Việt Nam* [Evaluation study on the formation and operation of Family and Juvenile Courts in Vietnam]. NXB. Lao động.

Báo điện tử Pháp luật thành phố Hồ Chí Minh. (2024, 27 tháng 6). *Tòa Tối cao trả lời ĐBQH về việc thành lập thêm Tòa Gia đình và người chưa thành niên* [The Supreme Court Responds to National Assembly Deputies Regarding the Establishment of Additional Family and Juvenile Courts]. Truy cập ngày 30 tháng 4, 2025, từ https://plo.vn/toa-toi-cao-tra-loi-dbqh-ve-viec-thanh-lap-them-toa-gia-dinh-va-nguoi-chua-thanh-nien-post797653.html

Cao, V. H., & Nguyễn, D. H. (2015, 28 tháng 9). *Một số vấn đề về tư pháp phù hợp với trẻ em* [Some Issues Regarding Child-Friendly Justice]. Trang thông tin điện tử Học viện Tòa án. Truy cập ngày 28 tháng 3, 2025, từ http://hvta.toaan.gov.vn/portal/page/portal/hvta/27676686/27677461?p_page_id=27677461&pers_id=28346379&folder_id=&item_id=122284560&p_details=1

Dammer, H. R., & Albanese, J. S. (2014). *Comparative criminal justice systems* (5th ed.). Wadsworth Cengage Learning.

Đào, L. T., & Trần, C. N. (2022). Cơ sở lý luận, chính trị, pháp lý cho việc xây dựng mô hình phiên tòa thân thiện, vì trẻ em trong tố tụng hình sự [Theoretical, Political and Legal Basis for Developing Child-Friendly Trial Models in Criminal Procedure]. Trong Trường Đại học Luật Hà Nội, *Kỷ yếu Hội thảo khoa học Mô hình phiên tòa thân thiện, vì trẻ em trong tố tụng hình sự* (pp. 8, 9).

Đào, L. T. (Chủ biên). (2024). *Triết lý xử lý người chưa thành niên vi phạm và thực tiễn xây dựng pháp luật trên thế giới* [Philosophies for Juvenile Offender Management and Legislative Practices Worldwide]. Nhà xuất bản Công an nhân dân.

Đỗ, T. H. V. (2023, 25 tháng 8). *Một số khó khăn, vướng mắc trong hoạt động của Tòa gia đình và người chưa thành niên* [Challenges in the Operation of Family and Juvenile Courts]. Tạp chí

Tòa án nhân dân điện tử. Truy cập ngày 02 tháng 5, 2025, từ https://tapchitoaan.vn/mot-so-kho-khan-vuong-mac-trong-hoat-dong-cua-toa-gia-dinh-va-nguoi-chua-thanh-nien9163.html

Đỗ, T. P. (2023). Nguyên tắc tiến hành tố tụng đối với người chưa thành niên từ chuẩn mực quốc tế đến điều kiện thực hiện tại Việt Nam [Procedural Principles for Juveniles: From International Standards to Implementation in Vietnam]. Trong Trường Đại học Luật Hà Nội, *Kỷ yếu hội thảo khoa học quốc tế: Tư pháp đối với người chưa thành niên – Kinh nghiệm quốc tế và bài học cho Việt Nam* (p. 250).

Hoàng, T. D. (2021). Chuẩn mực quốc tế về việc hoàn thiện pháp luật tố tụng hình sự về bảo đảm quyền con người của người dưới 18 tuổi [International Standards for Reforming Criminal Procedure Law to Ensure Human Rights for Juveniles]. *Tạp Chí Nghề Luật, 11*, 84.

Nguyễn, N. Ý (Chủ biên). (1999). *Đại Từ điển tiếng Việt* [Comprehensive Vietnamese Dictionary]. Nhà xuất bản Văn hóa thông tin.

Nguyễn, T. L. (2018). Quyền riêng tư của bị hại dưới 18 tuổi trong tố tụng hình sự [The Privacy Rights of Child Victims in Criminal Procedure]. *Tạp Chí Khoa Học Kiểm Sát, 2*, 18.

Phạm, M. T. (2017). Toà án chuyên trách dành cho người chưa thành niên – Thiết chế bảo vệ quyền và lợi ích cho người chưa thành niên tại một số quốc gia trên thế giới và Việt Nam [Specialized Juvenile Courts – An Institution for Protecting Juvenile Rights and Interests in Several Countries and in Vietnam]. Trong Trường Đại học Luật Hà Nội, *Kỷ yếu Hội thảo khoa học Quyền của người chưa thành niên trong pháp luật hình sự một số nước trên thế giới và kinh nghiệm cho Việt Nam* (p. 189–193).

Quỹ Nhi đồng Liên hợp quốc UNICEF Vietnam, & Viện Khoa học xét xử Tòa án nhân dân Tối cao. (2012). Mô hình tổ chức Tòa án chuyên biệt đối với người chưa thành niên trên thế giới [Models of Specialized Juvenile Courts Worldwide]. Trong *Báo cáo tổng quan về cơ sở lý luận và thực tiễn của sự cần thiết thành lập Tòa án chuyên trách đối với người chưa thành niên ở Việt Nam* (p. 83). Nhà xuất bản Thanh niên.

Reid, S., & Bromwich, R. (2019). *Youth and the law*. Edmond Montgomery Publications Limited.

Tòa án nhân dân tối cao. (2025, tháng 2). *Giới thiệu nội dung cơ bản của Luật Tư pháp người chưa thành niên Số 59/2024.QH15* [Introduction to the basic vontents of the Juvenile justice Law No. 59/2024/QH15]. Cổng thông tin điện tử phổ biến, giáo dục pháp luật quốc gia. Truy cập ngày 20 tháng 4, 2025, từ https://pbgdpl.gov.vn/Pages/tai-lieu-de-cuong.aspx?ItemID=370&l=TLDCGioiThieu

Trương, Q. V. (2019). Chính sách hình sự áp dụng đối với người chưa thành niên phạm tội - Từ lịch sử lập pháp đến quy định trong bộ luật hình sự năm 2015 [Criminal Policy Towards Juvenile Offenders – From Legislative History to the 2015 Criminal Code]. Trong Trường Đại học Luật Hà Nội, *Luật học Việt Nam – Những vấn đề đương đại* (p. 568). Nhà xuất bản Tư pháp.

Vũ, T. P. (2020). *Bảo vệ quyền con người của trẻ em bằng pháp luật hình sự Việt Nam* [Protecting the Human Rights of Children through Vietnamese Criminal Law]. Nhà xuất bản Công an nhân dân.

Chapter 13
Preventing Sexual Abuse of Children Under 16 Through Criminal Justice Mechanisms

Thao Huyen DIEP

Abstract Prevention of sexual offenses against persons under 16 years old is a system of solutions that embody both state and social characteristics, aiming to address the increase and development of such crimes. For crime prevention to be effective, it is essential to identify the legal regulations concerning this type of crime, as well as assess the extent and evolution of sexual abuse behaviors towards individuals under 16 in the current period. On that basis, it is necessary to propose preventive measures that focus on changing the mindset about crime prevention, improving the legal framework, raising community awareness, and building a safe and healthy environment for children.

13.1 Introduction

The phenomenon of sexual abuse against persons under the age of sixteen has long been a matter of public concern. However, the number of criminal cases continues to rise, with offenders becoming younger and offending patterns increasingly complex. The consequences of such offences are not limited to causing severe physical and psychological harm to victims but also result in long-term repercussions that adversely affect the development of children and the maintenance of social order and safety. Although Vietnamese law has established strict provisions, preventive effectiveness has not met expectations. In the context of rapid technological advancement, the online environment has become a common means of communication and connection, yet it also poses significant risks to children, particularly the risk of sexual abuse of persons under the age of sixteen. This reality presents new challenges for the protection of children.

Article history: Received 16 April 2025; Revised 18 July 2025; Accepted 18 August 2025.

T. H. DIEP (✉)
Tra Vinh University, Vinh Long Province, Viet Nam
e-mail: diepthao@tvu.edu.vn

N. Binh An et al. (eds.), *The Future of Child-Friendly Justice and Children's Rights in Vietnam*, https://doi.org/10.1007/978-981-95-3521-7_13

13.2 Recognition of Legal Provisions on Sexual Offences Against Persons Under Sixteen

Under the provisions of the 2015 Criminal Code as amended in 2017, sexual offences against persons under the age of sixteen are regulated in Chapter XIV on sexual offences, in which the victim is under sixteen years old. These include: Rape of a person under sixteen years old (Article 142); Sexual coercion of a person from thirteen years old to under sixteen years old (Article 144); Sexual intercourse or other sexual activities with a person from thirteen years old to under sixteen years old (Article 145); Obscene acts against a person under sixteen years old (Article 146); and Use of a person under sixteen years old for pornographic purposes (Article 147). Vietnamese criminal law relies on the age of the victim to determine the level of legal protection, with different age groups receiving different degrees of protection under criminal law, generally divided into three main categories: under thirteen years old; from thirteen to under sixteen years old; and from sixteen years old.

Pursuant to Article 142 of the 2015 Criminal Code as amended in 2017, rape of a person under sixteen years old is defined as the act of "using force, threatening to use force, or taking advantage of the victim's inability to defend himself or herself, or using another method to engage in sexual intercourse or other sexual activities with a person from thirteen years old to under sixteen years old against that person's will." The offence may be committed by using physical force on the victim's body or by verbal threats to coerce the victim. For sexual intercourse with a person under thirteen years old, even with the victim's consent, the perpetrator is still subject to criminal prosecution for rape of a person under sixteen years old. The law explicitly provides that in such cases the victim's consent has no legal effect to exclude the perpetrator's criminal liability.

Sexual coercion of a person from thirteen years old to under sixteen years old under Article 144 is defined as the act of "using any method to cause a person from thirteen years old to under sixteen years old, who is in a dependent situation or in a state of distress, to unwillingly engage in sexual intercourse or other sexual activities." This includes cases where the offender uses force, deception, inducement, promises, or threats to compel a person in a dependent or distressed situation to unwillingly allow sexual intercourse or other sexual activities, despite the victim's complete lack of desire for such acts. Where the victim is under thirteen years old, the offender shall be prosecuted for rape of a person under sixteen years old under Article 142.

Sexual intercourse or other sexual activities with a person from thirteen years old to under sixteen years old is defined as the act of "a person aged eighteen years or older engaging in sexual intercourse or other sexual activities with a person from thirteen years old to under sixteen years old, if the case does not fall under Article 142 or Article 144 of the 2015 Criminal Code as amended in 2017." The perpetrator must be at least eighteen years old and may be male or female. The act is carried out with the consent of both parties, without coercion from either side. This consent often arises from a romantic relationship, especially given that boys and girls tend to form such relationships at an early age. However, at this stage of physical and psychological development, children are not yet capable of full and accurate awareness of the matter.

Obscene acts against a person under sixteen years old under Article 146 are defined as acts committed by "a person aged eighteen years or older engaging in obscene acts against a person under sixteen years old without the intention of sexual intercourse or other sexual activities." The victim may be male or female, though in practice they are mainly female. The victim may be coerced to perform obscene acts, may consent to the perpetrator's obscene acts, or may voluntarily perform obscene acts on the perpetrator.

Use of a person under sixteen years old for pornographic purposes under Article 147 is defined as acts by "a person aged eighteen years or older enticing, inducing, or coercing a person under sixteen years old to perform pornographic acts or to directly witness pornographic performances in any form." This offence was first codified in the 2015 Criminal Code. Pornographic acts are understood as enticing, luring, inciting, promising, inducing, coercing, or using material benefits to have a person under sixteen years old perform or demonstrate pornographic acts to satisfy the offender's sexual desires, or to have the person under sixteen years old witness pornographic performances without engaging in sexual intercourse with the victim. Any pornographic act against a person under sixteen years old is considered a criminal offence, and victims may be male or female.

From the above analysis, sexual offences against persons under sixteen years old can be recognised as "*socially dangerous acts committed intentionally by a person with criminal liability capacity, infringing upon the inviolable right to sexual integrity, impairing normal physical development, or infringing upon the health, honour, and dignity of persons under sixteen years old.*"

13.3 Concept of the Crime Situation and the Prevention of Sexual Offences Against Persons Under Sixteen

13.3.1 Concept of the Crime Situation and the Situation of Sexual Offences Against Persons Under Sixteen

In the formation and development of criminology, there have been various approaches to the concept of the "crime situation." According to A. I. Alekseev, the crime situation is the objective manifestation of the state of crime in society, including indicators such as the number, structure, dynamics, geographic distribution, and trends of crime within a given period of time (Alekseev, 2004). Alekseev considers crime not as an isolated phenomenon but as the result of contradictions in the social structure, deficiencies in education, legal culture, and the effectiveness of social control. The study of the crime situation enables the identification of social factors leading to the increase or decrease of crime, thereby orienting appropriate intervention measures. Similarly, A. I. Dolgova views the crime situation as a negative social phenomenon reflecting deviations from social norms and the weakening of social institutions in controlling behaviour. Studying the crime situation helps to better understand social, economic, and cultural factors influencing criminal behaviour, thus contributing to the development of effective crime prevention measures (Dolgova, 2007).

In some criminological studies, the term "crime situation" is understood as a socio-legal phenomenon that reflects the degree and trend of crime within a specific period of time and in a defined space. It encompasses indicators such as the rate, types, and seriousness of criminal acts occurring in the community. It is not merely a collection of individual criminal cases but also a reflection of the social, cultural, and economic condition of a specific historical period. In contrast, "criminality" refers to the degree and trend of offending by an individual or a group, reflecting the existence of social, psychological, cultural, and economic factors that may lead to criminal behaviour, focusing on the characteristics, personality, and behaviour of the individual or group.

In Vietnam, the concept of "crime situation" has been discussed extensively by scholars. According to Prof. Dr. Nguyễn Ngọc Hòa, "The crime situation is the state and trend of movement of crimes (or groups of crimes, or a specific type of crime) that have occurred within a defined spatial unit and time unit" (Nguyễn Ngọc Hòa, 2015). Prof. Dr. Võ Khánh Vinh defines it as "a socio-legal and criminal phenomenon, historically changeable and class-based, comprising a unified totality (system) of crimes committed within a given society (nation) and within a specific period of time" (Võ Khánh Vinh, 2011). In the Criminology Textbook of Hanoi Law University, the crime situation is defined as "a negative social phenomenon contrary to criminal law, class-based and historically changeable, reflected in a totality of specific crimes that have occurred in society within a defined period of time" (Hanoi Law University, 2010). In the 2013 revised edition, the definition was stated as "the actual state and development of crime that has occurred within a defined time unit and spatial unit."

Under Article 4 of the Law on Children 2016, sexual abuse of persons under sixteen is understood as the act of using force, threatening to use force, coercing, enticing, or inducing a child to participate in activities related to sex, including rape, sexual coercion, sexual intercourse, obscene acts, and the use of children for prostitution or pornography in any form.

From the above theoretical foundations, the crime situation regarding sexual offences against persons under sixteen, from the perspective of legal science, is understood as the state and trend of movement of such offences that have occurred within a defined space and time.

13.3.2 Concept of Preventing Sexual Offences Against Persons Under Sixteen Through the Criminal Justice Mechanism

Crime prevention is a technical term within the field of criminology, widely used in criminological research both domestically and internationally (Farrington, 2000). The notion of crime prevention began to be studied more extensively in the seventeenth and eighteenth centuries, when philosopher Montesquieu expressed the view that "A good legislator should concern himself more with preventing crimes than with punishing them" (Katie Ann Martin, 2013). In the first edition of the Soviet Criminology Textbook, published in 1966, crime prevention was defined as "a system of interrelated measures carried out by state agencies and social organisations aimed at preventing crime and reducing or eliminating the causes of crime" (Herzenzon et al., 1966).

Crime prevention is one of the core areas of research and a key objective of criminology. Prof. Dr. Võ Khánh Vinh has stated that "Preventing the crime situation is a system of measures of different levels, state-based, social, and state-social in nature, aimed at remedying or neutralising (weakening or limiting) the causes and conditions of crime and thereby reducing and gradually eliminating the crime situation" (Võ Khánh Vinh, 1999). According to Assoc. Prof. Dr. Trịnh Tiến Việt, crime prevention is "a means of regulating the development of social relations for the purpose of limiting or eliminating the causes of crime, involving the interaction of socio-economic, educational-pedagogical, organisational, and legal measures, as a set of various methods of crime prevention" (Trịnh Tiến Việt, 2008).

Accordingly, "Prevention of sexual offences against persons under sixteen through the criminal justice mechanism" is understood as a system of measures of both state and social nature, implemented primarily through the activities of criminal justice bodies such as investigative agencies, the People's Procuracy, courts, and enforcement authorities. Preventive measures are not only legal in nature but also organisational-social, educational, and victim-support measures, designed to create a comprehensive, profound, and long-term prevention mechanism. These measures aim to address and gradually eliminate the causes and conditions giving rise to sexual offences against persons under sixteen, while reducing the occurrence of such crimes and moving towards effectively controlling this particularly serious and dangerous category of offences.

13.4 Assessment of the Extent and Trends of Sexual Offences Against Persons Under Sixteen in Vietnam from 2007 to 2023

Statistical data from reports of competent authorities indicate that this category of offences has not only increased in number but has also become more complex in modus operandi and more serious in its consequences (Table 13.1).

During the period from 2007 to 2023, the situation of sexual offences against persons under sixteen in Vietnam evolved with increasing complexity.

Specifically, between 2007 and 2010, the number of cases showed a downward trend from 1,068 cases in 2007 to 921 cases in 2010, representing a 13.76% decrease compared to the base year. Similarly, the number of defendants decreased from 1,181 to 1,023, a reduction of 13.38%. This decline can be attributed to the comprehensive implementation of the "Project on Combating Sexual Abuse of Children and Juvenile Crime" during this period, which resulted in positive prevention outcomes and effective enforcement of crime prevention policies.

Table 13.1 Extent of sexual offences against persons under sixteen nationwide (2007–2023)

Year	Sexual offences against persons under sixteen nationwide		% of cases compared to 2007	% of defendants compared to 2007
	Number of cases	Number of cases	%	%
2007	1.068	1.181	100	100
2008	1.028	1.113	96.25	94.24
2009	970	1.082	90.82	91.62
2010	921	1.023	86.24	86.62
2011	1.127	1.230	105.52	104.15
2012	1.278	1.381	119.66	116.93
2013	1.545	1.683	144.66	142.51
2014	1.382	1.433	129.40	121.34
2015	1.573	1.661	147.28	140.64
2016	1.342	1.415	125.66	119.81
2017	1.261	1.322	118.07	111.94
2018	1.166	1.227	109.18	103.90
2019	1.382	1.447	129.40	122.52
2020	1.167	1.214	109.27	102.79
2021	1.531	1.593	143.35	134.89
2022	2.287	2.300	214.14	194.75
2023	2.498	2.501	233.90	211.77

Source Supreme People's Court of Vietnam

However, in the period from 2011 to 2015, the number of cases increased again, from 1,127 cases in 2011 to 1,573 cases in 2015, an increase of over 47% compared to 2007. The number of defendants also rose to 1,661, an increase of 40.64% over the base year. Notably, in 2013, the number of cases reached 1,545, exceeding 1,500 for the first time. This was the period when social networks and the Internet developed rapidly. According to World Bank data, the proportion of Internet users in Vietnam increased from about 31% in 2010 to 48% in 2015 (Moore, 2016). Platforms such as Facebook and YouTube expanded quickly, becoming the primary communication channels for young people. However, the ease of accessing unfiltered content, including harmful and toxic information, was associated with increased risks of cyber-related crimes and greater exposure to harmful material.

From 2016 to 2020, there was a slight decline, with the highest figure in this period being 1,573 cases in 2015 and the lowest 1,167 cases in 2020. This decrease may reflect the initial impact of prevention and public awareness campaigns. Nevertheless, from 2021 to 2023, there was a sharp upward trend. The year 2022 was particularly notable, recording 2,287 cases and 2,300 defendants, equivalent to 214% and 194% respectively compared to 2007. This represents the highest figures in the entire survey period, with a rapid and marked increase (Fig. 13.1).

According to statistical data, from 2015 to 2021, more than 6,300 cases of sexual abuse were recorded nationwide, involving over 6,400 victims. Particularly, from 2020 to September 2023, there were as many as 7,483 cases of child sexual abuse nationwide, of which more than 80% were sexual offences—an extremely alarming proportion. In 2023 alone, there were 2,498 cases of child sexual abuse, representing an increase of 9.2% compared to 2022, with 82.2% of these involving sexual abuse. This situation may reflect the fact that the effectiveness of crime prevention policies

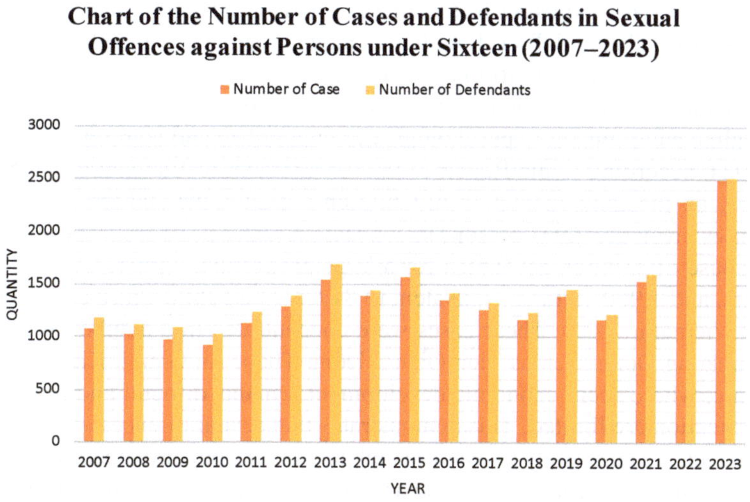

Fig. 13.1 Trends of sexual offences against persons under sixteen nationwide (2007–2023)

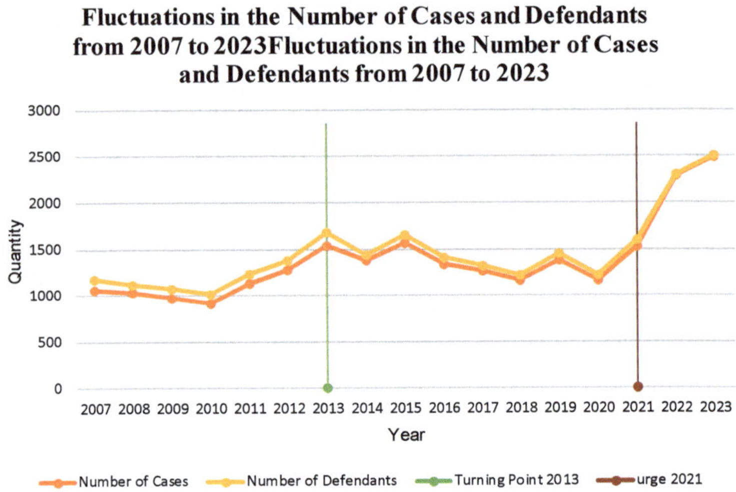

Fig. 13.2 Changes in the number of cases and number of defendants in sexual offences against persons under sixteen

in this area remains limited, and that the enhancement of social control has not been commensurate with the realities of society (Fig. 13.2).

The period from 2021 onwards marks a sharp increase, particularly in 2022 and 2023. This trend is not merely the result of random fluctuation but is strongly influenced by multiple social, economic, and technological factors. The COVID-19 pandemic disrupted socio-economic stability, placing many families under hardship and loosening parental supervision of children. Prolonged periods of online learning increased children's exposure to the Internet and social media platforms such as Facebook, YouTube, and TikTok without adequate parental oversight. This created opportunities for children to form early romantic relationships without proper guidance from family or school, or to be exploited by offenders who used sensitive images in the online environment to psychologically manipulate and commit acts of abuse.

In 2024, according to the Report of the Government of Vietnam to the National Assembly on the Implementation of Children's Rights, the authorities prosecuted 2,361 cases involving 2,931 persons in connection with acts of child abuse. Of these, sexual abuse of children accounted for a large proportion, with 1,927 cases, 2,106 offenders, and 1,960 victims, equivalent to 81.6% of all child abuse cases (Government of Vietnam, 2024). These cases were concentrated in a number of provinces in the Mekong Delta such as Tiền Giang, Đồng Tháp, An Giang, Kiên Giang, and Sóc Trăng, where socio-economic development remains difficult and resources for child protection are limited. This demonstrates that sexual offences against persons under sixteen are not merely transient social phenomena but have deep-rooted causes related to culture, education, social awareness, and economic conditions. Changing social habits, awareness, and institutional mechanisms requires long-term efforts;

thus, long-term prevention policies are needed to ensure continuity, stability, and effective coordination among agencies and organisations.

13.5 Preventive Solutions for Sexual Offences Against Persons Under Sixteen Through the Criminal Justice Mechanism

In practice, many preventive measures for sexual offences against persons under sixteen have been applied in most provinces and cities nationwide, and diverse research has been conducted from the perspectives of criminal law, criminology, and sociology. However, the incidence of such offences continues to rise. This indicates a need to change perceptions of crime prevention, especially the prevention of sexual offences, by clarifying which changes in the current period are influencing the increase in sexual offences against persons under sixteen, and whether the criminal justice mechanism for crime prevention is being implemented effectively.

13.5.1 Changing Perceptions of Prevention of Sexual Offences Against Persons Under Sixteen

First, an important preventive measure is the recognition that comprehensive legal protection must be expanded to cover not only girls but also boys, children with disabilities, and other vulnerable groups such as ethnic minority children, children in special circumstances, and street-working children. Ensuring the rights and safety of all children, regardless of gender, physical condition, living situation, or orientation, is consistent with the principle of non-discrimination under the United Nations Convention on the Rights of the Child. In addition, there must be a shift in social understanding of the concept of "consent" in sexual relations involving children. Some offenders have exploited children's lack of knowledge or psychological dependence to claim "consent" as justification, which represents a serious legal loophole. It is therefore necessary to eliminate any argument of consent where the victim is below the age of legal protection, while establishing clear, strict, and fair legal standards that form a solid basis for prosecuting offenders and protecting the personal rights and healthy development of children.

Second, prevention of sexual offences against persons under sixteen through the criminal justice mechanism requires unified and coordinated action between state agencies and social organisations to detect, prevent, and reduce this particularly serious category of crime. The procedural bodies, including the police, the People's Procuracy, the courts, and the criminal judgment enforcement agencies, play a central role, complemented by measures for victim support, community supervision, and social intervention. This approach aligns with the situational crime prevention theory developed by Clarke (2017), which emphasises reducing crime opportunities through environmental management, reorganisation of living conditions, increased supervision, and removal of conditions conducive to crime. This view is also consistent with the 1989 United Nations Convention on the Rights of the Child, particularly Article 19, which obliges State Parties to take "all appropriate legislative, administrative, social and educational measures to protect the child from all forms of physical or mental violence, injury or abuse, neglect or negligent treatment, maltreatment or exploitation, including sexual abuse" (United Nations, 1989).

Third, preventive efforts must be adapted to the context of technological development. In addition to traditional methods, attention must be given to non-traditional crime risks, such as the misuse of images and personal information of children and online sexual exploitation. As noted by Farrell et al. (2024), "The Internet has revolutionised crime, creating spaces for new crimes and new ways to commit old crimes." Necessary solutions include the proactive development of alert systems through location-tracking software, security cameras in schools and public areas, and the establishment of a national database on sexual offenders. As Brown and Rich (2023) emphasise, "There is no single, simple, universal approach to controlling child sexual abuse material; we need a range of approaches involving government, industry, and the online user community." These measures will enhance awareness of crime prevention, strengthen control, reduce recidivism risks, and create a safe environment for children's development.

Fourth, as Clarke (2017) has noted, "Preventing crime and stopping it from occurring is more important than detecting and punishing it." Crime prevention should be prioritised over post-offence detection and punishment. Instead of focusing only on addressing the consequences after offences have occurred, society should place greater emphasis on early intervention through effective preventive measures. Forecasting crime trends and identifying potential risks can help competent authorities implement timely preventive actions and minimise conditions conducive to offending. Early and proactive prevention is therefore the sustainable and effective approach to combating crime.

Fifth, raising community awareness of children's rights, particularly the inviolability of sexual integrity, should be a long-term strategy. Sustained public communication campaigns should be combined with community education to disseminate knowledge about children's rights. In many developed countries, models such as the National Child Protection Agency or the Independent Children's Rights Ombudsman have been established to safeguard children's rights and promptly address cases of abuse.

13.5.2 Overcoming Limitations in the Prevention of Sexual Offences Against Persons Under Sixteen

First, current prevention of sexual offences against persons under sixteen remains primarily focused on addressing the issue after the offence has occurred, revealing the ineffectiveness of early intervention and proactive prevention measures. Fundamental preventive mechanisms, such as identifying risks, monitoring deviant behaviour, assessing risk factors, or providing psychological support to children showing signs of harm, have not been systematically or consistently integrated. Notably, the criminal justice mechanism remains heavily punitive, especially towards juvenile offenders, often relying on severe measures such as detention, public trials, and custodial sentences. This approach not only undermines the effectiveness of strategies for preventing reoffending but also risks causing prolonged psychological harm, hindering reintegration, and increasing the likelihood of stigma. Meanwhile, more humane and rehabilitative approaches—such as diversion, community education, flexible probation, or behavioural therapy—are not yet widely applied. Given this reality, it is imperative to reshape the criminal justice mechanism towards a balanced integration of its punitive and preventive functions, with a particular emphasis on early intervention and flexible handling. Reference may be drawn from the Child Sexual Abuse Independent Inquiry (IICSA) and the "Child-Friendly Justice" model of the United Kingdom, which promote "child-sensitive interviewing" to minimise re-traumatisation during testimony, and the establishment of post-sentence monitoring systems for sexual offenders. This approach aligns with the principle enshrined in Article 40 of the United Nations Convention on the Rights of the Child, ensuring that children in conflict with the law are treated in a manner appropriate to their age and aimed at rehabilitation.

Second, a significant limitation in protecting victims under sixteen is the lack of specialised legal and psychological support mechanisms. The consistent presence of an independent legal representative, guardian, or psychologist throughout the criminal process is still not effectively implemented, leaving children without timely support in safeguarding both their rights and mental well-being, thereby increasing the risk of crisis and reluctance to cooperate with authorities. Furthermore, uncontrolled media coverage, including disclosure of identities or detailed descriptions of cases, has seriously infringed the privacy and dignity of child victims, violating legal and ethical standards in journalism. In Vietnam, the absence of a unified national database on child sexual abuse cases hinders statistical analysis, risk assessment, and early warning efforts. Inter-agency coordination among the police, courts, education, health, and social sectors remains fragmented, preventing a coherent and continuous intervention process. In light of these challenges, it is urgent to establish a comprehensive protection mechanism for child victims, including "single-session recorded testimony," assignment of investigators of the same gender, arrangement of child-friendly courtrooms or the use of protective screens, and ensuring the presence of legal and psychological support throughout the proceedings. These are core measures within the "Child-Friendly Justice" model effectively implemented in countries such as the United Kingdom, Sweden, and the Netherlands, which help minimise re-traumatisation and maximise protection of children's rights. At the same time, it is necessary to codify the principle of victim identity confidentiality in the media, with strict penalties for violations to ensure safety and dignity. The national database on sexual offences against children should be completed within the framework of digital governance, with interconnected data sharing across sectors, enabling prevention and risk warnings based on region, age, offence type, and recidivism rate. A monitoring mechanism should be established at both central and local levels to ensure a rapid and effective response in protecting children from the risk of abuse.

Third, strengthening inter-agency coordination in child protection in general, and in the prevention of sexual offences against persons under sixteen in particular, is essential. At present, provinces and cities nationwide are actively implementing the "Project on Combating Sexual Abuse of Children, Juvenile Offending, Domestic Violence, and Human Trafficking" (Project No. 4) led by the Ministry of Public Security. With the aim of creating a safe and healthy environment for children, localities have intensified public awareness campaigns and legal education on the prevention of child sexual abuse through mass media, workshops, and training for officials, teachers, parents, and students. In accordance with Decision No. 987/QĐ-BGDĐT dated 25 March 2020, which approved the Plan for Prevention and Intervention in Cases of School Violence and Child Sexual Abuse in Educational Institutions for the period 2020–2025, localities have established and strengthened Child Protection Steering Committees and developed networks of child protection collaborators at the grassroots level. Models such as "Safe Houses," "Safe Schools," and "Safe Communities" have also been widely implemented.

In addition, localities have actively partnered with international projects to enhance child protection. Notable examples include the "Child-Friendly Schools for Vulnerable Children" project funded by Save the Children, the "Ending Violence Against Children" project supported by World Vision Vietnam, and the "Strengthening Access to Justice and Protection for Children in Contact with the Law" project funded by UNICEF. As a result, the prevention of child sexual abuse has seen positive changes, reducing risks and safeguarding the legitimate rights of children nationwide. Provincial and municipal People's Committees have also prioritised and directed Task Forces under Scheme 06 to standardise and clean data for updating child information into local child management software. However, this process must be accelerated in the near future to ensure timely and effective protection.

13.5.3 Addressing Limitations from the Social, Family, and School Environment

Reforming approaches to sex education and self-protection skills within families and schools is an essential solution to protect children from the risk of sexual abuse, enabling them to understand their personal rights and how to protect themselves.

Within the family, parents should actively seek out and equip themselves with appropriate knowledge in order to guide their children naturally, age-appropriately, and without a deterrent tone. Rather than avoiding the topic, parents should create an open atmosphere that encourages children to share their thoughts on sexuality and privacy. Children need to be taught skills to identify inappropriate behaviour, understand bodily boundaries, and know how to react in dangerous situations. In particular, children should be taught to refuse and say "no" when they feel unsafe and to seek help from a trusted adult.

In raising children, parents are not only guides but also trusted companions. This companionship must be reflected in maintaining open communication, listening to, and respecting the child's feelings. Parents must reasonably monitor children's online activities, supervise peer relationships, and oversee interactions in a social media environment that is increasingly complex. According to the Ministry of Public Security, 59% of child sexual abuse cases are committed by neighbours or acquaintances (Ministry of Public Security, 2019). UNICEF reports that "up to 90% of cases of child sexual abuse involve perpetrators known to the child—including family members, relatives, neighbours, or teachers" (UNICEF, 2017). Therefore, children should never be left unsupervised, even with familiar individuals, unless there is absolute trust. Parents must also teach children to protect personal information, avoid sharing sensitive images, and refrain from meeting strangers online. For adolescents in their formative years who may develop early romantic feelings, parents should provide appropriate sex education to help them understand healthy relationships, safe boundaries, and self-protection. Equipping children with knowledge and skills from an early age is an effective preventive measure, helping them avoid abuse and grow up safely and confidently.

In parallel, schools should integrate sex education into the official curriculum, delivering it in a visual, interactive manner that focuses on self-defence skills, risk identification, and emergency responses. Teachers should be professionally trained to detect early signs of abuse, offer counselling, and provide support to students. Strengthening cooperation between families and schools through thematic sessions and discussion forums will enhance awareness, unify educational methods, and share experiences in child protection. This approach not only improves the effectiveness of sex education but also fosters a safe and healthy environment, enabling children to develop confidently and holistically. Furthermore, raising community awareness about preventing sexual offences against persons under sixteen is essential. Strong, continuous communication campaigns involving schools, local authorities, and social organisations should be implemented, along with building community surveillance networks to encourage the public to report abuse through hotlines or smart applications.

13.5.4 Legal Reform Solutions for the Prevention of Sexual Offences Against Persons Under Sixteen

First, regarding the offence of rape of a person under sixteen (Article 142), sexual intercourse with a person under thirteen is deemed rape regardless of the victim's consent. It is therefore necessary to review penalties in the current context, given that the maximum sentence can be life imprisonment, but the minimum penalty or additional mandatory measures such as compulsory education or rehabilitation programmes may need reconsideration. Lessons may be drawn from the practices of countries such as the United Kingdom, France, the United States, and the Republic of Korea in applying electronic monitoring or child access prohibition orders after release from prison, as well as defining the scope of such measures to ensure effective child protection without violating human rights.

Second, it is important to limit the overuse of pre-trial detention and prioritise age-appropriate handling. In practice, many offenders aged fourteen to under sixteen who are charged with very serious or especially serious crimes are subjected to pre-trial detention. Overuse of this measure can lead to negative consequences such as disruption of education, loss of reintegration opportunities, increased risk of reoffending, and diminished effectiveness of humanitarian policies for juvenile offenders. An essential preventive solution is to ensure that the justice mechanism adheres to the principle of non-discrimination and applies age-appropriate measures, particularly for juveniles who require special protection under the United Nations Convention on the Rights of the Child (United Nations, 1989, Articles 2 and 40). Alternatives to detention focusing on education, support, and rehabilitation should be given genuine priority instead of continuing the trend of early and overly broad criminalisation without due consideration for age-specific characteristics.

Third, the Draft Juvenile Justice Law 2025—expected to take effect on 1 January 2026—marks a significant step forward in judicial reform in Vietnam. Its goal is to establish a specialised, humane, and age-appropriate legal framework for juveniles in criminal proceedings. Current proposals provide for twelve diversionary measures as alternatives to imprisonment, including community-based education, restorative justice, behavioural rehabilitation, and supervised probation. These measures are designed to suit the psychological development and rehabilitation potential of children. Completion of this legal framework will help minimise the negative impacts of detention, while expanding opportunities for early intervention, psychological support, moral and vocational education, and sustainable reintegration. Particularly in the context of increasingly complex and difficult-to-control sexual offences against persons under sixteen, the provisions of this law will serve as a long-term preventive tool, rather than focusing solely on addressing consequences.

Based on this, there should be clear provisions and encouragement for the broad application of suitable alternatives such as restorative justice, mandatory community education, and personality rehabilitation programmes linked to vocational training. In parallel, the professional capacity of criminal justice agencies in psychology, sociology, and child protection should be enhanced to build a justice system that is not only strict but also fair, humane, and effective in preventing juvenile crime.

13.6 Conclusion

Preventing sexual offences against persons under sixteen through the criminal justice mechanism not only protects the safety and healthy development of children but also contributes to building a civilised and safe society. In the context of rapid digital technology development, online sexual abuse has become increasingly sophisticated, requiring educational, awareness-raising, and monitoring measures from families, schools, and competent authorities. Equipping children with self-protection skills, enhancing online safety awareness, and detecting warning signs in a timely manner help children actively avoid risks. At the same time, improvements to the legal framework and effective preventive solutions will strengthen the capacity to deter and handle abuse, creating a sustainable foundation for the safe development of children in the future.

Acknowledgements We acknowledge the support of time and facilities from Tra Vinh University (TVU) for this study.

References

Alekseev, A. I. (2004). *Криминология. Курс лекций* [Criminology: A course of lectures] (4th ed., revised and expanded). Moscow: Shchit-M Publishing.

Brown, R. (2023). *Eliminating online child sexual abuse material* (p. 167). Routledge.

Clarke, R. V. (2017). Situational crime prevention. In R. Wortley & M. Townsley (Eds.), *Environmental criminology and crime analysis* (2nd ed., pp. 259–294). Routledge.

Dolgova, A. I. (Ed.). (2007). *Криминология: Учебник для вузов* [Criminology: Textbook for universities]. Moscow, Russia: Norma.

Farrell, G., Tilley, N., & Tseloni, A. (2024). Why the crime drop? *Crime and Justice, 43*(1), 421–490.

Farrington, D. P. (2000). Explaining and preventing crime: The globalization of knowledge. *Criminology, 38*(1), 1–24.

Government of Vietnam. (2024). National report on the implementation of children's rights in 2024. Retrieved from Pháp Luật TP. Hồ Chí Minh Newspaper: https://plo.vn/so-vu-xam-hai-tre-em-bi-khoi-to-lan-dau-tien-giam-sau-4-nam-post790948.html

Hanoi Law University. (2010). *Criminology textbook*. People's Public Security Publishing House.

Herzenzon, A. A., Karpets, I. I., & Kudriavtsev, V. N. (Eds.). (1966). *Kriminologija*. Studopedia (theoretical reference).

Martin, K. A. (2013). *Domestic violence, sexual assault, and sex trafficking in the media: A content analysis* (p. 393). Master's Thesis. Available at ProQuest or institutional repository.

Ministry of Public Security. (2019). Report on the prevention and combat of child sexual abuse in 2019. Hanoi, Vietnam.

Moore, A. (2016, January 7). *Vietnam digital landscape 2015* [PowerPoint presentation]. http://www.vietnamdigitallandscape2015.com

Trịnh Tiến Việt. (2008). The concept of crime prevention from the criminological perspective. *VNU Journal of Science: Economics and Law, 2008*, 185–199.
UNICEF. (2017). *A familiar face: Violence in the lives of children and adolescents*. United Nations Children's Fund. https://www.unicef.org/publications/index_101397.html
United Nations. (1989). Convention on the rights of the child. *Treaty Series, 1577*, 3.
Võ Khánh Vinh. (1999). *Criminology textbook* (p. 150). Education Publishing House.
Võ Khánh Vinh. (2011). *Criminology textbook* (p. 160). People's Public Security Publishing House.
Võ Ngọc Hòa. (2015). *Criminology and the constituent elements of crime* (p. 252). Justice Publishing House.

Part IV
Emerging Challenges to Children's Rights in Vietnam

Chapter 14
Protecting Children's Privacy Rights in Cyberspace Under Vietnamese Law

Dang Thi Hong Tuyen

Abstract This article examines the protection of children's privacy rights in cyberspace under Vietnamese law, situating the analysis within the broader framework of human rights and data protection. The study begins by outlining the constitutional and statutory foundations of the right to privacy in Vietnam, tracing its historical development and clarifying its substantive content as applied to children. It then explores the specific legal provisions addressing children's privacy in the digital environment, including the Law on Children 2016, the Law on Cybersecurity 2018, the Law on Data 2024, and the Personal Data Protection Law 2025, as well as relevant decrees and the Code of Conduct on the Protection of Children in Cyberspace. The article critically assesses preventive measures, the roles of children, parents, state agencies, and private sector actors, and the current sanctioning mechanisms—criminal, civil, and administrative—available for addressing infringements. It identifies significant gaps in enforcement, regulatory limitations, and the absence of tailored sanctions for online violations. The findings underscore the need for legislative refinement, enhanced institutional coordination, and increased public awareness to address emerging risks such as biometric data misuse, targeted advertising, and the creation of enduring digital footprints. The article concludes with recommendations to strengthen legal protections and ensure a safe, rights-respecting digital environment for children in Vietnam.

14.1 Introduction

In the digital age, children have emerged as among the earliest and most active users of cyberspace, thereby facing heightened risks concerning the protection of their privacy in this distinct environment. Given the accessibility and openness of the digital space, the dissemination of children's personal information, including photographs,

Article history: Received 13 April 2025; Revised 23 July 2025; Accepted 03 August 2025.

D. T. H. Tuyen (✉)
Hanoi Law University, Ha Noi City, Viet Nam
e-mail: hongtuyenhlu@hlu.edu.vn

N. Binh An et al. (eds.), *The Future of Child-Friendly Justice and Children's Rights in Vietnam*, https://doi.org/10.1007/978-981-95-3521-7_14

names, school details, and daily routines, has become increasingly prevalent, particularly through social media platforms. While digital engagement yields benefits in education, entertainment, and social interaction, it simultaneously poses substantial threats to children's privacy, such as data breaches, targeted advertising, and potential exploitation for criminal purposes. Against this backdrop, the development and effective enforcement of a legal framework to safeguard children's privacy in the online environment is both urgent and indispensable. In Vietnam, various legal instruments have initially acknowledged children's fundamental rights in the digital environment and incorporated measures aimed at protecting their privacy. However, practical challenges and legal gaps persist in ensuring effective implementation. Therefore, this study seeks to examine the current Vietnamese legal framework governing personal privacy and children's privacy in cyberspace, evaluate the protective mechanisms in place, and assess the coherence and effectiveness of these regulations.

14.2 Overview of the Right to Privacy Under Vietnamese Law

Scholarly research has suggested that the concept of personal privacy in Vietnamese law can be traced back to the feudal era. The Hồng Đức Code of the Lê Dynasty, for example, stipulated in Article 2 that "anyone who arbitrarily enters the royal citadel shall be punished by flogging or demotion; entering a prohibited area shall result in penal servitude for military conscription… Officials who unlawfully enter the King's sleeping quarters or residence shall face the same penalties…". Similarly, the Gia Long Code (Hoàng Việt Luật Lệ) of the Nguyễn Dynasty prescribed in Article 268 that "those who are powerful and violent, relying on wealth and influence to oppress, intimidate, and humiliate ordinary people, causing them wrongful suffering…" and in Article 281 that "if individuals who are powerful and violent use coercion to detain people in private residences, interrogate them by force, or unlawfully confine them…". Although these ancient codes were not comprehensive by modern standards, they clearly demonstrate an early recognition of human dignity and personal rights. As observed by Trần Ngọc Tuấn (2024, p. 56), "the values of private life were respected to a certain extent, particularly in special contexts designated for specific subjects, demonstrating that the legal norms relating to privacy reflected social distinctions based on class and status".

In contemporary Vietnam, the protection of individual privacy rights has received increased attention and is now regulated in a more systematic manner. The 2013 Constitution affirms that the right to privacy is "inviolable" and guarantees, under the law, the security of information relating to private life, personal secrets, and family secrets. Furthermore, it protects the confidentiality of correspondence, telephone conversations, telegraphs, and other forms of private communication (Article 21, Constitution 2013). Building upon these constitutional guarantees, the Civil Code, the Criminal Code, and various specialized laws, including the Law on Electronic

Transactions, the Law on Cyberinformation Security, the Law on Information Technology, the Law on Telecommunications, and the Law on Post, establish specific provisions safeguarding privacy rights and personal data, and strictly prohibit acts that infringe upon such rights in the domains of postal services, telecommunications, cybersecurity, and the application and development of information technology.

Privacy is recognized as a fundamental and inviolable right of every individual under Vietnamese law. Article 21 of the 2013 Constitution stipulates that "(1) Everyone shall enjoy inviolability of private life, personal secrets, and family secrets, and shall be entitled to the protection of his or her honour and reputation. Information about private life, personal secrets, and family secrets shall be kept confidential by law. (2) Everyone has the right to the confidentiality of correspondence, telephone conversations, telegrams, and other forms of private communication. No one may illegally open, control, or seize other persons' correspondence, telephone conversations, telegrams, or private communications." From this provision, the categories of inviolable privacy rights can be identified as: (1) the right to information concerning private life, (2) the right to protection of personal secrets, (3) the right to protection of family secrets, and (4) the right to confidentiality of correspondence, telephone conversations, telegrams, and other forms of private communication. This constitutional guarantee also reflects Vietnam's commitment to the fundamental rights recognized in international treaties to which the country is a party (Cao Thanh Tâm, 2019).

The constitutional provisions on privacy set forth in the 2013 Constitution are further elaborated in the 2015 Civil Code. Article 38 of the 2015 Civil Code establishes the rights to private life, personal secrets, and family secrets as follows:

"1. The private life, personal secrets, and family secrets of a person are inviolable and protected by law. 2. The collection, preservation, use, and publication of information about an individual's private life must have the consent of that individual; the collection, preservation, use, and publication of information about family secrets must have the consent of all family members, unless otherwise provided by law. 3. The safety of mails, telephones, telegrams, and other forms of electronic information belonging to an individual shall be ensured and kept confidential. The opening, control, and retention of such communications may only be carried out in cases prescribed by law. 4. Contracting parties may not disclose information about each other's private life, personal secrets, or family secrets obtained during the formation or performance of a contract, unless otherwise agreed." (Article 38, Civil Code 2015).

Compared to the 2005 Civil Code, the 2015 Civil Code retains much of the earlier framework while introducing several notable amendments. First, the terminology was revised, replacing the phrase "right to privacy" (bí mật đời tư) with "right to private life" (quyền đối với đời sống riêng tư) and supplementing it with the distinct terms "personal secrets" and "family secrets". Second, substantively, Clause 1 of Article 38 in both Codes affirms the principle of inviolability and legal protection of personality rights. Clause 2 of the 2015 Code removes the previous provision allowing disclosure of information when the data subject has died, lost legal capacity, or not yet attained full civil capacity. Clause 3 remains largely unchanged from the 2005 Code, while Clause 4 introduces protection for privacy within contractual relations, a category typical of private law. Scholarly commentary suggests that the 2015 provisions represent more of a formal refinement than a substantive reform.

Nevertheless, the 2015 Civil Code contains four discernible innovations compared with its 2005 counterpart: (1) revised terminology to avoid conceptual ambiguities surrounding the notion of privacy; (2) inclusion of electronic data in Clause 3 to reflect technological advancements; (3) explicit provisions on data protection in contractual transactions; and (4) the addition of specific protections for family secrets (Cao Thanh Tâm, 2019).

It may be observed that the scope of the right to privacy protected under Vietnamese civil law remains relatively narrow, covering only private life, personal secrets, and family secrets. By contrast, prevailing theoretical perspectives on the right to privacy tend to interpret the scope of protection more broadly so as to encompass all matters relating to the individual concerned. This broader conception is not confined to private life or to personal and family secrets as defined under Vietnamese law, and it does not require distinguishing whether such matters constitute information or secrets (Trần Ngọc Tuấn, 2022).

14.3 Regulations on Children's Privacy Rights in Cyberspace Under Vietnamese Law

The rapid development of cyberspace has brought numerous benefits to children; however, it has also introduced potential risks that may directly affect them. Achievements in information technology in general, and the global Internet system in particular, have created significant advantages for children in various areas, including access to information, online learning, entertainment, and social networking (Daskalaki et al., 2020; Loutou et al., 2018). Nevertheless, these conveniences are accompanied by significant threats to children's right to privacy. Owing to its openness and ease of access, cyberspace has become an environment laden with risks concerning the protection of personal data, particularly for vulnerable groups such as children, who often lack sufficient awareness of privacy rights (Kravchuk, 2022; Livingstone & Byrne, 2023).

One of the most pressing concerns is the collection and use of children's personal data without stringent regulatory oversight. Social networking platforms, educational applications, and online games frequently require users to provide details such as name, age, address, and even location. Due to limited experience and insufficient understanding of information security, children are particularly susceptible to online scams. Many websites and applications present lengthy user agreements in small fonts and dense layouts, requiring consent to the terms and conditions before accessing services (Mizrahi, 2021). Most children do not carefully read these provisions and readily give consent, thereby creating opportunities for malicious actors to insert covert clauses enabling the collection and use of personal data.

A further common issue involves the infringement of children's right to privacy not only by online platforms but also inadvertently by adults with close familial ties who disclose images, age, name, or other personal information about a child on social networks. In Vietnam, many parents regularly post images of their children from infancy to adolescence without anticipating the long-term legal and practical consequences. Such actions create a lasting "digital footprint" that follows the child throughout life, increasing the risk of privacy violations (Dang & Doan, 2023). With the advancement of cyberspace, seemingly harmless information can be exploited for identity theft, impersonation, fraud, or other unlawful activities. Children may become victims of cybercrime when malicious actors extract personal data from social networks to generate facial recognition data, voice profiles, biometric identifiers, or fabricate false evidence for wrongful attribution of liability (European Parliamentary Research Service, 2025). More seriously, details about a child's residence, school, or daily routine, often inadvertently shared online by family members, can be exploited by offenders for abduction, abuse, or fraud (Bare, 2020). The increasing sophistication of targeted advertising also contributes to infringements of children's privacy. Algorithms tracking online behavior can monitor a child's browsing history and online habits to deliver personalized advertisements. A recent study found that approximately 90 per cent of 2,000 child-directed websites contained trackers, and about 27 per cent displayed personalized advertising (Moti et al., 2023).

In response to these challenges, Vietnam has promulgated a series of regulations aimed at protecting children's right to privacy in cyberspace. These provisions address the scope of the right, the requirement for children's views and consent regarding the use of their personal data online, and the mechanisms and methods for safeguarding such rights.

(i) *The right to privacy of children in cyberspace in Vietnam is currently recognized as a constitutional right derived from the general right to personal privacy*

As previously discussed, the right to personal privacy is among the fundamental human and civil rights enshrined in the 2013 Constitution (Article 21), and children, as subjects protected under the Constitution, naturally enjoy this right. Being members of a vulnerable group who have not yet fully developed the cognitive and physical capacity to protect themselves against harmful acts, children receive special protection in relation to their privacy rights (Phuong Nam, 2019). Under Clause 1 of Article 37 of the Constitution, children, defined as persons under 16 years of age, are entitled to protection, care, and education by the State, family, and society; they have the right to participate in matters concerning children; and any act of abuse, mistreatment, neglect, exploitation of labour, or other infringement of their rights is strictly prohibited. Accordingly, under the 2013 Constitution, the child's right to privacy is safeguarded in relation to private life information, personal secrets, family secrets, and the confidentiality of correspondence, telephone communications, telegrams, and other forms of private communications.

On the basis of these constitutional provisions, regulations on children's privacy in cyberspace have been elaborated in several legislative instruments, including the Law on Children 2016, the Law on Cybersecurity 2018, the Law on Data 2024, the

Personal Data Protection Law 2025, and various subordinate instruments such as Decree No. 56/2017/NĐ-CP dated 9 May 2017 of the Government detailing certain provisions of the Law on Children; Decree No. 13/2023/NĐ-CP dated 17 April 2023 on Personal Data Protection; Decree No. 15/2020/NĐ-CP dated 3 February 2020 on administrative sanctions in the fields of postal services, telecommunications, radio frequencies, information technology, and electronic transactions (as amended by Decree No. 14/2022/NĐ-CP dated 27 January 2022); and the Code of Conduct on the Protection of Children in Cyberspace issued under Decision No. 88/QĐ-BTTTT dated 21 January 2025 of the Minister of Information and Communications.

(ii) *The substantive content of children's right to privacy in cyberspace under Vietnamese law is fairly broad, derived from the interpretation of the notions of personal secrets and private life protected for children*

The right to privacy of children online is specifically addressed in the Law on Children 2016, the Law on Cybersecurity 2018, the Press Law 2016, and related implementing instruments. This legal framework has been continually updated alongside economic liberalization, the modernization of technological infrastructure, and the expansion of the Internet, reflecting the legislature's attention to this matter (Tăng Thị Thu Trang & Lê Thị Thu Huyền, 2022).

Clause 2 of Article 54 of the Law on Children 2016 stipulates that agencies, organizations, and individuals managing or providing information and communication products or services, and organizing activities in the online environment, must take measures to ensure the safety and confidentiality of the private life of children in accordance with the law. Similarly, Clause 1 of Article 29 of the Law on Cybersecurity 2018 provides that children have the right to protection, to access information, to participate in social activities, to play, to engage in entertainment, to maintain the confidentiality of their personal data and private life, and to exercise other rights when participating in cyberspace.

To clarify the provisions of Article 21 of the Constitution and Article 54 of the Law on Children, Decree No. 56/2017/NĐ-CP specifies in Article 33 that confidential information concerning the private life and personal secrets of a child includes their name, age, personal identifying characteristics, health information and private matters recorded in medical records, personal images, information concerning family members and caregivers, personal property, telephone numbers, personal mailing addresses, details regarding residence and place of origin, school and class details, academic results, friendship networks, and information on services provided to the child.

Furthermore, Clause 1 of Article 2 of Decree No. 13/2023/NĐ-CP defines personal data as information in the form of symbols, letters, numerals, images, sounds, or similar forms in an electronic environment that is associated with a specific individual or enables the identification of such individual, including both basic and sensitive personal data. The Law on Data 2024, which will take effect on 1 July 2025, further defines digital data as data relating to objects, phenomena, and events, including one or more forms such as sounds, images, numerals, letters, and symbols represented in digital form.

From these provisions, it is clear that the right to privacy of children in cyberspace in Vietnam encompasses the protection of personal secrets and private life, understood broadly to include information in digital form relating to their identity, health, images, family, property, contact details, residence, schooling, academic performance, social relations, and services provided to them. Nevertheless, because these provisions are largely enumerative, there remain categories of information that could reasonably be considered part of a child's private life or personal secrets but are not expressly regulated. With technological advancement, increasing volumes of digital data—whether directly identifiable or indirectly linkable—fall within the ambit of privacy, including behavioural data such as browsing history and IP addresses, and biometric identifiers such as fingerprints and facial data. Behavioural data can be misused for targeted advertising, while biometric data play an essential role in identity verification, access to online services, banking transactions, and other critical activities. The absence of specific provisions on these categories in the current legal framework creates significant legal gaps, which may lead to serious consequences for individual data subjects and for society as a whole.

(iii) *Regulations on the child's consent and the consent of parents or guardians in the processing of children's personal data in cyberspace*

Vietnamese law stipulates that the use and processing of children's personal data must obtain both the consent of the child and the consent of the child's parents or legal guardians. According to Article 6 of the Law on Children 2016, any act of disclosing or revealing information concerning the private life or personal secrets of a child without the consent of the child aged seven or older and the consent of the child's parents or legal guardians is strictly prohibited (Clause 11 of Article 6 of the Law on Children 2016). Similarly, under Clause 2 of Article 20 of Decree No. 13/2023/ND-CP, the processing of a child's personal data must obtain the consent of the child in cases where the child is seven years of age or older, in addition to the consent of the child's parents or legal guardians as prescribed by law. Under Vietnamese law, a child is defined as a person under sixteen years of age (Article 1 of the Law on Children 2016). Therefore, it can be understood that in all cases of processing a child's personal data in cyberspace—such as collection, analysis, aggregation, encryption, decryption, modification, deletion, destruction, anonymization, provision, disclosure, transfer, and any other operation performed on personal data (Clause 7 of Article 2 of Decree No. 13/2023/ND-CP)—the consent of the child's parents or legal guardians is required; and in cases where the child is seven years of age or older (from seven years to under sixteen years), the consent of the child is additionally required alongside the consent of the parents or legal guardians.

This provision under Vietnamese law demonstrates a divergence from international standards. The regulation in Vietnamese law on the dual consent mechanism for the processing of children's personal data in cyberspace, applicable to children aged seven and above (from seven to under sixteen years old), indicates that the processing of a child's personal data is subject to the will of the parents or legal guardians, even when the child has already attained a significant level of cognitive development at later stages (for example, from twelve to fifteen years old). This means that Vietnamese children do not possess any autonomous decision-making right with respect to authorizing the use of their personal information throughout the entire period of minority, effectively negating their right of self-determination and, in certain aspects, remaining inconsistent with the recommendation on evolving capacities of the child as enshrined in Article 5 of the United Nations Convention on the Rights of the Child (1989). Article 19 of General Comment No. 25 (2021) on children's rights in relation to the digital environment, adopted by the United Nations Committee on the Rights of the Child, further clarifies this requirement in cyberspace, where children may participate independently without parental or guardian supervision once they have reached a certain level of maturity and understanding.

14.4 Methods of Protecting Children's Right to Privacy in Cyberspace Under Vietnamese Law

14.4.1 Self-protection and Preventive Measures Against Infringement of Children's Right to Privacy in Cyberspace

First, the obligation of children to self-protect their own right to privacy

Vietnamese law provides that children, as data subjects and holders of personal data, have an obligation to protect their own personal data. Clause 1 of Article 10 of Decree No. 13/2023/NĐ-CP stipulates that data subjects are obliged to "protect their personal data and request other relevant organizations or individuals to protect their personal data". The Code of Conduct on Child Protection in Cyberspace (2025) sets out specific rules of conduct for children to apply in safeguarding their privacy online, including: (1) acquiring knowledge about risks in cyberspace and taking safety measures when engaging in online activities through computers, mobile phones, or tablets; (2) acting with caution and vigilance when engaging in cyberspace activities or searching for information on the Internet; (3) seeking advice and obtaining consent from parents or caregivers before connecting with strangers online; (4) exercising caution and responsibility when sharing or providing personal information, images, or private and confidential information about themselves or others in cyberspace; and (5) avoiding access to links or content of unknown origin and exiting and reporting any inappropriate content or conduct encountered.

Second, Vietnamese law prescribes the role of parents, guardians, and caregivers in the protection of children's right to privacy in cyberspace

Vietnamese law imposes a responsibility on parents to manage and supervise children when they participate in cyberspace. Clause 2 of Article 54 of the Law on Children 2016 provides that "Parents have the responsibility to provide education, impart knowledge, and guide skills so that children know how to protect themselves when participating in the online environment". Article 6 of the Code of Conduct on the Protection of Children in Cyberspace (2025) stipulates that parents, caregivers, and teachers must supervise and manage children's Internet use, control the content they access, upload, and share online, and manage their online relationships. The provision further requires parents to respect the child's autonomy, maintain regular communication, stay informed about risks, instruct preventive measures, report and guide the child to report harmful acts in cyberspace to competent authorities, and fulfill other related responsibilities. Clause 4 of Article 29 of the Law on Cybersecurity 2018 reinforces these obligations, stating that "Agencies, organizations, parents, teachers, caregivers of children, and other relevant individuals have the responsibility to ensure children's rights and to protect children when participating in cyberspace in accordance with the law on children".

These provisions demonstrate that Vietnamese law views parents, caregivers, and teachers as having an active duty to intervene in and strictly supervise children's online activities. This supervision may include checking login histories, installing security software, and restricting access to certain applications. Such an approach reflects Eastern cultural values, treating children as a vulnerable group in need of comprehensive protection and strong intervention from both the family and the State (Dang & Doan, 2023). However, allowing full control over all online activities may limit children's ability to develop self-protection skills and to learn safe online participation. Overreliance on parental control applications can lead to excessive digital surveillance, create psychological pressure, and negatively affect family relationships if there is insufficient transparency and communication. Excessive control may even constitute a violation of the child's own right to privacy (Wang et al., 2021). Furthermore, the absence of statutory limits or clear methods governing how parents, caregivers, and teachers may supervise or manage children's access and information-sharing online may result in misuse or overreach, such as covertly reading a child's digital diary.

Third, regarding the provisions on the responsibilities of stakeholders in the processing of children's personal data in cyberspace in different jurisdictions

In Viet Nam, stakeholders involved in the processing of children's personal data in cyberspace are divided into three main groups, each with specific responsibilities:

(i) The group of data controllers and operators, including media organizations, digital content creators on online platforms, Internet service providers, and providers of digital platforms.

Clause 2 of Article 29 of the Law on Cybersecurity 2018 provides that: operators of information systems, enterprises providing services on telecommunication networks, Internet networks, and value-added services in cyberspace are responsible for controlling the content of information on their information systems or services to ensure that such content does not cause harm to children or infringe upon children or their rights; they must prevent the dissemination of and remove information that is harmful to children or infringes upon children's rights; and they must promptly notify and coordinate with the specialized cyber-security protection units of the Ministry of Public Security for appropriate handling.

Article 36(2) of Decree No. 56/2017/ND-CP further stipulates that agencies, organizations, and enterprises providing services in the online environment must implement measures and tools to ensure the security and confidentiality of children's private life information, and must provide warning messages regarding potential risks when children provide or modify their private life information. In addition, organizations and enterprises operating or providing services in cyberspace are responsible for establishing mechanisms to receive information, assess, and classify the level of safety for children as reported by agencies, organizations, individuals, and children; to publish lists of online networks, services, and products according to their safety level for children; and to ensure the detection and removal of images, documents, and information inappropriate for children (Article 37(1)).

The Code of Conduct on Protection of Children in the Cyberspace 2025 stipulates that organizations, media enterprises and online content creators, Internet service providers, and digital platform providers have the responsibility to ensure the confidentiality of children's private life and personal information in accordance with the law, specifically to: "*Review and verify information before disseminating it, and ensure the confidentiality of children's private life and personal information in accordance with the law*" (Article 8(2)). In essence, the processing of personal data in cyberspace is identified as a digital service that brings socio-economic benefits to both the service provider and the data subject. However, unlike traditional business sectors that are subject to strict licensing conditions, the current legal framework in Viet Nam does not establish any special pre-clearance requirements for data controllers and data processors, particularly when the data subjects are children. This lack of stringent oversight stems from Viet Nam's open-door policy and its orientation toward attracting technology investment, as reflected in Resolution No. 52-NQ/TW dated 27 September 2019 of the Politburo on certain guidelines and policies to proactively participate in the Fourth Industrial Revolution, thereby creating favorable conditions for foreign enterprises (for example, TikTok, Facebook) to enter the market without imposing technical barriers (Dang & Doan, 2023).

(ii) The group of competent state agencies responsible for the protection of children's privacy in cyberspace. This group is extensive, encompassing numerous levels and sectors such as the Ministry of Public Security, the Ministry of Information and Communications, the Ministry of National Defense, the Ministry of Science and Technology, as well as other ministries, ministerial-level agencies, government agencies, and the People's Committees of provinces and centrally run cities.

The responsibilities of these agencies are set forth in the Law on Cybersecurity 2018. Specifically, Article 29(5) of the Law on Cybersecurity 2018 provides that: "*The specialized forces for cyber-security protection and other competent authorities shall be responsible for applying measures to prevent, detect, stop, and strictly handle acts of using cyberspace that are harmful to children or that infringe upon children or children's rights*".

Besides, Decree No. 56/2017/ND-CP also stipulates that agencies and organizations are responsible for implementing measures to protect children's right to privacy in cyberspace. Agencies, organizations, and individuals responsible for child protection in accordance with the law are entitled to request service providers and individuals participating in online environments to delete private life information of children to ensure their safety and the best interests of the child (Clause 3 of Article 36). State authorities in charge of information and communications and those responsible for child affairs are obliged to organize the reception of information, assessment, and classification of safety levels for children based on submissions from agencies, organizations, individuals, and children; to publish lists of information networks, services, and online products according to their level of safety for children; and to ensure the detection and removal of images, documents, and information inappropriate for children (Clause 1 of Article 37). Public security agencies are responsible for organizing and implementing support and intervention measures to protect children in the online environment (Clause 2 of Article 37).

(iii) Other relevant stakeholders include third parties, organizations, and individual users in cyberspace

According to Article 42 of the 2018 Law on Cybersecurity, users of cyberspace have the following responsibilities: to comply with the provisions of the law on cybersecurity; to promptly provide information related to cybersecurity protection, threats to cybersecurity, and acts of cybersecurity violations to competent authorities and cybersecurity protection forces.

Clause 3 of Article 29 of the 2018 Law on Cybersecurity stipulates that agencies, organizations, and individuals participating in cyberspace activities are responsible for cooperating with competent authorities in ensuring children's rights in cyberspace and in preventing harmful online content that may negatively affect children.

The Code of Conduct of 2025 provides that users in the online environment must comply with legal regulations on child protection in cyberspace; adhere to the terms of service of platform providers; refrain from sharing children's private and family life information online without the consent of their parents, caregivers, and the children themselves if they are at least 07 years old; report and notify VN-COP of harmful content and online acts of child abuse; and share measures to protect children online while promoting child protection programs among family members and the broader community.

14.4.2 Methods of Applying Sanctions Against Violations of Children's Right to Privacy in Cyberspace

Vietnamese law adopts a diversified sanctioning approach by concurrently applying three categories of legal sanctions. Although violations of children's right to privacy in cyberspace have not yet been specifically regulated in terms of sanctioning provisions, pursuant to Article 4 of Decree No. 13/2023/NĐ-CP, such violations may be subject to criminal, civil, and administrative sanctions.

(i) Regarding criminal sanctions. Acts infringing upon personal data may constitute criminal offenses under Article 159 of the 2015 Penal Code, which defines the offense of "Infringement upon the secrecy or safety of letters, telephones, telegrams, or other forms of private communication" and prescribes a maximum penalty of three years' imprisonment. They may also fall under Article 288 of the 2015 Penal Code, which defines the offense of "Illegally posting or using information on computer or telecommunication networks" and prescribes a maximum penalty of up to seven years' imprisonment. However, establishing criminal liability in accordance with the constituent elements of these offenses remains extremely difficult, and to date no case has been successfully prosecuted in Vietnam. A notable example is the public disclosure and sale of over 17,000 citizen identification records (Ministry of Science and Technology, 2021).

(ii) Regarding civil sanctions. Clause 1 of Article 9 of the 2015 Civil Code affirms: "All civil rights of individuals, legal persons, and other entities must be respected and protected by law." Clause 2 of this article enumerates five forms of civil sanctions applicable in cases of rights infringement, including: termination of the infringing act, public apology, public correction, performance of civil obligations, and compensation for damage.

(iii) *Regarding administrative sanctions.* Acts of infringement upon personal data may be subject to administrative penalties under Decree No. 15/2020/ND-CP. Article 102 of this Decree provides for a fine of up to VND 20,000,000 for the following acts: providing, exchanging, transmitting, or storing digital information for the purpose of threatening, harassing, distorting, slandering, or offending the reputation of organizations or the honor and dignity of individuals (Point g); disclosing information that constitutes state secrets or infringes upon private life, personal secrets, or family secrets, where such acts do not yet constitute criminal offenses (Point m). According to Point g, Clause 3 of Article 4 of the same Decree, the applicable fine levels are as follows: Violating organizations shall be fined from VND 10,000,000 to VND 20,000,000; violating individuals shall be fined from VND 5,000,000 to VND 10,000,000 (equivalent to half the fine imposed on organizations).

It can be observed that the current sanctioning mechanisms for violations involving personal data in general and infringements of children's right to privacy in cyberspace in particular remain insufficient and ineffective in terms of legal enforcement, lacking deterrent effect or adequate enforcement mechanisms of violations (Ministry of Science and Technology, 2021). Therefore, it is necessary to supplement, amend, and focus on harmonizing the applicable sanctioning mechanisms to meet the practical demands of state management in personal data protection, as well as in the fight against crimes and legal violations in this field. In addition, the current legal provisions only apply sanctions through three traditional forms and mainly address general violations, without regulations tailored to the particular nature of online infringements. Present regulations are generally applied in the form of administrative penalties or criminal liability for offenses related to personal privacy. However, due to the complexity and specificity of privacy violations in the cyberspace, however, applying of these general provisions faces many limitations, such as difficulties in identifying the constituent elements of crimes or administrative violations. The maximum administrative fine for acts infringing upon personal data is only VND 20 million (Article 102 of Decree No. 15/2020/ND-CP), while the profit gained from exploiting children's data by large technology platforms can reach hundreds of millions of U.S. dollars per year (Montgomery et al., 2021).

14.5 Conclusion

In the context of cyberspace becoming an increasingly essential environment for children's lives and development, the right to privacy must be regarded as a core component of both the legal and social protection systems. This study has shown that although Vietnam has made significant progress in constructing a legal framework, the implementation and protection of children's right to privacy in cyberspace still encounter substantial challenges. Risks such as personal data leakage, exploitation of online behaviors, personalized advertising, and the creation of a long-term "digital footprint" remain inadequately controlled.

Ensuring the protection of children's right to privacy requires not only a comprehensive and coherent legal framework but also close coordination among families, schools, technology enterprises, and state agencies. Responsibility rests not only with the law but with society as a whole in creating a cyberspace that is safe, humane, and compatible with the developmental characteristics of children. In the coming period, Vietnam needs to strengthen independent oversight mechanisms, enhance public awareness, and amend relevant legislation to keep pace with rapid technological advancements, thereby ensuring the highest level of protection for children's privacy in the digital environment.

References

Legal documents

Ministry of Information and Communications. (2025). *Code of Conduct on the Protection of Children in Cyberspace, Decision No. 88/QĐ-BTTTT (Bộ quy tắc ứng xử về bảo vệ trẻ em trong môi trường mạng*, Quyết định số 88/QĐ-BTTTT).

Academic Documents

Bare, C. (2020). The undisclosed dangers of parental sharing on social media: A content analysis of sharenting images on Instagram. *Electronic Theses and Dissertations*, Paper 3732. https://dc.etsu.edu/cgi/viewcontent.cgi?article=5179&context=etd

Cao Thanh Tâm. (2019). The right to privacy in current Vietnamese civil law. Industry and Trade Magazine (Quyền về đời sống riêng tư theo pháp luật dân sự Việt Nam hiện hành). *Tạp chí Công thương*. https://tapchicongthuong.vn/quyen-ve-doi-song-rieng-tu-theo-phap-luat-dan-su-viet-nam-hien-hanh-62272.htm

Dang, M. T., & Doan, T. A. (2023). Children's data protection in Vietnam: Legal framework and challenges. *Journal of Law and Sustainable Development, 11*(12), e02675. https://ojs.journalsdg.org/jlss/article/view/2675/1237

Daskalaki, E., Psaroudaki, K., Karkanaki, M., & Fragopoulou, P. (2020). Understanding the online behavior and risks of children: Results of a large-scale national survey on 10–18 year olds. *arXiv*. https://arxiv.org/pdf/2008.10274

European Parliamentary Research Service. (2025). Children and deepfakes: Risks and policy options (Briefing No. PE 775.855). *European Parliament*. https://www.europarl.europa.eu/RegData/etudes/BRIE/2025/775855/EPRS_BRI(2025)775855_EN.pdf

Kravchuk, N. (2022). Privacy of a child in the digital environment: New risks unaddressed. *Legal Issues in the Digital Age*, 2(1), 11–20. https://cyberleninka.ru/article/n/privacy-of-a-child-in-the-digital-environment-new-risks-unaddressed-1/viewer

Livingstone, S., & Byrne, J. (2023). Science for policy to protect children in cyberspace. *Science, 380*(6644), 123–125. https://scholarsphere.psu.edu/resources/51b7f2ae-2900-4b20-b349-f1f17aa5b080

Loutou, S., Tselios, N., & Altanopoulou, P. (2018). The effect of Twitter-mediated activities on learning outcome and student engagement: A case study. *arXiv*. https://arxiv.org/pdf/1803.01343

Ministry of Science and Technology of Vietnam. (2021). Sanctions for violations of regulations on personal data protection (Chế tài xử lý các hành vi vi phạm quy định bảo vệ dữ liệu cá nhân). https://mst.gov.vn/che-tai-xu-ly-cac-hanh-vi-vi-pham-quy-dinh-bao-ve-du-lieu-ca-nhan-197149685.htm

Mizrahi, B. F. (2021). Risky fine print: A novel typology of ethical risks in mobile app user agreements. *Villanova Law Review, 66*(3), Article 1. https://digitalcommons.law.villanova.edu/vlr/vol66/iss3/1

Montgomery, K. C., Chester, J., & Milosevic, T. (2021). Children and digital marketing: Rights, risks, and responsibilities. *Journal of Business Research, 132*, 797–804. https://doi.org/10.1016/j.jbusres.2021.04.059

Moti, Z., Şenol, A., Bostani, H., Zuiderveen Borgesius, F., Moonsamy, V., Mathur, A., & Acar, G. (2023). Targeted and troublesome: Tracking and advertising on children's websites. *arXiv*. https://arxiv.org/pdf/2308.04887

Phương Nam. (2019). Legal regulations on protecting children's privacy. Justice Newspaper (Quy định của pháp luật về bảo vệ quyền riêng tư của trẻ em). *Báo Công lý*. https://congly.vn/quy-dinh-cua-phap-luat-ve-bao-ve-quyen-rieng-tu-cua-tre-em-10364.html

Tăng Thị Thu Trang & Lê Thị Thu Huyền. (2022). Law on protecting children's privacy in cyberspace (Pháp luật bảo vệ quyền riêng tư của trẻ em trên không gian mạng). *Tạp chí Pháp luật về quyền con người*, số 05/2022. https://qcn.hcma.vn/Content/phap-luat-bao-ve-quyen-rieng-tu-cua-tre-em-viet-nam-tren-khong-gian-mang-422416

Trần Ngọc Tuấn. (2022). Privacy theory: Suggestions for improving regulations on personal privacy in Vietnam (Lý thuyết về quyền riêng tư: Gợi mở đối với việc hoàn thiện quy định quyền riêng tư cá nhân tại Việt Nam). *Tạp chí Pháp luật về quyền con người*, số 01/2022. https://qcn.hcma.vn/Content/ly-thuyet-ve-quyen-rieng-tu-goi-mo-doi-voi-viec-hoan-thien-quy-dinh-quyen-rieng-tu-ca-nhan-tai-viet-na-6211

Trần Ngọc Tuấn. (2024). *The right to privacy of individuals under Vietnamese civil law [Doctoral dissertation] (Quyền về đời sống riêng tư của cá nhân theo quy định pháp luật dân sự Việt Nam* [Luận án Tiến sĩ]). Trường Đại học Luật TP.HCM.

Wang, Y., Zhao, J., & Shadbolt, N. (2021). *Protection or punishment? A qualitative study of parental control apps use and children's digital rights in China.* https://arxiv.org/pdf/2109.05347

Chapter 15
Protecting Children's Rights in International Trade Disputes: A Legal Perspective from Vietnam on Products Infringing Intellectual Property Rights

Tran Minh Chien, Pham Hoang Phuc, and Huynh Thi Ngoc Diem

Abstract This article examines the intersection between children's rights and international trade law, focusing on the risks posed by intellectual property (IP)-infringing products such as counterfeit toys, pharmaceuticals, and educational materials. Through a legal analysis of Vietnam's domestic framework and comparative insights from WTO and FTA practices, the study identifies critical enforcement gaps and regulatory misalignments. It proposes targeted reforms in legal definitions, sanctions, cross-border cooperation, and digital trade governance. The paper argues that protecting children in the context of global trade is both a legal obligation and a moral imperative, essential to fostering a sustainable and rights-based trading system.

15.1 Introduction

Children's rights, including the rights to life, protection, development, and participation, are increasingly becoming a central concern in international trade. In recent years, international trade disputes have not only revolved around purely economic interests, but are also associated with human rights and moral issues, especially children's rights. In the context of globalization and integration, goods flowing across borders can directly affect children: from toys, food, pharmaceuticals to cultural

Article history: Received 05 April 2025; Revised 01 July 2025; Accepted 08 August 2025.

T. M. Chien (✉)
Hung Vuong University of Ho Chi Minh City, Ho Chi Minh City, Viet Nam
e-mail: chientm@dhv.edu.vn

P. H. Phuc
Yersin University of Dalat, Lam Dong Province, Viet Nam
e-mail: phucph@yersin.edu.vn

H. T. N. Diem
Vietnam Women's Academy, Ha Noi City, Viet Nam
e-mail: diemhtn@hvpnvn.edu.vn

N. Binh An et al. (eds.), *The Future of Child-Friendly Justice and Children's Rights in Vietnam*, https://doi.org/10.1007/978-981-95-3521-7_15

and educational products. Notably, many products that violate intellectual property rights, including counterfeit and pirated goods, pose significant threats to the rights and interests of children. Vietnam, as a member of the World Trade Organization since 2007 and an early ratifier of the United Nations Convention on the Rights of the Child in 1990, faces the critical challenge of harmonizing its international trade obligations with its domestic duty to protect children's rights. This paper provides an in-depth analysis of the legal framework for the protection of children's rights in international trade disputes, focusing on the legal aspects of products infringing intellectual property rights in Vietnam. Accordingly, this paper compares Vietnamese legal standards with relevant international frameworks, identifies key similarities and differences, and proposes legal reforms to strengthen child protection amid deeper global integration.

15.2 International Legal Framework on Children's Rights and International Trade

Children's rights are widely recognized in international human rights treaties. The 1989 United Nations Convention on the Rights of the Child (CRC), which Vietnam was the first Asian country to ratify (Ministry of Labour, War Invalids and Social Affairs, 2015)—sets a foundational standard, requiring countries to ensure that the best interests of children are the top priority in all decisions related to children (Article 3 of the CRC) (Saluzzo, 2022). The UN Committee on the Rights of the Child has interpreted that the principle of the best interests of the child must be embedded within national economic and trade policies, rather than confined to the social domain (Saluzzo, 2022). This implies that when designing trade policies, such as those governing imports and exports, governments must account for their potential impacts on children, ensuring that they do not sacrifice their long-term interests for the sake of short-term growth goals (Saluzzo, 2022). Besides the CRC, the International Labour Organization's (ILO) standards are also important in trade: the two basic conventions on child labour are ILO Convention No. 138 on the Minimum Working Age (1973) and No. 182 on the Worst Forms of Child Labour (1999) (Van Daalen & Hanson, 2019). Viet Nam ratified ILO 182 in 2000 and recently ratified ILO 138 (in 2019), demonstrating its commitment to the elimination of child labour (LDVN Lawfirm, 2022). According to the 2018 national survey report, Vietnam has more than 1 million children (accounting for 5.3% of children aged 5–17) working early, of which about 520,000 children work in heavy, hazardous conditions (VietnamPlus, 2020). These figures show the urgency of integrating child protection into trade and economic development policies.

In the field of trade, the current WTO system does not have any specific provisions to protect human rights or children's rights, due to the opposition of many developing countries concerned about "plugging" labor conditions into trade (Saluzzo, 2022). Right from the first WTO Ministerial Meeting (Singapore 1996), the proposal to include labor issues, including child labor, on the WTO agenda was rejected, with the majority view that the WTO is not the right forum to address this issue (Saluzzo, 2022). Instead, the ILO is considered to be the appropriate professional organization for labor standards (Saluzzo, 2022). As a result, WTO agreements—including the Agreement on Trade-Related Intellectual Property Rights (TRIPS)—do not directly address children's rights or child labour. Nonetheless, WTO member states retain limited flexibility to advance child protection objectives under exceptions provided by the GATT and GATS agreements (Charnovitz, 1998). Specifically, Article XX of the GATT allows members to apply trade restrictions necessary to protect "social ethics" or "human health and life"—this is an important basis for justifying child protection measures. For example, the ban on the import of goods produced by child labor can be argued to protect public morality (since the exploitation of child labor is considered unethical) (Saluzzo, 2022).

Similarly, a ban on the circulation of toys or foods that are toxic to children can be justified under the public health protection exception. However, applying these exceptions is not simple. So far, no WTO lawsuit has directly arbitrated the import ban on child labor, and the legality of such discriminatory measures based on process and production methods (PPMs) remains controversial. WTO precedents (e.g., the case of Shrimp—Turtle and EC—Seal Products) show that the WTO is willing to recognize non-commercial justice values (environment, animal ethics) within the scope of exceptions (World Trade Organization, 1998), but to convince that children's rights fall under the category of "public morality" (Ministry of Labor, War Invalids and Social Affairs, 2020) must be rigorously justified, and any measures applied must avoid arbitrary or unjustifiable discrimination. Some scholars have suggested that products made through the exploitation of children can be considered "not like" to legally produced products, in order to circumvent the principle of most-favored-nation and national treatment, but this approach has not been accepted by the WTO's dispute settlement body.

Against this backdrop, countries and trade blocs have found other ways to integrate child protection standards into trade. On the one hand, many countries have adopted unilateral measures: the United States has long banned the import of goods produced by forced labor or forced child labor under Section 307 of the Tariff Act of 1930, and the "domestic demand" loophole exemption was eliminated in 2016 (Engels et al., 2025), through which any product with forced child labor components is absolutely prohibited from importing. The European Union is also working towards a law banning goods related to forced labor (News European Parliament, 2024). On the other hand, in new-generation free trade agreements (FTAs), the chapter on "Trade and Sustainable Development" often binds parties to respect basic labor standards, including a commitment to eliminate child labor (Nguyen & Ngo, 2022). For example, the EVFTA Agreement (EU-Viet Nam) clearly stipulates the obligation of each party to fully implement its rights at the ILO, especially "the effective elimination of child labour" (Article 13.4 of the EVFTA) (Navasartian, 2020). The EVFTA also requires Vietnam to make efforts to ratify ILO conventions that have not yet joined (Navasartian, 2020)—in fact, Vietnam has approved the plan to ratify Conventions 105 (2020) and 87 (2023) according to the roadmap (Navasartian, 2020).

While these commitments are more cooperative than sanctions (the EVFTA does not have a mechanism to punish violations of labor commitments) (Navasartian, 2020), they create significant political pressure. In general, international law is gradually shaping a common norm that requires harmony between trade and the protection of vulnerable groups, including children (Navasartian, 2020). "The best interests of children" is not only a social slogan but also a measure for the country's economic and trade policies in the era of globalization (Navasartian, 2020).

15.3 Risks to Children's Rightsfrom Products that Infringe on Intellectual Property

Intellectual property (IP) infringing products mainly include counterfeit goods, counterfeit goods, pirated goods (infringement of trademarks, designs, patents) and copyright infringing goods (pirated copies of books, films, software, etc.). These products cause damage to IP rights holders, but at the same time, they also have the potential to have a negative impact on consumers—especially children and vulnerable groups. *The following main risks can be analyzed:*

15.3.1 Firstly, Safety and Health Risks from Counterfeit Goods and Low-Quality Goods

Children have the right to the highest health and safety protection, but in fact, many IP-infringing goods circulating on the market do not meet safety standards, leading to infringement of this right of children. Typically, the problem of counterfeit and counterfeit children's toys. Due to the pursuit of profits, counterfeit goods establishments often do not comply with technical regulations, use cheap, toxic materials (Ullman & Kang, 2021). Imitation toys of famous cartoon characters rampant in the cheap Vietnamese market attract young children, but there are hidden dangers: many items have small details that are easy to fall apart, causing the risk of choking for young children; Many items made from recycled plastic, unsafe paints contain heavy metals such as lead and cadmium that exceed the permissible level dozens of times (Ullman & Kang, 2021).

A survey in Vietnam shows that up to 70% of toys on the market are unknown, the origin of which is unknown—most of them are cheap Chinese goods—making it very difficult for parents to distinguish between real and fake and less aware of the potential harm (VietNam Briefing, 2024). A study in Nam Dinh found that 37.5% of children's toy samples in kindergartens contained lead, with an average content of up to 2,207 mg/kg (24 times the limit of 90 mg/kg) (VietNam Briefing, 2024). In Hanoi, nearly 10% of the surveyed toys contain lead with an average content of 625 mg/kg, 7 times the safe level (VietNam Briefing, 2024). Lead poisoning seriously affects children's brain and physical development; In fact, pediatricians in Viet Duc warn that many children who suck on cheap plastic toys for a long time can accumulate lead, causing brain damage, pneumonia, and gastrointestinal poisoning (VietNam Briefing, 2024). In a typical case in 2014, 37 primary school students in Dak Nong had to be hospitalized in an emergency due to playing with "toy grenades" smuggled from China—a type of plastic bag containing an explosive chemical that produces toxic pungent smoke (Tuoi Tre Online, 2014). This dangerous toy is sold publicly at a very cheap price, and as a result, a series of children have difficulty breathing, convulsions, and fainting due to inhalation of toxic fumes (Tuoitrenews, 2014). The incident raises deep concerns about the toxicity of many toys of unknown origin that are rampant.

Not only toys, but other consumer products for children such as milk, confectionery, and clothes are also counterfeited and imitated, causing harm (VOV, 2025). For example, counterfeit children's clothing often uses inexpensive dyes that contain azo or skin allergens (Thoa, 2014). Milk bottles and pacifiers made from recycled plastic can stop being contaminated with toxins (such as BPA) (VnExpress Newspaper, 2010). Especially serious are counterfeit and low-quality goods in the field of pharmaceuticals and children's food (Phong, 2025). Counterfeit medicines and supplements have caused tragedies around the world: A 2019 study published in the American Journal of Tropical Medicine & Hygiene estimated that every year more than 250,000 children globally die from counterfeit or substandard medicines (Taylor, 2019). In particular, counterfeit malaria drugs alone killed about 155,000 children, and poor quality antibiotics for pneumonia claimed the lives of the same number (Taylor, 2019). Recently, the World Health Organization (WHO) has warned about fake cough syrups containing toxic chemicals (diethylene glycol, ethylene glycol) from India circulating in Gambia and Indonesia, causing hundreds of children to die from acute kidney failure (Thiagarajan, 2023). These figures and facts underscore that counterfeiting is not only an economic damage but also a public health problem, directly infringing on children's right to life and healthcare.

In Vietnam, although there are no complete statistics, the authorities have detected many cases of counterfeit western medicines and counterfeit functional foods circulating (Yen & Ngan, 2024). The case of VN Pharma importing fake cancer drugs (2017) is a wake-up call about the management gap in the pharmaceutical sector. For children—a group vulnerable to drugs that do not ensure quality—the circulation of counterfeit drugs and fake vaccines is a serious violation of the right to health protection. Obviously, the fight against counterfeit goods is also about protecting the lives and health of children. The laws of many countries consider the production and trading of counterfeit food and medicines to be a serious crime. In Vietnam, the current Criminal Code separately stipulates the crimes of producing and trading counterfeit goods as food, food, food additives (Article 193) and curative drugs and preventive drugs (Article 194) with a very strict penalty frame (up to 15 years in prison and a fine of 1–3 billion VND) (Mai, 2024). This shows the policy of severely handling counterfeit goods that directly affect public health, especially vulnerable groups such as children.

15.3.2 Second, the Risk Associated with Violations of the Right to Development and Access to Education

An often overlooked aspect is the impact that both the enforcement and lack of enforcement of intellectual property rights may have on children's rights to education and cultural development. Children have the right to access appropriate education, information and culture (CRC, Articles 28, 29, 17). However, imbalances in IP protection sometimes create barriers to the enforcement of these rights. On the one hand, copyright infringement of cultural and educational products for children can negatively affect the healthy development environment. For example, pirated storybooks, cartoons, and video games are often uncensored in content and quality, and may contain inappropriate or dangerous elements (for instance, pirated cartoons embedded with harmful advertisements or video games altered to include excessive violence) (Phuong, 2024). This infringes on children's right to access safe content.

On the other hand, excessive IP protection can also hinder children's right to access knowledge. In many developing countries, high-priced copyrighted textbooks and learning materials are beyond the reach of poor students (El Labban, 2013). If the law does not have a reasonable educational exception mechanism that allows copying for teaching, children may be deprived of equal learning opportunities. Recognizing this, international IP law makes certain exceptions: the Berne Convention (Article 10(2)) allows the citation of works for teaching; The TRIPS Agreement also allows countries to provide exceptions or limitations to copyright as long as it does not infringe on the legitimate interests of the owner (Article 13 of the TRIPS).

In practice, certain countries, such as India, have enacted detailed regulations permitting the publication of low-cost textbook editions or the translation of works specifically for educational use under exceptional circumstances (Khan, 2023). Vietnam has also internalized a number of educational exceptions in the IP Law (for example, Article 25 of the IP Law allows the use of published works for illustration in non-commercial teaching). However, these exceptions are relatively narrow, and their application is limited (Huyen, 2022). It is therefore essential to achieve a balanced approach that simultaneously prevents the unauthorized printing of counterfeit textbooks, which are often error-ridden and harmful to children's learning, while ensuring that authentic educational resources remain affordable or are accompanied by support schemes for disadvantaged children. Children's rights require the state to take proactive measures so that all children have access to knowledge and technology for their development (Saluzzo, 2022).

In the context of digital transformation, many educational and entertainment content for children moves across borders (games, online videos), posing challenges in controlling malicious content and copyright infringement (An, 2024). Vietnam has promulgated the Law on Cyber Security 2018 and Decree 56/2017/ND-CP on protecting children in the cyber environment, which prohibits the act of providing content harmful to children's development (Article 29 of the Law on Cyber Security

2018 and Article 35 of Decree 56/2017/ND-CP). Coordination between IP enforcement and content management is necessary to both protect healthy works and prevent harmful products from reaching children.

15.3.3 Third, Child Labor in the Supply Chain of Goods Infringing on Intellectual Property

A significant yet often indirect consequence of producing and distributing IP-infringing goods is the heightened risk of child labor exploitation. Establishments that make counterfeit and counterfeit goods often operate underground, out of control, and it is easy to hire children to work illegally to reduce costs. International reality shows that industries such as counterfeit garments, counterfeit shoes, counterfeit toys... in some developing countries, child labor is employed due to the simple nature of outsourcing and the need for low-cost labor (Transnational Alliance to Combat Illicit Trade, 2021). Although there is no official data on the percentage of child labor in the production of counterfeit goods, there is every reason to be concerned that this illegal supply chain is creeping into the use of children.

Children may be involved in various stages of illicit production, such as labeling, packaging, or transporting counterfeit goods, typically without any form of labor protection. Such practices constitute a grave violation of children's rights to protection from economic exploitation (CRC, Article 32). In Vietnam, the Children's Law 2016 prohibits the act of "exploiting child labor" and "using children to work illegally labor law" (Article 28). The Labor Code 2019 also prohibits the use of people under the age of 18 in heavy, toxic, dangerous or exploitative work in any form (Article 143). However, implementation in practice is still difficult, especially in the informal economic sector. According to a 2018 survey, the majority of child workers in Vietnam work in agriculture and households (84%), but there is also a segment in industry and services (16%) (VietnamPlus, 2020). If counterfeit processing facilities are located in households, it is very likely that children in the household are also involved in auxiliary work (the report shows that 40.5% of working children in Vietnam are unpaid domestic workers in their own households) (International Labour Organization, 2020). This situation is often overlooked under the guise of "family labor," yet in reality, it involves children's participation in production chains that serve adult economic interests.

Therefore, the fight against counterfeit and contraband goods also contributes to the elimination of the environment that tolerates child labor. Multinational corporations are now increasingly interested in social responsibility in their supply chains, committing not to use child labor or forced labor. For example, LEGO—a major toy company that is investing in a factory in Vietnam—claims to be in absolute compliance with labor standards and will strictly inspect subcontractors for no child labor (The LEGO Group, 2020). Pressure from consumers and international partners forces Vietnamese businesses in the supply chain (including indirect outsourcing) to say no to child labor (Doan & Sa, 2024).

Thus, safeguarding children's rights entails not only ensuring the safety of the end products but also enforcing ethical standards throughout the production process. Vietnamese law has strong sanctions (criminal and administrative) for the act of using children to work illegally (Article 296 of the Criminal Code, Article 29 of Decree 12/2022/ND-CP). What remains crucial is the need to intensify inspections, particularly within high-risk industries such as garment manufacturing, footwear, and handicrafts. These sectors are especially prone to hosting counterfeit operations where child labor may be prevalent (Alliance, 2019). At the same time, improve family livelihoods to reduce the motivation for children to work early (Nissen, 2018). At the international level, the linkage of trade with labor standards is being promoted: the EVFTA as stated affirms the obligation to eliminate child labor (Navasartian, 2020); The United States prohibits the import of goods with signs of forced child labor (Engels et al., 2025). These moves indirectly put pressure on Vietnam to address the root of child labor if it wants to take advantage of commercial interests and avoid international disputes over reputation.

15.4 Vietnam's Legal Framework for Products Infringing Intellectual Property Rights in Child Protection

Vietnam has developed a relatively comprehensive legal framework encompassing intellectual property rights, child protection, and product safety, thereby establishing a legal foundation for addressing the challenges posed by IP-infringing goods affecting children.

First of all, in terms of intellectual property rights, Vietnam promulgates the Intellectual Property Law 2005 (amended in 2009, 2019, 2022) to implement the TRIPS Agreement. The law stipulates rights to trademarks, inventions, designs, copyrights, etc. and strictly prohibit the infringement of these rights (Article 28 of the Intellectual Property Law). To handle infringements, the law allows for many sanctions: civil, administrative, criminal and border control.

In practice, Vietnam frequently imposes administrative sanctions for violations involving counterfeit trademarks and piracy. Market management teams (PMs) in coordination with the economic police often inspect and confiscate counterfeit goods in the domestic market (Luu, 2025). For example, in 2022, the management force has inspected about 72,641 cases, detected and handled over 43,964 cases of violations on counterfeit and counterfeit goods, collecting and remitting VND 348.2 billion to the budget (Bac Giang Newspaper, 2023). Particularly during the peak of the Mid-Autumn Festival in 2022, provincial authorities successively seized large quantities of smuggled children's toys, including items of a violent nature and lacking proper documentation (Thu, 2022). Typically, in Bac Ninh, the management seized 101 plastic guns and 17 plastic swords of violent toys sold to children, administratively sanctioning the shop owner 6 million VND and confiscating all goods (Thu, 2022). In Lai Chau, it was discovered that a car carrying 304 sets of paperless plastic gun sword toys, the management department fined 6 million VND and confiscated the shipment worth about 11 million VND (Thu, 2022). These figures indicate that such violations remain widespread. Although administrative penalties are frequently imposed, the level of fines remains relatively low compared to the potential profits from counterfeit trade, thereby limiting their deterrent effect.

While criminal sanctions are more stringent, they are less frequently applied due to the high thresholds required for prosecution and the difficulty of establishing criminal intent. The Criminal Code 2015 (amended in 2017) devotes a number of provisions to handle the crime of IP infringement. In addition to the crimes of counterfeit goods as mentioned, Article 226 of the Penal Code stipulates the crime of infringing upon copyright and related rights (copying and trading of smuggled works on a commercial scale) with a maximum penalty of 3 years in prison. Article 225 stipulates the crime of infringing upon industrial property rights (production, trading of counterfeit trademarks or large-scale geographical indications) with a fine of up to 5 years in prison and a fine of up to 1 billion VND for individuals. However, initiating criminal proceedings requires the demonstration of significant damage or large-scale operations, which limits the number of cases that are successfully prosecuted. Border control for IP-infringing goods has also been implemented under Article 51 of TRIPS. Vietnamese Customs authorities are empowered to suspend customs clearance, seize, and process goods suspected of IP infringement, either upon request from rights holders or when clear indications of violation are identified. For example, Customs has repeatedly blocked shipments of toys and children's clothing with counterfeit trademarks of origin from China into the country (Online Finance Magazine, 2017). In 2020, Huu Nghi Border Gate Customs (Lang Son) seized 12 tons of consumer goods and children's toys suspected of counterfeiting famous brands (Rolex, Prada, Gucci...) (Tuoitrenews, 2022). These border measures help prevent violating goods early, avoiding wide circulation causing harm to users. However, due to limited resources, Customs mainly inspects by focus, and numerous shipments of smuggled goods continue to evade inspection due to resource limitations and loopholes in the enforcement system.

Regarding the protection of consumer rights and product safety, Vietnam has the Law on Protection of Consumer Rights 2023, the Law on Product Quality 2007 and national technical regulations (QCVN) for products related to children. Typically, QCVN Regulation 3:2019/BKHCN on safety of children's toys was issued in 2019 to control the content of toxic chemicals and the physical and mechanical properties of toys (VietNam Briefing, 2024). From 01/01/2021, children's toys manufactured or imported into Vietnam are required to be certified in accordance with QCVN 3:2019 and affixed with the CR mark (SGS, 2019). These regulations align with international safety standards (ISO 8124, ASTM F963), particularly regarding permissible levels of heavy metals and toxic substances in toys (ISSQ, 2024). The promulgation of QCVN 3:2019 partly stems from studies showing the level of lead contamination in toys as mentioned above, creating a legal tool to deal with unsafe toys (VietNam Briefing, 2024). In addition, Vietnam also has regulations prohibiting the sale of violent and anti-educational toys. Decree 69/2018/ND-CP lists “toys harmful to children’s personality education and health or to social security, order and safety” in the list of goods banned from trading (Appendix I). In fact, the arrests of violent swords and toy guns mentioned above are all based on this regulation to confiscate and destroy (Thu, 2022). Thus, the law has tools to protect children from toxic toys both physically and mentally. The problem lies in the implementation stage: due to real profits and demand, violent toys and cheap toys of unknown origin are still rampant, requiring functional forces to further strengthen inspection and handling, especially on children’s holidays.

Regarding the protection of children’s rights, the Children’s Law 2016 is a foundational document, stipulating 25 groups of children’s rights in accordance with the CRC (Yen, 2019). This law affirms that every child (under 16 years old) has the right to live safely, to receive health care, to be educated, to be protected from all forms of abuse. Notably, the right to be protected from labor exploitation and trafficking, kidnapping, violence, and abuse is clearly stipulated (Articles 28 and 29)—creating a legal basis for handling acts of forced child labor in illegal production facilities. However, the Children’s Law currently defines a child as an individual under the age of 16, which is lower than the international standard established by the CRC and ILO, where the threshold is under 18 (LDVN Lawfirm, 2022). As a result, adolescents aged 16 to 17 may not be fully protected under child-specific legal mechanisms, despite remaining minors under international law. For example, a 17-year-old who works in a counterfeit factory will not be protected by the Children’s Law, but only under the general labor law. This is the difference of Vietnamese law compared to the CRC and ILO, and it has been recommended that Vietnam should expand the definition of children to under 18 years old to be consistent with international practice (LDVN Lawfirm, 2022). However, the current law (Labor Code 2019) also has its own regulations to protect minors under 18 years old when working (Chapter XI) such as prohibiting night work, prohibiting heavy and hazardous work. These regulations partly fill the protection gap for the 16–17 age group.

Overall, Vietnam’s legal framework on IP, consumer protection and child protection has provisions applicable to the issue of IP-infringing goods affecting children. The relationship between these areas of law is reflected in the fact that: the act of producing and trading counterfeit goods infringes on IP and at the same time violates criminal law; counterfeit goods that are not safe for children in violation of the Law on Product Quality and the Law on Children; The use of children in the production of counterfeit goods seriously violates the Labor Law and the Children’s Law. Vietnamese law is generally compatible with basic international standards (TRIPS, CRC, ILO)—for example: Vietnam has criminal sanctions for commercial acts of IP infringement in accordance with the requirements of Article 61 of TRIPS; there are regulations prohibiting child labor in accordance with ILO 138 and 182; have product safety regulations close to international standards (Article 212 of the IP Law). Nonetheless, significant discrepancies remain in terms of enforcement capacity and the overall effectiveness of legal implementation. Developed countries often have strong judicial systems, businesses and consumers are willing to initiate civil lawsuits for acts of IP infringement or harm to users. In Vietnam, disputes are mainly handled administratively, few cases are brought to court, leading to sanctions that are not enough deterrent, and recidivism is still common (Thu, 2022). In addition, social awareness of the harm of counterfeit goods is not high—many parents still carelessly buy cheap toys of unknown origin for their children without anticipating all the dangers (VietNam Briefing, 2024). Compared to international law, Vietnam has some minor differences: as stated, the definition of the age of children is different from the CRC (LDVN Lawfirm, 2022); or the scope of copyright protection is narrower. However, these differences are not too big and are gradually narrowing in the integration process (for example, the IP Law 2022 has amended many contents to be in line with the CPTPP and EVFTA agreements).

15.5 Practice of International Trade Disputes Related to Products Infringing Intellectual Property Rights and Children's Rights

Although children's rights are not frequently invoked in WTO or FTA jurisprudence, several illustrative cases offer valuable insights for Vietnam.

U.S.-China case (Dispute DS362, 2009): The U.S. brought a complaint against China for insufficient enforcement of intellectual property rights, including the widespread availability of counterfeit goods and pirated media, which allegedly fostered a "feeling of impunity" (World Trade Organization, 2009). Although this lawsuit does not mention the child factor, it indirectly affects children because China at that time was rampant with fake toys and cartoons. The WTO Dispute Settlement Body's ruling partly requires China to lower the criminal threshold to handle more infringements (Saluzzo, 2022). After the lawsuit, China stepped up the "Sword Stick" campaign to destroy hundreds of counterfeit toy factories, including the discovery of many establishments employing underage labor (Paben, 2017). This demonstrates that trade-related pressure can compel governments to enhance IPR enforcement, which in turn may reduce the prevalence of child labor in counterfeit supply chains.

Child labour in textile exports: Some countries such as Bangladesh and Pakistan were threatened with trade sanctions in the 1990s due to the use of children in factories (Bhattacharya, 1996). In response to trade sanctions, Bangladesh entered into an agreement with the ILO in 1995, committing to eliminate child labor from its garment sector; the result was thousands of children are withdrawn from the factory and transferred to school (Saluzzo, 2022). Although not part of the formal WTO mechanism, this is a real-life example of how the threat of trade disputes can promote the protection of children. Vietnam currently also exports a lot of textiles, garments, leather and footwear—industries that import partners (US, EU) strictly require without child labor (Long, 2024). If any Vietnamese enterprise violates, the risk of losing orders or being sued under the FTA mechanism is very high (Nguyen & Ngo, 2022). Therefore, the industry itself has developed a code of conduct prohibiting child labor, actively complying with it to avoid trade risks.

Public health-related disputes: The Australian case—Cigarette Packaging (Plain Packaging, DS435, DS441) (2012–2020) is not directly about children but strongly relates to adolescent health rights (World Trade Organization, 2020). Australia enacted a law to remove cigarette brand packaging, a measure to reduce the attractiveness of cigarettes to young people, which was sued by tobacco companies for trademark infringement (Support the Guardian, 2012). The WTO ultimately ruled Australia's measure did not violate trade agreements, for reasons of acceptable public health protection, and the measure did not create undue trade restrictions (Fenton-Glynn, 2019). This victory affirms a principle: when there is a conflict between IP rights (trademarks) and health rights (especially of minors who are susceptible to drug addiction), international law prioritizes health protection. The lesson for Vietnam is that there is a legal basis for implementing trade restrictions (such as banning the advertising of alcoholic beverages aimed at children, controlling imported violent video games) if the goal is to protect adolescents from harm. The WTO has paved the way for arguments on human rights and health in trade disputes (Marceau, 2002).

Disputes over access to essential medicines: In the early 2000s, the United States complained to South Africa and Thailand about the compulsory licensing of HIV-treated ARVs (which also affect HIV-infected children)—allegedly violating TRIPS (Halbert, 2002). Although it has not yet reached the WTO, public pressure has caused pharmaceutical companies to withdraw their lawsuits, leading to the 2001 Doha Declaration affirming that TRIPS must not obstruct the right of countries to protect people's health. Vietnam is in a similar situation with Tamiflu in 2005: before the H5N1 avian influenza pandemic threatened, Vietnam lacked special medicines for the population (including children) (IPS Correspondents, 2005). The government has prepared steps to enforce the license by temporarily suspending Roche's patent monopoly on Tamiflu, allowing the domestic company to produce for emergency needs (Yeh, 2007). In the end, Roche had to agree to a controlled transfer to Vietnamese production (UK, 2021). This case shows Vietnam's decision to prioritize the right to life and access to essential medicines, even at the expense of exclusive IP rights, aligns with TRIPS flexibilities and reflects the humanitarian spirit underpinning international law. This is a precious precedent, affirming that Vietnamese law knows how to flexibly apply exceptions for public health (Articles 27.2 and 31 of TRIPS) to ensure children's right to medical care.

From the above cases, it can be seen that the general trend is that children's rights and human values are increasingly upheld in international trade, although they are not always directly invoked. In some cases, children's rights serve as "public morality" that guides the interpretation of commercial law. As one study observed: "the adjudication of commercial disputes today has more consideration of non-commercial values" (Saluzzo, 2022). This creates a premise for Vietnam and other countries to confidently integrate the goal of child protection into the implementation of trade commitments, as long as it is within the legal framework.

15.6 Evaluation of Vietnamese Law and International Practice from a Comparative Perspective

Through the analysis, some of the following main aspects can be compared:

Degree of internalization of international treaties: Vietnam has joined most of the relevant international conventions (CRC, ILO 138, 182, TRIPS, CPTPP, EVFTA...) and internalized it quite completely. Compared to many jurisdictions, Vietnam has demonstrated commendable progress in aligning its domestic legal framework with international obligations. For example, as soon as the EVFTA required it, Vietnam ratified the remaining core labour conventions and amended the 2019 labour law to allow the establishment of independent workers' organisations—a progress ahead of some other ASEAN countries. However, there is still a gap as the definition of "child" is not under 18 years old (LDVN Lawfirm, 2022). Many countries (UK, Australia, Japan...) consider people under 18 to be completely children, while Vietnam separates 16–17 as "minors", which can cause this group to be less protected. This divergence warrants reconsideration to ensure greater consistency with prevailing international standards (VietNam Net, 2019).

Legal framework for handling IP-infringing goods: Vietnamese and international laws are similar in that it considers the production and trading of counterfeit goods to be a serious illegal act. Vietnam's legal sanctions (civil, administrative, criminal) formally satisfy TRIPS obligations. Compared to developed countries, Vietnam's sanctions system has all kinds of types, but the application is still different. In the United States and the EU, IP rights holders actively use civil courts, claiming large damages - a very high deterrent effect (for example, the Nike case sued smuggled shoe factories using child labor to claim millions of dollars in compensation) (Van, 2011). In Vietnam, most cases stop at administrative sanctions with low fines (several tens of millions of VND) (Thu, 2022), which is not enough to prevent the recurrence of violations. Moreover, the enforcement of criminal judgments in this field is still problematic—very few cases are severely imprisoned, often only fines are the main ones, leading to the perception that "many counterfeits, few fines" still exist. This is a practical difference between Vietnam and developed countries in terms of the effectiveness of IP law enforcement.

Ensuring product safety for children: Vietnam has issued QCVN 3:2019 on toys, equivalent to international standards—a positive similarity (VietNam Briefing, 2024). Countries such as the United States have the Consumer Product Safety Act (CPSIA 2008) which strictly regulates the quality inspection of children's toys (e.g. absolute ban on lead, phthalates) (HQTS, 2024). The EU has a very strict Toy Safety Directive 2009 (European Parliament, 2021). In comparison, Vietnam's QCVN 3:2019 does not have a mechanism to closely monitor each import shipment like the US/EU, but the basic chemical limit standard is equivalent. Vietnam currently lacks a robust product recall mechanism for hazardous goods, which is a critical gap in consumer protection. In the United States, the Product Safety Commission (CPSC) regularly orders the recall of dangerous toys (such as the recall of 18 million lead-contaminated Chinese toys in 2007) (Linh & Ngoc, 2007). In Vietnam, there is a voluntary recovery mechanism but few businesses implement it due to unclear sanctions. This is a difference that needs to be overcome by increasing the responsibility of manufacturers/importers for the safety of children's products.

Law on child labor: Viet Nam has a fairly complete legal framework prohibiting child labor, similar to ILO conventions. However, enforcement in the informal sector remains challenging, as is the case in many developing countries. Developed countries have almost completely eliminated child labor since the twentieth century; Vietnam has only decreased from 15.5% (2012) to 5.3% (2018) of working children (VietnamPlus, 2020). Compared to the region, this rate is 2% lower than the Asia–Pacific average (VietnamPlus, 2020), showing that Vietnam is on the right track. Another point is that the sanctioning of the act of using child labor in Vietnam mainly stops at an administrative fine of several tens of millions, very few cases are criminally prosecuted (the Penal Code is guilty of "exploiting children" Article 150 but requires serious exploitation). Meanwhile, in many countries, child labor can be subject to facility closure and even criminal prosecution against employers. The deterrence of Vietnamese law in this area needs to be improved.

In general, while Vietnamese and international legal frameworks share the common objective of safeguarding children's rights, the critical challenge for Vietnam lies in improving enforcement capacity to translate formal commitments into effective practice. The biggest difference lies in the distance between written law and the law of reality.

15.7 Proposal to Improve Vietnamese Law

In order to strengthen the protection of children's rights in trade, especially for IP-infringing products, Vietnam needs to continue to improve laws and enforcement mechanisms in the following key directions:

Finalize definitions and scope of protection: Consider amending the Children's Law to align the legal definition of "child" with the CRC standard by setting the threshold at under 18 years of age (LDVN Lawfirm, 2022). This will help better protect the 16–17-year-old group against risks such as labor exploitation in the production of counterfeit goods. At the same time, supplementing specific regulations on the responsibilities of families and owners of production establishments in not allowing children to participate in illegal business labor.

Increasing sanctions for violations affecting children: Re-examining the framework of administrative sanctions in the fields of trade, consumption, and IP - proposing higher fines for violations affecting children or goods harmful to children. For example, selling hazardous toys to children should be treated as an aggravating factor in determining the severity of sanctions. Currently, the maximum administrative fine for counterfeit goods (according to Decree 98/2020/ND-CP) is 200 million VND for individuals, 400 million for organizations; it can be considered to further increase the "profit on children's health" nature of the behavior. For criminal cases, the guidelines for the application of the Penal Code should emphasize the prosecution of cases of counterfeit production of food and pharmaceuticals for children as serious crimes (which can be considered as "endangering the lives of many people" to apply the highest frame). Public adjudication of severe cases may serve a strong deterrent function and foster public awareness (Nguyen, 2016).

Improving the efficiency of IP law enforcement and consumer protection: Strengthening the capacity of market management, customs, and economic police forces in detecting and handling counterfeit goods (Hung, 2024). Equipped with rapid testing equipment (lead spectrometer, chemical test kit) to detect on the spot toys and food suspected of being poisoned. An interdisciplinary enforcement mechanism should be institutionalized. Upon detection of suspicious shipments, agencies responsible for product standards, child protection, and consumer safety must coordinate swiftly. Currently, the 389 National Steering Committee on Anti-Smuggling and Counterfeiting has promoted its initial coordination role (Thu, 2022) and needs to integrate the task of assessing the impact of violations on vulnerable groups (children, patients, etc.). In addition, IP rights holders (toys, fashion, and food companies) are encouraged to actively participate in supporting the authorities to distinguish between real and fake goods (Bac Giang Newspaper, 2023), thereby increasing the ability to detect infringing goods.

Strengthening e-commerce management: The trend of trading counterfeit and counterfeit goods has shifted sharply to e-commerce platforms and social networks, where many buyers are tech-savvy teenagers. The law needs to keep up by assigning clearer responsibilities to e-exchange owners in preventing IP-infringing goods and unsafe aviation. Decree 85/2021/ND-CP has initially required e-commerce floors to remove infringing products when there is feedback, but enforcement is still limited. Sanctions are needed if the floor tolerates the sale of violent toys and food of unknown origin to children. At the same time, develop an AI tool to automatically scan online counterfeit advertising keywords for early warning.

Promote propaganda and education: In parallel with sanctions, raising public awareness of the harm of counterfeit goods to children is key. The authorities should coordinate with the youth union and women's union to organize communication campaigns: "Say no to toxic toys", "Buy genuine products for your child's future". Include this content in the consumer education program in schools so that children themselves know how to distinguish safe items. When consumers—especially parents—are well aware that buying cheap counterfeit goods may be at the expense of their children's health and safety, they will be more cautious (VietNam Briefing, 2024). The lesson from the EU shows that people can be effective "eyes and ears": the EU has a RAPEX system for consumers to report dangerous products (Citical Catalyst, 202). Vietnam should also set up a hotline/website channel to receive reports about unsafe goods for children, through which the authorities intervene in a timely manner.

International cooperation: Strengthen cooperation with regional and international countries to prevent the production and trade of counterfeit goods across borders. The majority of counterfeit toys and children's clothing in Vietnam are of foreign origin (mainly China) (VietNam Briefing, 2024), so it is necessary to coordinate with China to eradicate these establishments at the root. ASEAN can build a mechanism to share information about counterfeit shipments, establish common standards for product safety (similar to EU standards) to prevent low-quality goods right from regional borders. Vietnam can also propose APEC and WTO to exchange experiences in integrating child protection goals in trade policies. Through multilateral forums, Viet Nam affirms its stance that fair trade must go hand in hand with sustainable and humane development—in which children enjoy a healthy and safe trade environment (Saluzzo, 2022).

Amending and supplementing relevant legal documents: Studying and amending the IP Law in the direction of increasing the role of the court in handling violations (empowering the court to proactively apply temporary emergency measures to dangerous IP infringing goods to quickly recover from circulation). Develop the Law on Consumer Product Safety (currently there is an ordinance) to have a stronger and more comprehensive legal framework on goods quality management, traceability and recall of hazardous products. In that law, a separate chapter on children's products is set aside with strict requirements. In addition, issue an updated list of toxins prohibited in children's products (e.g. supplement to the list of endocrine disruptors—which the EU is considering) (Endocrine Disruptor list, 2024).

The above recommendations come from practical requirements and reference to international experience. Effective implementation not only better protects Vietnamese children, but also helps Vietnam meet its commitments in the new generation of FTAs, improve the national image of respect for human rights, thereby facilitating deep integration.

15.8 Conclusion

Protecting children's rights in international trade disputes, especially related to IP-infringing products, is a multidimensional issue that requires a comprehensive approach. The above analysis shows that IP-infringing products such as counterfeit and counterfeit goods can cause serious harm to children—from health and physical safety to the right to access education and be protected from exploitation. International law and Vietnam both increasingly emphasize the responsibility of the state in ensuring trade at the service of people, not harming vulnerable subjects. Vietnam has made much legislative progress, but enforcement needs to be further strengthened. Comparison with the international community shows that Vietnam's legal architecture is broadly consistent with international norms; however, challenges remain in mobilizing the requisite institutional capacity and political will to ensure rigorous and consistent enforcement. In the context of integration, Vietnam has the opportunity to access technical assistance and experience from advanced countries to improve the situation. The improvement of the law and effective enforcement not only protect the country's future generations, but also contribute to building a healthy and transparent trade environment, creating trust for international partners. A legal system that places children at the heart of development serves as a key indicator of a nation's commitment to human dignity, social progress, and sustainable integration into the global order (Saluzzo, 2022). With political will and concerted efforts, Vietnam can reconcile the requirement to protect children's rights with international trade obligations, so that "no child is left behind" in the economic development process.

References

Legal Documents

Agreement on Trade-Related Aspects of Intellectual Property Rights (TRIPS)

Berne Convention for the Protection of Literary and Artistic Works. (1886)

Comprehensive and Progressive Agreement for Trans-Pacific Partnership (CPTPP)

Consumer Product Safety Act (CPSA). (1972)

Convention on the Rights of the Child (CRC). 1989

Criminal Code 2015 (amended and supplemented in 2017) No. 100/2015/QH13, dated November 27, 2015, of the National Assembly of the Socialist Republic of Vietnam.

Criminal Procedure Code 2015 No. 101/2015/QH13, dated November 27, 2015, of the National Assembly of the Socialist Republic of Vietnam.

Decree 12/2022/ND-CP dated January 17, 2022, of the Government regulating the management of consumer rights protection activities.

Decree 56/2017/ND-CP dated May 9, 2017, of the Government regulating the quality management of products and goods.

Decree 69/2018/ND-CP dated May 15, 2018, of the Government regulating food safety management.

Decree 85/2021/ND-CP dated August 25, 2021, of the Government regulating intellectual property management.

Decree 98/2020/ND-CP dated August 26, 2020, of the Government regulating the quality management of products and goods.

Free Trade Agreement between the European Union and Vietnam (EVFTA)

Labor Code 2019 No. 45/2019/QH14, dated November 20, 2019, of the National Assembly of the Socialist Republic of Vietnam.

Law on Children 2016 No. 102/2016/QH13, dated April 5, 2016, of the National Assembly of the Socialist Republic of Vietnam.

Law on Food Safety 2010 No. 55/2010/QH12, dated June 17, 2010, of the National Assembly of the Socialist Republic of Vietnam.

Law on Intellectual Property 2005 (amended and supplemented in 2009) No. 50/2005/QH11, dated November 29, 2005, of the National Assembly of the Socialist Republic of Vietnam.

Law on Product and Goods Quality 2007 No. 05/2007/QH12, dated November 21, 2007, of the National Assembly of the Socialist Republic of Vietnam.

Law on Protection of Consumer Rights 2010 No. 59/2010/QH12, dated November 17, 2010, of the National Assembly of the Socialist Republic of Vietnam.

Tariff Act, 1930

References According to Citations

Alliance. (2019). *Ending child labour, forced labour and human trafficking in global supply chains*. https://www.ilo.org/sites/default/files/wcmsp5/groups/public/%40ed_norm/%40ipec/documents/publication/wcms_716930.pdf

An, T. (2024). Cyberspace and children: Factors that make children vulnerable. *Information Security Magazine*. https://www.nait.vn/pckns/khong-gian-mang-va-tre-em-nhung-yeu-to-khien-tre-de-bi-anh-huong-1598.html

Anh, N. T. H. (2021). Compulsory patent licensing for crucial vaccines in Vietnam. *Vietnam Investment Review*. https://vir.com.vn/compulsory-patent-licensing-for-crucial-vaccines-in-vietnam-86562.html

Bac Giang Newspaper. (2023). *In 2022, handling over 43,964 cases of violations of counterfeit and counterfeit goods*. https://www.baobacgiang.vn/nam-2022-xu-ly-tren-43964-vu-vi-pham-hang-gia-hang-nhai.bbg

Bhattacharya, D. (1996). International trade, social labelling and developing countries: The case of Bangladesh's Garments export and use of child labor. *Annuaire Suisse - Tiers Monde, 15*, 215–238.

Charnovitz, S. (1998). The moral exception in trade policy. *Virginia Journal of International Law, 38*, 689.

Critical Catalyst. (2021). *Consumer product safety and RAPEX*. https://www.gov.si/en/topics/consumer-product-safety-and-rapex/

Doan, G., & Sa, T. (2024). Challenges and efforts of Viet Nam in eliminating child labour. *Dan Tri Newspaper*. https://dantri.com.vn/lao-dong-viec-lam/thach-thuc-va-nhung-no-luc-cua-viet-nam-trong-viec-xoa-bo-lao-dong-tre-em-20241223100313424.htm

Engels, E., et al. (2025). *European forced labour regulation entered into force - what should businesses expect?* https://sustainability.freshfields.com/post/102jxs7/european-forced-labour-regulation-entered-into-force-what-should-businesses-expect

European Parliament. (2024). *Products made with forced labour to be banned from EU single market*. https://www.europarl.europa.eu/news/en/press-room/20240419IPR20551/products-made-with-forced-labour-to-be-banned-from-eu-single-market

El Labban, N. A. M. (2013). *Copyright: A roadblock to education in developing countries? (Master's thesis)*. The American University in Cairo.

European Parliament. (2021). *The EU toy safety directive*. https://www.europarl.europa.eu/RegData/etudes/BRIE/2021/662632/EPRS_BRI(2021)662632_EN.pdf

Endocrine Disruptor List. (2024). *Substances identified as endocrine disruptors at EU level*. https://edlists.org/the-ed-lists/list-i-substances-identified-as-endocrine-disruptors-by-the-eu

Fenton-Glynn, C. (2019). *Children's Rights and sustainable development: Interpreting the UNCRC for future generations (Part IV - Children's Rights in a Globalised World)*. Cambridge University Press.

Halbert, D. (2002). Moralized discourses: South Africa's intellectual property fight for access to AIDS drugs. *Seattle Journal for Social Justice, 1*(2), Article 2.

Hung, Q. (2024). Handled 17,584 cases of violations on trading in counterfeit and low-quality goods. *Customs online*. https://haiquanonline.com.vn/xu-ly-17584-vu-vi-pham-ve-kinh-doanh-hang-gia-hang-kem-chat-luong-185860.html&link=autochanger

HQTS. (2024). *A complete guide to CPSIA testing compliance requirements*. https://www.hqts.com/cpsia-testing-compiance-guide/

Huyen, P. M. (2022). Improving Vietnam's law on copyright exceptions in the industrial revolution 4.0. *Journal of Science, Hanoi Open University, 90*, 63.

ISSQ. (2024). *Regulations on conformity of children's toys according to QCVN 3:2019/BKHCN*. https://issq.org.vn/vien-issq-quy-dinh-ve-hop-quy-do-choi-tre-em

IPS Correspondents. (2005). *HEALTH: Drug resistance leads Vietnam to revise bird flu fight*. https://www.ipsnews.net/2005/12/health-drug-resistance-leads-vietnam-to-revise-bird-flu-fight/

International Labour Organization. (2020). *Viet Nam's child labour rate lower than region's average by 2 percentage points*. https://www.ilo.org/resource/news/viet-nam%E2%80%99s-child-labour-rate-lower-region%E2%80%99s-average-2-percentage-points

Khan, A. (2023). Role of copyright law in education and academics. *Juris Center*. https://jurisc entre.com/2023/05/24/role-of-copyright-law-in-education-and-academics/

Luu, Q. (2025). The imprint of the general department of market surveillance over more than 06 years of operation under the vertical industry model. *Ministry of Industry and Trade*. https://dms.gov.vn/tin-chi-tiet/-/chi-tiet/dau-an-tong-cuc-quan-ly-thi-truong-qua-hon-06-nam-hoat-dong-theo-mo-hinh-nganh-doc-3103-2.html

LDVN Lawfirm. (2022). *Some issues in the provisions of the law on child protection from violence*. https://fdvnlawfirm.vn/tin-tuc/some-issues-in-the-provisions-of-the-law-on-child-protection-from-violence.html

Long, N. Q. (2024). *To strengthen the competitiveness of Vietnam's textile and garment export products and enterprises in the EU market*. https://vioit.moit.gov.vn/ftas/du-an-evfta/tang-cuong-ket-noi-det-may/xay-dung-thuong-hieu-da-giay-viet-nam-tai-thi-truong-eu-cac-co-hoi-va-thach-thuc-159.391.html

Linh, H., & Ngoc, M. (2007). *Mattel recalls more than 18 million toys 'made in China'*. https://tienphong.vn/mattel-thu-hoi-hon-18-trieu-do-choi-made-in-china-post92993.tpo

Marceau, G. (2002). WTO dispute settlement and human rights. *European Journal of International Law, 13*(4).

Minh Phong. (2025). *Investigation of fake health food production lines for children*. https://baochinhphu.vn/bo-y-te-canh-bao-khong-mua-su-dung-2-loai-thuc-pham-cho-tre-bi-nghi-gia-102250425115800937.htm

Mai, B. (2024). Regarding the crimes of producing and trading counterfeit goods according to the provisions of the Criminal Code 2015. *People's Court Magazine*. https://tapchitoaan.vn/ve-cac-toi-san-xuat-buon-ban-hang-gia-theo-quy-dinh-cua-bo-luat-hinh-su-nam-201512399.html

Ministry of Labor, War Invalids and Social Affairs. (2015). *Celebrating the 25th Anniversary of Viet Nam's Ratification of the UN Convention on the Rights of the Child*. https://molisa.gov.vn/baiviet/24042?tintucID=24042

Ministry of Labor, War Invalids and Social Affairs. (2020). *Ensuring of child's rights implementation and children protection requires the strong and practical solution*. https://molisa.gov.vn/baiviet/222588?tintucID=222588

Nguyen, K. (2016). Mobile trials: Promote the effects of education, deterrence and crime prevention. *Vietnam Law Newspaper*. https://baophapluat.vn/xet-xu-luu-dong-day-manh-tac-dung-giao-duc-ran-de-va-phong-ngua-toi-pham-post218586.html

Nguyen, C., & Ngo, P. H. (2022). Elimination of child labor in Vietnam's new generation of free trade agreements. *Lentera Hukum, 9*(1).

Navasartian, A. (2020). EU-Vietnam free trade agreement: Insights on the substantial and procedural guarantees for labour protection in Vietnam. *European Papers*. https://www.europeanpapers.eu/europeanforum/eu-vietnam-free-trade-agreement-guarantees-for-labour-protection-in-vietnam

Nissen, A. (2018). Can WTO member states rely on citizen concerns to prevent corporations from importing goods made from child labour? *Utrecht Law Review, 14*(2), 71.

Online Finance Magazine. (2017). *Customs has prevented many counterfeit Chinese goods "Made in Vietnam"*. https://tapchitaichinh.vn/hai-quan-da-ngan-chan-nhieu-hang-trung-quoc-gia-mao-made-in-vietnam.html

Paben, J. (2017). China announces 'Sword' crackdown on illegal scrap plastic imports. *Resource Recycling*. https://resource-recycling.com/plastics/2017/02/15/china-announces-sword-crackdown-illegal-scrap-plastic-imports/

Phuong, L. (2024). Pirated books, fake books: Seriously affecting students' knowledge. *Government e-newspaper*. https://baochinhphu.vn/sach-lau-sach-gia-anh-huong-nghiem-trong-toi-kien-thuc-hoc-sinh-102240817155573378.htm

Support the Guardian. (2012). *Australia passes plain-packaging cigarette law*. https://www.theguardian.com/world/2011/nov/10/australia-plain-packaging-cigarette-law

SGS. (2019). *Vietnam announces new technical regulation for toy safety*. https://www.sgs.com/en/news/2019/12/safeguards-18419-vietnam-announces-new-technical-regulatioon-for-toy-safety

Saluzzo, S. (2022). Looking for the best interests of the child (BIC) in the least expected places: Can it really make a difference? Zoom In. *Questions of International Law*. https://www.qil-qdi.org/the-best-interests-of-the-child-in-international-trade-policies-some-remarks-on-child-labour-and-trade/

Transnational Alliance to Combat Illicit Trade. (2021). *The human cost of illicit trade: Exposing demand for forced labor in the dark corners of the economy*. TRACIT.org.

The LEGO Group. (2020). *The LEGO group modern slavery statement 2020*. https://www.lego.com/cdn/cs/aboutus/assets/blt137c3bf64e1c1706/Modern_Slavery_Statement_2020_-_FINAL_-_Signed.pdf

Thu, H. (2022). Dangers when choosing smuggled toys, of unknown origin. *e-Magazine Anti-Counterfeiting and Trade Fraud Techniques*. https://kythuatchonghanggia.vn/chong-hang-gia/nguy-hai-khi-chon-lua-do-choi-nhap-lau-khong-ro-nguon-goc-xuat-xu-12067

Tuoitrenews. (2022). *Police break up counterfeit consumer goods ring in southern Vietnam*. https://news.tuoitre.vn/police-break-up-counterfeit-consumer-goods-ring-in-southern-vietnam-10365095.htm

Tuoitrenews. (2014). *37 students suffer from harmful Chinese grenade-shaped toys*. https://news.tuoitre.vn/37-students-suffer-from-harmful-chinese-grenade-shaped-toys-10324857.htm

Taylor, P. (2019). *Report takes stock of child death toll from fake meds. Securing industry*. https://www.securingindustry.com/pharmaceuticals/report-takes-stock-of-child-death-toll-from-fake-meds/s40/a9440/

Thiagarajan, K. (2023). *Whatever happened to the case of 66 child deaths linked to cough syrup from India? Goats and Soda*. https://www.npr.org/sections/goatsandsoda/2023/08/31/1196893607/whatever-happened-to-the-case-of-66-child-deaths-linked-to-cough-syrup-from-indi

Thai, Y., & Nguyen, N. (2024). Counterfeit drugs, real worries. *People's e-newspaper*. https://daibieunhandan.vn/thuoc-gia-noi-lo-that-post356162.html

Thoa, L. (2014). Australia recalls thousands of jeans containing carcinogens. *Labor Newspaper*. https://nld.com.vn/suc-khoe/uc-thu-hoi-hang-ngan-quan-jean-chua-chat-gay-ung-thu-20140509110420274.htm

Ullman, K., & Kang, A. (2021). Counterfeited goods and the safety of our children. *NJRD Law Firm*. https://www.njordlaw.com/counterfeited-goods-and-safety-our-children

Van, H. (2011). Nike faces allegations of worker exploitation. *Youth online*. https://tuoitre.vn/nike-doi-mat-voi-cao-buoc-boc-lot-cong-nhan-446666.htm

Van Daalen, E., & Hanson, K. (2019). The ILO's shifts in child labour policy: Regulation and abolition. *International Development Policy, 11*, 134.

VietNam Net. (2019). *Legal age for children should be adjusted for better protection*. https://vietnamnet.vn/en/legal-age-for-children-should-be-adjusted-for-better-protection-564056.html

VietnamPlus. (2020). *Vietnam's child labour rate 2 percentage points lower than region's average: Survey*. https://en.vietnamplus.vn/vietnams-child-labour-rate-2-percentage-points-lower-than-regions-average-survey-post193407.vnp

VietNam Briefing. (2024). *Vietnam's toy market: An overview 2024*. https://www.vietnam-briefing.com/news/vietnams-toy-market-industry-overview-2024.html/

VnExpress Newspaper. (2010). *Confused by the bottle for babies with toxic substances*. https://vnexpress.net/hoang-mang-boi-binh-sua-cho-tre-co-chat-doc-hai-2274581.html

VOV. (2025). *200 types of fake health food products for children*. https://vov.vn/thi-truong/200-loai-san-pham-thuc-pham-bao-ve-suc-khoe-gia-danh-cho-tre-em-post1194747.vov

World Trade Organization. (1998). *India etc versus US: 'shrimp-turtle'*. https://www.wto.org/english/tratop_e/envir_e/edis08_e.htm

World Trade Organization. (2009). *China - Measures affecting the protection and enforcement of intellectual property rights: Report of the Panel (WT/DS362/R).*

World Trade Organization. (2020). *Australia - Certain measures concerning trademarks, geographical indications and other plain packaging requirements applicable to tobacco products and packaging: Reports of the Appellate Body (WT/DS435/AB/R, WT/DS441/AB/R).*

Yen, N. T. (2019). Children's rights in Vietnamese law today. *Legal e-Magazine*. https://phaply.net.vn/quyen-tre-em-trong-phap-luat-viet-nam-hien-nay-a210359.html

Yeh, B. T. (2007). Influenza antiviral drugs and patent law issues (CRS Report for Congress No. RL33159). *Congressional Research Service.*

Tuổi trẻ online. (2014). *The blue face of China's "grenade" smash is exploded: 37 students are hospitalized.* https://tuoitre.vn/xanh-mat-luu-dan-trung-quoc-dap-la-no-37-hs-nhap-vien-590747.htm

Chapter 16
Protecting Children's Data Privacy in the Age of AI: Legal Lessons from the U.S. And EU

Le Ho Trung Hieu and Vu Thi Bich Hai

Abstract Children today have many opportunities to access modern technology, especially artificial intelligence (AI), which helps support their right to access information and education. However, some AI applications may collect and process children's personal data, posing risks of privacy violations if not strictly controlled. Many countries, including Vietnam, have issued regulations on protecting privacy and personal data, but limitations remain in addressing the challenges posed by AI. Ensuring the right to privacy of children in the context of digital transformation requires an approach that balances the benefits of digital technology with the best interests of the child. This study employs the method of normative legal analysis to examine the legal systems of the United States (U.S.) and the European Union (EU) and subsequently uses comparative legal analysis to propose solutions for improving Vietnamese law in protecting the privacy and personal data of children in the AI era.

16.1 Introduction

In the digital era, children are increasingly exposed to AI technologies from an early age, through interactions with virtual assistants, smart social media platforms, and AI-powered educational applications. It is undeniable that AI offers significant benefits for children, enabling them to expand their knowledge, transform their learning methods, and enhance digital engagement. However, alongside the benefits that AI brings are growing concerns over violations of children's privacy. The uncontrolled collection, analysis, and use of children's personal data, which may

Article history: Received 16 April 2025; Revised 12 July 2025; Accepted 05 August 2025.

L. H. T. Hieu
Tra Vinh University, Vinh Long Province, Viet Nam
e-mail: lhthieu2404@sdh.tvu.edu.vn

V. T. B. Hai (✉)
Faculty of Law, Van Lang University, Ho Chi Minh City, Viet Nam
e-mail: hai.vtb@vlu.edu.vn

N. Binh An et al. (eds.), *The Future of Child-Friendly Justice and Children's Rights in Vietnam*, https://doi.org/10.1007/978-981-95-3521-7_16

even be exploited for commercial purposes, can seriously undermine their holistic development, including physical, psychological, and moral well-being. In 2023, the United Nations Children's Fund (UNICEF), in collaboration with the World Economic Forum (WEF), issued a warning about the risks AI may pose to children (Linh, 2023). These concerns encompass privacy, safety, and the effects on behavior and mental health. Social media platforms have been identified as a major source of risk, as AI algorithms not only learn from and retain children's search and interaction behaviors but may also inadvertently sustain or amplify content that is potentially harmful to them (Linh, 2023). Accordingly, it is imperative to establish a robust legal framework to protect children's privacy in the context of digital transformation. Although Vietnam has enacted basic provisions to safeguard children's privacy, the legal system governing AI remains limited. This calls for further legal research and reform to ensure the protection of children's privacy in the digital age.

16.2 Global Awareness of the Legal Implications of AI on Children's Right to Privacy

International legal frameworks recognize the right to privacy as an essential aspect of human rights. According to the 1948 Universal Declaration of Human Rights (UDHR), the right to privacy is enshrined in Article 12, which states "*no one shall be subjected to arbitrary interference with his/her privacy, family, home, or correspondence, nor to attacks upon his/her honor or reputation. Everyone has the right to the protection of the law against such interference or attacks*". Privacy reflects the intrinsic worth of individuals and embodies the fundamental human desire for autonomy in social relations. It must be safeguarded against arbitrary or unlawful intrusions. As a universal, inalienable, and non-transferable right, privacy is recognized and protected by law and enforceable by competent authorities (Aitken et al., 2024, p. 15). Children constitute a particularly vulnerable group due to their age, physical health, and cognitive development. Accordingly, they are entitled to a higher level of care and special protection, particularly from violations of their right to privacy (Milkaite & Lievens, 2019). At present, the right to privacy is recognized as a fundamental children's right under the United Nations Convention on the Rights of the Child (UNCRC), a legally binding international treaty ratified by over 195 countries and territories. The Preamble of the Convention affirms "*children, due to their physical and mental immaturity, require special safeguards and care, including appropriate legal protection.*" This principle is reflected in earlier instruments including "*the 1924 Geneva Declaration of the Rights of the Child, the 1959 United Nations Declaration of the Rights of the Child, the UDHR, the International Covenant on Civil and Political Rights (ICCPR), the International Covenant on Economic, Social and Cultural Rights (ICESCR), and various other international statutes and instruments issued by specialized agencies and international organizations working for the welfare of children"*. Regarding the right to privacy of children, Article 16 of the UNCRC provides "*no child shall be subjected to arbitrary or unlawful interference with their privacy, family, home, or correspondence, nor to unlawful attacks on their honor and reputation*". The law shall protect the child against such interventions or attacks. This provision acknowledges that children have the right to be protected from intrusions into their private life, including the gathering, storage, and use of personal data, as well as interference in family relationships, residential settings, and communications. Moreover, it requires Member States to establish legal mechanisms ensuring the effective implementation of this right in practice.

With the rapid advancement of AI systems in the digital era, the irresponsible use of this technology poses emerging challenges that may adversely affect children's right to privacy (Zheng & Shu, 2023). Specifically, AI typically functions through the collection, processing, and analysis of massive quantities of data, including personal data. Personal data constitutes a core component of the right to privacy, encompassing identifiable or potentially identifiable information such as names, addresses, biometric details, online behavior, and even emotional data (Zheng & Shu, 2023). The Council of Europe issued Convention No. 108 on the Protection of Individuals with Regard to Automatic Processing of Personal Data in 1981. According to Article 2(a) of the Convention, personal data is defined as any information relating to an individual who is either identified or identifiable. Without transparent and responsible governance, children's personal data, closely linked to their personality rights, may be stored unlawfully and, more critically, misused in ways that result in discrimination or psychological harm. Currently, there is no single legally binding and comprehensive international convention governing AI, but a variety of soft law instruments, such as declarations, recommendations, and guidelines, have been issued by international organizations to establish ethical and legal frameworks for the safe, transparent, and accountable development and use of AI, including privacy-related concerns. Regarding children's privacy, the 2021 Report No. 25 (A/HRC/31/64) of the United Nations Committee on the Rights of the Child emphasizes that children are a particularly vulnerable group in digital environments, especially where AI is applied in education, entertainment, and social media. The gathering of personal data of children without clear and informed consent may result in commercial exploitation, discriminatory practices, and negative impacts on their development. Accordingly, states have a duty to guarantee that AI systems are unable to infringe upon children's right to privacy and to promote the design of digital technologies that are safe, transparent, and accountable. Processing children's personal data of children must be age-appropriate, developmentally suitable, and aligned with the best interests of the child, in compliance with the principles of data minimization and informational self-determination.

16.3 The U.S. and EU Legal Frameworks on Children's Personal Data and Privacy in the Age of AI

16.3.1 The U.S.

The U.S. is a pioneering country with a foundational legal framework for protecting the right to privacy of children in the online environment, regulated at both federal and state levels (Livingstone et al., 2025). At the federal level, this issue is regulated by the Children's Online Privacy Protection Act (COPPA) (Milkaite & Lievens, 2019). Effective since 2000 and last amended in 2012, COPPA sets out specific provisions for safeguarding children's privacy online. Administered by the Federal Trade Commission (FTC), the Act requires operators of websites or online services directed to children under the age of 13, or that knowingly collect personal data from them, to comply with the following requirements: informing parents about their practices regarding the collection of children's personal data (Section 312.4); obtaining verifiable parental consent prior to collecting, using, or disclosing such information (Section 312.5); enabling parents to revoke their consent and request deletion of the child's data (Section 312.6(a)(2)); providing parental access to review their children's personal data (Section 312.6(a)(3)); prohibiting conditions that require a child to disclose more personal information than is reasonably necessary to participate in online activities (Section 312.7); and implementing appropriate measures to ensure the confidentiality, security, and integrity of the collected information (Section 312.8). COPPA also includes a "safe harbor" provision (Section 312.11), allowing industry groups or other entities to develop self-regulatory guidelines that the FTC may approve as a means of compliance with the statute. At the state level, certain jurisdictions have enacted legislation building upon COPPA, adapting its principles to local contexts. For instance, Texas passed the Protecting Kids Online through Parental Empowerment Act (PKOPEA) of 2024, which prohibits digital service providers from selling, sharing, or disclosing children's personally identifiable information without parental consent (Section 509.052(b)). Additionally, providers are required to offer tools that enable parents to manage and monitor privacy settings on their children's accounts (Section 509.054(b)).

At present, the U.S. has yet to adopt a unified federal law governing the deployment of AI technologies, The federal system and differing perspectives among governmental authorities regarding AI constitute major obstacles to the establishment of a comprehensive legal framework applicable across the entire territory. At the federal level, within just a year, the Executive Order issued by President Joe Biden on the "*Safe, Secure, and Trustworthy Development and Use of AI*" in 2023 was repealed and replaced by President Donald Trump's Executive Order on "*Removing Barriers to American Leadership in AI*." in 2025 (The White House, 2025a, 2025b). With respect to the influence of AI on privacy and personal data, in 2023, the U.S. Senate publicly debated the licensing of AI systems, the establishment of an independent regulatory body, and several proposed federal bills, including: the Artificial Intelligence Research, Innovation, and Accountability Act, which requires transparency and risk assessment mechanisms for high-risk AI systems with high risks; and the American Privacy Rights Act, which seeks to ensure individuals' rights to opt out of significant algorithmic decision-making processes. However, these legislative proposals have faced political opposition and, to date, have not been enacted (Davtyan, 2024).

At the state level, several states have adopted their own AI-specific legislation tailored to local conditions and priorities. Nonetheless, these laws generally do not emphasize the right to individual's privacy, particularly that of children (Thomson et al., 2025). For instance, Colorado enacted the first state AI law in 2024, which defines the legal liability of developers and deployers of high-risk AI applications involved in automated decision-making and discriminatory practices, yet it does not address privacy concerns. Later the same year, Utah enacted the AI Policy Act, requiring individuals and entities to disclose their use of generative AI in consumer interactions (Thomson et al., 2025). Meanwhile, numerous state privacy laws have undergone amendments to account for AI's impact on privacy. These amendments address automated decision-making processes and AI-related data processing, particularly in contexts involving user profiling or high-risk applications. Notably, California's privacy legislation covers such matters in Sections 11, 14, and 20, while Colorado's 2023 Privacy Act addresses them in Sections 6-1-1306 and 6-1-1309.

16.3.2 The EU

In the EU, privacy rights have long been protected and are enshrined in numerous key legal instruments of the Union. Notably, Article 8 of the Charter of Fundamental Rights of the European Union provides that "*everyone has the right to the protection of personal data, the right to access and rectify such data, and that data must be processed fairly, transparently, and based on consent or other legitimate legal grounds*". The EU has further reinforced these protections through a harmonized data protection regime applicable to all organizations, including businesses, public authorities, and non-profits, that process the personal data of EU residents, known as the General Data Protection Regulation (GDPR). Chapter III of the GDPR explicitly recognizes several data protection rights for all individuals, including children, such as "*the rights to access, rectification, erasure, restriction of processing, objection to processing, and protection against automated decision-making*". Additionally, the GDPR imposes obligations on data controllers to implement suitable safeguards for protecting personal data (Smyr & Ulianova, 2022, p. 4).

In relation to children, the GDPR provides stricter safeguards compared to those for adults. These include requirements for parental consent, transparency in data processing, prohibitions against subjecting children to automated decision-making, and the allocation of responsibility for securing child data among the European Data Protection Board (EDPB), the European Commission, Member States, data controllers, and age verification authorities (Faisal, 2022, p. 120). Article 8 of the GDPR provides that the processing of children's personal data in the context of offering information society services is lawful only if the child is at least 16 years old and capable of giving consent. For children under the age of 16, parental consent is required. However, Member States may lower the age threshold, provided it is not below 13 years old. For example, Hungary and Finland set the age at 16, Switzerland at 15, and Spain at 14 (Aitken et al., 2024, p. 23). The regulation mandates that data controllers must take reasonable steps to verify that parental consent has been given. Importantly, this provision only applies to information society services, which are services normally provided for remuneration, at a distance, by electronic means, and at the individual request of the recipient (Pujiyanto et al., 2023).

Recital 58 of the GDPR emphasizes transparency, requiring that information be provided to children in a manner that is concise, clear, accessible, and easy to understand. If a data breach presents a high risk to the rights and freedoms of an individual, including a child, the data controller must notify the affected individual without undue delay (Article 34 GDPR). Furthermore, the GDPR prohibits children from being subjected to automated decision-making processes. In the landscape of digital transformation and the AI era, the GDPR includes several provisions aimed at mitigating the impact of automated technologies like AI on the privacy and personal data of children. Specifically, Recital 71 and Article 22 of the GDPR grant individuals "*the right not to be subject to a decision based solely on automated processing, including profiling, that produces legal or similarly significant effects*". Such processing is permitted only when based on explicit consent, when necessary for entering into or performing a contract, or when authorized by Union or Member State law. Importantly, automated decision-making should not apply to children (Faisal, 2022, p. 131).

The EU has also adopted the Artificial Intelligence Act (the AI Act), the first comprehensive legal framework governing AI technologies, which has effect on August 1, 2024. Its objective is to ensure the development and application of AI technologies are carried out safely, transparently, and responsibly. This Act not only lays the foundation for AI governance but also complements existing data protection and privacy mechanisms, especially concerning children, who are recognized as a vulnerable group in the digital environment (Le, 2024, p. 867). Specifically, under Article 5(1)(a) of the AI Act, the use of AI systems is prohibited if they "*exploit vulnerabilities of specific groups, such as children*", in a way that may negatively affect their physical or mental health or behavioral development or autonomy. Additionally, the Act provides a classification system for AI applications based on levels of risk. High-risk technologies, such as facial recognition, emotion analysis, and automated decision-making, are subject to stringent restrictions or outright bans. Furthermore, Article 10 of the AI Act requires that AI systems rely on high-quality, representative, unbiased, and non-discriminatory data, and that processing personal data must fully comply with the GDPR.

16.4 Vietnamese Law on Children's Personal Data and Privacy in the Age of AI: Challenges and Recommendations

16.4.1 Vietnamese Law on Children's Personal Data and Privacy in the Age of AI

Vietnam became the earliest nation in Asia and the second globally to finalize the ratification for the UNCRC on February 20, 1990 (Burr, 2002). Article 37 of the 2013 Constitution of Vietnam formally recognizes children's rights. This provision states: "*children shall be protected, cared for, and educated by the State, family, and society; and shall have the right to participate in issues concerning children*". It is strictly prohibited to abuse, maltreat, exploit the labor of, or violate children's rights in any form. Throughout the nation's development, the protection and care of children have consistently been prioritized in policymaking. Under Article 21 of the 2013 Constitution, the right to privacy is protected, stipulating that no one may violate their private life, personal secrets, or correspondence, including letters and telecommunications. Article 38 of the 2015 Civil Code further establishes that "*private life, personal secrets, and family secrets are inviolable and protected by law*". Accordingly, the privacy rights of all individuals, including children, are constitutionally guaranteed and must be protected by the State.

Since the adoption of the 2013 Constitution, additional regulations concerning children's privacy rights have been progressively detailed in a range of specialized legal documents. The most prominent among these is the 2016 Law on Children, along with guiding documents as Decree No. 56/2017/ND-CP, and other relevant statutes including the 2016 Press Law and the 2018 Cybersecurity Law (Dang & Doan, 2023, p. 8). The 2016 Law on Children emphasizes the principle of comprehensive child protection, particularly the respect for and assurance of children's rights to personal data confidentiality, privacy, and family secrets. The law forbids revealing or disseminating this information without the consent of both the child and their parents or guardians, in cases where the child is 7 years old or older.; for children under the age of 7, consent must be provided solely by their parents or guardians. Decree No. 56/2017/ND-CP provides specific elements of personal information and privacy of children, such as full name, image, health records, academic information, residential address, relationships (friends and caregivers), property, communication methods, and services used exclusively by children. Additionally, the 2016 Press Law prohibits the dissemination of information that may negatively affect the comprehensive physical or mental development of children (Clause 9, Article 9), reflecting the State's concern for the influence of media on children. Similarly, Article 29 of the 2018 Cybersecurity Law establishes a legal mechanism to protect the personal information of children on online platforms.

Amidst the rapid advancement of digital technology, particularly the Internet and AI, children's privacy rights face serious threats due to the potential collection, use, and dissemination of their personal data without proper control. These challenges highlight the urgent need for a comprehensive legal framework to protect children in the digital space. A significant development is Decree No. 13/2023/ND-CP, which took effect on July 1, 2023, marking Vietnam's first comprehensive regulation on personal data protection. Under Clause 1, Article 20, personal data of children is classified as sensitive data and must be subject to special protection based on the principle of serving the best interests of the child. Notably, Clause 2, Article 20 requires that processing personal data of children aged 7 or over must obtain the consent of both the child and their parents or guardians; for children under the age of 7, only the consent of parents and guardians is required. The Decree also grants children and their guardians the right to be informed, the right to consent or refuse data processing, the right to access, correct, or delete data, the right to withdraw consent, and the right to claim compensation for data breaches. Data controllers and processors are obligated to verify age, ensure transparency in data usage, and delete data when it is no longer necessary or upon legitimate requests. Furthermore, on November 30, 2024, the National Assembly passed the Data Law, which is the first legislation to manage, develop and protect digital data. This law clearly identifies risks associated with data processing, including risks to privacy rights (Clause 1, Article 25). To mitigate these risks, it requires state agencies to establish early-warning and appropriate protection mechanisms during data processing. Data controllers are responsible for conducting risk assessments, implementing data protection measures, promptly responding to incidents, developing risk management frameworks, and reporting periodically to regulatory authorities.

Vietnam has also set out strategic orientations for AI development in Decision No. 127/QĐ-TTg dated January 26, 2021, approving the "National Strategy on Research, Development, and Application of Artificial Intelligence until 2030", although there is still no specific law comprehensively governing AI-related activities until recently. In pursuit of legal reform, in June 2024, the National Assembly passed Resolution No. 129/2024/QH15, adding the Law on the Digital Technology Industry to the 2025 legislative agenda. In September 2024, the Government submitted the draft law comprising 8 chapters and 72 articles, which was debated for the first time in November 2024. The law was passed on June 14, 2025. Importantly, Chapter VII of the law is dedicated to AI, with a strong focus on privacy rights (Vinh, 2024). Clause 1 of this chapter lays out principles for the development, provision, and application of AI, emphasizing human-centered design, inclusiveness, fairness, non-discrimination, and the protection of ethical values, human rights, and privacy. Article 52 of the law specifies the obligations of entities involved in developing, deploying, and operating AI systems to protect privacy and personal data. These entities must promptly address requests to access, correct, supplement, or delete personal data in accordance with the law and clearly notify users if the AI system poses risks to safety, security, or privacy. This represents a vital step in shaping legal policy to safeguard privacy in the context of AI development, especially for children.

16.4.2 Challenges and Recommendations

First, regarding the age threshold requiring parental and child consent for data processing and the disclosure of children's personal information: Article 8 of Decree No. 13/2023/ ND-CP and Clause 2, Article 6 of the 2016 Law on Children currently set the age threshold at 7 years old. However, this threshold should be reconsidered. Compared to the U.S. and EU, Vietnam's age threshold requiring both parental and child consent for processing personal data of children is relatively low. According to psychologist (Piaget, 1977), children between 7 and 11 years old begin to develop logical reasoning skills for simple matters but are not yet capable of handling abstract or complex matters. Therefore, at this age, children are still at risk of being unable to make appropriate decisions and may face risks associated with personal data processing. Today, children are increasingly exposed to new technologies, including AI, which create opportunities for learning beyond the home and school environments (Zheng & Shu, 2023). However, this also heightens the risk of privacy violations, particularly when personal data is collected and analyzed unlawfully for the purpose of training technological systems. To uphold the principle of the best interests of the child, Vietnamese law needs to adjust the age threshold for requiring consent in personal data processing (Dang & Doan, 2023, p. 16). Specifically, for children under the age of 7, notification and parental or guardian consent are required. Regarding children from 7 to 11 years old, notification and the consent of parents and guardians are required, along with an assessment of the child's cognitive ability by the data processor, who must report to the competent state authority to determine whether the child's additional consent is also needed. For children aged 11 and older, notification and joint consent from both the child and their parents or guardians are required.

Second, current Vietnamese law lacks specific provisions on protecting personal data from the AI-related risks. Meanwhile, the EU has developed an AI Act alongside the GDPR, which protects personal data, including that of children. In the U.S., in addition to COPPA, some states have amended their personal data protection laws to address AI-related issues, including automated decision-making and AI data processing in user profiling or high-risk applications. Based on international experience, Vietnam's personal data protection laws should include specific AI-related regulations (Le, 2024, p. 873). In particular, data processors should be required to inform data subjects about automated personal data processing and clearly explain the risks and impacts of algorithms, AI, and automated decision-making systems. They should also grant data subjects the right to opt out, and the right to refuse (Cannataci, 2021, p. 21). For personal data of children, the law should mandate that data processors develop mechanisms to assess the child's cognitive abilities and report to the competent state authority to guarantee the best interests of the child. Data processing must also comply with the legally defined age thresholds. Furthermore, the law should establish a clear classification system for AI models and strictly prohibit the use of high-risk AI, especially with respect to children's personal data and privacy (Cannataci, 2021, p. 22).

Third, current personal data protection regulations in Vietnam were only issued through sub-law documents, specifically Decree No. 13/2023/ND-CP. By contrast, the U.S. and EU have enacted dedicated statutes passed by their legislatures. As a result, the legal effect of these regulations in Vietnam is still limited, with relatively low stability and binding power (Nam & Hong, 2023, p. 42). This situation significantly affected the ability to protect privacy and personal data security, including that of children, especially in the context of rapidly advancing digital technology and AI. Recently, the 2024 Data Law has come into effect. However, the law only addresses privacy risks among various types of data risks, without providing mechanisms for identifying such risks or clarifying the responsibilities of involved parties in managing data to safeguard privacy. Therefore, further refinement or a dedicated law on personal data protection may be urgently needed in the current digital transformation era (Greenleaf, 2024, p. 24).

Fourth, Vietnam has not yet enacted a dedicated law to regulate the research, development, and application of AI. The absence of such a law means that there are no comprehensive regulations to guide and control AI-related activities, especially concerning human rights, personal data, and privacy. Accordingly, going forward, Vietnam should draw lessons from the EU and several U.S. states in establishing a complete legal framework for AI. Initially, Vietnam should urgently pass a Digital Technology Industry Law to manage AI effectively in the digital era. This law should clearly regulate the responsibilities of AI operators, deployers, processors, and users, as well as classify AI systems by risk levels and specify prohibited practices (Le, 2024, p. 873).

Fifth, the 2016 Law on Children should be amended to include a separate chapter on protecting children in the digital environment. Currently, Article 54 only provides general guidelines regarding the obligations of agencies, organizations, and families in protecting children online and requires the development of privacy protection measures. A new chapter should be detailed and include provisions on the responsibilities of schools, families, and society in educating and raising awareness about online safety; mechanisms for creating safe digital content and age-appropriate content classification; development of internet safety protection systems; measures to prevent addictive and violent online content; allowing children and families to report harmful content and establishing effective channels for complaint reception and resolution. Additionally, the law should clearly define the responsibilities of state management agencies in monitoring, inspecting, and handling violations to ensure effective implementation of regulations on protecting the privacy of children in the digital environment.

16.5 Conclusion

In the landscape of children being exposed to AI at an increasingly young age, protecting their privacy and personal data has become particularly urgent. While AI opens many opportunities for children's cognitive development, it also carries risks in collecting and using personal data, threatening the holistic development of children. Around the world, countries have adopted different approaches to protect children: the United States has passed a specific law to guarantee children's privacy in the online environment, while the European Union has integrated child protection regulations into broader frameworks such as the GDPR. Despite differences in form, these mechanisms all base their principles on protecting the best interests of the child. With the rapid development of AI, each country has its own approach to regulation, but currently, the EU is a leader in having passed a specialized law on AI. In Vietnam, protecting children's privacy and personal data under Vietnamese laws still faces some limitations. The 2016 Child Law does not have clear regulations on protecting children in the digital platform; personal data regulations are still at the subordinate legal text level, with low legal effectiveness; the age threshold requiring parental consent is still low; and the mechanisms for supervision and assessment have not been established. Additionally, the legal framework for AI is still in the stage of orientation and consultation with stakeholders.

References

Aitken, M., Mahomed, S., Briggs, M., & Atabey, A. (2024). Mapping study on the rights of the child and artificial intelligence: Legal frameworks that address AI in the context of children's rights. Council of Europe. https://rm.coe.int/cdenf-2024-04-mapping-study-children-and-artificial-intelligence-/1680b212f8

Burr, R. (2002). Global and local approaches to children's rights in Vietnam. *Childhood, 9*(1), 49–61. https://doi.org/10.1177/0907568202009001235

Cannataci, J. A. (2021). *Artificial intelligence and privacy, and children's privacy: Report of the Special Rapporteur on the right to privacy* (A/HRC/46/37). United Nations Human Rights Council. https://digitallibrary.un.org/record/3901302

Dang, M. T., & Doan, T. A. (2023). Children's data protection in Vietnam: Legal framework and challenges. *Journal of Law and Sustainable Development, 11*(12), e2675. https://doi.org/10.55908/sdgs.v11i12.2675

Davtyan, T. (2024, September 9). The U.S. approach to AI regulation: Federal laws, policies, and strategies explained. SSRN. https://doi.org/10.2139/ssrn.4954290

Faisal, K. (2022). Certain legal aspects of children's right to protect personal data in the context of AI under the European Union data protection laws. *Viestintäoikeuden vuosikirja, 2022*, 106–137. https://www.edilex.fi/viestintaoikeuden-vuosikirja/1000870008.pdf

Greenleaf, G. (2024). Vietnam's 2024 draft data privacy law is ambitious and ambiguous. *Privacy Laws & Business International Report, 192*, 22–25. https://ssrn.com/abstract=5124884

Le, T. M. (2024). EU AI Act and its relationship with Vietnamese law in creating a legal policy for AI regulation. *International Journal of Religion, 5*(10), 867–874. https://doi.org/10.61707/jp3pks38

Linh, T. (2023, March 23). Protecting children in cyberspace. Nhan Dan Online. https://en.nhandan.vn/protecting-children-in-cyberspace-post123701.html

Livingstone, S., Lievens, E., Graham, R., Pothong, K., Steinberg, S., & Stoilova, M. (2025). Children's privacy in the digital age: US and UK experiences and policy responses. In D. A. Christakis & L. Hale (Eds.), *Handbook of children and screens* (pp. 491–497). Springer. https://doi.org/10.1007/978-3-031-69362-5_67

Milkaite, I., & Lievens, E. (2019). Children's rights to privacy and data protection around the world: Challenges in the digital realm. *European Journal of Law and Technology, 10*(1). https://ejlt.org/index.php/ejlt/article/view/674/912

Nam, B. T. N., & Hong, N. N. P. (2023). Addressing the challenges of data privacy protection law in Vietnam. *VNU Journal of Science: Legal Studies, 39*(1), 30–44. https://js.vnu.edu.vn/LS

Piaget, J. (1977). The role of action in the development of thinking. In L. S. Siegel, D. M. Brodzinsky & R. M. Golinkoff (Eds.), *Knowledge and development* (pp. 17–42). Springer US. https://doi.org/10.1007/978-1-4615-8888-2_2

Pujiyanto, M. E., Hamidah, S., & Sulistyo, F. (2023). Children data privacy: A comparative analysis on the United States of America, European Union and Indonesian law. *International Journal of Social Science Research and Review, 6*(2), 381–387. https://doi.org/10.47814/ijssrr.v6i2.1013

Smyr, D., & Ulianova, E. (2022). Legal issues of children's personal data protection. *Open Journal for Legal Studies, 5*(1), 1–10. https://doi.org/10.32591/coas.ojls.0501.01001s

The White House. (2023). *Executive order on the safe, secure, and trustworthy development and use of artificial intelligence.* https://www.whitehouse.gov/briefing-room

The White House. (2025a, January 23). White house fact sheet: President Donald J. Trump takes action to enhance America's AI leadership. The American Presidency Project. https://www.presidency.ucsb.edu/documents/white-house-fact-sheet-president-donald-j-trump-takes-action-enhance-americas-ai

The White House. (2025b, January). *Executive order on removing barriers to American leadership in artificial intelligence.*

Thomson, A. C., Waltzman, H. W., Allen, K., & Von Borstel, M. P. (2025, February 25). *Protecting the next generation: How states and the FTC are holding businesses accountable for children's online privacy.* Mayer Brown. https://www.mayerbrown.com/en/insights/publications/2025/02/protecting-the-next-generation-how-states-and-the-ftc-are-holding-businesses-accountable-for-childrens-online-privacy

Vinh, H. (2024, October 9). Digital technology law to drive economic and technology breakthroughs. VnEconomy. https://vneconomy.vn/digital-technology-law-to-drive-economic-and-technology-breakthroughs.htm

Zheng, G., & Shu, J. (2023). In the name of protection—A critical analysis of China's legal framework of children's personal information protection in the digital era. *SSRN*. https://doi.org/10.2139/ssrn.4459480

Chapter 17
The Right to Education for Ethnic Minority Children in Vietnam

Nguyen Thi Thu Huong

Abstract This article examines the right to education of ethnic minority children in Vietnam. Employing a human rights-based approach together with analytical and synthetic methods, it clarifies the concept of ethnic minority children and their right to education under Vietnamese law, as well as the current legal provisions governing this right. The study adopts a qualitative analysis combined with the synthesis of secondary sources to identify achievements, limitations, and barriers in the realization of the right to education. Based on the findings, it proposes solutions to enhance the effectiveness of implementation, ensuring equity in access to education and promoting comprehensive development for ethnic minority children in Vietnam.

17.1 The Concept of Ethnic Minority Children and Their Right to Education in Vietnam

17.1.1 The Concept of Ethnic Minority Children

Children are individuals undergoing physical, intellectual, and mental development who require appropriate protection, care, and education. The 1989 United Nations Convention on the Rights of the Child defines a child as a person below the age of eighteen, unless under national law majority is attained earlier (Article 1). Accordingly, national legal systems may set a lower age threshold. In Vietnam, the Law on Children 2016 defines a child as a person under sixteen years of age (Article 1).

Ethnic groups are dispersed across Vietnam with varying population sizes. The group with the largest population, constituting the majority, is referred to as the "majority ethnic group", while smaller groups are called "ethnic minorities". Under Decree No. 05/2011/ND-CP on Ethnic Affairs, "ethnic minorities" are groups with

Article history: Received 24 April 2025; Revised 04 July 2025; Accepted 06 August 2025.

N. T. T. Huong (✉)
Thai Nguyen University of Sciences, Thai Nguyen Province, Viet Nam
e-mail: huong.ntt@tnus.edu.vn

N. Binh An et al. (eds.), *The Future of Child-Friendly Justice and Children's Rights in Vietnam*, https://doi.org/10.1007/978-981-95-3521-7_17

smaller populations than the majority; the "majority ethnic group" constitutes over 50% of the national population; "ethnic minorities with very small populations" are those with fewer than 10,000 people.

Vietnam is home to 54 ethnic groups, each with its own cultural identity, language, and customs. The Kinh people are the majority, while the other 53 are ethnic minorities (Government, 2025a, 2025b), including 16 with very small populations (Government, 2017). Therefore, in Vietnam, ethnic minority children are persons under sixteen years of age belonging to ethnic groups with smaller populations than the majority and possessing their own cultural identity, language, and customs.

17.1.2 The Concept of the Right to Education of Ethnic Minority Children

The right to education is a fundamental human right recognized in international and national legal instruments. Article 26 of the 1948 Universal Declaration of Human Rights affirms that "everyone has the right to education." The 1989 Convention on the Rights of the Child provides that "States Parties recognize the right of the child to education." This right ensures equal access to education without discrimination based on gender, ethnicity, economic conditions, or social status.

The right to education of ethnic minority children means that all such children must have the opportunity to access and benefit from education appropriate to their economic, cultural, and social conditions. It includes equality and non-discrimination in education and the obligation of the State to guarantee its realization. In practice, differences in economic conditions, geography, language, culture, and other specific factors create barriers to educational access for ethnic minority children. Consequently, in addition to enjoying the same rights as majority children, they are entitled to specific preferential policies in the field of education. These measures contribute to enabling them to fully exercise their right to education.

17.2 The Current Legal Framework on the Right to Education of Ethnic Minority Children in Vietnam

17.2.1 Legal Recognition of the Right

The right to education of ethnic minority children is enshrined in the Constitution, which is the highest legal instrument in Vietnam. Article 5 of the 2013 Constitution provides that "All ethnicities are equal, united, respect and assist one another for mutual development; all acts of ethnic discrimination and division are prohibited." Article 39 stipulates that "Citizens have the right and obligation to study," and Clause

3 of Article 61 states that "The State gives priority to educational development in mountainous areas, islands, and regions inhabited by ethnic minorities."

This right is further detailed in statutory and sub-statutory instruments. Article 16 of the 2016 Law on Children affirms that "Children have the right and are entitled to equal opportunities in learning and education." Clause 1 of Article 13 of the 2019 Law on Education provides that "All citizens, regardless of ethnicity, are equal in learning opportunities." Accordingly, in Vietnam, ethnic minority children have the legal right to equality and non-discrimination in education.

17.2.2 Measures to Ensure the Right in Practice

17.2.2.1 Preferential Admission Policies

(a) Admission at Higher Age Thresholds

Clause 1 of Article 28 of the 2009 Law on Education sets the entry age for grade one at six, for grade six at eleven, and for grade ten at fifteen. For ethnic minority students, admission may occur at an age higher than the prescribed age (Point b, Clause 2, Article 28). This provision addresses obstacles such as the need to assist the family or the long distance to school, which may prevent enrollment at the standard age. Without such a policy, these children could be denied access to schooling. However, differences in age among classmates may cause psychological and cognitive disparities, affecting integration in learning. Therefore, this is only a temporary solution; in the long term, the State must ensure adequate living conditions and infrastructure so that ethnic minority children can attend school at the standard age.

(b) Direct Admission and Priority Points in Upper Secondary Enrollment

Ethnic minority students often live in remote areas with limited educational resources. To reduce competitive pressure and increase opportunities for upper secondary education, they may be granted direct admission or priority points in entrance examinations. Students from very small ethnic minority groups, as well as ethnic minority or Kinh students who meet one of the following conditions, such as attending lower secondary boarding schools for ethnic minorities, having disabilities, or achieving high results in specific competitions, are eligible for direct admission. Others may receive an additional 1.0 priority point (Article 14 of Circular No. 30/2024/TT-BGDĐT). However, to maintain consistent quality in upper secondary education, such measures should be temporary. It is necessary to improve the quality of lower secondary education in ethnic minority areas so that ethnic minority students can meet the same entrance requirements as Kinh students.

17.2.2.2 Financial Support Measures

(a) *Tuition Exemption*

The State implements a policy of exempting tuition fees for all primary school students from grade 1 to grade 5. Tuition fees are also exempted for five-year-old preschool children (effective from 01 September 2024) and lower secondary school students (effective from 01 September 2025); students attending boarding schools for ethnic minorities; and students belonging to ethnic minorities with very small populations (Article 15 of Decree No. 81/2021/ND-CP).

(b) *Tuition Reduction*

Preschool children and students from ethnic minority groups, except those from ethnic minorities with very small populations, residing in particularly disadvantaged villages or hamlets, communes classified as Zone III in ethnic minority and mountainous areas, or communes in especially difficult coastal, island, and bãi ngang areas are entitled to a 70 percent reduction in tuition fees. Ethnic minority children and Kinh children are entitled to a 50 percent tuition reduction if their parents are receiving monthly allowances for occupational accidents or occupational diseases, or if their families are classified as poor households (Article 16 of Decree No. 81/2021/ND-CP).

(c) *Assistance with Learning Expenses*

Ethnic minority children and Kinh children in preschool and general education are entitled to assistance with learning expenses if they fall into one of the following categories: (1) orphaned of both parents; (2) with disabilities; (3) having parents belonging to poor households; (4) residing in particularly disadvantaged villages or hamlets, communes classified as Zone III in ethnic minority and mountainous areas, or communes in especially difficult coastal, island, and bãi ngang areas. The support level is VND 150,000 per student per month (Clause 4 of Article 18 and Clause 10 of Article 20 of Decree No. 81/2021/ND-CP).

Students from ethnic minorities with very small populations attending preschools, general education schools, semi-boarding schools for ethnic minorities, or boarding schools for ethnic minorities are entitled to monthly learning support at rates equivalent to 30 percent, 40 percent, 60 percent, or 100 percent of the statutory base salary (Article 4 of Decree No. 57/2017/NĐ-CP). With the statutory base salary in 2025 being VND 2,340,000, the corresponding monthly support levels are VND 702,000; VND 936,000; VND 1,404,000; and VND 2,340,000.

Financial support policies demonstrate the State's responsibility in sharing the financial burden with families of ethnic minority students. However, there remain certain shortcomings. First, the tuition exemption policy does not cover preschool children under the age of five. Second, the level of learning expense support for ethnic minority students is still low compared to the actual cost of living.

(d) *Support for Lunch, Accommodation, and Rice for Semi-boarding Students*

Ethnic minority children and Kinh children attending semi-boarding preschools are entitled to lunch support when they simultaneously meet the following four conditions: (1) aged from three months to three years; (2) having permanent residence in communes classified as Zone II or Zone I in ethnic minority and mountainous areas; (3) enrolled in public preschool institutions located in communes classified as Zone III, Zone II, Zone I, communes with particularly disadvantaged villages in ethnic minority and mountainous areas, or communes in especially difficult coastal, island, and bãi ngang areas; (4) belonging to one of the following categories: children from poor households; children without caregivers; children who are children of persons with meritorious service to the revolution; children with disabilities (Clause 1 of Article 4 of Decree No. 66/2025/NĐ-CP).

Ethnic minority children and Kinh children attending semi-boarding primary schools and lower secondary schools are entitled to lunch support when they meet the following three conditions: (1) having permanent residence in communes classified as Zone III, Zone II, Zone I, communes with particularly disadvantaged villages in ethnic minority and mountainous areas, or communes in especially difficult coastal, island, and bãi ngang areas; (2) living at least 4 kms away from school for primary students and at least 7 kms for lower secondary students, or in areas with difficult terrain and transportation; (3) belonging to one of the following categories: the student and his or her father or mother or legal guardian have permanent residence in a commune or village classified as particularly disadvantaged; the student belongs to a poor household and the family has permanent residence in a commune classified as Zone II or Zone I in ethnic minority and mountainous areas (Point a, Clause 2, Article 4 of Decree No. 66/2025/NĐ-CP).

Ethnic minority students attending semi-boarding upper secondary schools are entitled to lunch support when they meet the following two conditions: (1) living at least 10 kms away from school, or in areas with difficult terrain and transportation; (2) belonging to one of the following categories: the student and his or her father or mother or legal guardian have permanent residence in a commune or village classified as particularly disadvantaged; the student belongs to a poor household or has permanent residence in a commune classified as Zone II or Zone I in ethnic minority and mountainous areas (Point b, Clause 2, Article 4 of Decree No. 66/2025/NĐ-CP).

The support level depends on the level of education. Children attending semi-boarding preschools and general education schools receive VND 360,000 per month and VND 936,000 per month respectively; students who arrange their own accommodation receive VND 360,000 per month; supported students also receive 15 kg of rice per month (Clauses 1 and 2 of Article 6 of Decree No. 66/2025/NĐ-CP).

Students attending boarding schools for ethnic minorities are entitled to additional benefits such as policy scholarships at 80 percent of the statutory base salary, rewards of VND 600,000 for good students and VND 800,000 for excellent students, provision of personal items and learning materials, travel expense support, and rice support (Clause 3 of Article 6 of Decree No. 66/2025/NĐ-CP).

Policies on lunch and rice support have significant meaning in attracting children to attend school. Many children eat only vegetables at home, but when attending school they can have meat, which makes them eager to go to school (VOV Northwest Reporters Group, 2024). These policies have contributed to increasing the school attendance rate and reducing the dropout rate. However, there are still shortcomings in financial support policies. First, to be eligible for benefits, ethnic minority children must simultaneously meet multiple conditions, which means that some children from poor ethnic minority households are not entitled to lunch, rice, or accommodation support because they do not satisfy all the conditions. Second, the eligibility criteria for each group of students are different, which creates difficulties in the application process. Third, the lunch support policy for preschool children applies only to those aged from three months to three years, leaving children aged from four to six years ineligible.

17.2.2.3 Language Support Measures

Vietnamese is the official language used in educational institutions (Clause 1 of Article 11 of the 2009 Law on Education), therefore the State places significant emphasis on teaching Vietnamese to ethnic minority children, particularly in the period before they enter grade one. The State has issued various legal documents regulating the teaching of Vietnamese, such as Circular No. 23/2023/TT-BGDĐT on the teaching and learning of Vietnamese for ethnic minority children prior to entering grade one, and the Scheme "Enhancing Vietnamese for Preschool Children and Primary School Students in Ethnic Minority Areas for the 2016–2020 period with orientation to 2025."

In order to prevent the decline or disappearance of ethnic minority languages, the State also pays close attention to the teaching of ethnic minority languages. The State has issued many documents ensuring the availability of materials and equipment for teaching ethnic minority languages. These include Decree No. 82/2010/NĐ-CP on the teaching and learning of ethnic minority spoken and written languages in general education institutions and continuing education centres; Circular No. 01/2025/TT-BGDĐT issuing the list of minimum teaching equipment for ethnic minority languages in general education institutions, continuing education centres, and vocational and continuing education centres; and Decision No. 142/QĐ-TTg dated 27 January 2022 approving the Programme "Improving the Quality of Teaching Ethnic Minority Languages in the General Education Curriculum for the 2021–2030 period."

Currently, some languages of ethnic minority groups are spoken by very few people and are at risk of complete extinction, yet they have not been given investment for teaching. Examples include the Cơ Lao Đỏ language in Trùng Sán, Hà Giang; the Ơ Đu language in Con Cuông, Nghệ An; and the Tu Dí (Bố Y) language in Mường Khương, Lào Cai. Other languages that are now spoken by only a small number of people include Pu Péo, Cơ Lao Trắng, and La Chí in Hà Giang; and Rục, Mày, Sách, and Arem in Quảng Bình (Tung, 2021).

17.2.2.4 Measures to Ensure the Quality and Quantity of Teachers

To ensure adequate numbers and quality of teachers for teaching ethnic minority languages, the State regulates the organisation of training, retraining, and certification in ethnic minority languages for teacher training, as well as the standards for teachers of ethnic minority languages (Circular No. 09/2023/TT-BGDĐT). Teachers of ethnic minority languages are entitled to a job responsibility allowance equivalent to 0.3 of the general minimum wage (Clause 1 of Article 9 of Decree No. 82/2010/NĐ-CP).

To support teachers working in areas with extremely difficult socio-economic conditions, and to help teachers in boarding or semi-boarding schools for ethnic minorities reduce material difficulties, remain committed to their work, and fulfil their teaching duties for ethnic minority students, the State provides allowances and subsidies in addition to salaries (Decree No. 76/2019/NĐ-CP and Decree No. 61/2006/NĐ-CP).

17.2.2.5 Measures to Ensure Schools and Classrooms

The State establishes boarding schools for ethnic minorities and semi-boarding schools for ethnic minorities for the benefit of ethnic minority students and Kinh students from families with long-term residence in areas with extremely difficult socio-economic conditions. A semi-boarding school for ethnic minorities must have at least 50 percent ethnic minority students, and a boarding school for ethnic minorities must have at least 90 percent ethnic minority students (Point a, Clause 2, Article 3 of Circular No. 03/2023/TT-BGDĐT and Clause 3 of Article 9 of Circular No. 04/2023/TT-BGDĐT).

Boarding and semi-boarding schools for ethnic minorities receive certain forms of support to ensure adequate learning conditions for students. These include investment in physical facilities and equipment, financial support for the procurement, supplementation, and repair of tools, financial support for organising annual health check-ups for students, financial support for electricity costs, financial support for cooking meals for students, and financial support for managing semi-boarding students outside of regular school hours (Article 7 of Decree No. 66/2025/NĐ-CP).

17.3 The Practical Implementation of the Right to Education of Ethnic Minority Children in Vietnam

17.3.1 Achievements in the Implementation of the Right to Education of Ethnic Minority Children in Vietnam

17.3.1.1 First, the Number of Ethnic Minority Children Attending School and Attending at the Appropriate Age has Shown an Increasing Trend

The number of ethnic minority children attending school has increased at all educational levels. Compared to the 2019–2020 academic year, in the 2021–2022 academic year the number of ethnic minority primary school students was 1,628,141 (an increase of 85,386 students); lower secondary school students numbered 999,780 (an increase of 83,577 students); and upper secondary school students numbered 348,776 (an increase of 24,466 students) (Thi, 2023). As of May 2024, the total number of ethnic minority children attending preschool was 820,156, accounting for 16 percent of all children attending school nationwide. A total of 99.1 percent of ethnic minority children attending school received enhanced Vietnamese language instruction (Xuyen, 2024).

The proportion of ethnic minority children attending school at the appropriate age and being able to read and write has increased at all levels. The rates of ethnic minority children attending school at the appropriate age at the primary, lower secondary, and upper secondary levels are 96.9 percent, 81.6 percent, and 47.0 percent respectively. The literacy rate among ethnic minority persons aged 15 and above in the national common script is 80.9 percent (Committee for Ethnic Minority Affairs & General Statistics Office, 2020, p. 77).

17.3.1.2 Second, Ethnic Minority Children have been able to Participate in Classes on their Own Spoken and Written Languages

Nationwide, the teaching and learning of six ethnic minority languages in general education schools has been officially implemented, with curricula and textbooks issued by the Ministry of Education and Training. These languages are Mong, Cham, Khmer, Gia Rai, Ba Na, and E De, taught in 22 provinces and cities, involving 756 schools, 5,267 classes, and 174,562 students (Tung, 2021).

17.3.1.3 Third, the System of Schools, Satellite Campuses, and Specialised Schools for Ethnic Minority Students has Increased in Both Number and Quality

Nationwide, there are nearly 21,600 schools and 26,500 satellite campuses in ethnic minority areas. Compared to 2015, the number of schools has increased by more than 3,800, while the number of satellite campuses has decreased by about 2,300. The proportion of permanent school buildings nationwide has improved significantly, from 77.1 percent in 2015 to 91.3 percent in 2019 (Committee for Ethnic Minority Affairs & General Statistics Office, 2020, p. 74).

The network of boarding and semi-boarding schools for ethnic minorities has expanded in both quantity and quality. There are currently 318 boarding schools for ethnic minorities with about 101,918 students, and 1,139 semi-boarding schools with about 245,080 students (Hung & Hung, 2022). Boarding and semi-boarding schools have a very high rate of permanent infrastructure, exceeding 93 percent. Notably, 15 boarding schools in border communes have achieved 100 percent permanent school and classroom facilities (Committee for Ethnic Minority Affairs & General Statistics Office, 2020).

17.3.1.4 Fourth, the Number and Quality of Teachers in Ethnic Minority Areas have Improved

The total number of teachers working in schools and satellite campuses in ethnic minority areas is nearly 525,000, of which 134,900 are ethnic minority teachers, accounting for 25.7 percent. The quality of teachers in ethnic minority areas has improved significantly, with 68.8 percent holding a university degree or higher (Committee for Ethnic Minority Affairs & General Statistics Office, 2020, pp. 47–48).

17.3.2 Limitations in the Implementation of the Right to Education of Ethnic Minority Children in Vietnam

17.3.2.1 First, there Remain Ethnic Minority Children who do not Attend School or who Attend at an Inappropriate Age

The rate of ethnic minority children out of school, including those who have never attended or have dropped out, remains nearly three times higher than that of the Kinh majority. There are 19 out of 53 ethnic minorities with more than 20 percent of children out of school, including the Brau (35.4 percent) and Xtieng (35.3 percent). Some ethnic minorities have upper secondary school attendance rates at the appropriate age below 30 percent, such as Mong, Ba Na, Gia Rai, Mnong, Raglay, and

Xtieng (Committee for Ethnic Minority Affairs & General Statistics Office, 2020, p. 75).

The proportion of ethnic minority children not attending school varies considerably by educational level and tends to increase at higher levels. At the primary level, for every 100 children of school age about 2 are not attending; at the lower secondary level this number rises to 13, and at the upper secondary level to 46. About 13.3 percent of ethnic minority children do not attend lower secondary school. Some groups have much higher rates, such as Brau (45.2 percent), Xtieng (39.6 percent), and Gia Rai (36.3 percent). Among upper secondary school-age ethnic minority students, non-attendance exceeds 50 percent. Nearly 30 percent of ethnic minority students are not attending school at the appropriate age (Committee for Ethnic Minority Affairs & General Statistics Office, 2020, p. 77).

17.3.2.2 Second, Many Ethnic Minority Children are not Proficient in Vietnamese

About 21 percent of ethnic minority people aged 15 and over are not proficient in reading and writing Vietnamese. Literacy rates in Vietnamese for ethnic minorities (male 86.7 percent, female 75.1 percent) remain much lower than for the Kinh majority (male 97 percent, female 94.6 percent). Some of the lowest rates are found among the Mang (46.2 percent), La Hu (46.9 percent), Lu (49.7 percent), and Mong (54.3 percent) (Committee for Ethnic Minority Affairs & General Statistics Office, 2020, p. 77). One reason for limited Vietnamese proficiency is the lack of a uniform language environment. In many localities, children use Vietnamese only at school, while at home and in the community they speak mainly their mother tongue. In addition, some local teachers frequently use ethnic minority languages in teaching and communication, further reducing opportunities for students to practise Vietnamese in the school environment (Minh, 2024).

17.3.2.3 Third, Some Ethnic Minority Children Cannot Speak or Write in their Own Ethnic Language

In Vietnam, 32 out of 53 ethnic minorities have their own written language. However, the proportion of ethnic minority people aged 15 and over who can read and write their own language is low, at 15.9 percent. The highest rates are among the E De (38.8 percent), followed by the Ba Na (31.7 percent) and Hoa (31.4 percent), while the lowest rates are among the Co and Lu (0.8 percent) (Committee for Ethnic Minority Affairs & General Statistics Office, 2020, p. 78).

17.3.2.4 Fourth, Schools and Teachers do not Fully Meet Needs

Some general education schools in ethnic minority areas still lack adequate living and learning facilities, such as classrooms, functional rooms, semi-boarding accommodation, kitchens, sanitation facilities, and drinking water, with classroom quality being poor. The proportion of permanent satellite campuses remains relatively low, at only 54.4 percent. Many localities have not eliminated temporary classrooms built from bamboo and thatch (Committee for Ethnic Minority Affairs & General Statistics Office, 2020, p. 45).

The number of teachers with appropriate qualifications and knowledge of ethnic minority culture and language remains limited. In ethnic minority communes, more than 700 teachers still have qualifications below the upper secondary level (Committee for Ethnic Minority Affairs & General Statistics Office, 2020, pp. 47–48). Furthermore, many young teachers lack practical experience and have limited skills in encouraging ethnic minority students to attend school. Very few localities have a team of teachers fluent and competent in teaching ethnic minority languages that are in danger of disappearing (Duong, 2023).

17.3.3 Barriers Affecting the Implementation of the Right to Education of Ethnic Minority Children in Vietnam

17.3.3.1 First, Legal and Institutional Barriers

The right to education of ethnic minority children has been recognised and guaranteed in many current legal documents. However, Vietnam has not yet enacted a specific and comprehensive law on ethnic affairs. This has resulted in education policies for ethnic minority groups lacking an overall and coherent framework. Current legislation also lacks clarity and consistency in determining eligibility for benefits across different groups. Some support policies such as tuition exemption and reduction, scholarships, rice support, and provision of books and school supplies have been implemented, but the level of support remains low and does not meet the actual needs of students.

17.3.3.2 Second, Financial Barriers

Many ethnic minority families live in difficult economic circumstances and cannot afford educational expenses such as textbooks, uniforms, and transportation. Children are often required to work at an early age to help their families, leading to school dropout. According to statistics, the poverty and near-poverty rates of ethnic minority households remain 3.5 times higher than the national average. Poor ethnic minority households account for 22.3 percent and near-poor households account for 13.2 percent of all ethnic minority households nationwide (Hung & Hung, 2022).

17.3.3.3 Third, Transportation Barriers

Ethnic minority people live scattered across the territory of Vietnam, but mainly in remote and mountainous areas with difficult access to transportation and long distances from schools. Children from 14 out of 53 ethnic minority groups have to travel distances ranging from 20 to 50 kms through dangerous forest and mountain roads to reach school (Duong, 2023). In addition, the road network has not been fully upgraded. Only 80 percent of villages and hamlets have hardened roads to commune centres, while 9,474 villages and hamlets still have mainly dirt or temporary roads, with travel mainly by motorbike or bicycle (Government, 2019a, 2019b, p. 11). In some localities, the consolidation of classes and school sites has resulted in many students having to travel more than 10 kms to school without adequate means of transport, contributing to increased dropout rates (Tung, 2021).

17.3.3.4 Fourth, Language Barriers

Many ethnic minority children are not proficient in Vietnamese, which makes it difficult for them to acquire knowledge. Although there is a policy of bilingual education (ethnic minority language and Vietnamese), its implementation has not been fully effective (Hoang, 2019).

17.3.3.5 Fifth, Perception Barriers

Many ethnic minority families have low levels of educational attainment and limited awareness of the role of education. It is still common for students to leave school to help their families with farming and animal husbandry. In addition, early marriage before the legal age remains in some ethnic minority areas, causing many children, especially girls, to drop out. In 2018, the early marriage rate among ethnic minorities was 21.9 percent. The Mong had the highest rate at 51.5 percent, followed by the Co Lao (47.8 percent), Mang (47.2 percent), and Xinh Mun (44.8 percent) (Committee for Ethnic Minority Affairs & General Statistics Office, 2020, p. 61).

17.4 Recommendations to Improve the Effectiveness of Implementing the Right to Education of Ethnic Minority Children in Vietnam

17.4.1 Review and Improve the Legal System on the Right to Education of Ethnic Minority Children

First, the State should enact a unified and comprehensive law on ethnic affairs. Such a law would specify human rights and the right to equality among ethnic groups. The content should include priority policies to promote the comprehensive development of ethnic minority regions, recognising and guaranteeing the rights of ethnic minority people in areas such as education, healthcare, employment, language, and the preservation and promotion of cultural identity.

Second, regulations on the right to education of ethnic minority children should be developed using an approach tailored to the specific circumstances of each ethnic group and locality. Policy design should be based on comprehensive surveys of terrain, population distribution, infrastructure, and socio-economic conditions of each ethnic minority area, rather than solely relying on administrative classification by Zones I, II, and III. Based on these assessments, separate policies should be issued for each region, with particular attention to ethnic minorities with low rates of access to education.

Third, the scope of beneficiaries of financial support policies should be expanded. Regulations should be supplemented to exempt tuition fees for preschool children under the age of five and to provide lunch subsidies for ethnic minority children aged four to six. The number of conditions required to receive lunch subsidies should be reduced so that more ethnic minority children can benefit from this policy.

Fourth, the level of financial support for students should be increased according to a set roadmap.

In order to help ethnic minority students focus on their studies without being burdened by economic pressures, the amount of financial support for learning expenses, lunch subsidies, accommodation, and rice for semi-boarding students should be increased to approach the minimum living standard. This policy should be implemented according to a reasonable roadmap, in line with the State budget's capacity, with priority given to poor households in ethnic minority areas with extremely difficult socio-economic conditions, and should include mechanisms for regular monitoring and evaluation to adjust the policy in accordance with actual changes.

17.4.2 Develop a Teaching Workforce with Competence, Qualifications, and Knowledge of Ethnic Minority Cultures

Teacher training institutions should organise training courses on teaching methods suited to local cultures, and provide training on counselling skills and how to persuade parents to send their children to school. Training should be provided for teachers capable of teaching ethnic minority languages at risk of extinction.

Schools in ethnic minority areas should prioritise the recruitment of teachers who are members of ethnic minorities or Kinh teachers who can speak at least one local ethnic minority language. The ability of teachers to communicate in ethnic minority languages will facilitate communication and support for students in the process of integration and learning, especially during the transition from preschool to grade one.

17.4.3 Ensure Adequate Quantity and Quality of Schools and Classrooms

Resources should be prioritised for the construction of permanent classrooms, with the gradual elimination of temporary classrooms, focusing investment on school sites in remote areas where infrastructure is severely degraded.

The planning and construction of schools and classrooms should be based on scientific criteria that take into account geographical conditions, population density, and transportation accessibility of each region. The consolidation of school sites should be carefully considered to avoid mechanical implementation that forces children to travel long distances to school.

17.4.4 Strengthen Communication on the Right to Education of Children and the Harms of Early Marriage

Schools and local authorities should actively promote information on the right to education of ethnic minority children and the impact of early marriage on children's education. Communication programmes should be implemented in both Vietnamese and local ethnic minority languages to raise awareness among parents and communities about children's right to education. To increase the effectiveness of communication activities, schools should coordinate with respected community figures such as village elders and heads of hamlets.

17.4.5 Promote Socialisation of Educational Activities

More Vietnamese language literacy classes should be organised for ethnic minority parents. This not only improves their Vietnamese proficiency but also enables them to better support their children's education.

Organisations and individuals should be encouraged to participate in building essential infrastructure such as bridges, roads, and schools to facilitate safe access to education for students.

17.4.6 Strengthen Economic Development and Poverty Reduction Efforts in Ethnic Minority Areas

Economic development and poverty reduction in ethnic minority areas should be implemented in a synchronised manner, linked to the cultural characteristics, natural conditions, and specific strengths of each locality. This is a fundamental solution to ensuring the livelihoods of ethnic minority people, thereby creating conditions for their children to fully attend school.

17.5 Conclusion

The right to education of ethnic minority children is fully recognised in the Vietnamese legal system. However, several legal, economic, social, and geographical barriers still hinder their access to this right. The State must adopt comprehensive solutions to reduce and eliminate these barriers, thereby promoting the effective implementation of the right to education for ethnic minority children. This will contribute to ensuring equal access to education and achieving the goal of sustainable development where no one is left behind.

References

Committee for Ethnic Minority Affairs & General Statistics Office. (2020). *Results of the 2019 survey on the socio-economic situation of 53 ethnic minority groups*. Statistical Publishing House.

Duong, N. (2023). Access to quality education is a challenge for ethnic minority children. Retrieved from Dân trí: https://dantri.com.vn/xa-hoi/tiep-can-giao-duc-chat-luong-la-thach-thuc-voi-tre-em-dan-toc-thieu-so-20231204213042551.htm

Government. (2006). Decree No. 61/2006/ND-CP on policies for teachers and educational administrators working in special schools in areas with extremely difficult socio-economic conditions. Retrieved from Chinhphu.vn: https://vanban.chinhphu.vn/?pageid=27160&docid=15321

Government. (2010). Decree No. 82/2010/ND-CP on the teaching and learning of ethnic minority languages and scripts in general education institutions and continuing education centres. Retrieved from Chinhphu.vn: https://vanban.chinhphu.vn/default.aspx?pageid=27160&docid=95695

Government. (2011). Decree No. 05/2011/ND-CP on ethnic affairs. Retrieved from Chinhphu.vn: https://vanban.chinhphu.vn/?pageid=27160&docid=98691

Government. (2017). Decree No. 57/2017/ND-CP on preferential policies for admission and educational support for preschool children, students, and university students from very small ethnic minority groups. Retrieved from Thư viện pháp luật: https://thuvienphapluat.vn/van-ban/Giao-duc/Nghi-dinh-57-2017-ND-CP-uu-tien-tuyen-sinh-ho-tro-hoc-tap-tre-mau-giao-hoc-sinh-sinh-vien-dan-toc-348922.aspx

Government. (2019a). Master plan for socio-economic development of ethnic minority and mountainous areas and areas with extremely difficult conditions for the period 2021–2030. Hanoi.

Government. (2019b). Decree No. 76/2019/ND-CP on policies for officials, public employees, workers, and armed forces personnel working in areas with extremely difficult socio-economic conditions. Retrieved from Chinhphu.vn: https://vanban.chinhphu.vn/?pageid=27160&docid=198019

Government. (2021). Decree No. 81/2021/ND-CP regulating tuition fee collection and management mechanisms for institutions in the national education system and policies on tuition exemption, reduction, and support for learning expenses; service prices in education and training. Retrieved from Chinhphu.vn: https://vanban.chinhphu.vn/default.aspx?pageid=27160&docid=203950

Government. (2025a). Decree No. 66/2025/ND-CP on policies for nursery children, students, and trainees in ethnic minority and mountainous areas, coastal and island areas, and education institutions with such beneficiaries. Retrieved from Chinhphu.vn: https://vanban.chinhphu.vn/?pageid=27160&docid=213123

Government. (2025b). List of ethnic groups in Vietnam. Retrieved from Chinhphu.vn: https://chinhphu.vn/dan-toc/danh-sach-cac-dan-toc-viet-nam-10000494

Hoang, P. (2019). Limited Vietnamese proficiency: A barrier to learning for ethnic minority students. Retrieved from Dân trí: https://dantri.com.vn/giao-duc/han-che-tieng-viet-rao-can-hoc-tap-cua-hoc-sinh-dan-toc-thieu-so-20191010044812348.htm

Hung, P. H., & Hung, D. K. (2022). Current situation and solutions to eradicate illiteracy among ethnic minority and mountainous children. Retrieved from Tạp chí Kinh tế và Dự báo Online: https://kinhtevadubao.vn/thuc-trang-va-giai-phap-xoa-mu-chu-cho-tre-em-dan-toc-thieu-so-va-mien-nui-21231.html

Minh, B. (2024). Mong ethnic minority children overcome language barriers to learn and speak Vietnamese. Retrieved from Hoà Bình điện tử: https://baohoabinh.com.vn/16/189564/Tre-em-dan-toc-Mong-buoc-qua-rao-can-de-hoc-va-noi-tieng-Viet.htm

Thi, K. (2023). Innovating approaches to educational support in ethnic minority and mountainous areas: Perspectives from the "lowlands" of education. Retrieved from Dân tộc và phát triển: https://baodantoc.vn/doi-moi-tiep-can-ho-tro-giao-duc-o-vung-dong-bao-dtts-va-mien-nui-nhin-nhan-o-vung-trung-cua-giao-duc-bai-1-1702216178923.htm

Tung, D. T. (2021). Implementation of laws on the right to education of ethnic minority people in Vietnam. Retrieved from Tạp chí Điện tử Lý luận Chính trị: https://lyluanchinhtri.vn/thuc-hien-phap-luat-ve-quyen-hoc-tap-cua-nguoi-dan-toc-thieu-so-o-viet-nam-961.html

VOV Northwest Reporters Group. (2024). Boarding meals "attract" disadvantaged students to school. Retrieved from VOV Voice of Vietnam: https://vov.vn/xa-hoi/bua-an-ban-tru-keo-hoc-sinh-vung-kho-den-truong-post1073166.vov

Xuyen, M. (2024). Ethnic minority children account for 16% of total students enrolled nationwide. Retrieved from Hậu Giang online: https://baohaugiang.com.vn/giao-duc/tre-em-la-nguoi-dan-toc-thieu-so-den-truong-chiem-16-trong-tong-so-hoc-sinh-136792.html

Chapter 18
Business Cooperation Contracts and Education Rights of the Child in Vietnam

Vu Thi Bich Hai and Le Ho Trung Hieu

Abstract Education in Vietnam has been increasingly developed so the demand for cooperation between domestic and foreign investors has also risen. Business cooperation contracts (BCC contracts) have become common in the field of education. However, education today is not only a business sector but also carries the mission of human development. Therefore, an educational BCC contract must balance the economic interests of investors with community responsibility, in which the protection of children's rights is included. This chapter clarifies certain legal issues concerning educational BCC contracts under Vietnamese law in relation to the right of the child to education in Vietnam and proposes recommendations to improve the legal framework of Vietnam on this matter.

18.1 Introduction

Education is a sector that every country prioritizes for investment. In the current era of integration, education business in Vietnam attracts strongly both domestic and foreign investment, creating a significant contribution to economic development. Investment through the form of BCC contracts in this field has received increasing attention and the improvement of law on educational BCC contracts has become urgent.

Article history: Received 01 April 2025; Revised 21 July 2025; Accepted 19 August 2025.

V. T. B. Hai
Tra Vinh University, Vinh Long Province, Viet Nam
e-mail: vtbhai2404@sdh.tvu.edu.vn

L. H. T. Hieu (✉)
Faculty of Law, Van Lang University, Ho Chi Minh City, Viet Nam
e-mail: hieu.lht@vlu.edu.vn

N. Binh An et al. (eds.), *The Future of Child-Friendly Justice and Children's Rights in Vietnam*, https://doi.org/10.1007/978-981-95-3521-7_18

18.2 Overview of Business Cooperation Contracts in Education

Investment in education can change the world in a positive direction. Understanding and applying this philosophy, Vietnam has concentrated resources on this activity and considers it a top national policy (Article 61, Constitution 2013).

Compared to previous historical periods, the perception of education in Vietnam today has shifted. The State recognizes education as a sector permitted for business and accordingly has specified corresponding business lines. Education business is oriented toward developing the knowledge of different groups, including children. In Vietnam, alongside public education, private education has increasingly affirmed its position through quality and scale. Cooperation in doing business in education not only brings economic value but also carries profound humanitarian significance in human development.

According to Clause 14 Article 3 of the Law on Investment 2020 (as amended) ("LDT 2020"), an educational BCC contract is a contract signed by investors to cooperate in doing business in education without establishing a new economic organization. Profit and products distributed are the outcomes that investors aim to achieve through this cooperative activity. The business cooperation activities often conducted in this field may include trading educational products (books, stationery), direct establishment of educational institutions, franchised education business (such as AMES English, Wise English, Superbrain), online course business, preschool education business, educational software (Trường doanh nhân HBR, 2024), joint education, joint training and so on. A BCC contract may also be signed between a school and an enterprise to organize classes at the enterprise (Campbell, 1985), such as internships and practicum guidance with fees.

"Commercialization of education" is a current trend of development. With Vietnamese cultural tradition, national identity and the influence of education, the learner has always been the central subject for the adjustment of policies and regulations. At the same time, the quality of education through business cooperation activities also depends much on the learner (experience, health, disposition, attitude) to reach the educational result of knowledge, skills, autonomy and accountability of the learner (Bảo, 2020). The regulation of the State over educational BCC contracts is indispensable in order to achieve the above goals and to establish a fair investment environment.

Educational BCC contracts have the following characteristics:

Firstly, domestic or foreign investors are the subjects of this contract. Normally, at least one party has professional activities in education and the parties exploit each other's advantages in business to achieve investment efficiency. However, during their business cooperation, no new economic organization is established. This leads to the fact that the parties must still act in their own names when entering into relations with third parties although such transactions are for the purpose of the educational BCC contract.

Secondly, the purpose of an educational BCC contract is not only directed at profit seeking but also at developing humanitarian values in training and human development.

Thirdly, apart from investment and civil law, this contract must also comply with provisions of educational law and relevant international treaties. Certain special BCC contracts (such as international cooperation projects) require approval from the competent State authority. An educational BCC contract concerning children, though having a commercial nature, must ensure the right of this group to access education, must not infringe upon children's rights, and must be transparent and fair (including non discrimination on the basis of gender, ethnicity, or family circumstances). It must prioritize the interests of children (for example, tuition levels appropriate so that children from different economic backgrounds can realize the right to education, with preferential policies for children in mountainous or island areas, children with disabilities, and children from poor families).

18.3 Provisions of Vietnamese Law on Business Cooperation Contracts in Education

At present, BCC contracts in general are regulated under the LDT 2020. Since such contracts are concluded in a specific sector, educational BCC contracts must also comply with the Law on Education 2019, the Law on Higher Education 2012 (as amended and supplemented), the Law on Children 2016 (as amended and supplemented in 2018), Decree 86/2018/NĐ-CP dated 06 June 2018 (as amended and supplemented by Decree 124/2024/NĐ-CP dated 05 October 2024) ("Decree 86/2018/NĐ-CP"), other guiding instruments as well as the general provisions on cooperation contracts under the Civil Code 2015, the United Nations Convention on the Rights of the Child 1989 (UNCRC), and other international treaties to which Vietnam is a member. Meanwhile, in China, educational business cooperation between Chinese and foreign educational institutions is regulated in a specific legal instrument called the Law on Sino Foreign Cooperative Education 2003 (as amended and supplemented in 2016). The objective of this law is to promote the development of education through international cooperation while safeguarding national sovereignty, political and ideological orientation, and educational quality (Zou et al., 2022, p. 2).

In Vietnam, educational BCC contracts must ensure the rights of the group of users of educational products and services who are persons under 18 years old. In this respect, certain points need to be emphasized:

Firstly, an educational BCC contract must meet the conditions of conditional business investment lines.

Education and training belong to the system of business lines in Vietnam according to Decision 27/2018/QĐ-TTg dated 06 July 2018, including preschool education, general education, vocational education, higher education, other forms of education (sports and recreation, culture and arts, other unclassified education), and educational support services. Each type of educational activity must comply with different specific conditions.

Because of this characteristic, when entering into a BCC contract, each party must carefully examine its own legal capacity and that of its partner, as well as the activities for which it is responsible, to ensure the validity of the cooperation. Each party may independently verify the information provided by the partner with competent authorities such as business registration offices, investment condition certifying agencies, or state education management authorities. If a BCC contract is concluded in preschool education, it is necessary to scrutinize the requirements concerning personnel, classrooms, educational equipment, etc., according to Decree 125/2024/NĐ-CP dated 05 October 2024. At the same time, the State supervises such activities to ensure that the outcomes of the BCC contract truly generate value for investors.

Secondly, the contractual clauses of educational BCC contracts.

Clause 1 Article 28 LDT 2020 provides for the "principal contents" in such contracts. However, since the law uses the wording "principal" rather than "mandatory", it may be understood that not all educational BCC contracts must include all such provisions. Regarding the contributions of each investor, typically one party contributes financial resources or facilities, while the other provides conditions related to the issuance of diplomas and certificates, so that party directly performs training and business management activities. Due to the long term nature of education, these contracts usually last from 5 to 20 years. The parties may also include other terms in the contract provided they do not contravene legal provisions. The parties may agree to use assets formed during the cooperation to establish an enterprise that matches their business orientation.

Currently, educational institutions often sign with each other or with enterprises a "Memorandum of Understanding" (MOU). The contents of an MOU may involve matters such as training (design and appraisal of curricula, practical skill training, expert exchange), scientific research (seminars, conferences, surveys, appraisal, textbooks), and other cooperation (promotion, communication of both parties' images). In practice, enterprises may receive interns, prioritize recruitment, and provide scholarships, while universities conduct media and introduce the enterprise's brand. Such agreements usually only record general orientations of cooperation, while each specific cooperative activity requires a separate detailed agreement. When signing MOUs, the parties also determine that they are not binding, as they are only of orientational nature, similar to a "framework agreement". Thus, it can be said that the MOU is merely the first step for the parties to reach a final agreement before implementing specific activities. After signing an MOU, if the parties proceed with business cooperation, the document they sign thereafter will be the BCC contract.

Thirdly, an educational BCC contract with a foreign investor.

There are three most common forms at present: (i) joint education, (ii) joint training, and (iii) joint organization of foreign language proficiency examinations for foreign certificates (Clauses 4 and 5 Article 2, Article 6 Decree 186/2018/NĐ-CP).

If joint education is implemented by "private" educational institutions at preschool and general education levels, joint training is implemented at the higher education level. The joint organization of foreign language proficiency examinations has become popular in recent years to meet learners' demands, such as the joint organization of Cambridge English examinations between the University of Cambridge and Anh Viet Foreign Language—Informatics Center (Ministry of Education and Training, 2023), Eco Valley Vietnam Education and Training Joint Stock Company (Ministry of Education and Training, 2024), and others.

Economic development leads to the improvement of people's material and spiritual life. Parents are also willing to pay for their children to study joint programs and training according to international standards (Dezan, 2025). At the same time, international foreign language certificates such as TOEIC, IELTS, TOEFL, CEFR are required conditions for various purposes including tourism, overseas study, employment, and immigration. As of 30 June 2024, there were 605 educational projects by foreign investors with more than 4.57 billion USD, and approximately 430 joint training programs with foreign institutions at 65 domestic universities (Tiến, 2024). Among them, the United Kingdom, with its long educational tradition, is regarded as a leading exporter of education (Hà, 2024) and has strong business cooperation activities with investors in Vietnam, such as the British Council, Cambridge Education Organization, and BUV. The Memorandum of Understanding on cooperation in vocational education between Vietnam and the United Kingdom signed in April 2022 is the basis for investors of both countries to cooperate in business.

Fourthly, the executive office of a foreign investor in Vietnam

This office is established so that the foreign investor can administer and manage the investment project under the educational BCC contract in Vietnam (Articles 49 and 50, LDT 2020). This executive office is entitled to have its own seal, to open bank accounts, to implement policies for labor recruitment, and to sign and perform business activities under the educational BCC contract that the parties have concluded. However, this office must be distinguished from the "representative office of foreign education in Vietnam" under Decree 86/2018/NĐ-CP, which is a "dependent unit" of a foreign educational organization or institution in Vietnam established for the purpose of promoting cooperation and investment in education. The authority to approve the establishment of a representative office of foreign education in Vietnam belongs to the Ministry of Education and Training, whereas the executive office of a foreign investor must be registered with the investment management authority at the place where the office is located.

Fifthly, settlement of disputes in educational BCC contracts

The settlement of disputes concerning educational BCC contracts may be conducted through various methods. Among these, negotiation and conciliation are prioritized; if these are not successful, investors may resolve disputes before Arbitration or Court (Clause 1 Article 14, LDT 2020).

It can be said that the advantage of promoting business cooperation in education, particularly in the private sector, does not only enhance educational quality by allowing learners to access competitive education but also becomes a driving force of development. However, the socialization and commercialization of education through the BCC contract model, if not strictly supervised, may transform education into mere commercialization, reducing the deeper values of training, human development, and the protection of learners' rights in general and of children in particular.

In practice, the implementation of educational BCC contracts has encountered certain obstacles between educational investors, such as in managing the process of contract performance, monitoring educational quality, profit distribution, allocation of risks, and especially in reconciling the perspectives between business benefits in education and the rights of children. Nevertheless, it is important to distinguish an educational BCC contract from other forms of capital mobilization.

In reality, the following case occurred: International School A (primary, lower secondary, and upper secondary levels) in Ho Chi Minh City called upon parents to sign an "educational investment package contract" with the content of mutual cooperation. Parents contributed an amount ranging from 3 to 5 billion VND depending on the program and level of study, for the duration of their child's enrollment at the school. Upon completion of the study, the entire sum contributed by parents would be reimbursed (Nhân & Khánh, 2024). Subsequently, the school faced a financial crisis and could not pay salaries to teachers, who then collectively refused to teach, resulting in infringement of students' rights. It can be observed that the above contract between parents and the school was not a form of BCC contract for profit sharing between the two parties and did not contain provisions on controlling the business process. Instead, it was a form of capital mobilization (loan) by the school from parents, with parents receiving interest in the form of tuition exemption or reduction for their children. The school's mobilization of capital from parents was thus an ordinary civil transaction voluntarily established between the parties. Within this relationship, parents found it very difficult to determine the purposes for which the school used the funds (education investment, real estate, securities, etc.). Determining whether the school violated its educational commitments was also not the primary concern of parents, since their initial objective was to find a school for their children. In this situation, parents faced the choice between continuing to contribute money for their children to remain at School A or transferring their children to another institution, while facing the serious risk of losing the invested amount.

In the United States, educational risk contingency funds have been established to assist learners of private schools when such incidents occur. Under the Coronavirus Response and Relief Supplemental Appropriations Act 2021 (CRRSA Act), the United States Department of Education provided emergency support to private schools against the Covid 19 pandemic through the EANS program (D.E, 2021). In Germany, the Organisation for Economic Co operation and Development (OECD) has measures to support private schools in crisis by way of salary subsidies, loans, and tax exemptions or reductions (OECD, 2023, p. 377). Vietnamese law at present has no specific provisions governing capital mobilization in education or state support when such situations arise. Therefore, parents must carefully identify and understand the type of contract when concluding agreements in order to avoid disputes.

The improvement of law on educational BCC contracts in line with the current orientation toward child friendly justice also presents significant challenges in balancing the interests of investors (profit) with the entitlements of learners, especially children (tuition fees, curriculum, facilities, and services).

18.4 Recommendations for Improving Vietnamese Law on Business Cooperation Contracts in Education Under the Orientation of Child Friendly Justice in Vietnam

Firstly, investment conditions in education in Vietnam are currently provided from legal instruments at the level of statutes (LDT 2020, Law on Education 2019, Law on Higher Education 2012 as amended, Law on Children 2016 as amended in 2018) to sub statutory instruments (Decrees, Circulars). This multiplicity of instruments has unintentionally become a barrier for investors, particularly foreign investors when investing in Vietnam. Therefore, the author recommends consolidating these conditions into one legal instrument, specifically within the corresponding specialized law, so that application becomes more convenient. This approach is also similar to the provisions of China in the Law on Sino Foreign Cooperative Education 2003 (as amended in 2016).

Secondly, in Australia, a country with a developed education system, corporate social responsibility (CSR) in education is built upon a combination of mandatory regulations on education and safety standards for learners, protection of the rights and comprehensive development of learners regardless of origin, gender, or socio economic circumstances, together with voluntary policies, national and international standards. The parties in a BCC contract must ensure compliance with the rules and principles in the Corporations Act 2001, the Australian Consumer Law 2010 (as amended in 2017), and the Education Services for Overseas Students Act 2000. At the same time, the parties are encouraged to implement the National Standard on Corporate Social Responsibility (AS 8003–2003) and international CSR principles such as the UN Global Compact and ISO 26000 on social responsibility (Shatnawi et al., 2022, p. 1468). From this Australian experience, the author recommends supplementing the Law on Education and the Law on Children with provisions on CSR of the parties to ensure educational quality and profit objectives when entering into BCC contracts involving learners who are children.

Thirdly, educational BCC contracts directly affect learners as third parties to the contractual relationship. There is a view that it is necessary to establish a "model contract" for educational business cooperation in order to guarantee clarity and uniformity of clauses concerning the minimum rights of learners. However, from the perspective of contractual nature, an educational BCC contract is concluded between investors with respect to educational activities and not between investors and learners. Therefore, if mandatory application of a model contract is imposed, it may limit the freedom of business and freedom of contract of investors. Instead, in order to protect learners' rights, including children, in a fair and transparent manner, it should be stipulated that when a transaction with a third party is established under a BCC contract, the content of that transaction must be clear, understandable, and must prioritize protection for the weaker third party in the established transaction.

Fourthly, with respect to joint education, Vietnamese law restricts cooperation at preschool and general education levels to "private institutions", while public institutions are not permitted to engage in this form. From the perspective of state management, BCC contracts in public educational institutions are not recognized as autonomous in developed educational systems such as Australia and the United States. Instead, the laws of these countries only allow such contracts in areas under state control, for example in Australia including cooperation with enterprises for vocational training and employment support, student exchange, and orientation of joint programs (Allens, 2016, p. 14). However, in the trend of educational socialization, public schools are increasingly granted autonomy and competition between public and private schools has become intense. Thus, this restriction may become a developmental barrier for public schools and create unequal treatment between public and private institutions. Therefore, Vietnam should consider extending regulations on joint education with foreign partners at preschool and general education levels to also include "public preschool institutions" and "public general education institutions".

Fifthly, one of the important conditions for conducting joint activities is the "assurance of educational quality". To meet this condition, Clause 2 Article 4 of Decree 186/2018/NĐ-CP requires that the cooperating institutions must undergo quality accreditation in accordance with Vietnamese law. In reality, there are cases where one cooperating party (as a party to the BCC contract) acts only as an intermediary for marketing and student recruitment, without directly engaging in training or education. In such cases, requiring both cooperating parties to be subject to quality accreditation is unnecessary (Dương, 2024). Therefore, the author suggests revising this provision so that quality accreditation is mandatory only for the cooperating party that directly conducts educational and training activities.

Sixthly, in countries such as Australia, Canada, and the United Kingdom, contract disputes are often resolved through non judicial methods to maintain relations between the parties after disputes, reduce losses, and protect business secrets. Many educational BCC contracts such as training cooperation, joint programs, and cross border research projects are preferentially resolved by methods limiting the decision making authority of third parties, such as negotiation and conciliation (Oyeyoade, 2022, p. 7). In Vietnam, settlement of disputes in educational BCC contracts involving the rights of third parties, particularly children, should include provisions giving priority to negotiation and conciliation to avoid negative impacts on learners who are children. At the same time, it is necessary to add principles ensuring that even when disputes arise, the parties must continue educational activities so that children's learning is not interrupted during dispute settlement.

18.5 Conclusion

Business cooperation in education is an inevitable trend in the development of Vietnamese education, aiming at training human resources in close connection with economic growth. The recommendations presented in this chapter contribute to further improving the legal framework to protect the parties in educational BCC contracts, in association with the implementation of corporate social responsibility of investors in safeguarding children's rights. At the same time, the State should adopt preferential policies when investing in this field. In addition, legal dissemination must be strengthened to raise investors' awareness, so that the implementation of law on educational BCC contracts moves toward child friendly justice and effective protection of children's rights in Vietnam.

References

Allens. (2016). *The public private partnership law review* (2nd ed.). Law Business Research Ltd.

Bảo, L. N. (2020, December 30). Một số vấn đề pháp lý đặt ra khi thương mại hóa giáo dục [Some legal issues raised when commercializing education]. *Tạp chí Công thương*. https://tapchicongthuong.vn/mot-so-van-de-phap-ly-dat-ra-khi-thuong-mai-hoa-giao-duc-77648.htm

Campbell, C. P. (1985, August 22). *Working partnerships: A joint venture in vocational education*. ERIC. https://eric.ed.gov/?id=ED260293

Dezan, S. (2025). *Education in Vietnam: Opportunities and challenges*. Vietnam Briefing. https://www.vietnam-briefing.com/ng-business-guide/vietnam/sector-insights/industry-spotlight-vietnam-s-growing-appetite-for-education

D.E. (2021). *Emergency assistance to non public schools program*. U.S. Department of Education. https://www.education.nh.gov/who-we-are/division-of-learner-support/bureau-of-instructional-support/emergency-assistance-non?utm

Dương, N. N. (2024, November 14). Quy định hợp tác, đầu tư trong lĩnh vực giáo dục – cải cách nhưng chưa triệt để [Regulations on cooperation and investment in education – reform but not thorough]. *Thời báo Kinh tế Sài Gòn*. https://thesaigontimes.vn/quy-dinh-hop-tac-dau-tu-trong-linh-vuc-giao-duc-cai-cach-nhung-chua-triet-de/

Hà, T. T. K. (2024, April 18). Hợp tác giáo dục Việt Nam Anh: Thực trạng và triển vọng [Vietnam UK educational cooperation: Situation and prospects]. *Tạp chí Cộng sản*. https://www.tapchicongsan.org.vn/web/guest/the-gioi-van-de-su-kien/-/2018/915002/hop-tac-giao-duc-viet-nam---anh--thuc-trang-va-trien-vong.aspx

Ministry of Education and Training. (2023). *Quyết định 248/QĐ-BGDĐT ngày 16/01/2023 phê duyệt liên kết tổ chức thi cấp chứng chỉ tiếng Anh Cambridge*. [Decision No. 248/QĐ-BGDĐT dated January 16, 2023 on approval of cooperation in organizing Cambridge English examinations]

Ministry of Education and Training. (2024). *Quyết định 02/QĐ-BGDĐT ngày 02/01/2024 phê duyệt liên kết tổ chức thi cấp chứng chỉ tiếng Anh Cambridge*. [Decision No. 02/QĐ-BGDĐT dated January 2, 2024 on approval of cooperation in organizing Cambridge English examinations]

Nhân, T., & Khánh, B. (2024, January 4). Từ vụ việc Trường quốc tế AISVN: Để không "nắm dao đằng lưỡi" [From the AISVN International School case: To avoid holding the blade side of the knife]. *Tuổi Trẻ*. https://tuoitre.vn/tu-vu-viec-truong-quoc-te-aisvn-de-khong-nam-dao-dang-luoi-20240401091327465.htm

Organisation for Economic Co operation and Development. (2023). Education at a glance 2023: OECD indicators. *OECD Publishing*. https://doi.org/10.1787/e13bef63-en

Oyeyoade, S. (2022). Developing dispute resolution policy for conflicts settlement in public private partnership (PPP) projects in educational institutions [Policy brief]. *F1000Research, 11*, 1400. https://doi.org/10.12688/f1000research.127531.1

Shatnawi, A., Al Gasawneh, J., Mansur, H., & Alresheedi, A. (2022). The effect of board nationality and educational diversity on CSR performance: Empirical evidence from Australian companies. *Uncertain Supply Chain Management, 10*(6), 1467–1478. https://doi.org/10.5267/j.uscm.2022.6.009

Tiến, L. (2024, September 27). Việt Nam thu hút hơn 4,57 tỉ USD từ các dự án đầu tư của nước ngoài vào giáo dục [Vietnam attracts more than 4.57 billion USD from foreign investment projects in education]. *Giáo dục Việt Nam.* https://giaoduc.net.vn/viet-nam-thu-hut-hon-457-ti-usd-tu-cac-du-an-dau-tu-cua-nuoc-ngoai-vao-giao-duc-post245817.gd

Trường doanh nhân HBR. (2024, November 20). Kinh doanh giáo dục là gì? 7 hình thức kinh doanh hot nhất hiện nay [What is educational business? 7 most popular forms today]. https://hbr.edu.vn/kinh-doanh-giao-duc

Zou, B., Wang, X., & Yu, C. (2022). The impact of Sino foreign cooperative universities in China on Chinese postgraduate students' learning performances in the United Kingdom and United States. *Frontiers in Psychology, 13*, 1–12. https://doi.org/10.3389/fpsyg.2022.1012614

MIX
Papier aus verantwortungsvollen Quellen
Paper from responsible sources
FSC® C105338

If you have any concerns about our products,
you can contact us on
ProductSafety@springernature.com

In case Publisher is established outside the EU,
the EU authorized representative is:
Springer Nature Customer Service Center GmbH
Europaplatz 3, 69115 Heidelberg, Germany

Printed by Libri Plureos GmbH
in Hamburg, Germany